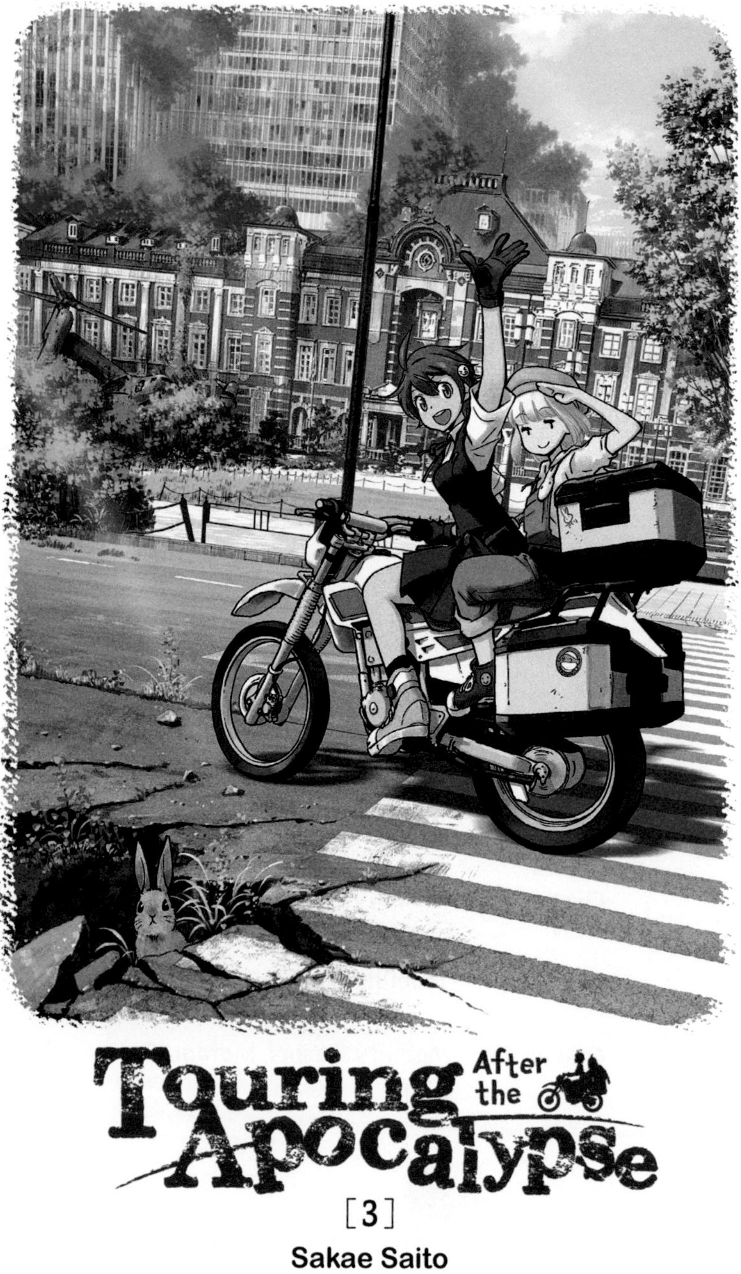

Touring After the Apocalypse

[3]

Sakae Saito

CONTENTS

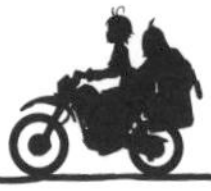

Touring After the Apocalypse

Chapter 12

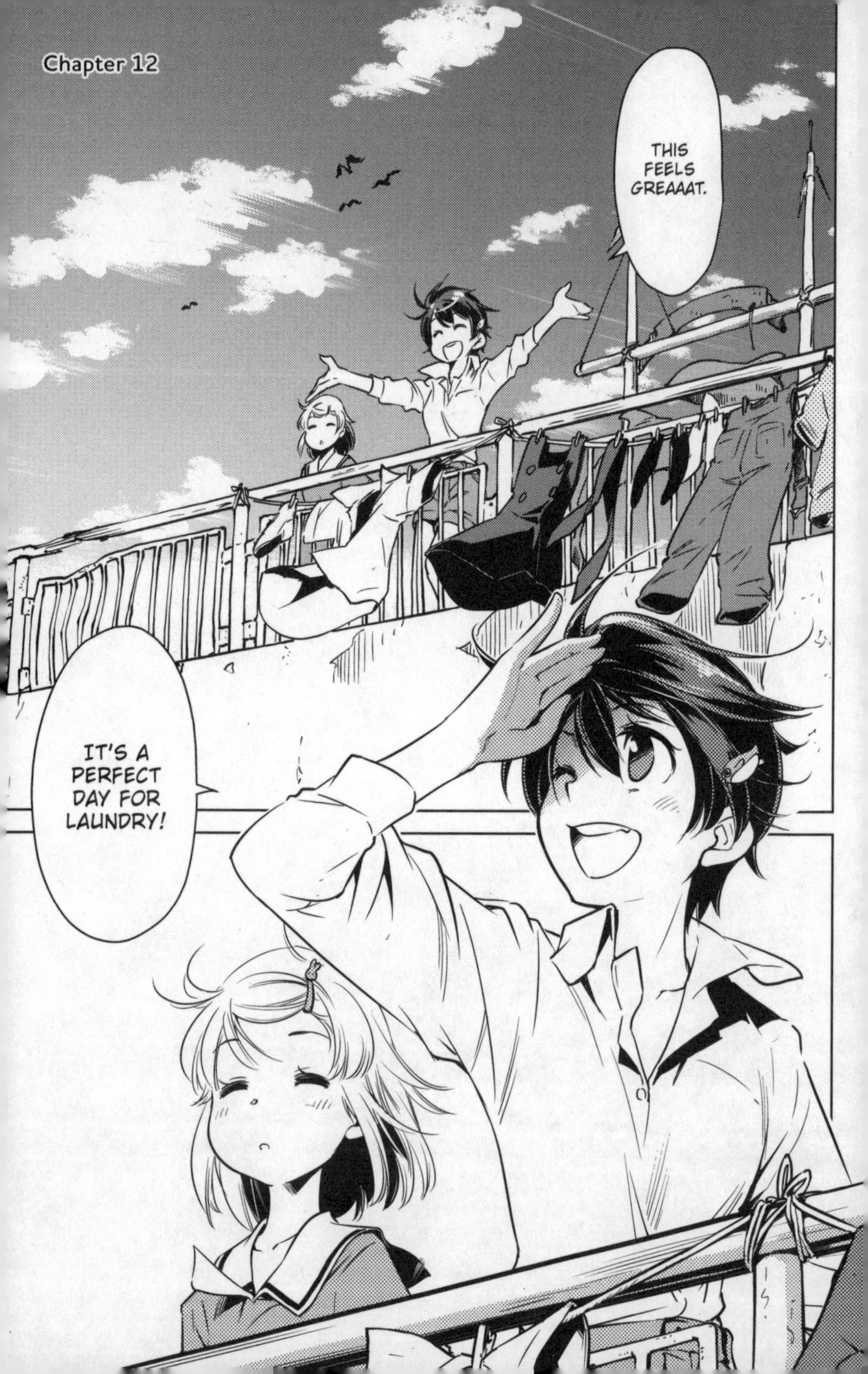
THIS FEELS GREAAAT.
IT'S A PERFECT DAY FOR LAUNDRY!

Chapter 12 | Umihotaru, Departure

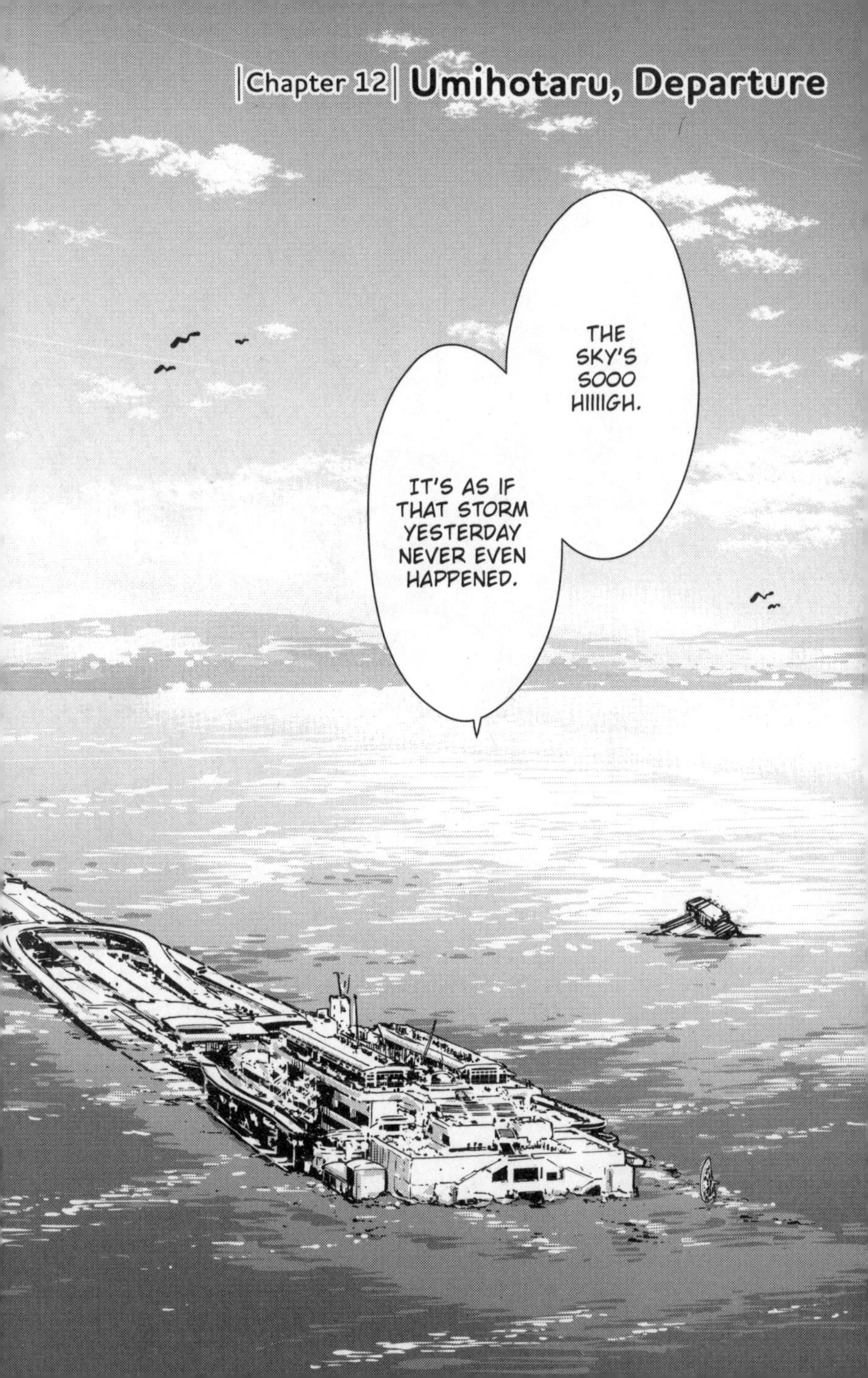
THE SKY'S SOOO HIIIIGH.
IT'S AS IF THAT STORM YESTERDAY NEVER EVEN HAPPENED.

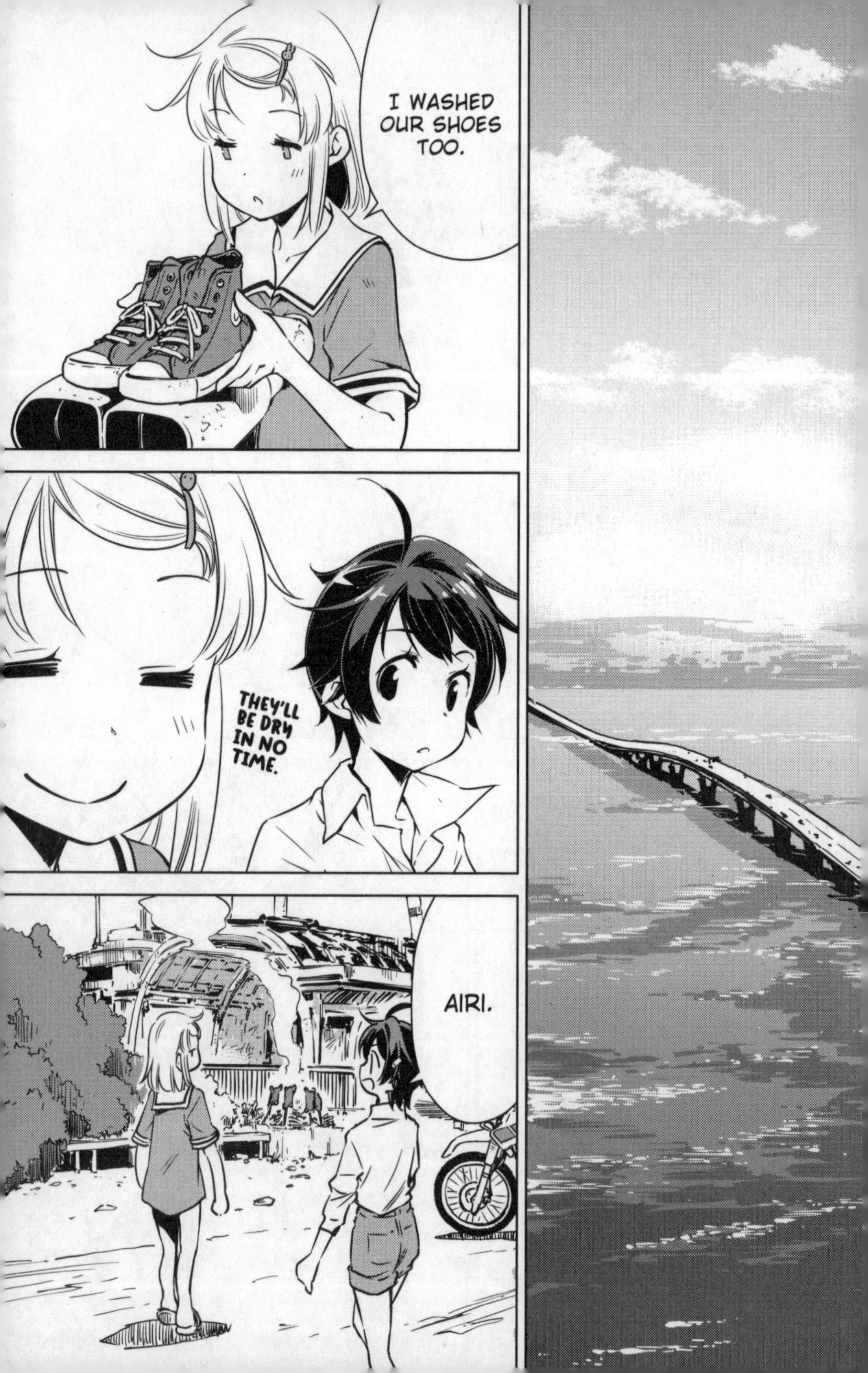
I WASHED OUR SHOES TOO.
THEY'LL BE DRY IN NO TIME.
AIRI.

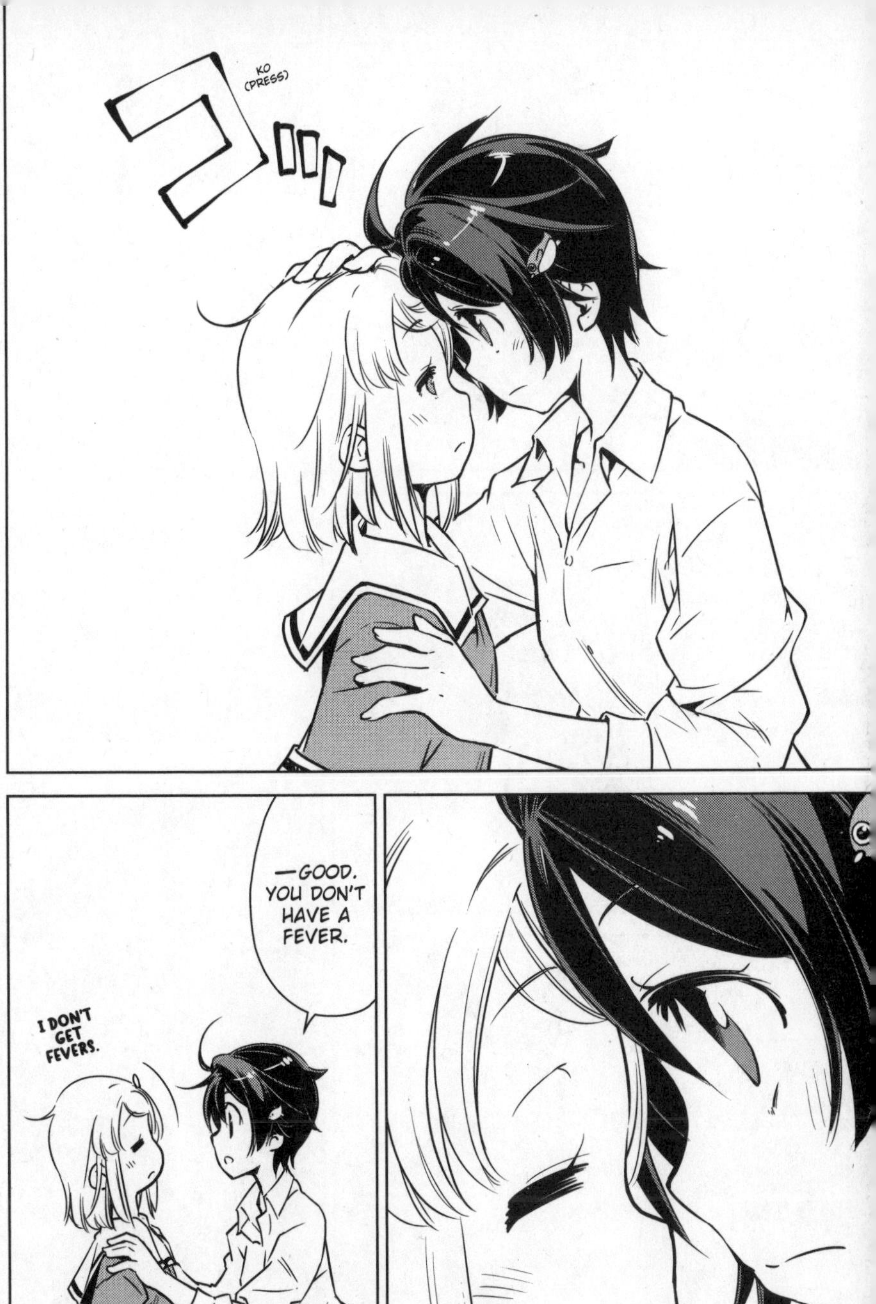
KO (PRESS)
—GOOD. YOU DON'T HAVE A FEVER.
I DON'T GET FEVERS.

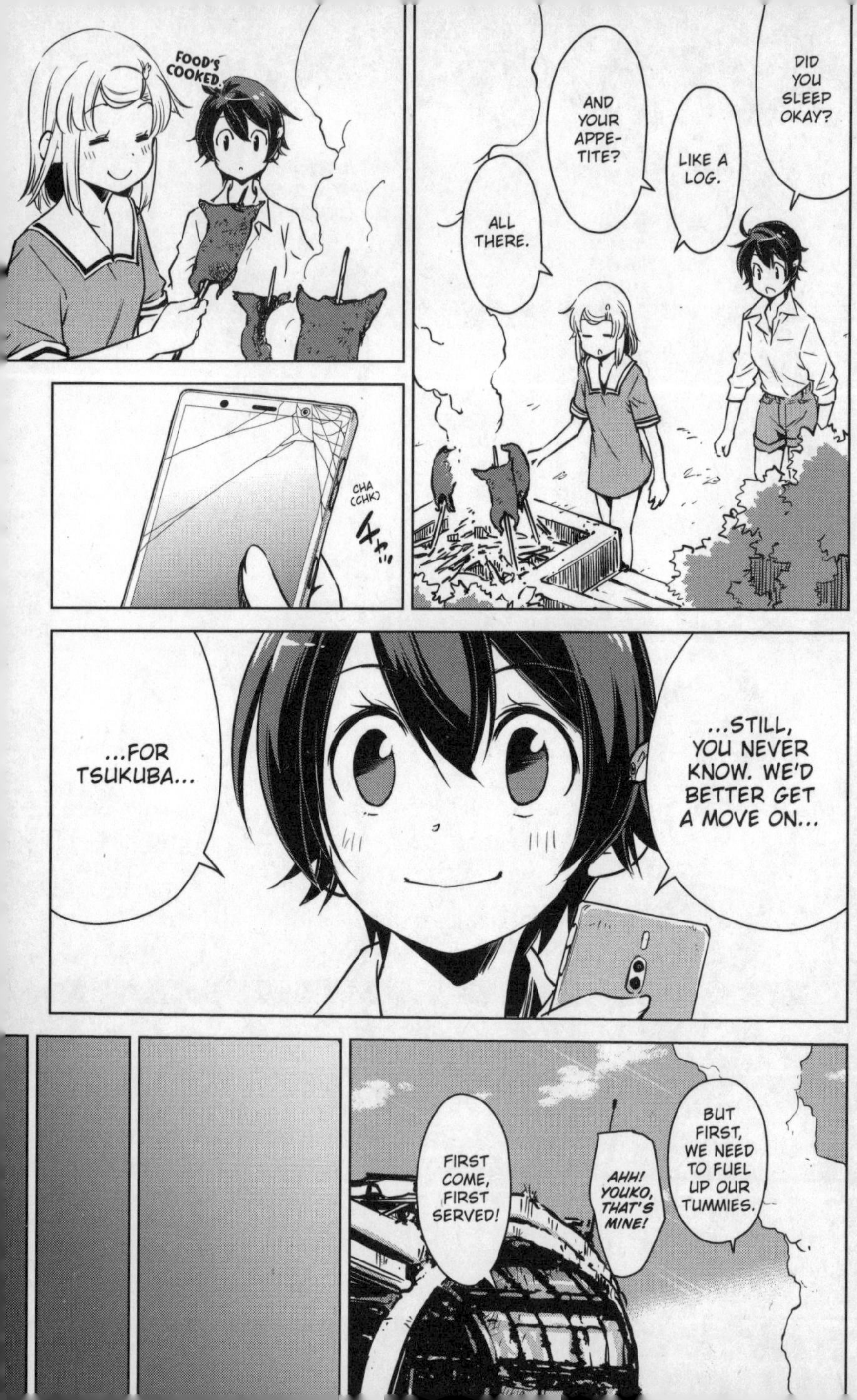
DID YOU SLEEP OKAY?
LIKE A LOG.
AND YOUR APPE-TITE?
ALL THERE.
FOOD'S COOKED.
CHA (CHK)
...STILL, YOU NEVER KNOW. WE'D BETTER GET A MOVE ON...
...FOR TSUKUBA...
BUT FIRST, WE NEED TO FUEL UP OUR TUMMIES.
AHH! YOUKO, THAT'S MINE!
FIRST COME, FIRST SERVED!

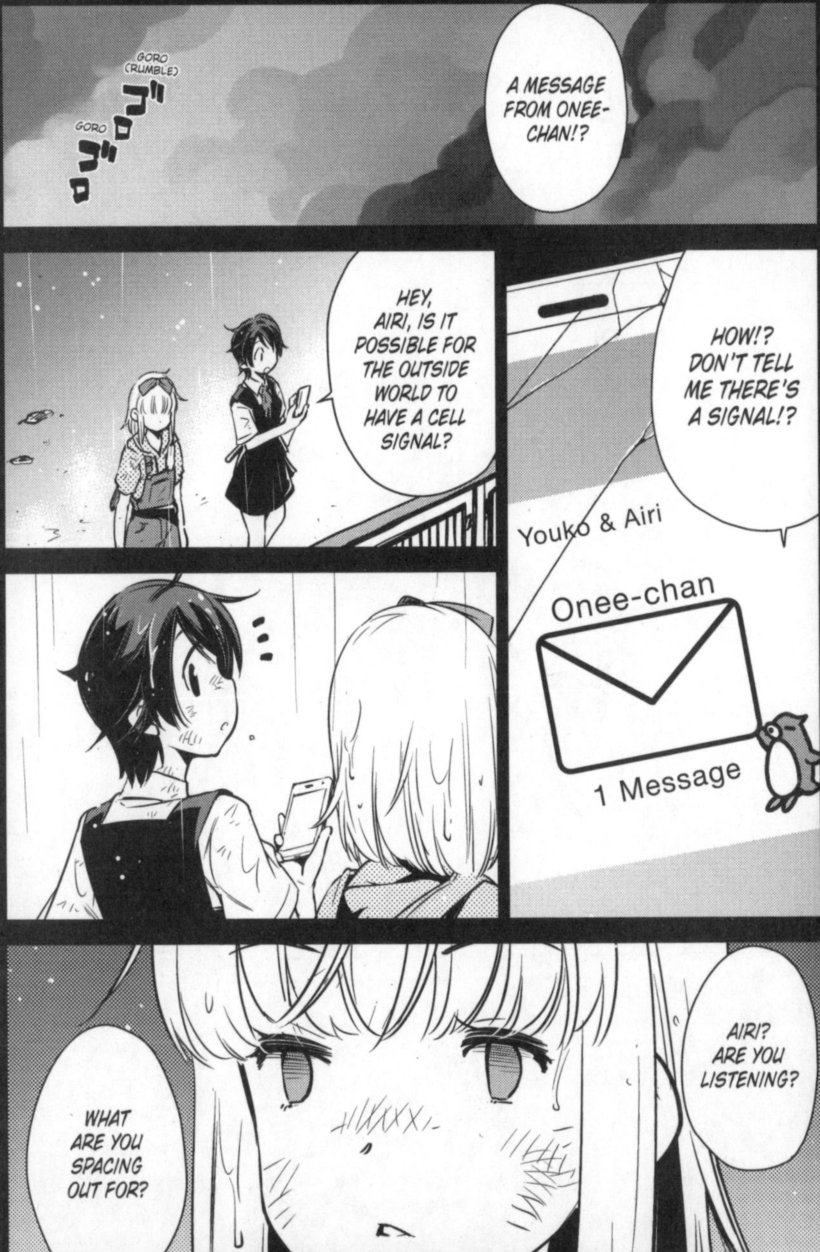
A MESSAGE FROM ONEE-CHAN!?
GORO (RUMBLE)
ゴロ
GORO
ゴロ
HOW!? DON'T TELL ME THERE'S A SIGNAL!?
Youko & Airi
Onee-chan
1 Message
HEY, AIRI, IS IT POSSIBLE FOR THE OUTSIDE WORLD TO HAVE A CELL SIGNAL?
AIRI? ARE YOU LISTENING?
WHAT ARE YOU SPACING OUT FOR?

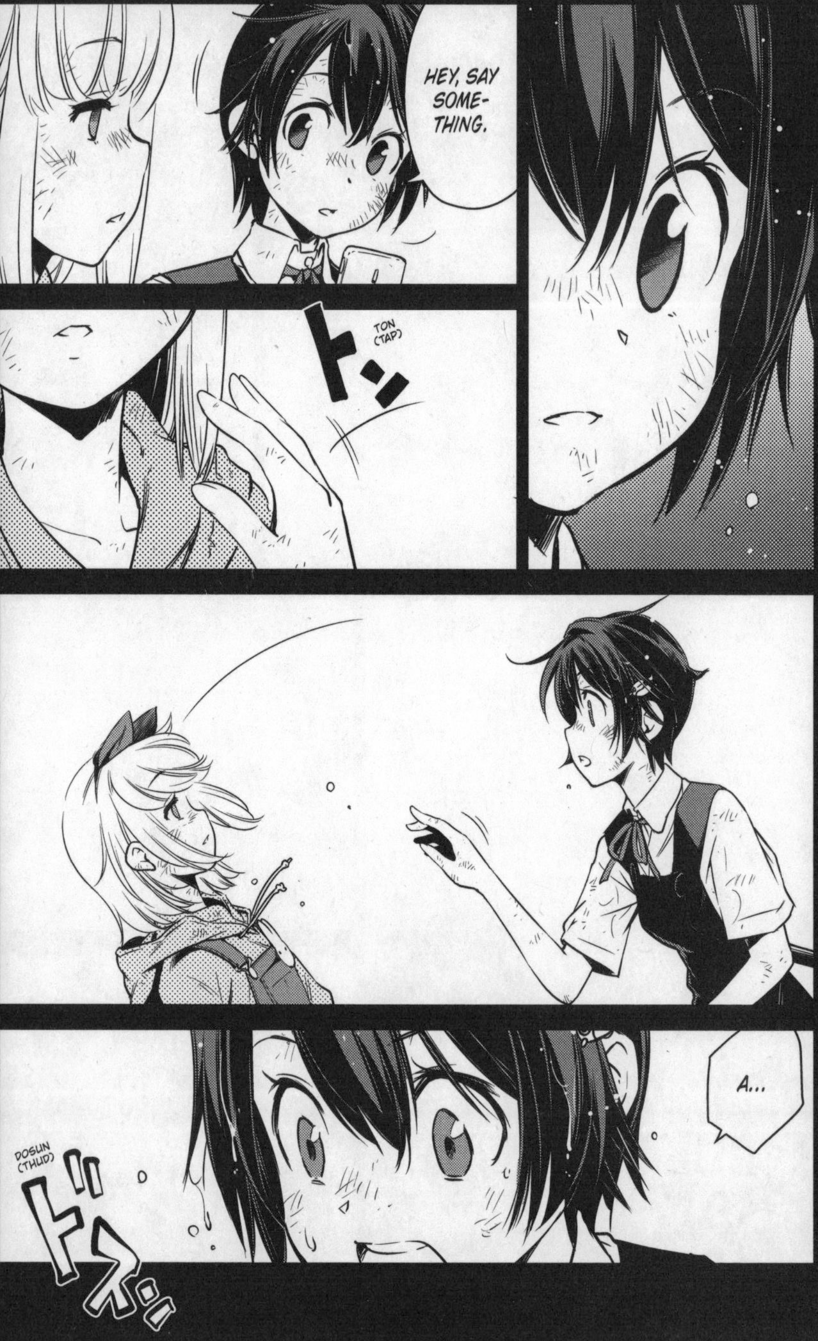
HEY, SAY SOME-THING.
トッ
TON (TAP)
A...
ドスッ
DOSUN (THUD)

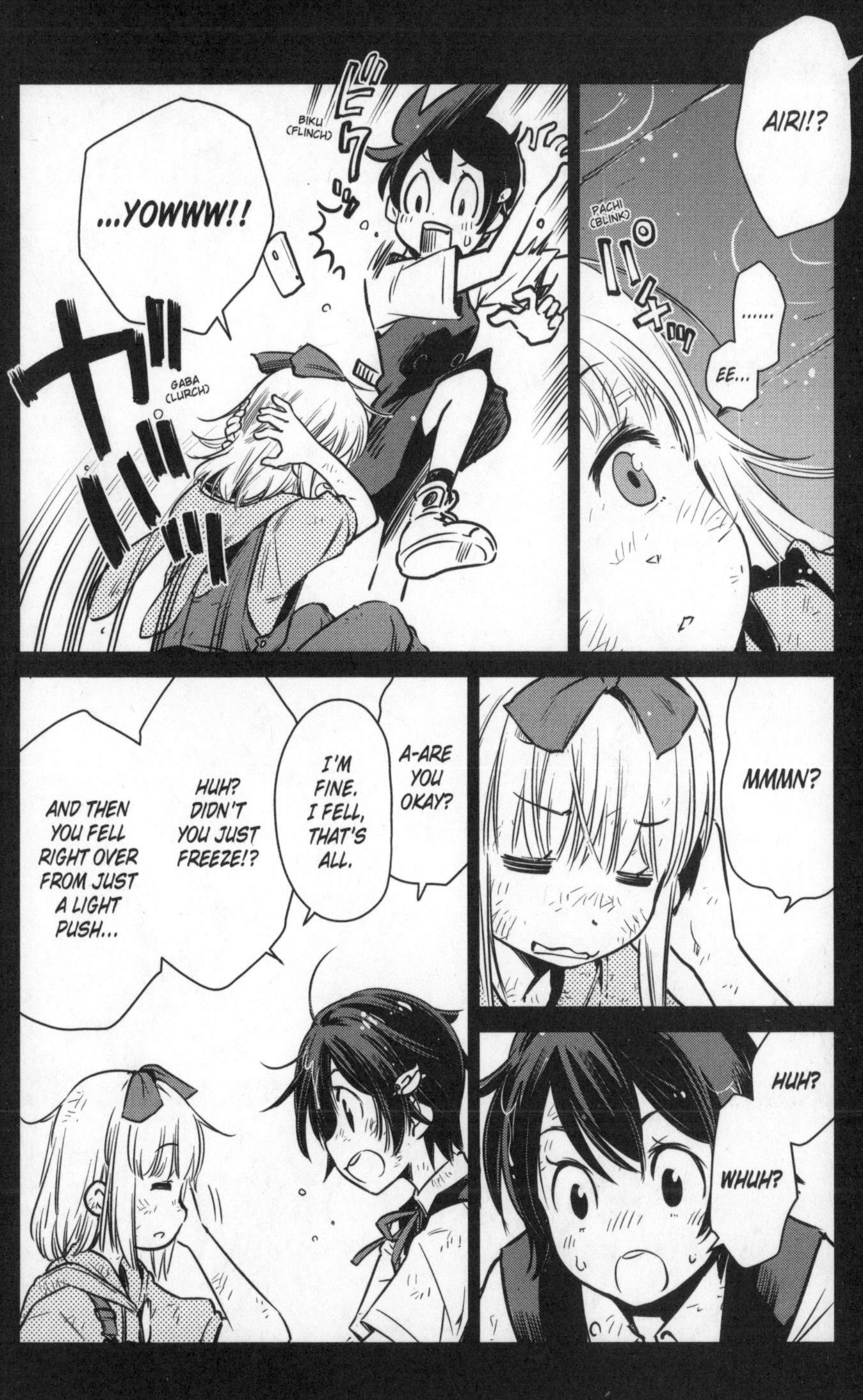
AIRI!?
PACHI (BLINK)
......
EE...
BIKU (FLINCH)
...YOWWW!!
GABA (LURCH)
MMMN?
HUH?
WHUH?
A-ARE YOU OKAY?
I'M FINE. I FELL, THAT'S ALL.
HUH? DIDN'T YOU JUST FREEZE!?
AND THEN YOU FELL RIGHT OVER FROM JUST A LIGHT PUSH...

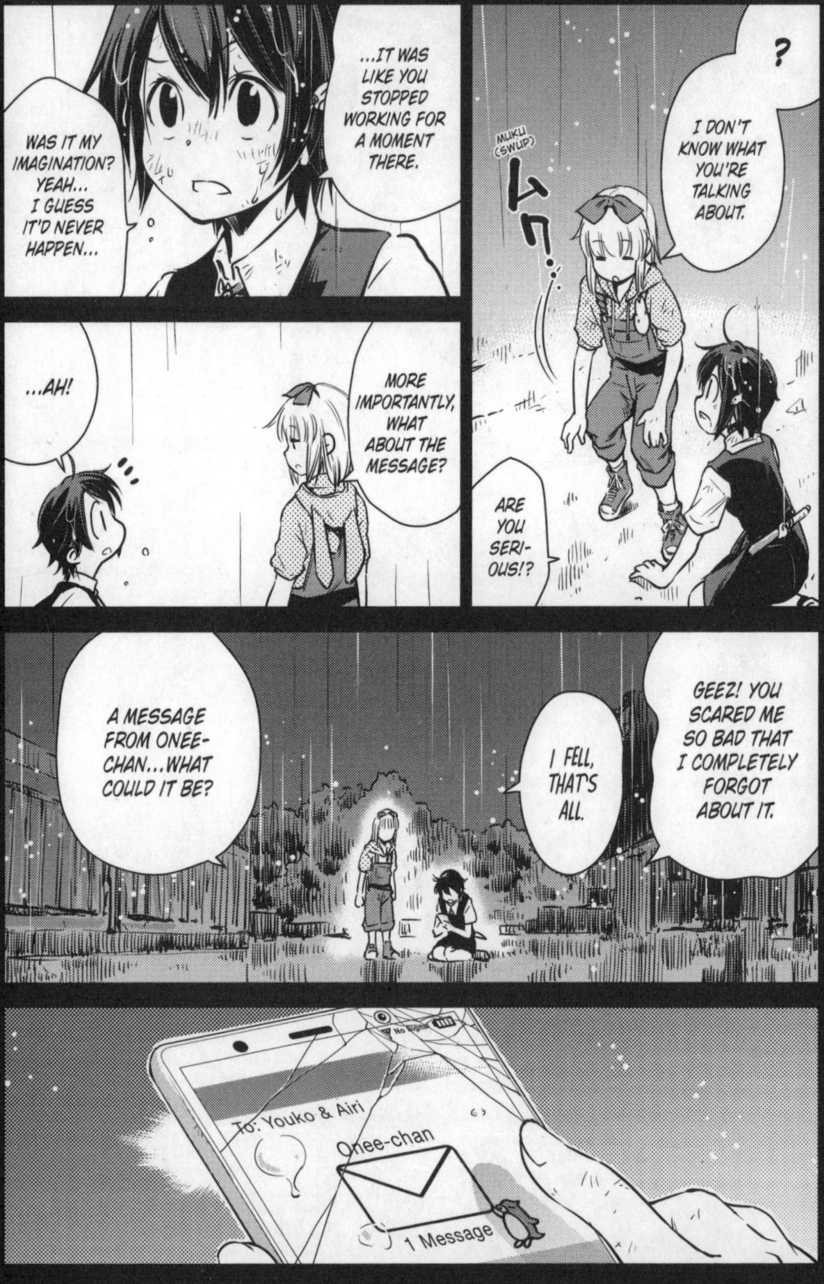
?
I DON'T KNOW WHAT YOU'RE TALKING ABOUT.
MUKU (SWUP)
ARE YOU SERI-OUS!?
...IT WAS LIKE YOU STOPPED WORKING FOR A MOMENT THERE.
WAS IT MY IMAGINATION? YEAH... I GUESS IT'D NEVER HAPPEN...
MORE IMPORTANTLY, WHAT ABOUT THE MESSAGE?
...AH!
GEEZ! YOU SCARED ME SO BAD THAT I COMPLETELY FORGOT ABOUT IT.
I FELL, THAT'S ALL.
A MESSAGE FROM ONEE-CHAN...WHAT COULD IT BE?
To: Youko & Airi
Onee-chan
1 Message

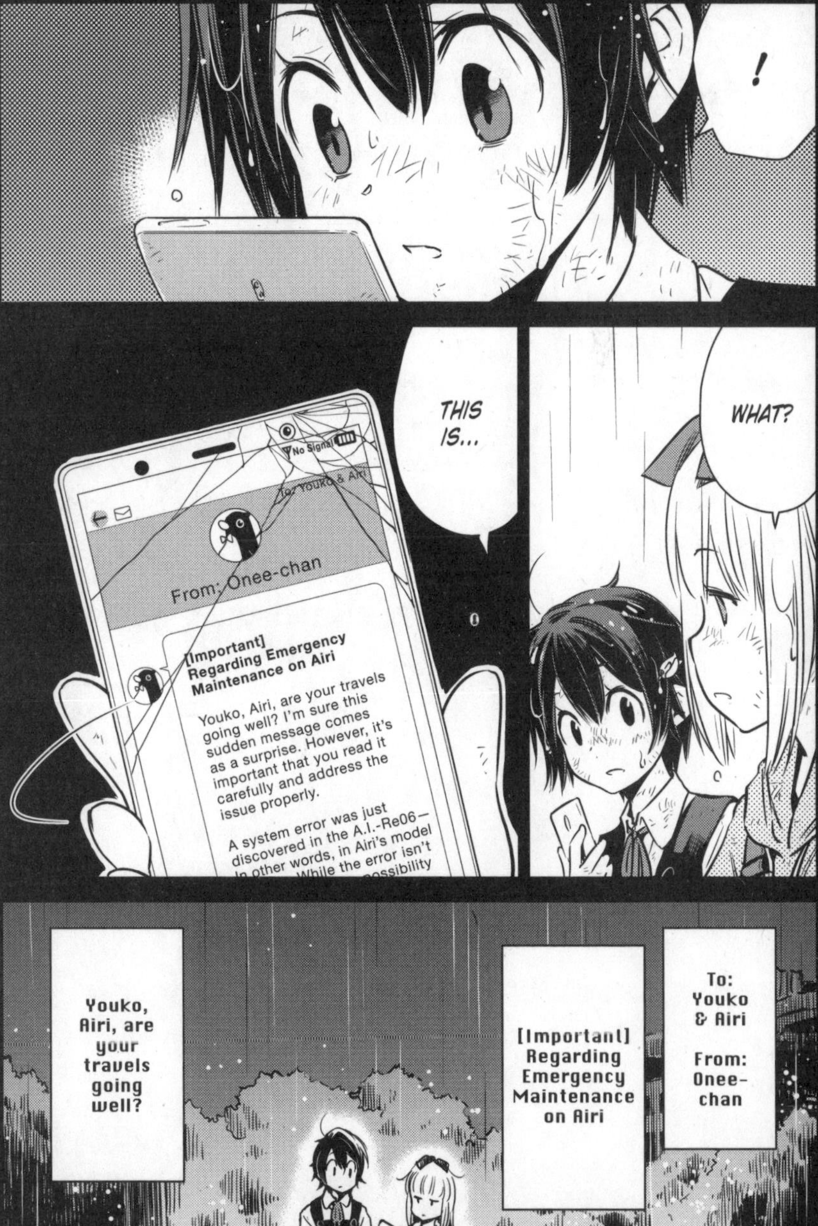
!
WHAT?
THIS IS...
No Signal
To: Youko & Airi
From: Onee-chan
[Important] Regarding Emergency Maintenance on Airi
Youko, Airi, are your travels going well? I'm sure this sudden message comes as a surprise. However, it's important that you read it carefully and address the issue properly.
A system error was just discovered in the A.I.-Re06—
To: Youko & Airi
From: Onee-chan
[Important] Regarding Emergency Maintenance on Airi
Youko, Airi, are your travels going well?

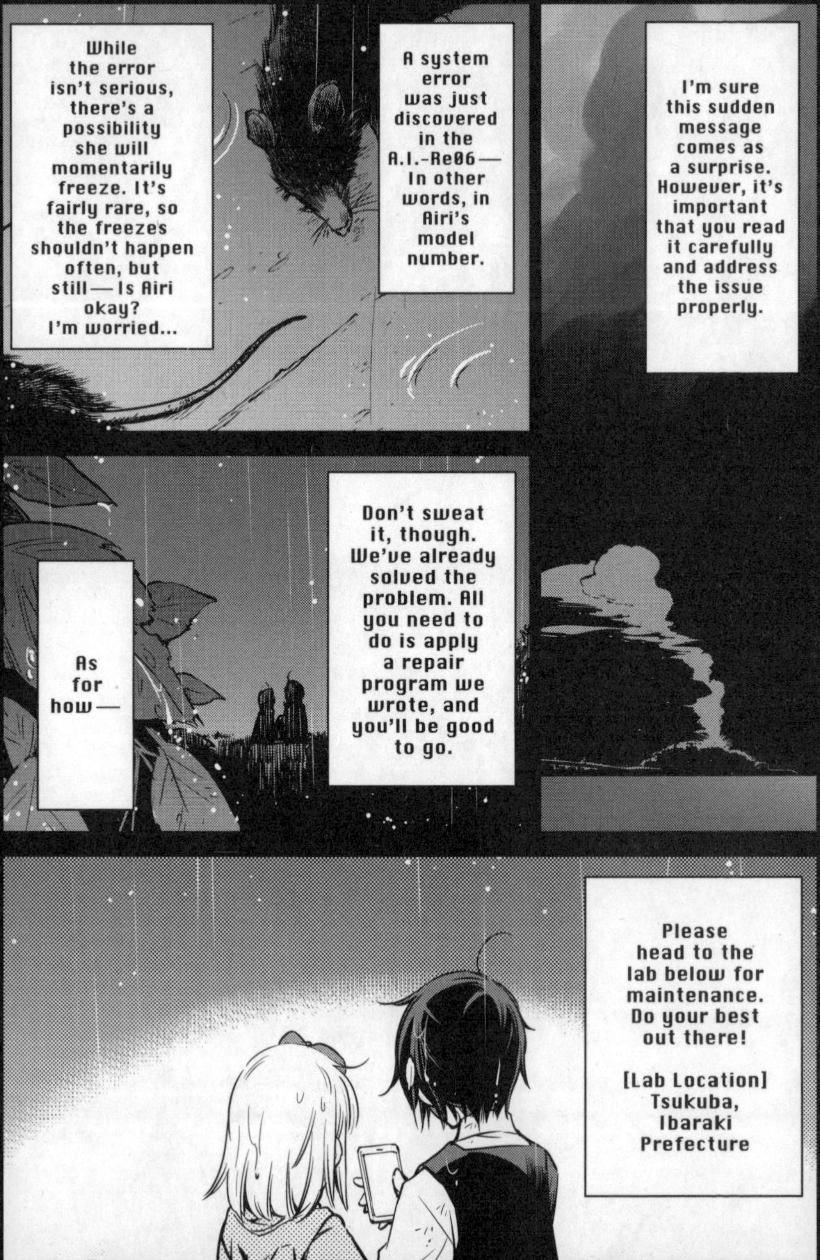
I'm sure this sudden message comes as a surprise. However, it's important that you read it carefully and address the issue properly.
A system error was just discovered in the A.I.-Re06— In other words, in Airi's model number.
While the error isn't serious, there's a possibility she will momentarily freeze. It's fairly rare, so the freezes shouldn't happen often, but still— Is Airi okay? I'm worried...
Don't sweat it, though. We've already solved the problem. All you need to do is apply a repair program we wrote, and you'll be good to go.
As for how—
Please head to the lab below for maintenance. Do your best out there!
[Lab Location] Tsukuba, Ibaraki Prefecture

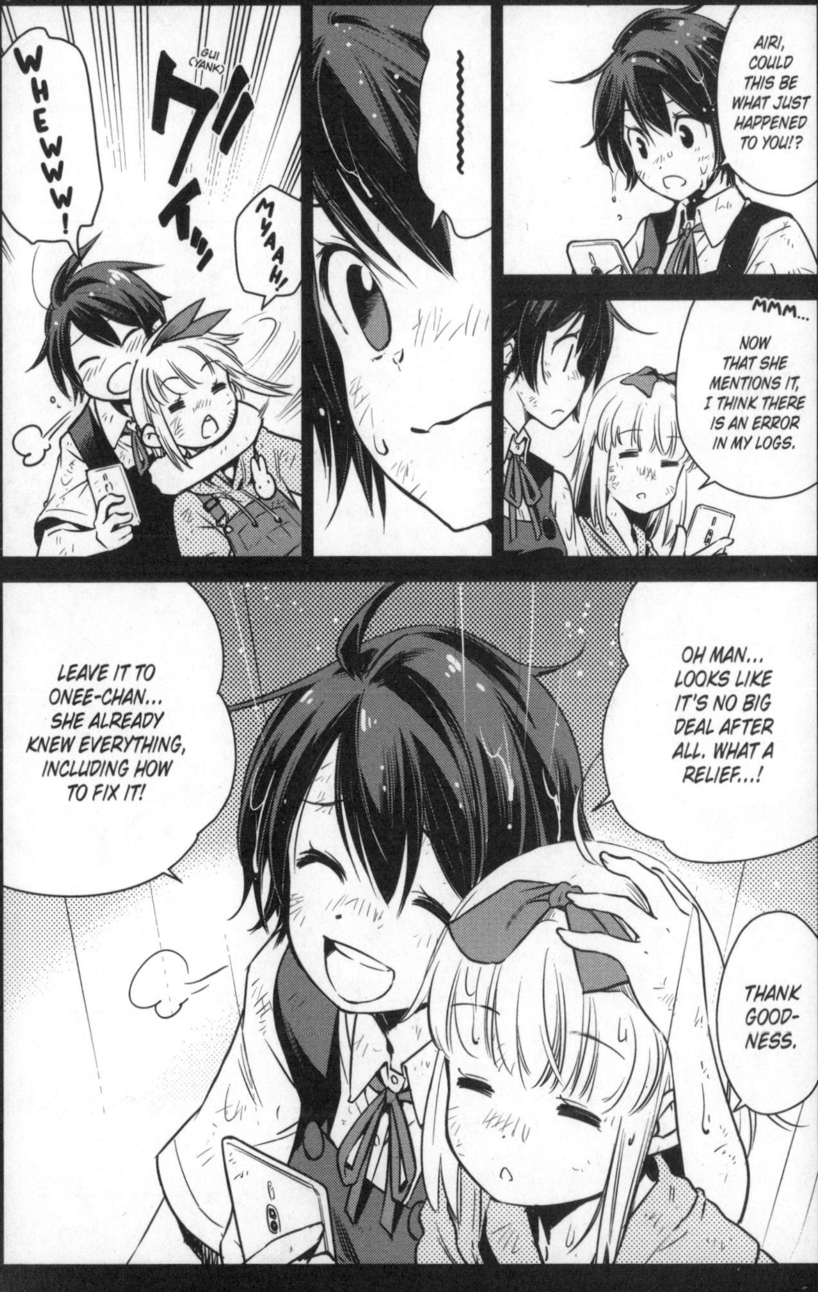
AIRI, COULD THIS BE WHAT JUST HAPPENED TO YOU!?
MMM...
NOW THAT SHE MENTIONS IT, I THINK THERE IS AN ERROR IN MY LOGS.
GUI (YANK)
MYAAAH!
WHEWWWW!
OH MAN... LOOKS LIKE IT'S NO BIG DEAL AFTER ALL. WHAT A RELIEF...!
LEAVE IT TO ONEE-CHAN... SHE ALREADY KNEW EVERYTHING, INCLUDING HOW TO FIX IT!
THANK GOOD-NESS.

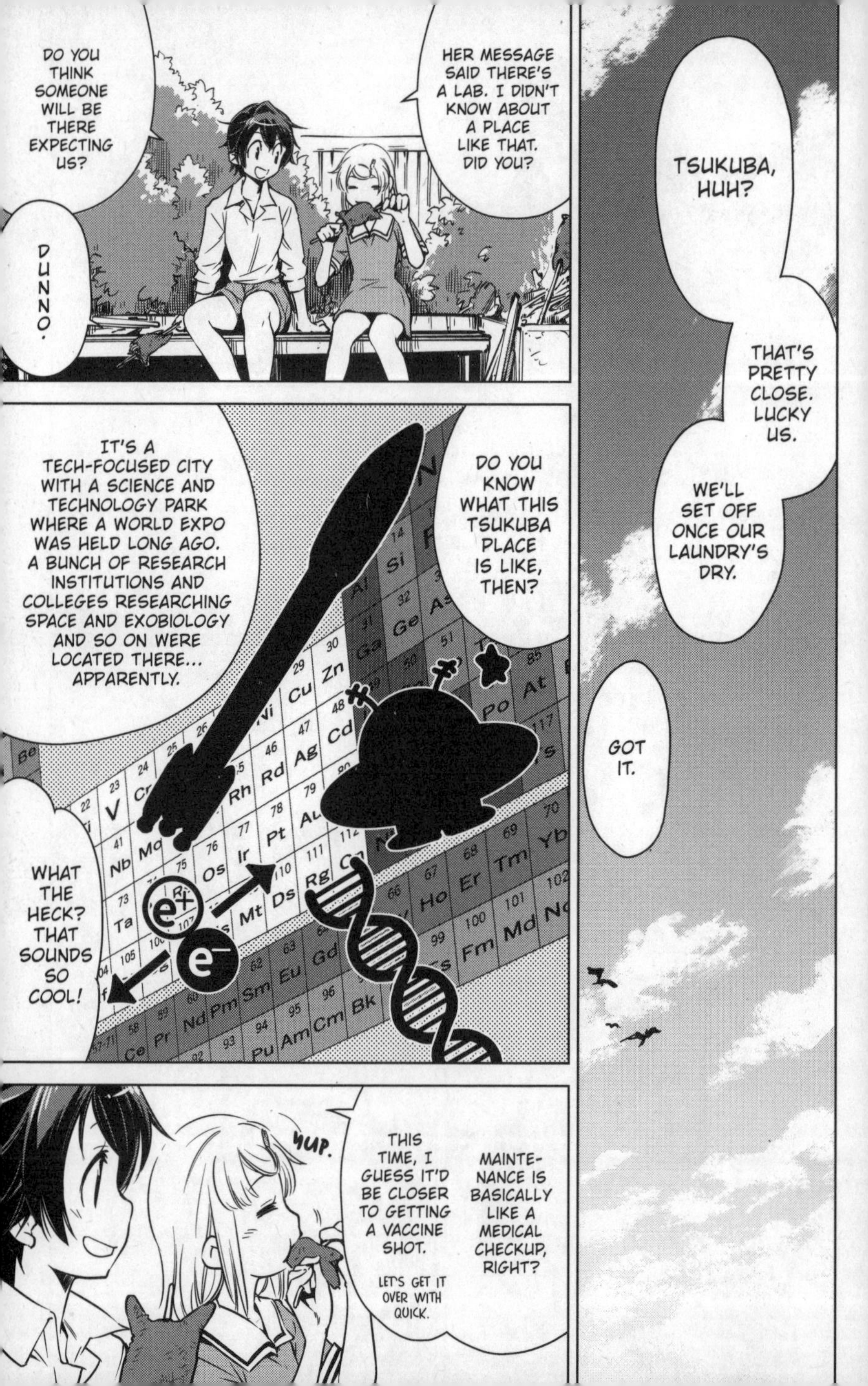
TSUKUBA, HUH?
THAT'S PRETTY CLOSE. LUCKY US.
WE'LL SET OFF ONCE OUR LAUNDRY'S DRY.
GOT IT.
HER MESSAGE SAID THERE'S A LAB. I DIDN'T KNOW ABOUT A PLACE LIKE THAT. DID YOU?
DO YOU THINK SOMEONE WILL BE THERE EXPECTING US?
DUNNO.
DO YOU KNOW WHAT THIS TSUKUBA PLACE IS LIKE, THEN?
IT'S A TECH-FOCUSED CITY WITH A SCIENCE AND TECHNOLOGY PARK WHERE A WORLD EXPO WAS HELD LONG AGO. A BUNCH OF RESEARCH INSTITUTIONS AND COLLEGES RESEARCHING SPACE AND EXOBIOLOGY AND SO ON WERE LOCATED THERE... APPARENTLY.
WHAT THE HECK? THAT SOUNDS SO COOL!
MAINTE-NANCE IS BASICALLY LIKE A MEDICAL CHECKUP, RIGHT?
YUP.
THIS TIME, I GUESS IT'D BE CLOSER TO GETTING A VACCINE SHOT.
LET'S GET IT OVER WITH QUICK.

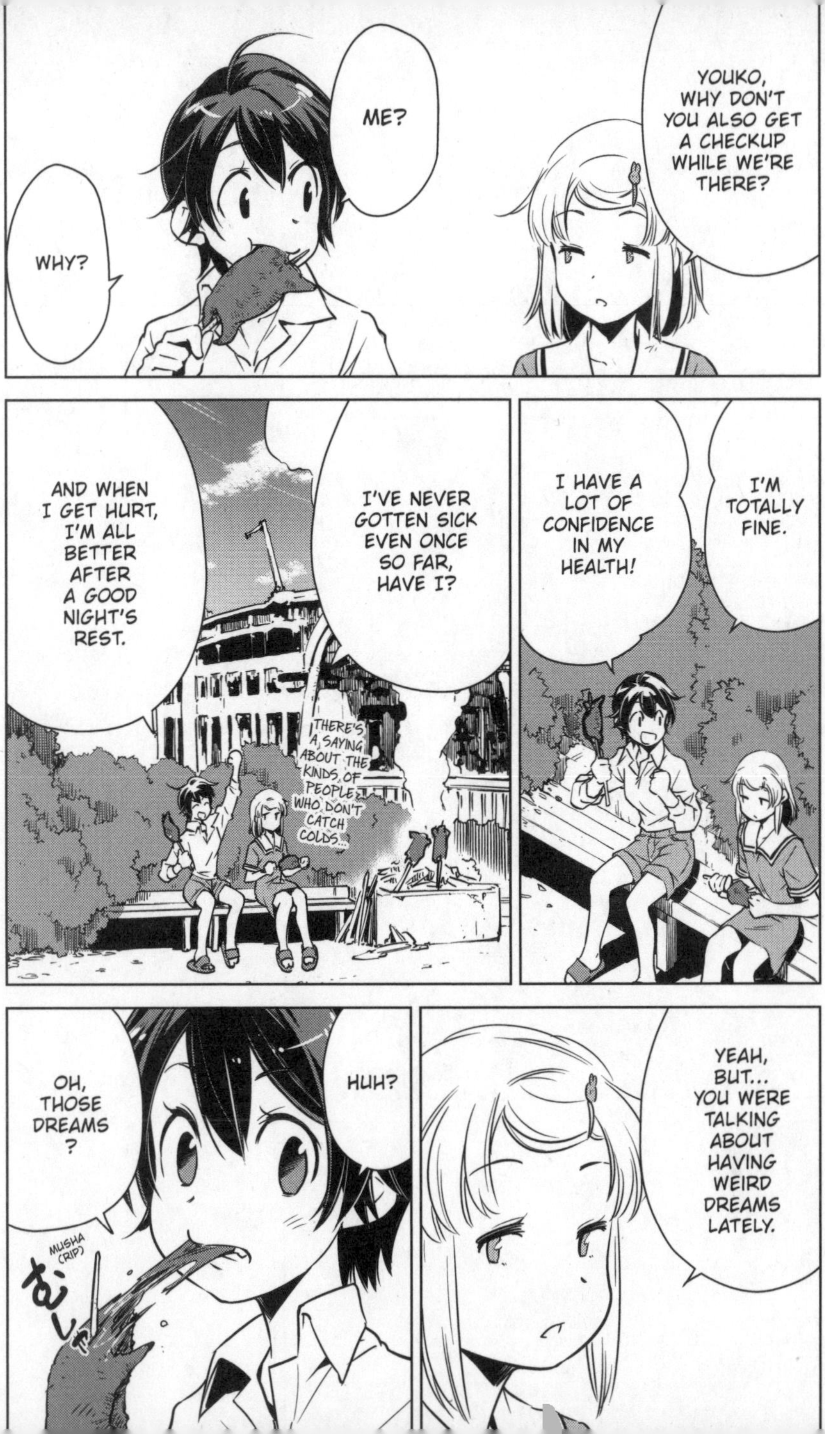
YOUKO, WHY DON'T YOU ALSO GET A CHECKUP WHILE WE'RE THERE?
ME?
WHY?
I'M TOTALLY FINE.
I HAVE A LOT OF CONFIDENCE IN MY HEALTH!
I'VE NEVER GOTTEN SICK EVEN ONCE SO FAR, HAVE I?
AND WHEN I GET HURT, I'M ALL BETTER AFTER A GOOD NIGHT'S REST.
THERE'S A SAYING ABOUT THE KINDS OF PEOPLE WHO DON'T CATCH COLDS...
YEAH, BUT... YOU WERE TALKING ABOUT HAVING WEIRD DREAMS LATELY.
HUH?
OH, THOSE DREAMS?
MUSHA (RIP)

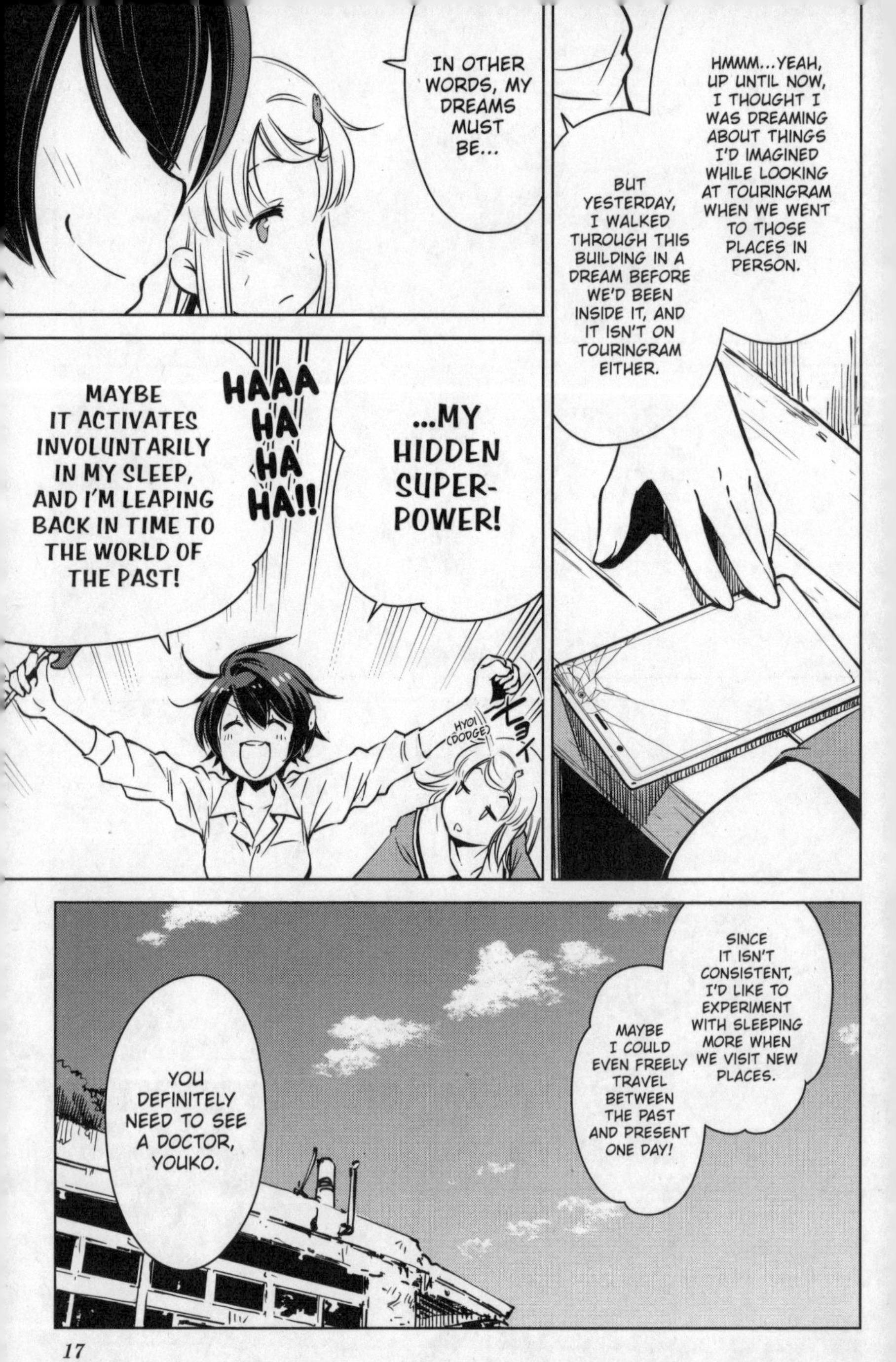
HMMM...YEAH, UP UNTIL NOW, I THOUGHT I WAS DREAMING ABOUT THINGS I'D IMAGINED WHILE LOOKING AT TOURINGRAM WHEN WE WENT TO THOSE PLACES IN PERSON.
BUT YESTERDAY, I WALKED THROUGH THIS BUILDING IN A DREAM BEFORE WE'D BEEN INSIDE IT, AND IT ISN'T ON TOURINGRAM EITHER.
IN OTHER WORDS, MY DREAMS MUST BE...
...MY HIDDEN SUPER-POWER!
HAAA HA HA HA!!
MAYBE IT ACTIVATES INVOLUNTARILY IN MY SLEEP, AND I'M LEAPING BACK IN TIME TO THE WORLD OF THE PAST!
HYOI (DODGE)
SINCE IT ISN'T CONSISTENT, I'D LIKE TO EXPERIMENT WITH SLEEPING MORE WHEN WE VISIT NEW PLACES.
MAYBE I COULD EVEN FREELY TRAVEL BETWEEN THE PAST AND PRESENT ONE DAY!
YOU DEFINITELY NEED TO SEE A DOCTOR, YOUKO.

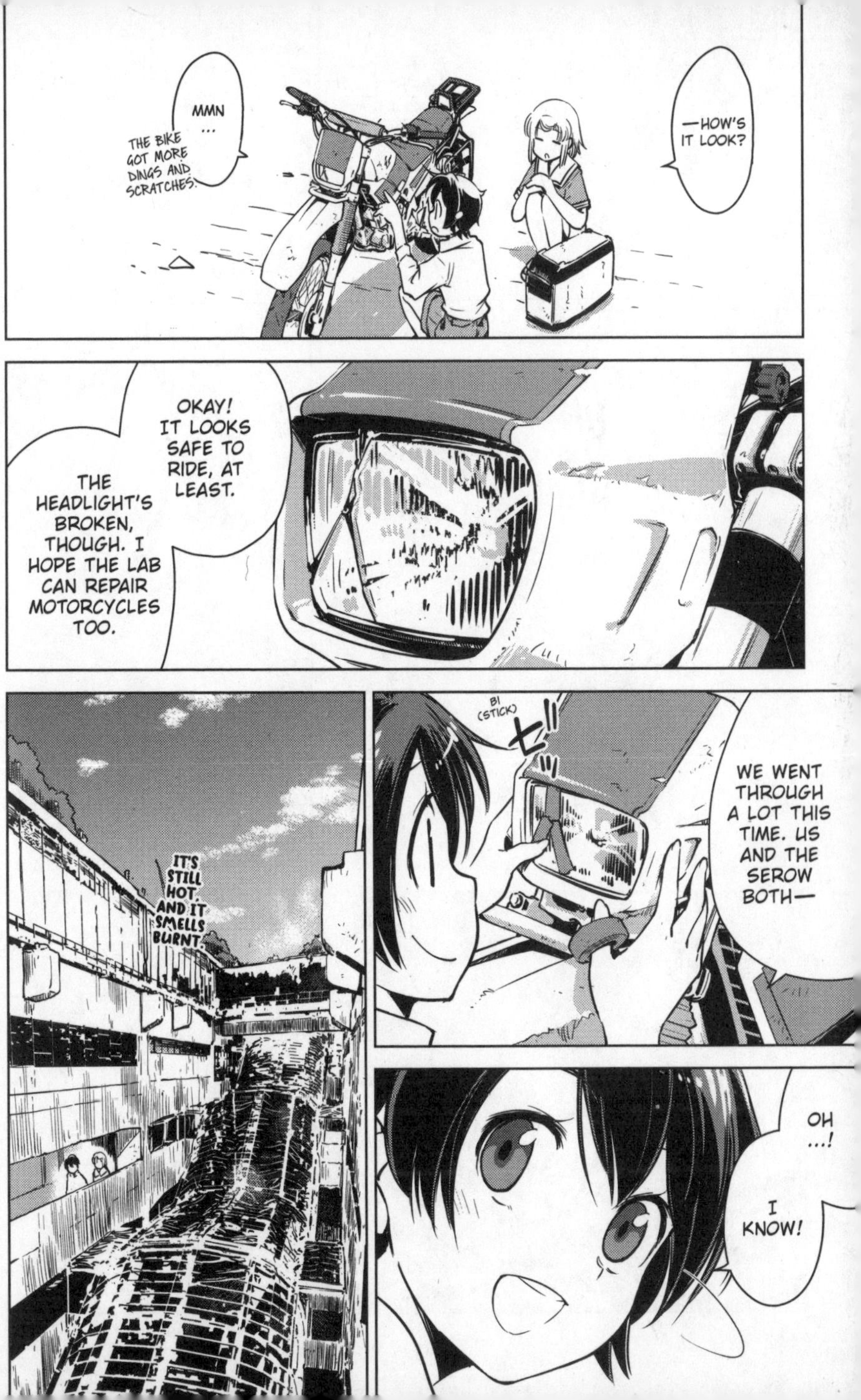
—HOW'S IT LOOK?
MMN ...
THE BIKE GOT MORE DINGS AND SCRATCHES.
OKAY! IT LOOKS SAFE TO RIDE, AT LEAST.
THE HEADLIGHT'S BROKEN, THOUGH. I HOPE THE LAB CAN REPAIR MOTORCYCLES TOO.
WE WENT THROUGH A LOT THIS TIME. US AND THE SEROW BOTH—
BI (STICK)
OH ...!
I KNOW!
IT'S STILL HOT. AND IT SMELLS BURNT.

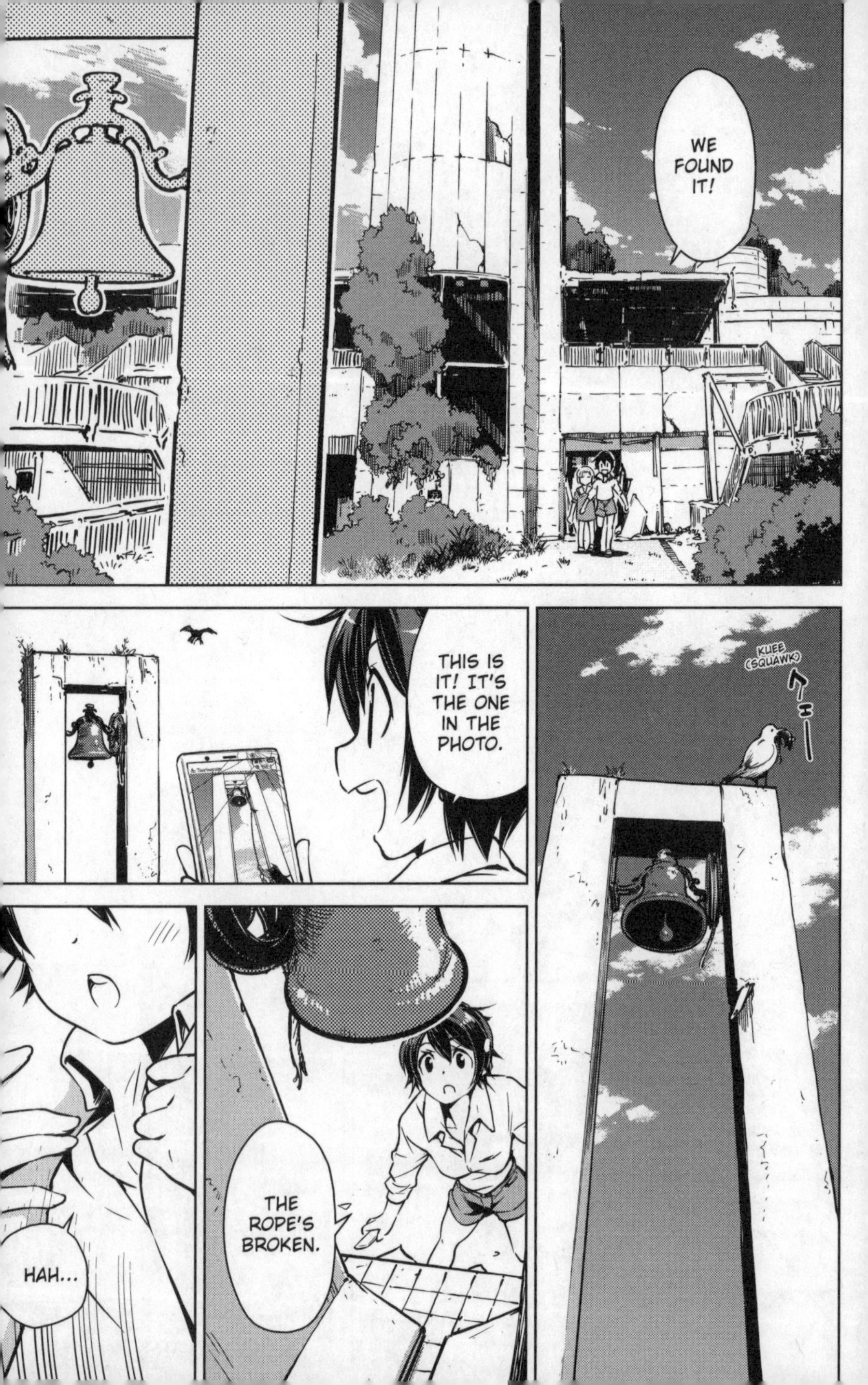
WE FOUND IT!
KUEE (SQUAWK)
THIS IS IT! IT'S THE ONE IN THE PHOTO.
THE ROPE'S BROKEN.
HAH...

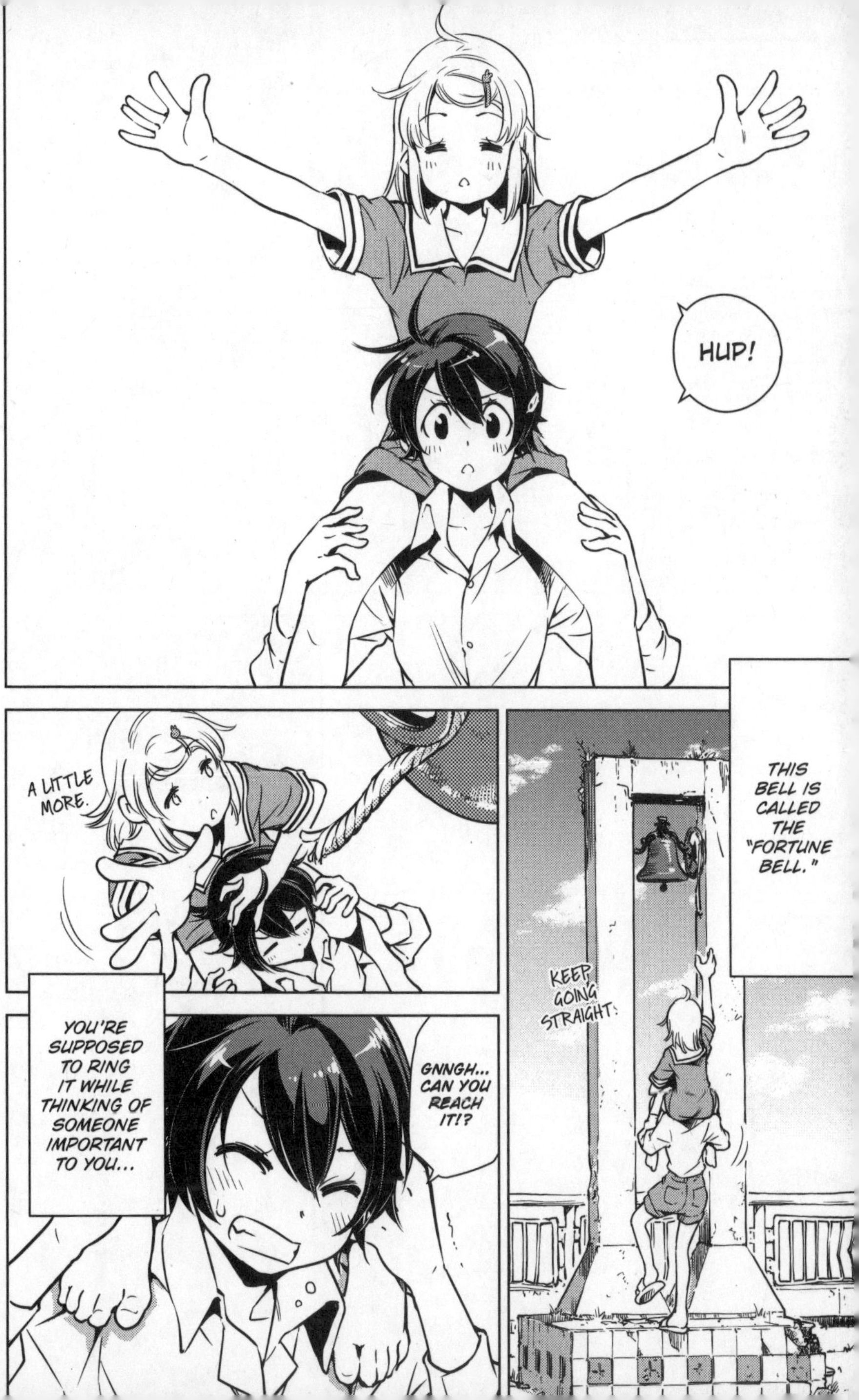
HUP!
THIS BELL IS CALLED THE "FORTUNE BELL."
KEEP GOING STRAIGHT.
A LITTLE MORE.
GNNGH... CAN YOU REACH IT!?
YOU'RE SUPPOSED TO RING IT WHILE THINKING OF SOMEONE IMPORTANT TO YOU...

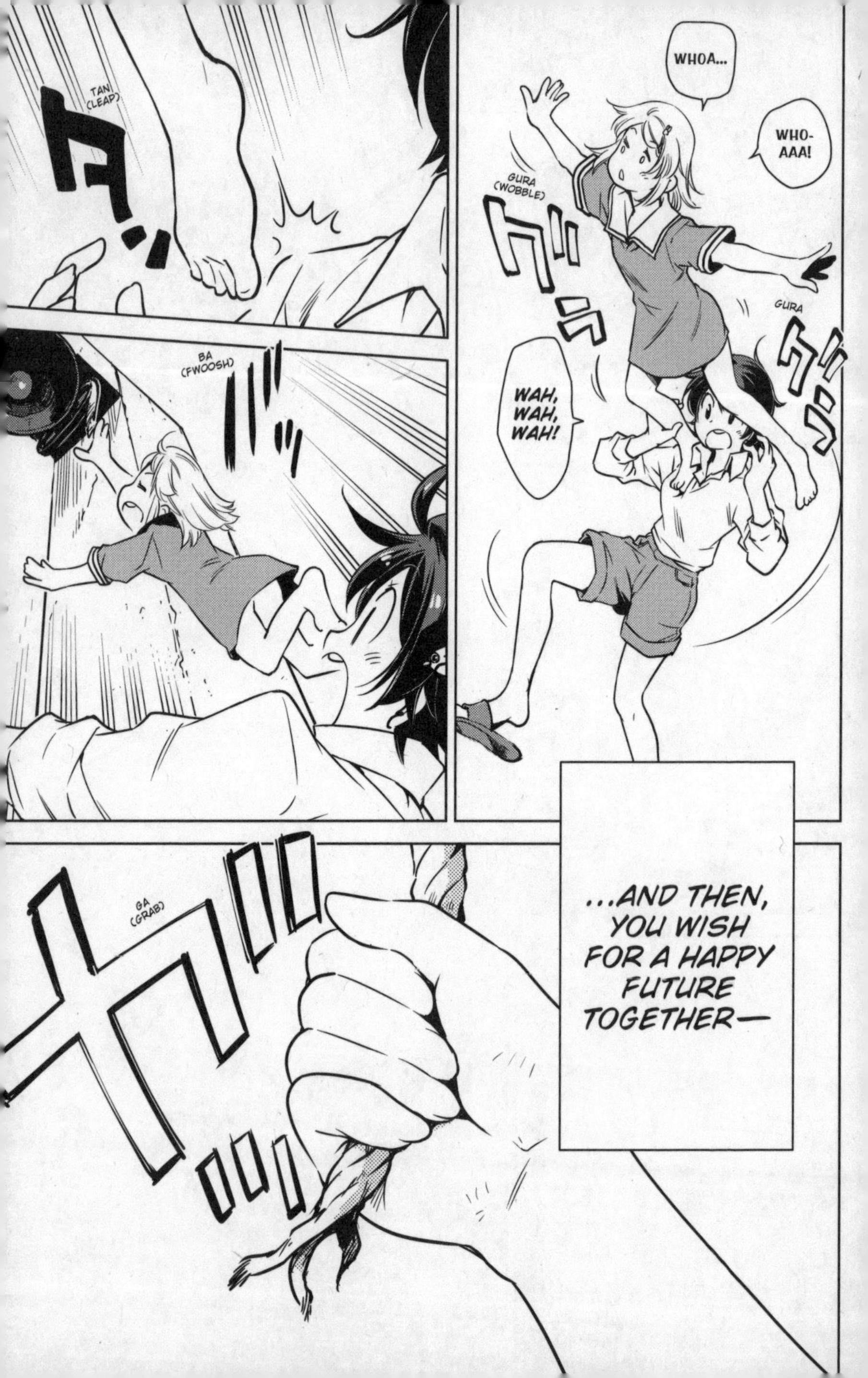
WHOA...
WHO-AAA!
GURA (WOBBLE)
GURA
WAH, WAH, WAH!
TAN (LEAP)
BA (FWOOSH)
...AND THEN, YOU WISH FOR A HAPPY FUTURE TOGETHER—
GA (GRAB)

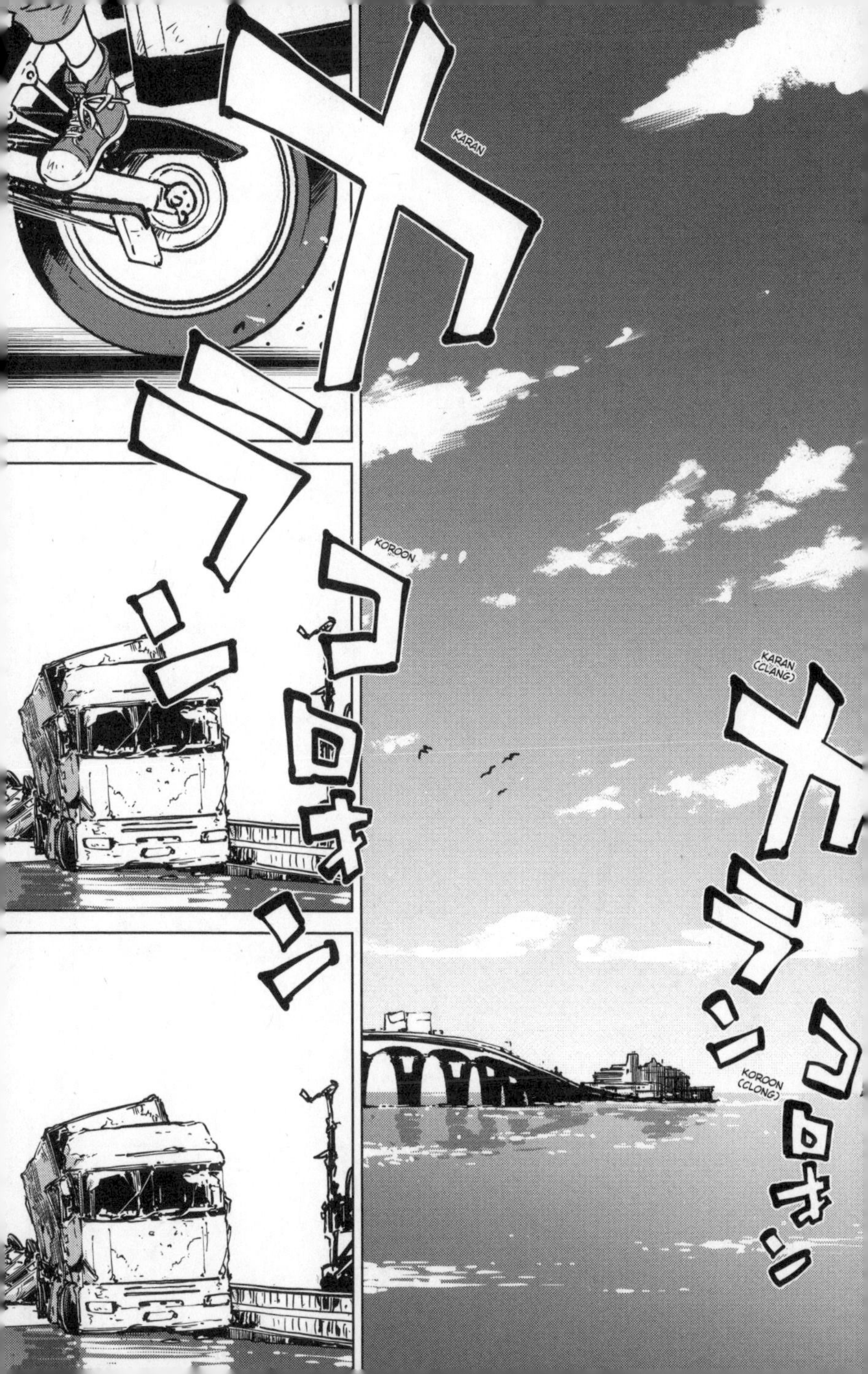
KARAN (CLANG)
KOROON (CLONG)
KARAN
KOROON

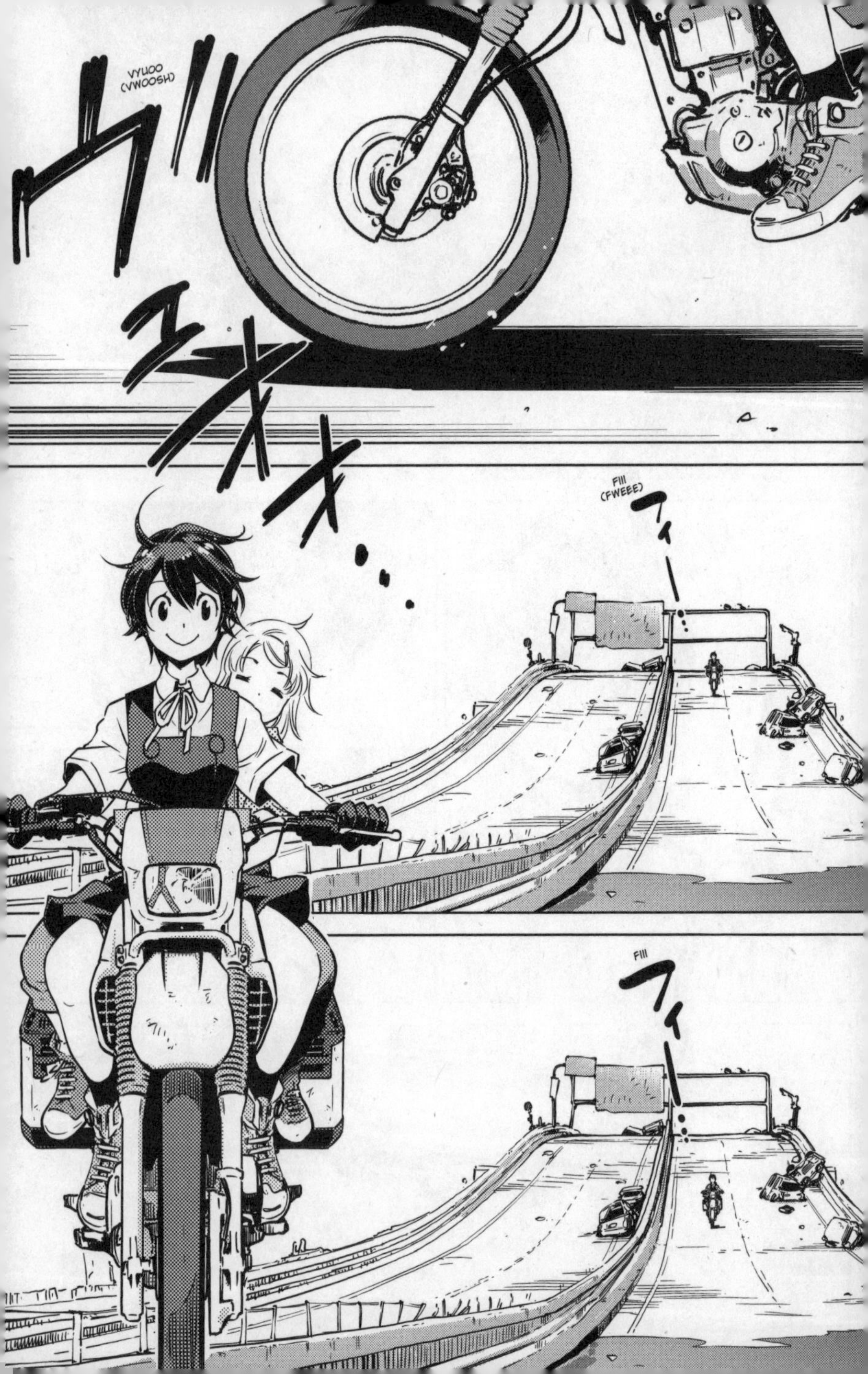
VYUOO
(VWOOSH)
FIII
(FWEEE)
FIII

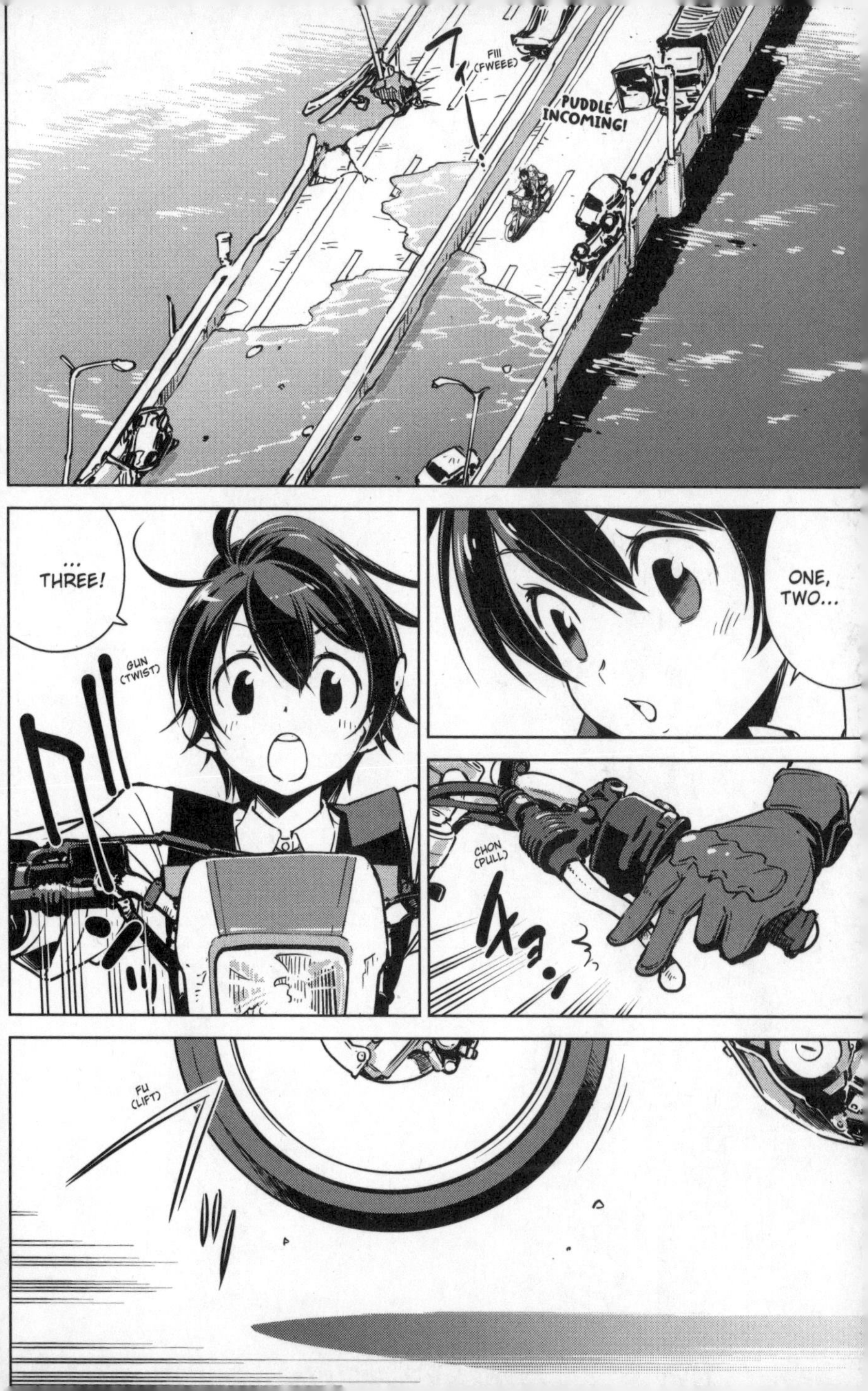
FIII
(FWEEE)
PUDDLE INCOMING!
ONE, TWO...
CHON
(PULL)
... THREE!
GUN
(TWIST)
FU
(LIFT)

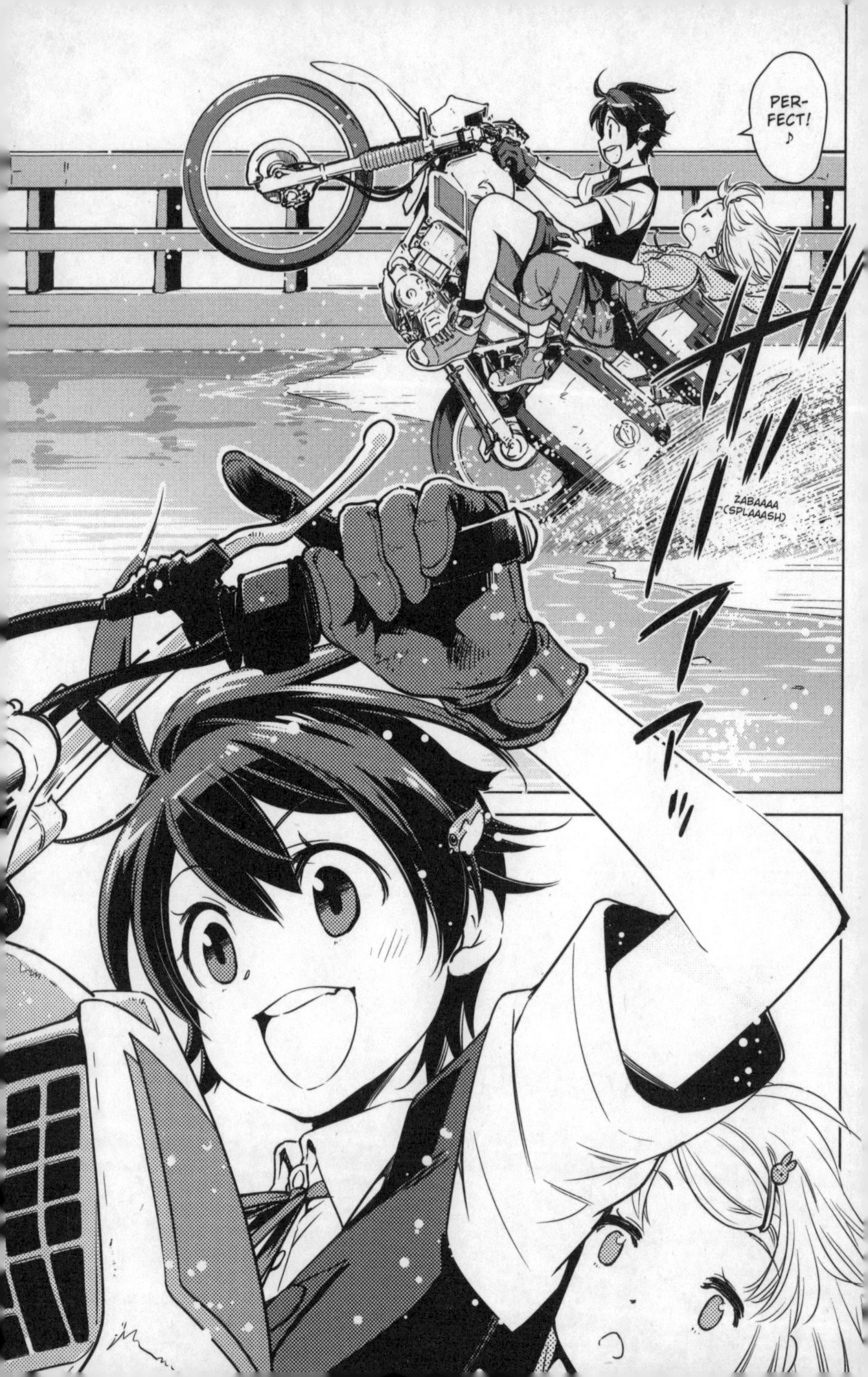
PER-
FECT!
♪
ZABAAAA
(SPLAAASH)

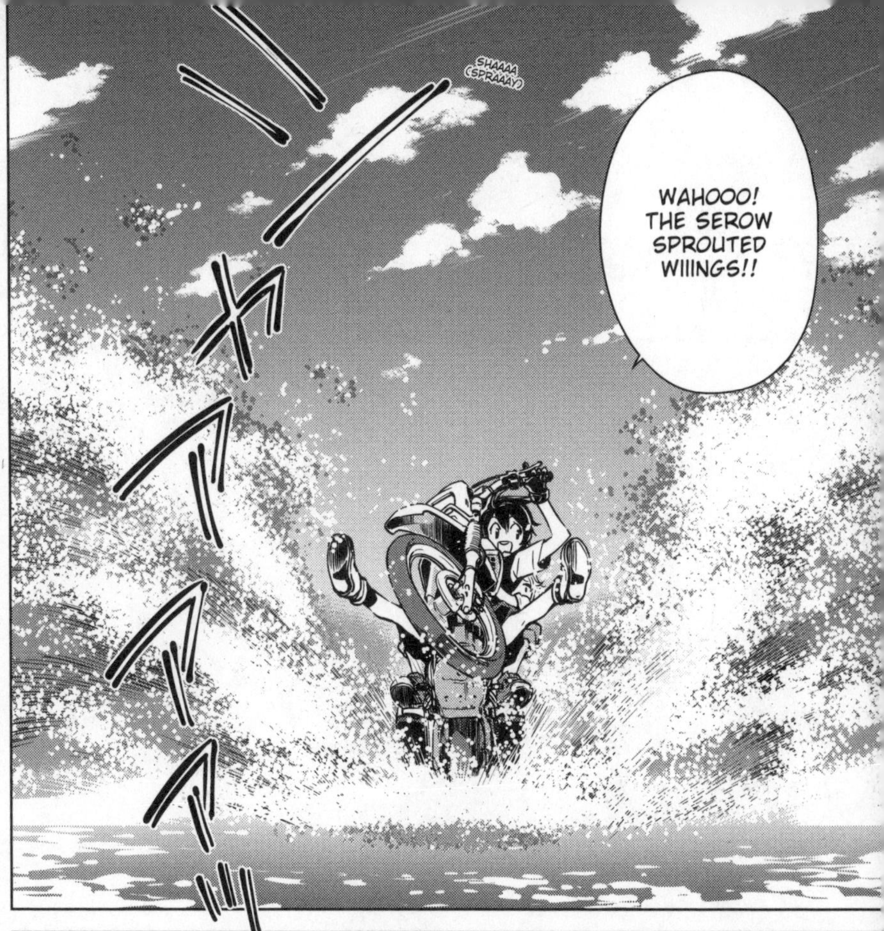
WAHOOO! THE SEROW SPROUTED WIIINGS!!
SHAAAA (SPRAAAY)
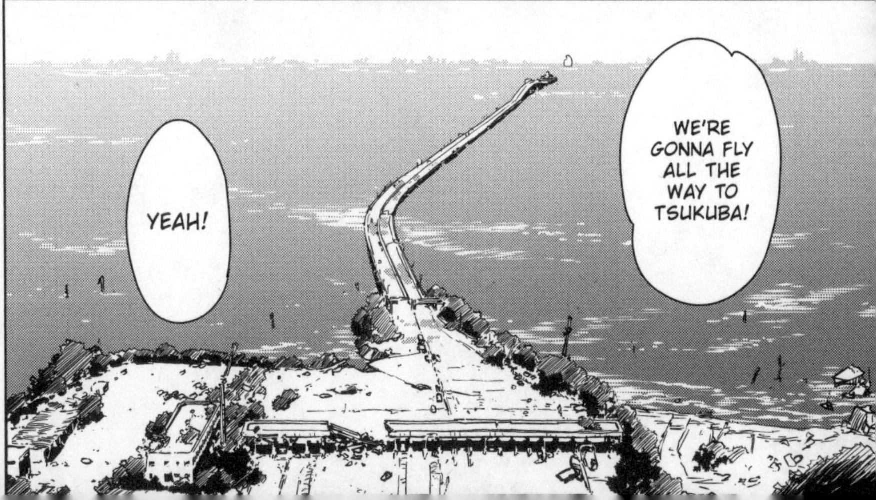
WE'RE GONNA FLY ALL THE WAY TO TSUKUBA!
YEAH!

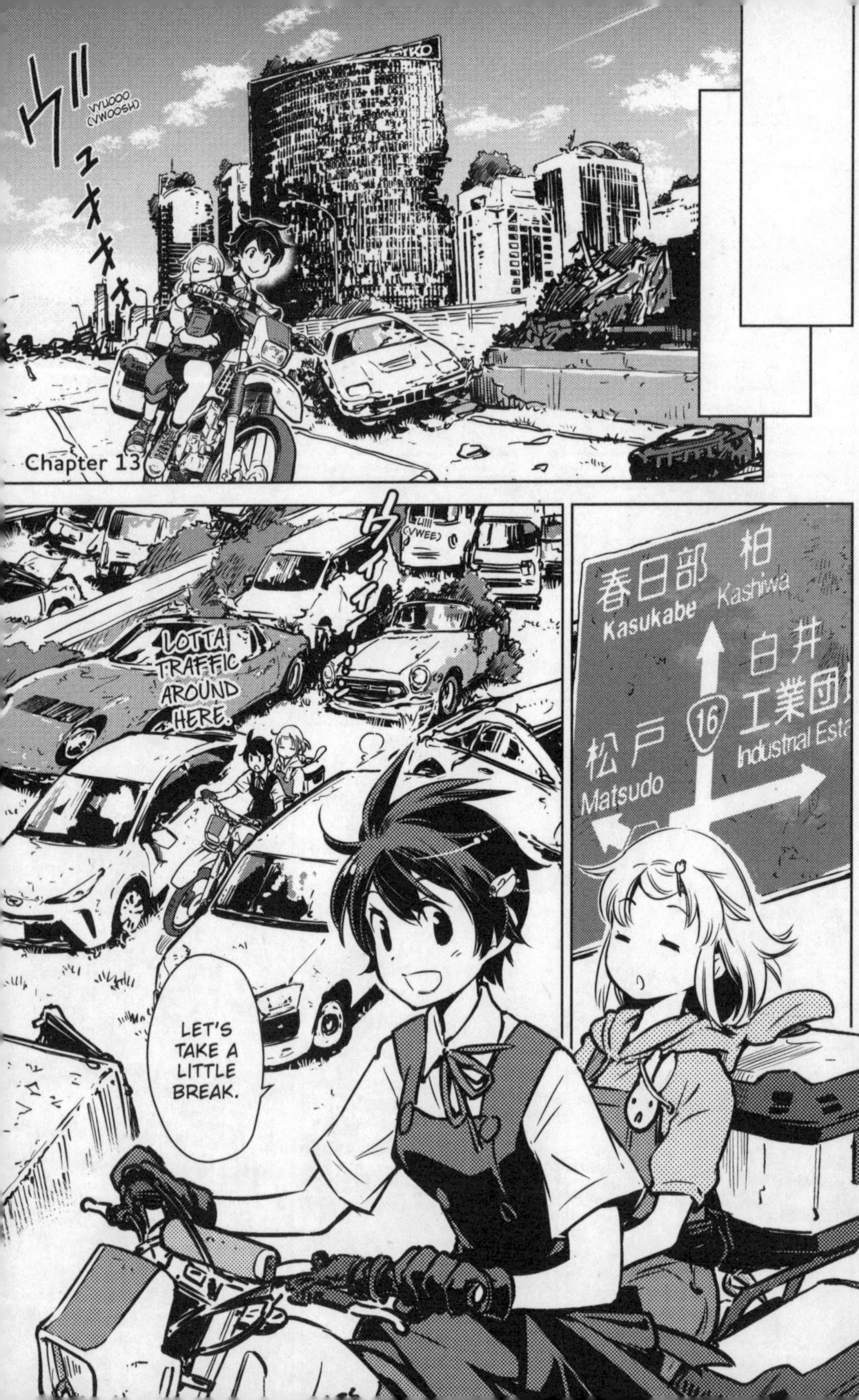
Chapter 13
VYUOOO (VWOOSH)
春日部 柏
Kasukabe Kashiwa
白井
工業団
Industrial Esta
16
松戸
Matsudo
LET'S TAKE A LITTLE BREAK.
(VWEE)
LOTTA TRAFFIC AROUND HERE.

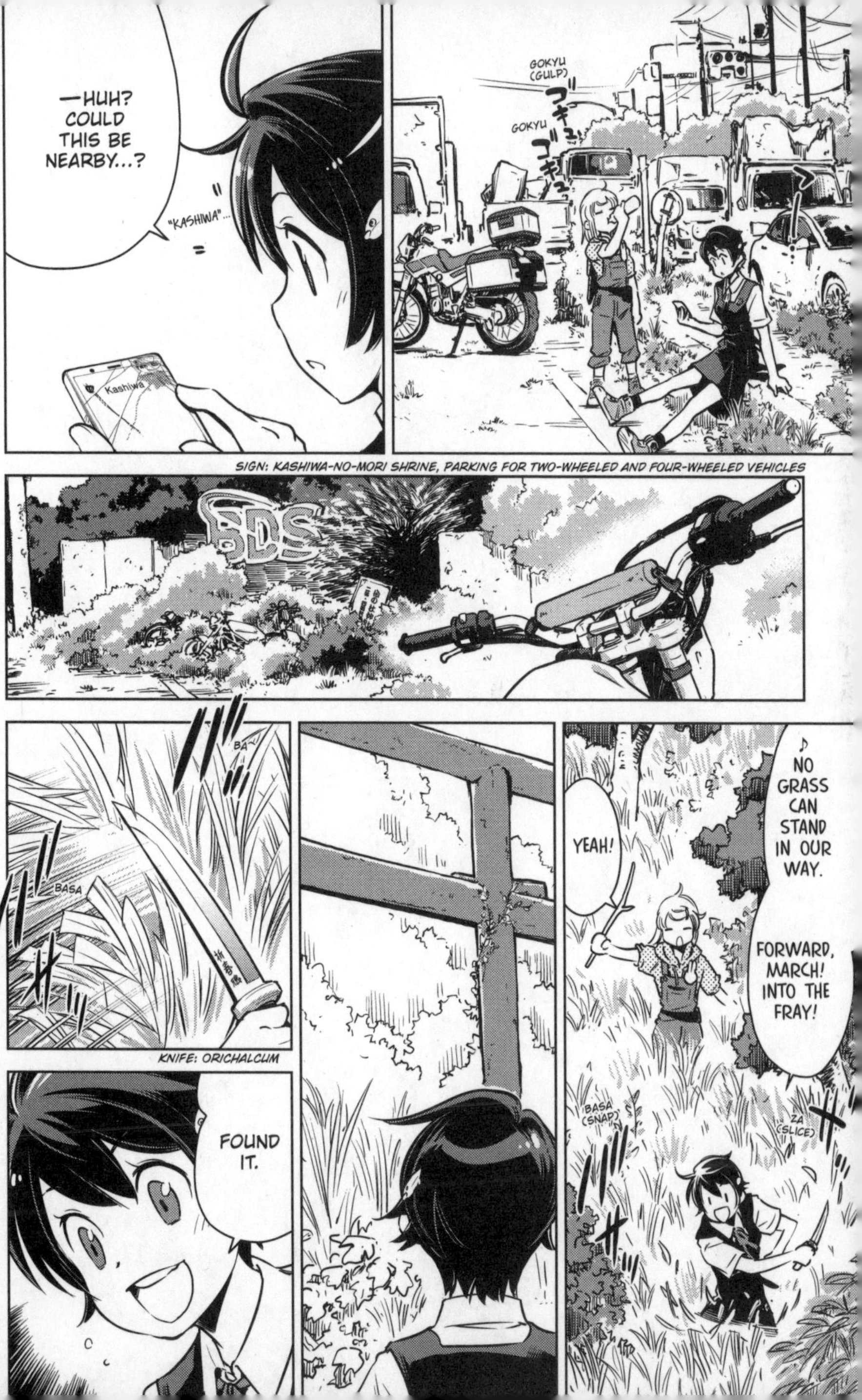
GOKYU (GULP)
ゴキュ
GOKYU
ゴキュ
—HUH? COULD THIS BE NEARBY...?
"KASHIWA"...
Kashiwa
SIGN: KASHIWA-NO-MORI SHRINE, PARKING FOR TWO-WHEELED AND FOUR-WHEELED VEHICLES
♪ NO GRASS CAN STAND IN OUR WAY.
YEAH!
FORWARD, MARCH! INTO THE FRAY!
BASA (SNAP)
ZA (SLICE)
BA
BASA
KNIFE: ORICHALCUM
FOUND IT.

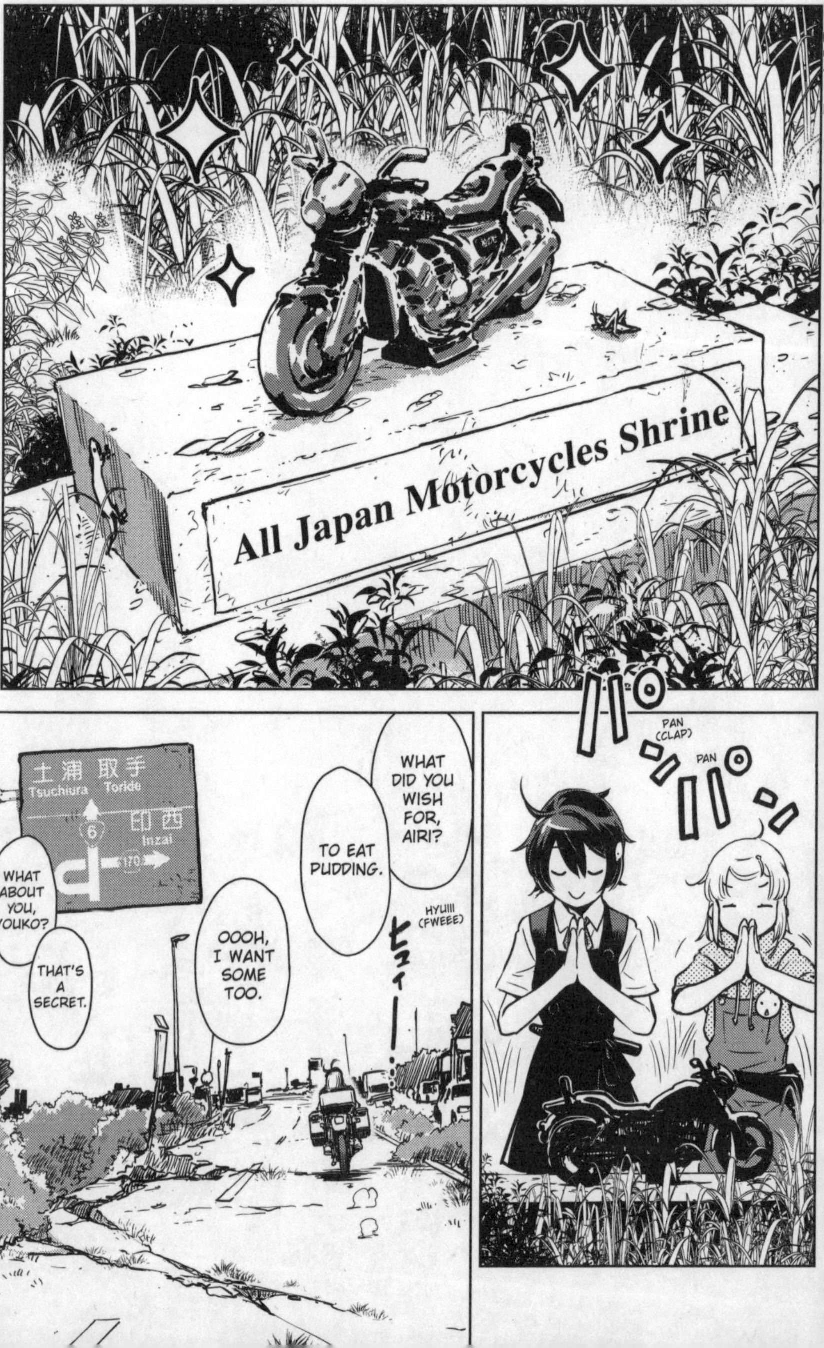
All Japan Motorcycles Shrine
PAN (CLAP)
PAN
WHAT DID YOU WISH FOR, AIRI?
TO EAT PUDDING.
HYUIII (FWEEE)
OOOH, I WANT SOME TOO.
土浦 取手
Tsuchiura Toride
6
印西
Inzai
170
WHAT ABOUT YOU, YOUKO?
THAT'S A SECRET.
NO FAIR!

Chapter 13 | Tsukuba

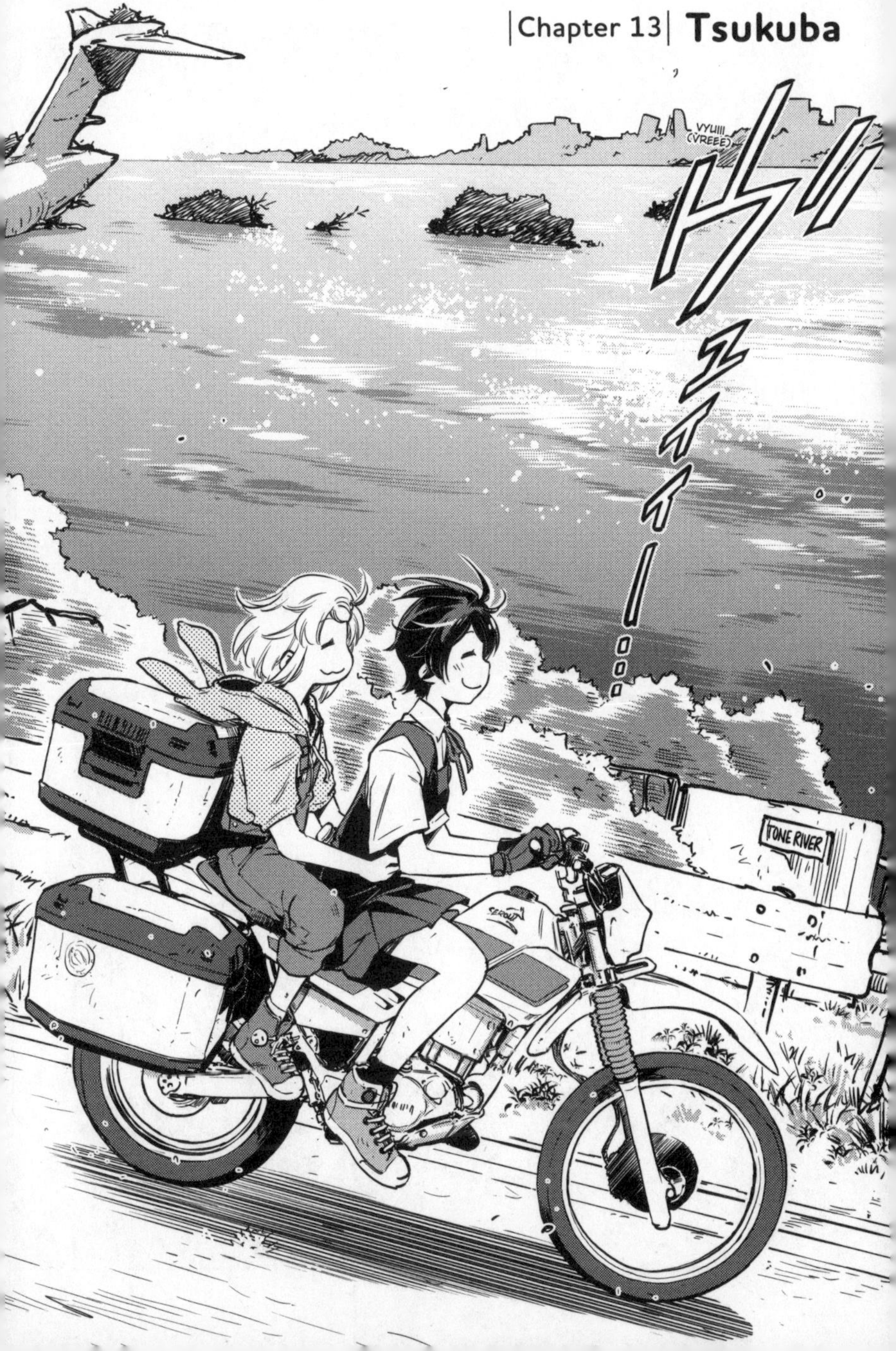
VYUIII
(VREEE)
TONE RIVER

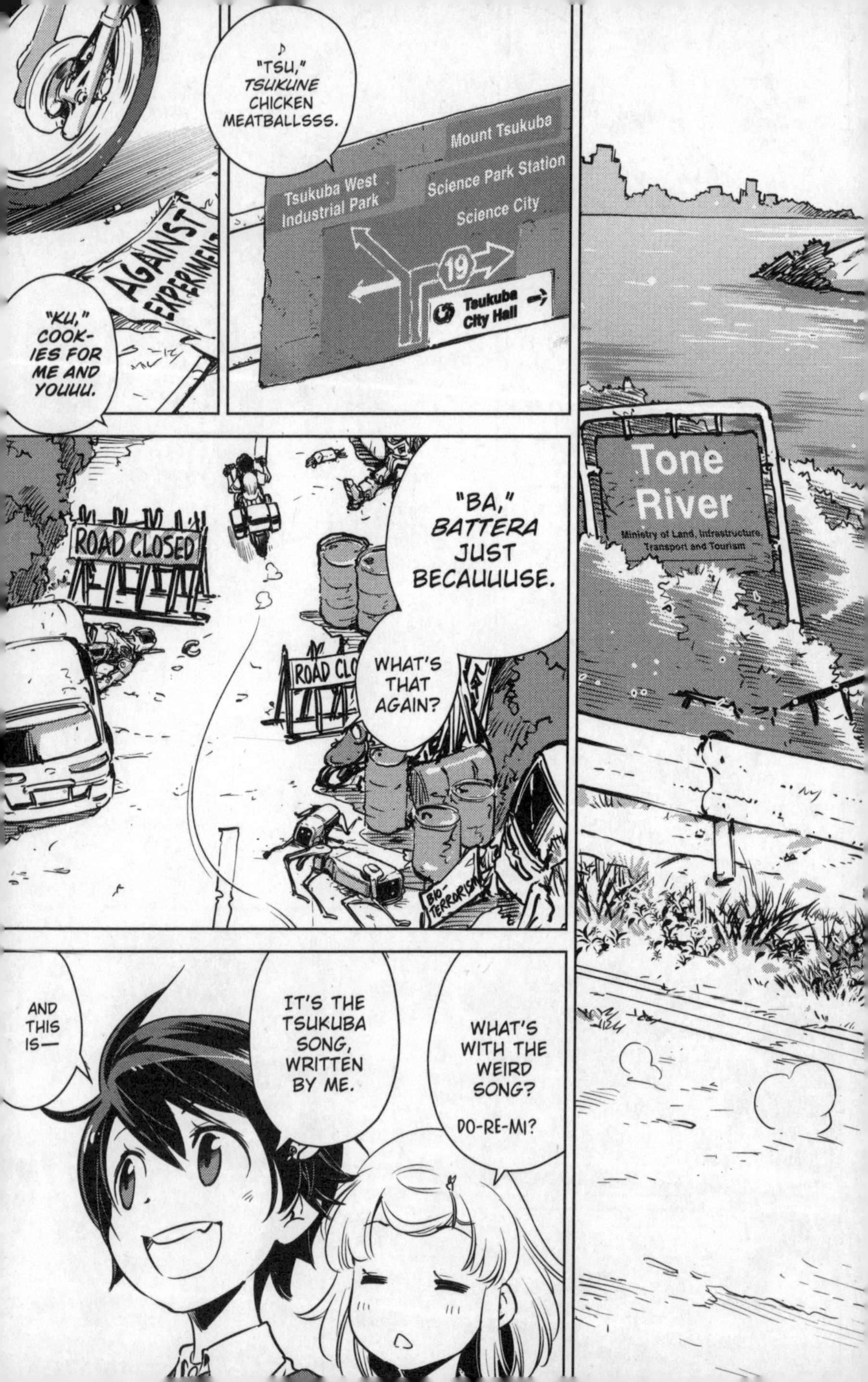
Tone River
Ministry of Land, Infrastructure, Transport and Tourism
♪ "TSU," TSUKUNE CHICKEN MEATBALLSSS.
Mount Tsukuba
Science Park Station
Science City
Tsukuba West Industrial Park
19
Tsukuba City Hall
AGAINST EXPERIMEN
"KU," COOKIES FOR ME AND YOUUU.
"BA," BATTERA JUST BECAUUUSE.
WHAT'S THAT AGAIN?
ROAD CLOSED
ROAD CLO
BIO-TERRORISM
WHAT'S WITH THE WEIRD SONG?
DO-RE-MI?
IT'S THE TSUKUBA SONG, WRITTEN BY ME.
AND THIS IS—

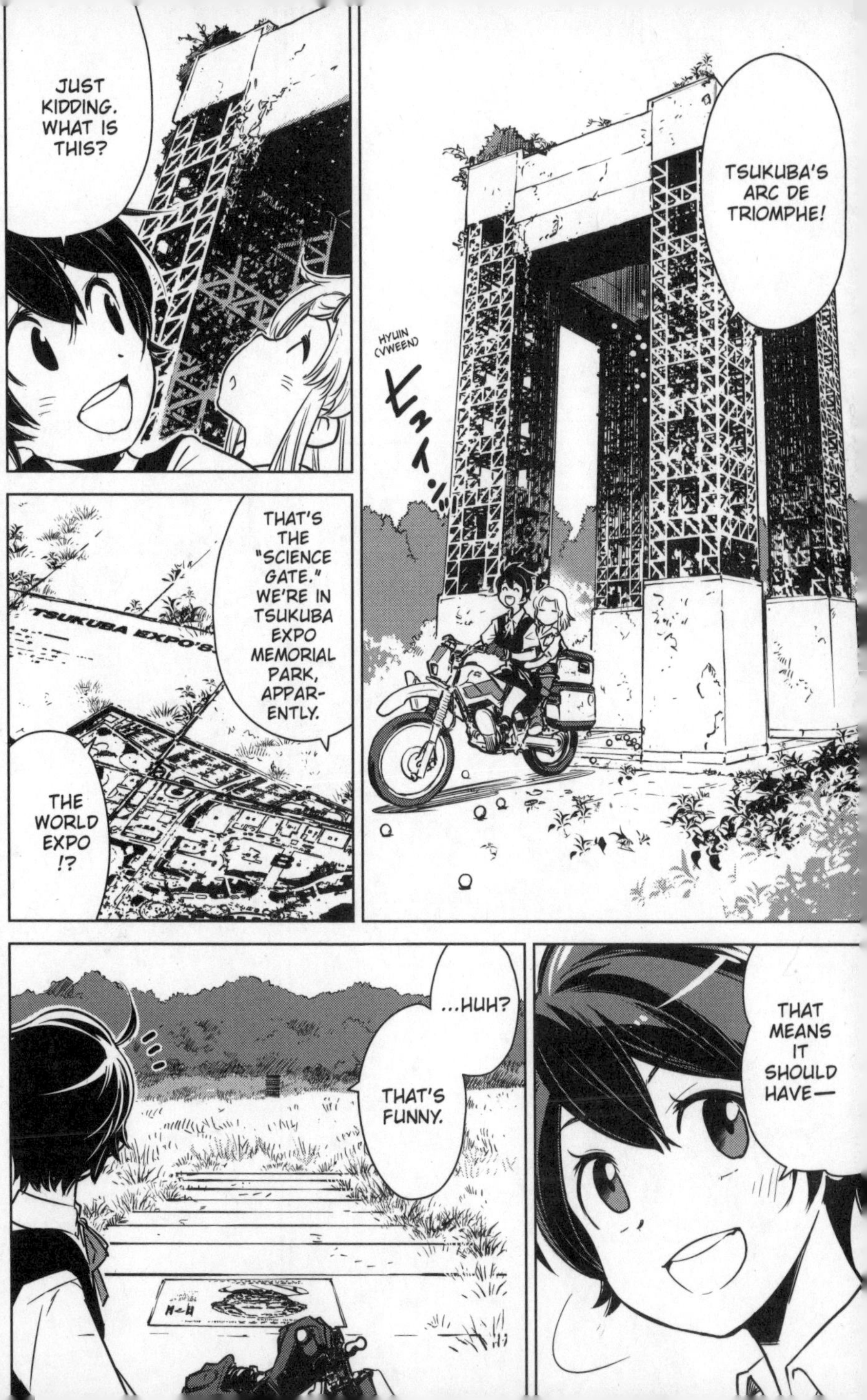
TSUKUBA'S ARC DE TRIOMPHE!
HYUIN (VWEEND)
JUST KIDDING. WHAT IS THIS?
THAT'S THE "SCIENCE GATE." WE'RE IN TSUKUBA EXPO MEMORIAL PARK, APPARENTLY.
TSUKUBA EXPO'S
THE WORLD EXPO !?
THAT MEANS IT SHOULD HAVE—
...HUH?
THAT'S FUNNY.

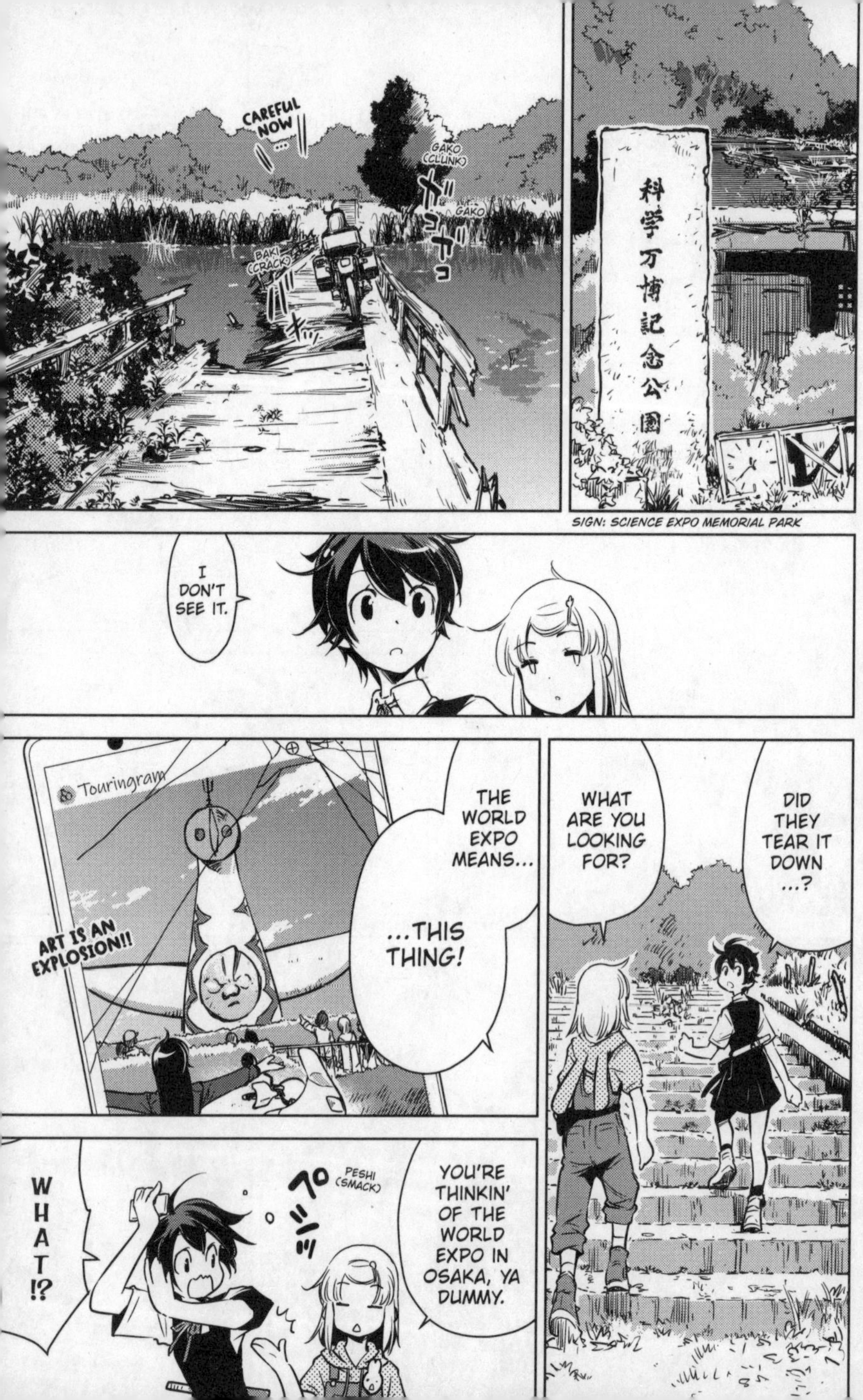
科学万博記念公園
SIGN: SCIENCE EXPO MEMORIAL PARK
CAREFUL NOW...
GAKO (CLUNK)
GAKO
BAKI (CRACK)
I DON'T SEE IT.
DID THEY TEAR IT DOWN ...?
WHAT ARE YOU LOOKING FOR?
THE WORLD EXPO MEANS...
...THIS THING!
Touringram
ART IS AN EXPLOSION!!
YOU'RE THINKIN' OF THE WORLD EXPO IN OSAKA, YA DUMMY.
PESHI (SMACK)
WHAT!?

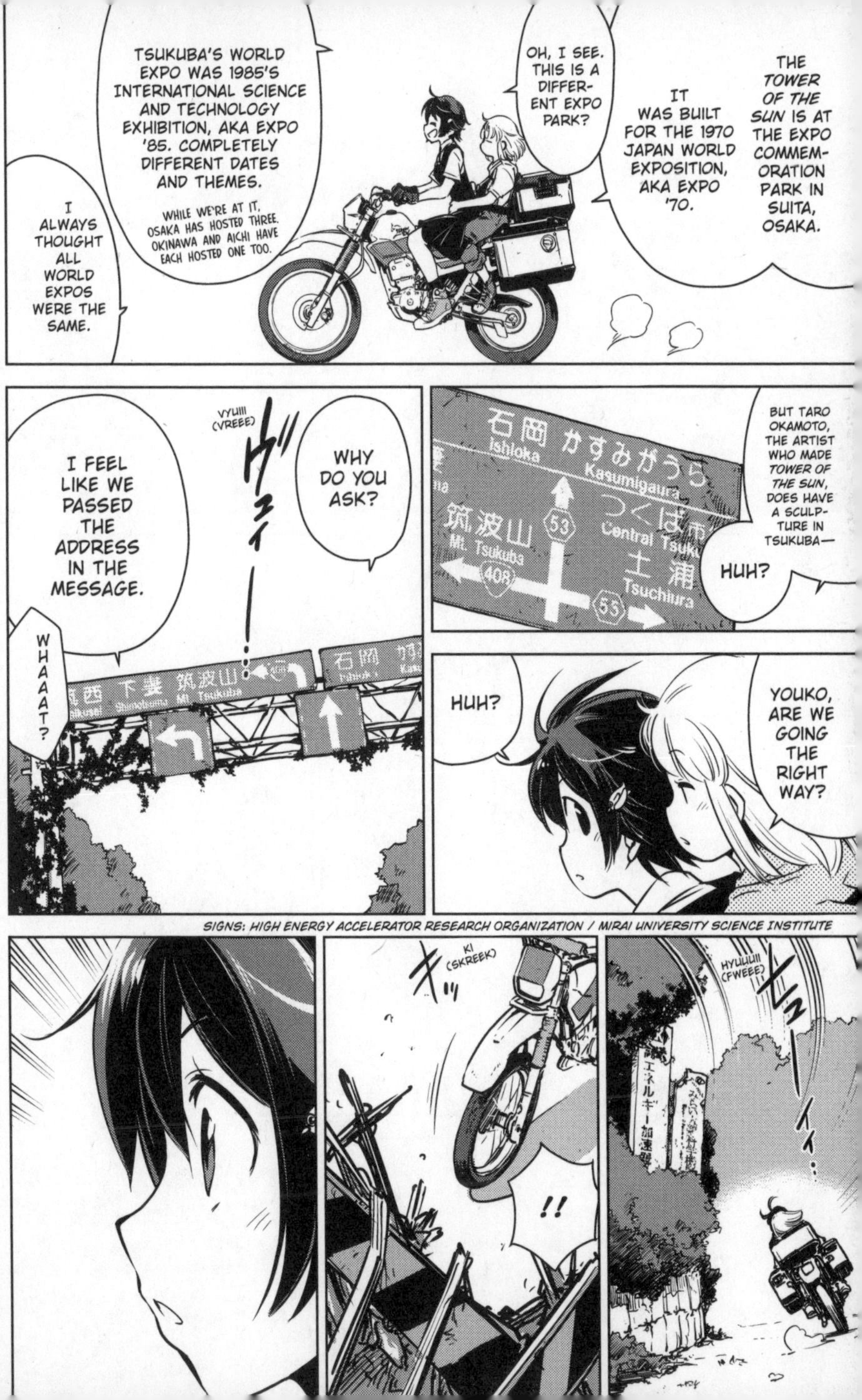
THE TOWER OF THE SUN IS AT THE EXPO COMMEMORATION PARK IN SUITA, OSAKA.
IT WAS BUILT FOR THE 1970 JAPAN WORLD EXPOSITION, AKA EXPO '70.
OH, I SEE. THIS IS A DIFFERENT EXPO PARK?
TSUKUBA'S WORLD EXPO WAS 1985'S INTERNATIONAL SCIENCE AND TECHNOLOGY EXHIBITION, AKA EXPO '85. COMPLETELY DIFFERENT DATES AND THEMES.
WHILE WE'RE AT IT, OSAKA HAS HOSTED THREE. OKINAWA AND AICHI HAVE EACH HOSTED ONE TOO.
I ALWAYS THOUGHT ALL WORLD EXPOS WERE THE SAME.
石岡 かすみがうら
Kasumigaura
筑波山
Mt. Tsukuba
53
408
土浦
Tsuchiura
55
BUT TARO OKAMOTO, THE ARTIST WHO MADE TOWER OF THE SUN, DOES HAVE A SCULPTURE IN TSUKUBA—
HUH?
YOUKO, ARE WE GOING THE RIGHT WAY?
HUH?
VYUIII (VREEE)
WHY DO YOU ASK?
I FEEL LIKE WE PASSED THE ADDRESS IN THE MESSAGE.
WHAAAAT?
筑波山
Mt. Tsukuba
下妻
Shimotsuma
石岡
SIGNS: HIGH ENERGY ACCELERATOR RESEARCH ORGANIZATION / MIRAI UNIVERSITY SCIENCE INSTITUTE
HYUUUII (FWEEE)
KI (SKREEK)
!!

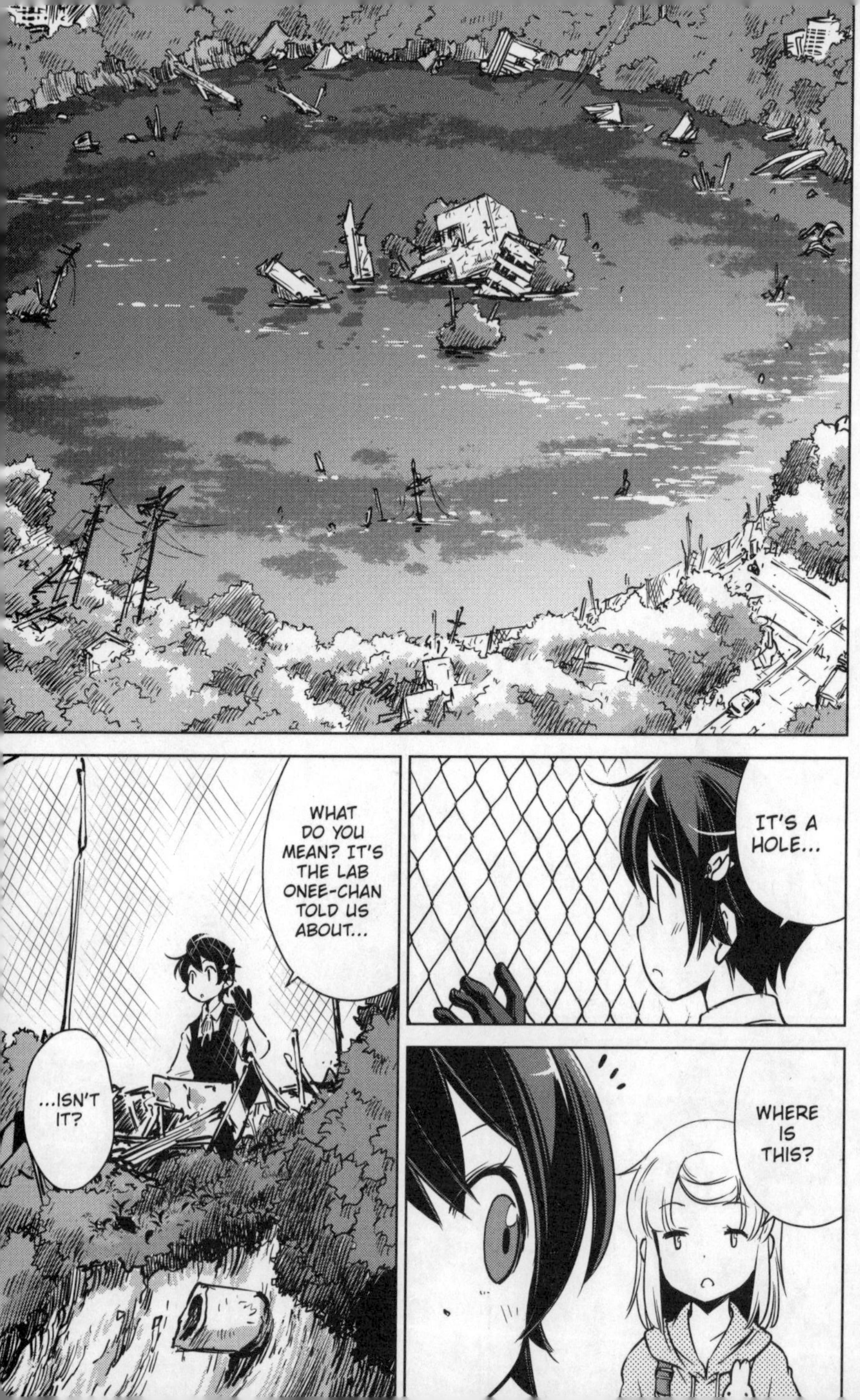
IT'S A HOLE...
WHERE IS THIS?
WHAT DO YOU MEAN? IT'S THE LAB ONEE-CHAN TOLD US ABOUT...
...ISN'T IT?

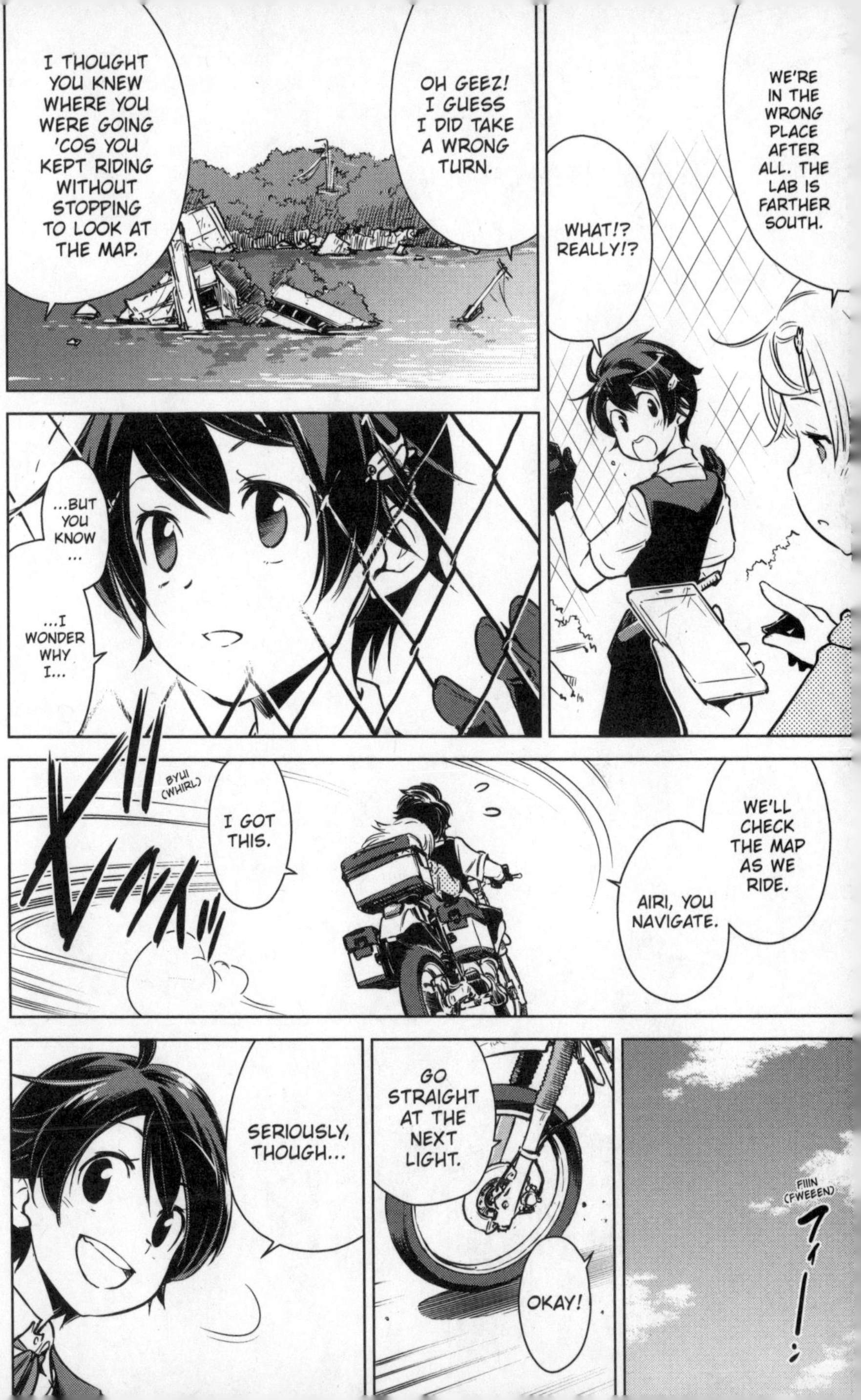
WE'RE IN THE WRONG PLACE AFTER ALL. THE LAB IS FARTHER SOUTH.
WHAT!? REALLY!?
OH GEEZ! I GUESS I DID TAKE A WRONG TURN.
I THOUGHT YOU KNEW WHERE YOU WERE GOING 'COS YOU KEPT RIDING WITHOUT STOPPING TO LOOK AT THE MAP.
...BUT YOU KNOW...
...I WONDER WHY I...
WE'LL CHECK THE MAP AS WE RIDE.
AIRI, YOU NAVIGATE.
I GOT THIS.
BYUI (WHIRL)
FIIIN (FWEEEND)
GO STRAIGHT AT THE NEXT LIGHT.
OKAY!
SERIOUSLY, THOUGH...

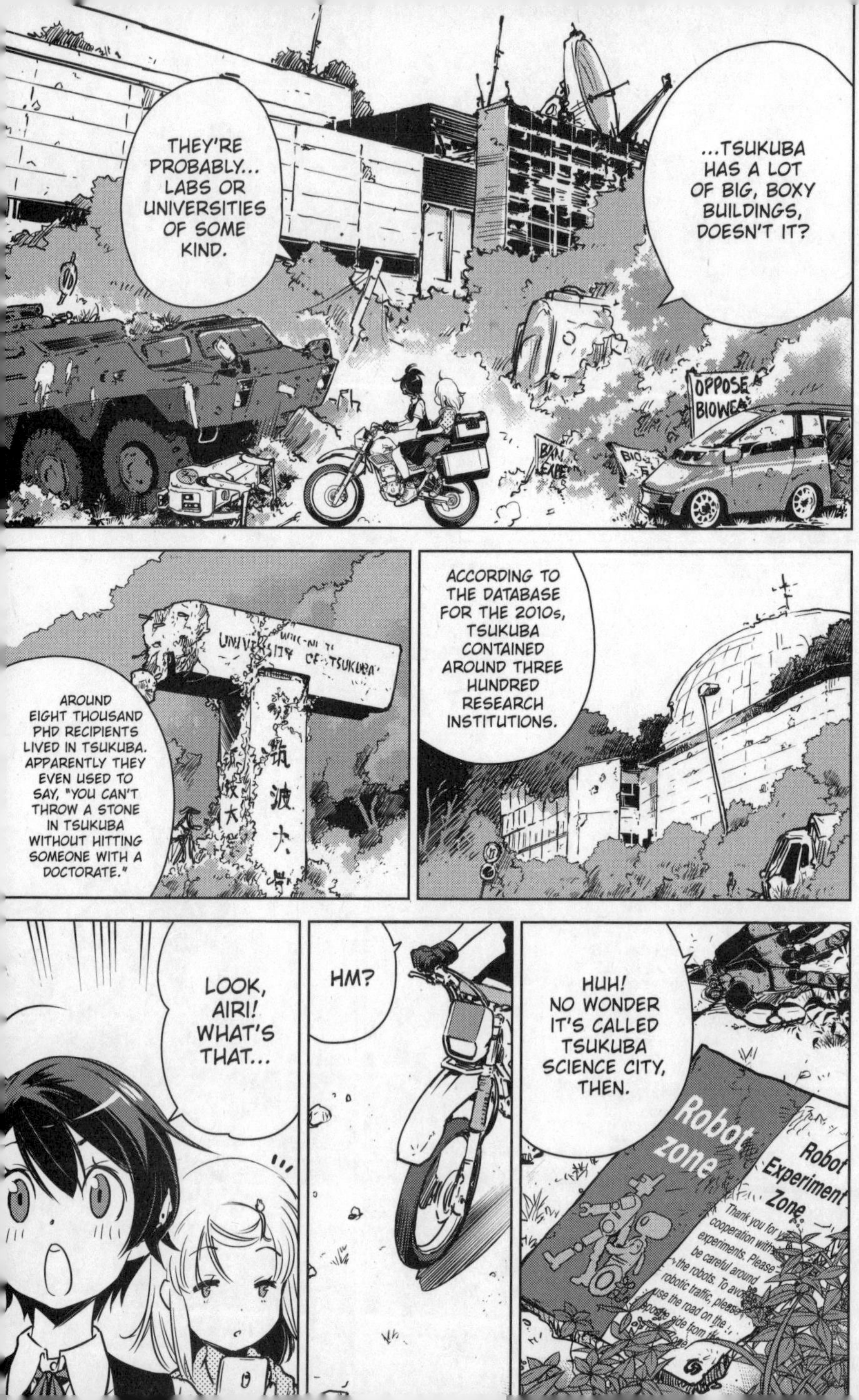
...TSUKUBA HAS A LOT OF BIG, BOXY BUILDINGS, DOESN'T IT?
THEY'RE PROBABLY... LABS OR UNIVERSITIES OF SOME KIND.
OPPOSE BIOWEA
ACCORDING TO THE DATABASE FOR THE 2010s, TSUKUBA CONTAINED AROUND THREE HUNDRED RESEARCH INSTITUTIONS.
UNIVERSITY OF TSUKUBA
筑波大学
AROUND EIGHT THOUSAND PHD RECIPIENTS LIVED IN TSUKUBA. APPARENTLY THEY EVEN USED TO SAY, "YOU CAN'T THROW A STONE IN TSUKUBA WITHOUT HITTING SOMEONE WITH A DOCTORATE."
HUH! NO WONDER IT'S CALLED TSUKUBA SCIENCE CITY, THEN.
Robot zone
Robot Experiment Zone
HM?
LOOK, AIRI! WHAT'S THAT...

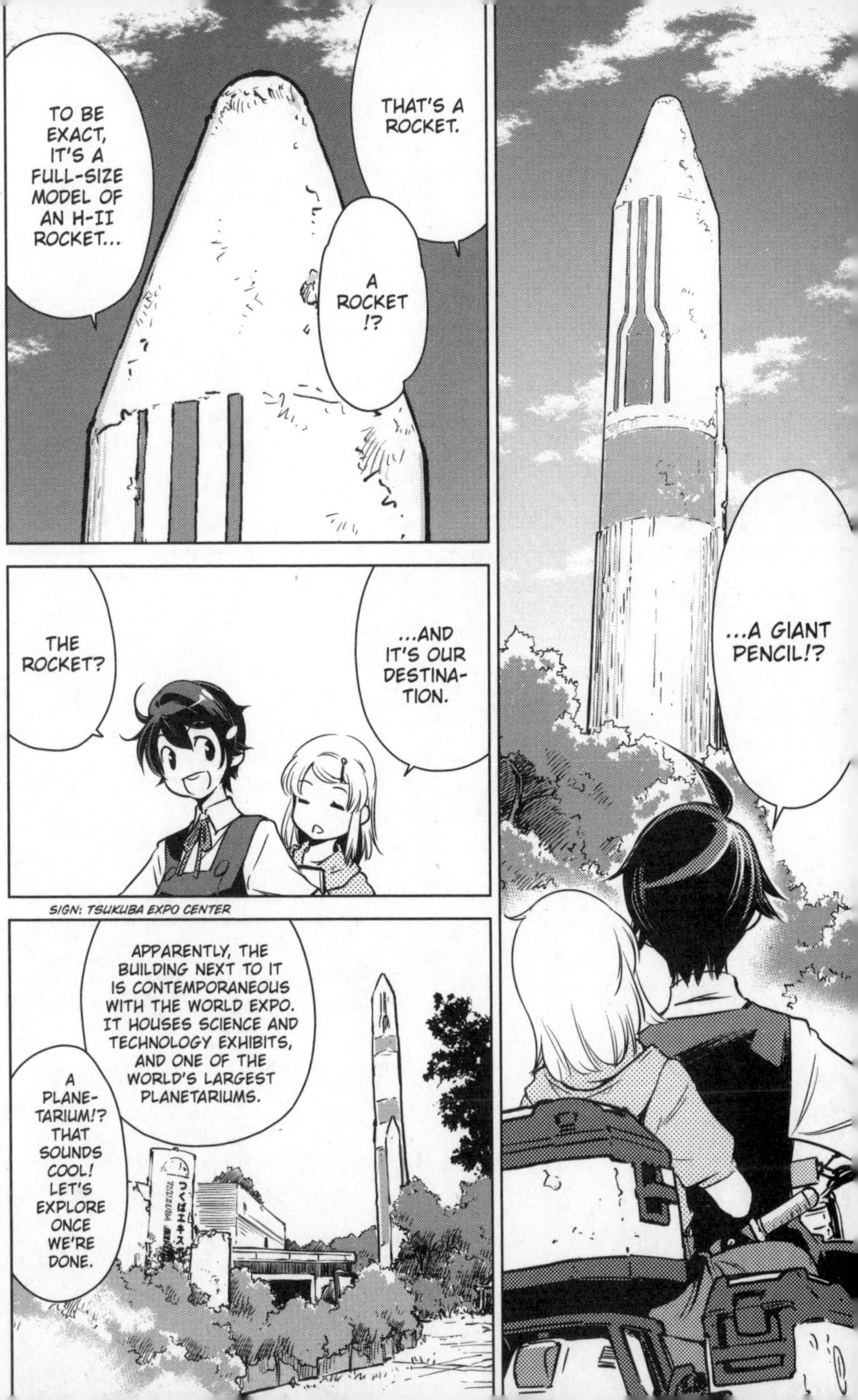
...A GIANT PENCIL!?
THAT'S A ROCKET.
A ROCKET!?
TO BE EXACT, IT'S A FULL-SIZE MODEL OF AN H-II ROCKET...
...AND IT'S OUR DESTINATION.
THE ROCKET?
SIGN: TSUKUBA EXPO CENTER
APPARENTLY, THE BUILDING NEXT TO IT IS CONTEMPORANEOUS WITH THE WORLD EXPO. IT HOUSES SCIENCE AND TECHNOLOGY EXHIBITS, AND ONE OF THE WORLD'S LARGEST PLANETARIUMS.
A PLANETARIUM!? THAT SOUNDS COOL! LET'S EXPLORE ONCE WE'RE DONE.

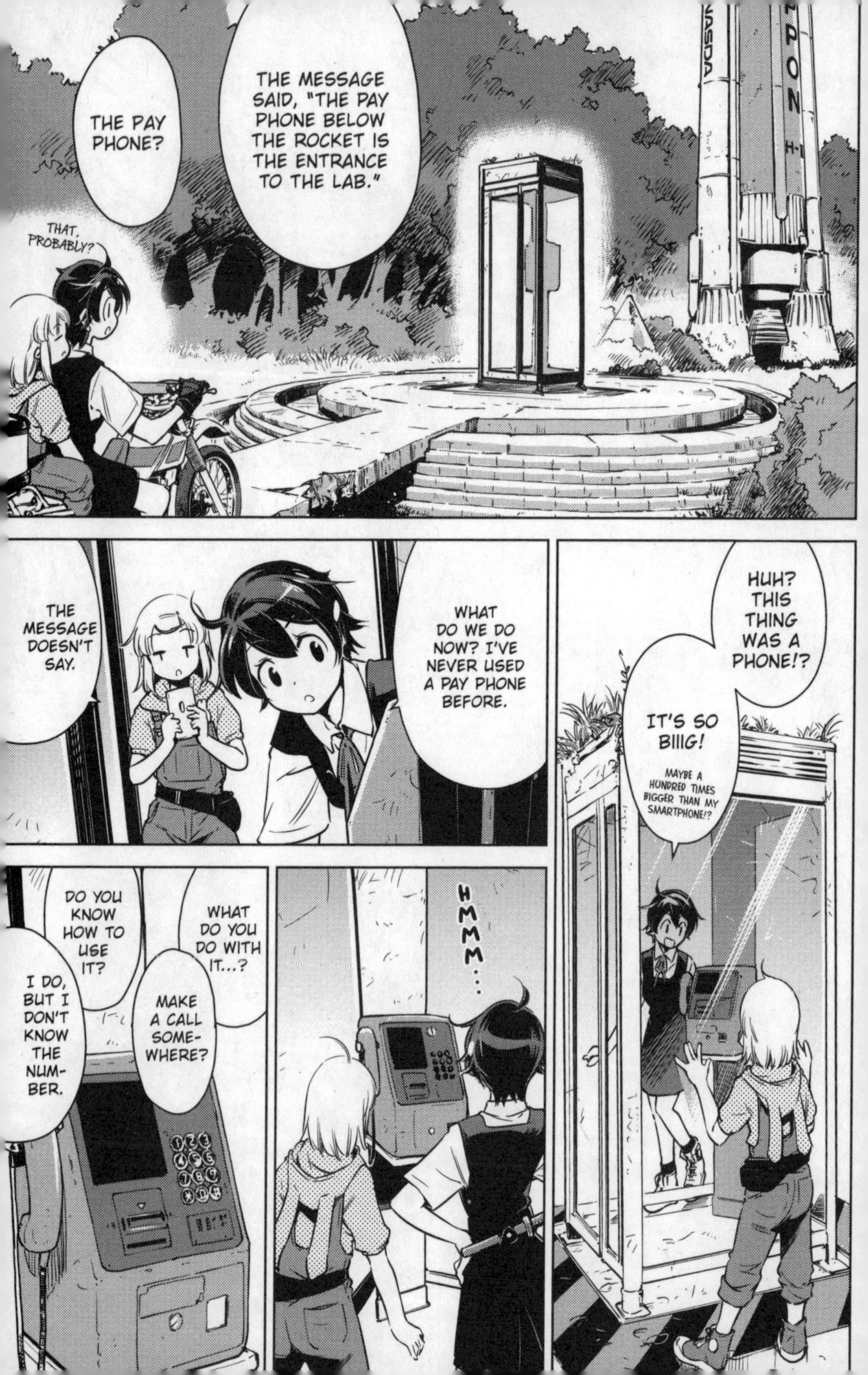
THE MESSAGE SAID, "THE PAY PHONE BELOW THE ROCKET IS THE ENTRANCE TO THE LAB."
THE PAY PHONE?
THAT, PROBABLY?
NASDA
HUH? THIS THING WAS A PHONE!?
IT'S SO BIIIG!
MAYBE A HUNDRED TIMES BIGGER THAN MY SMARTPHONE!?
WHAT DO WE DO NOW? I'VE NEVER USED A PAY PHONE BEFORE.
THE MESSAGE DOESN'T SAY.
HMMM...
WHAT DO YOU DO WITH IT...?
DO YOU KNOW HOW TO USE IT?
MAKE A CALL SOMEWHERE?
I DO, BUT I DON'T KNOW THE NUMBER.

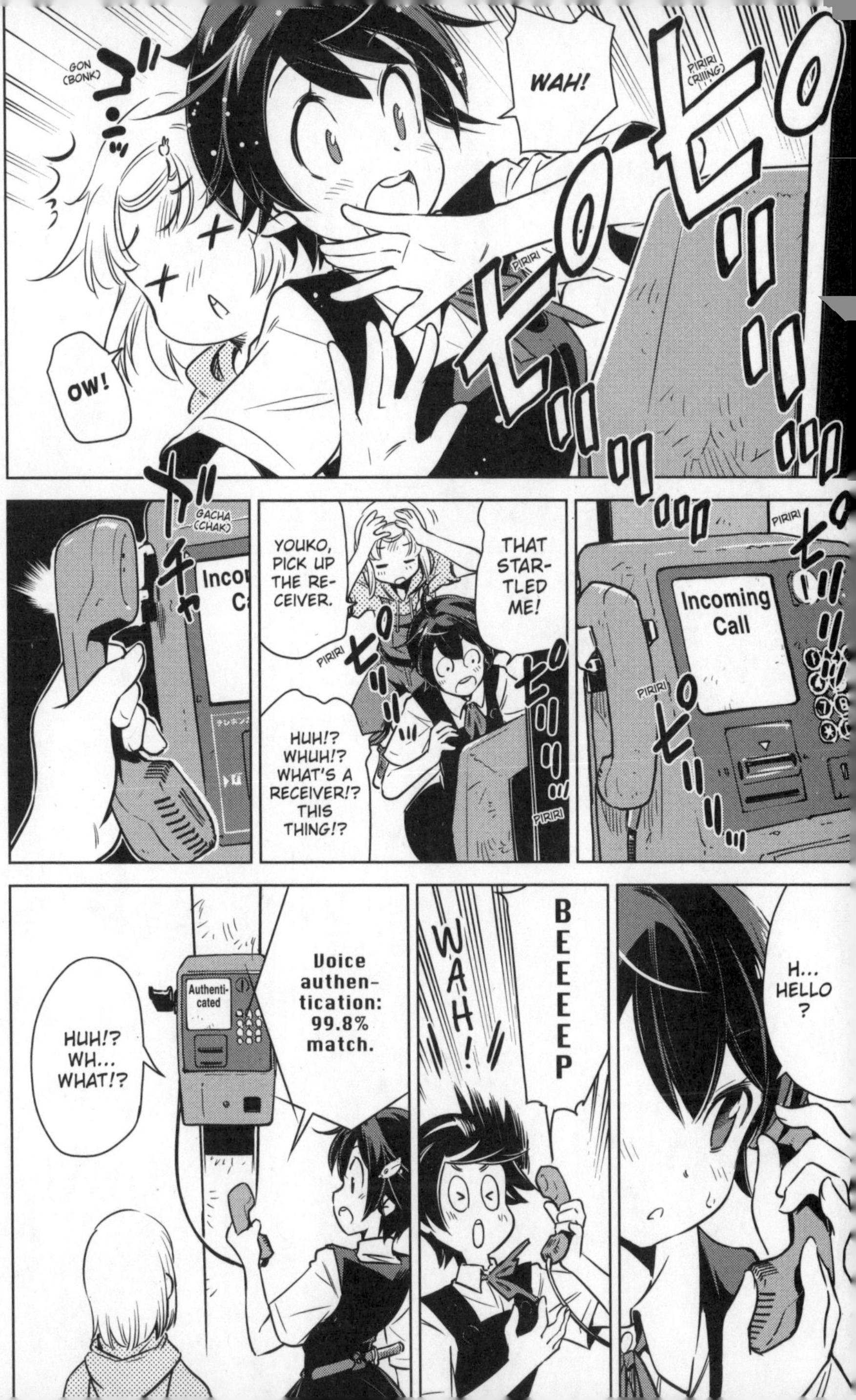
PIRIRI (RIIING)
WAH!
GON (BONK)
PIRIRI
OW!
PIRIRI
Incoming Call
PIRIRI
THAT STAR-TLED ME!
YOUKO, PICK UP THE RE-CEIVER.
PIRIRI
HUH!? WHUH!? WHAT'S A RECEIVER!? THIS THING!?
PIRIRI
GACHA (CHAK)
H... HELLO ?
BEEEEP
WAH!
Voice authen-tication: 99.8% match.
Authenti-cated
HUH!? WH... WHAT!?

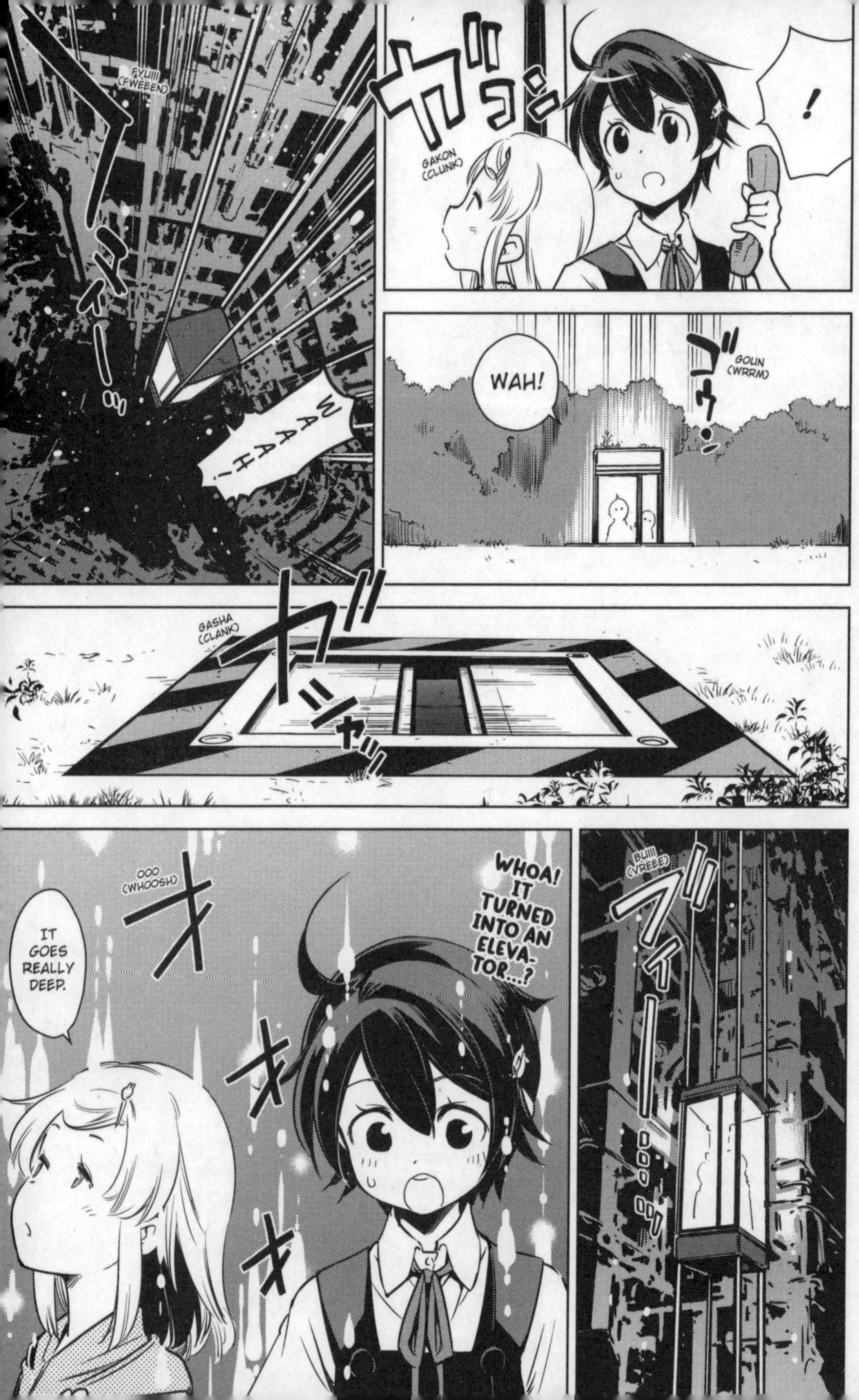
!
GAKON (CLUNK)
GOUN (WRRM)
WAH!
FYUIII (FWEEEN)
WAAAH!
GASHA (CLANK)
BUIII (VREEE)
WHOA! IT TURNED INTO AN ELEVATOR...?
OOO (WHOOSH)
IT GOES REALLY DEEP.

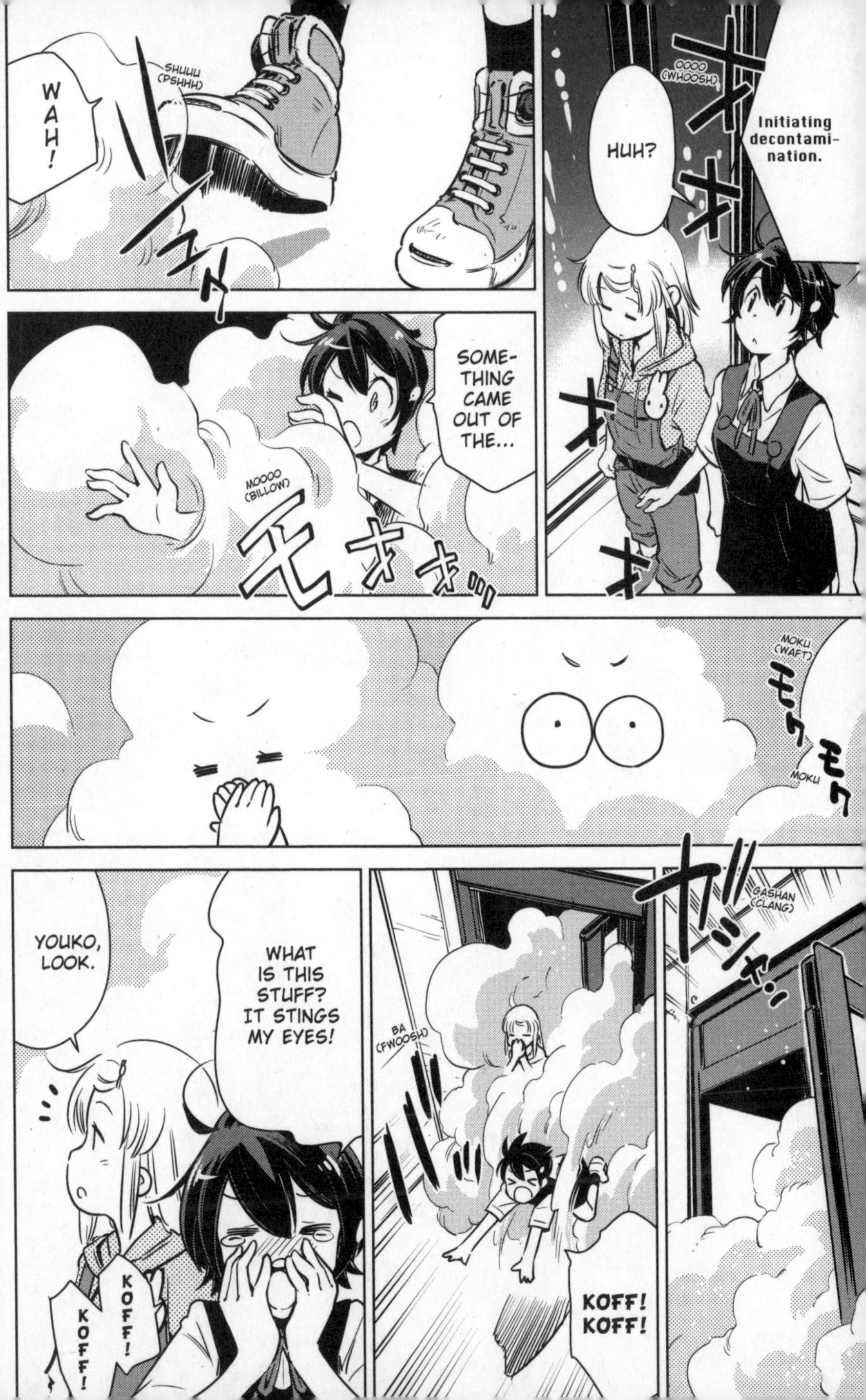
Initiating decontamination.
OOOO (WHOOSH)
HUH?
SHUUU (PSHHH)
WAH!
SOMETHING CAME OUT OF THE...
MOOOO (BILLOW)
MOKU (WAFT)
MOKU
GASHAN (CLANG)
BA (FWOOSH)
KOFF! KOFF!
WHAT IS THIS STUFF? IT STINGS MY EYES!
YOUKO, LOOK.
KOFF!
KOFF!

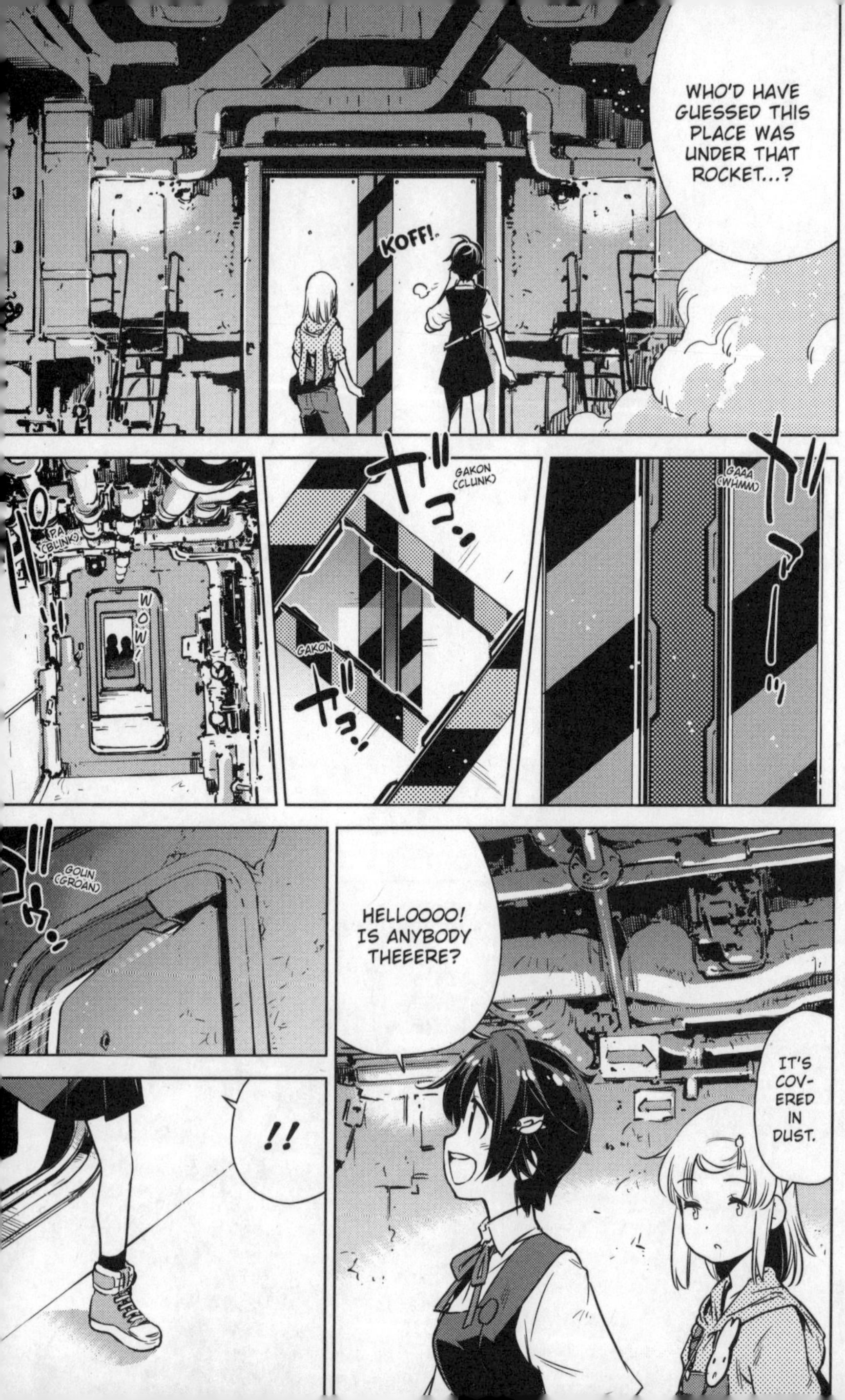
WHO'D HAVE GUESSED THIS PLACE WAS UNDER THAT ROCKET...?
KOFF!
GAAA (WHMM)
GAKON (CLUNK)
GAKON
PA (BLINK)
WOW!
HELLOOOO! IS ANYBODY THEEERE?
IT'S COV-ERED IN DUST.
GOUN (GROAN)
!!

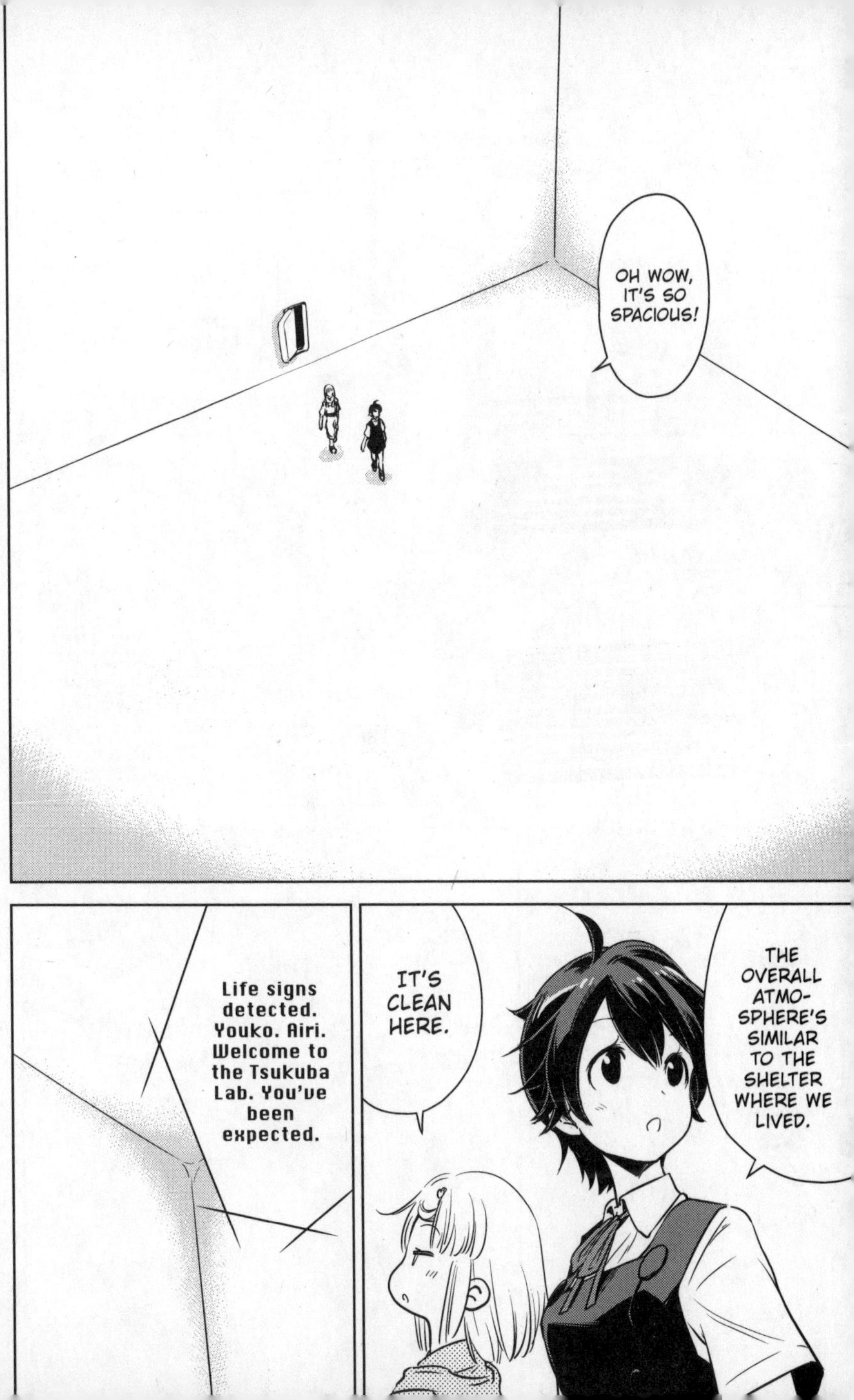
OH WOW, IT'S SO SPACIOUS!
THE OVERALL ATMOSPHERE'S SIMILAR TO THE SHELTER WHERE WE LIVED.
IT'S CLEAN HERE.
Life signs detected. Youko. Airi. Welcome to the Tsukuba Lab. You've been expected.

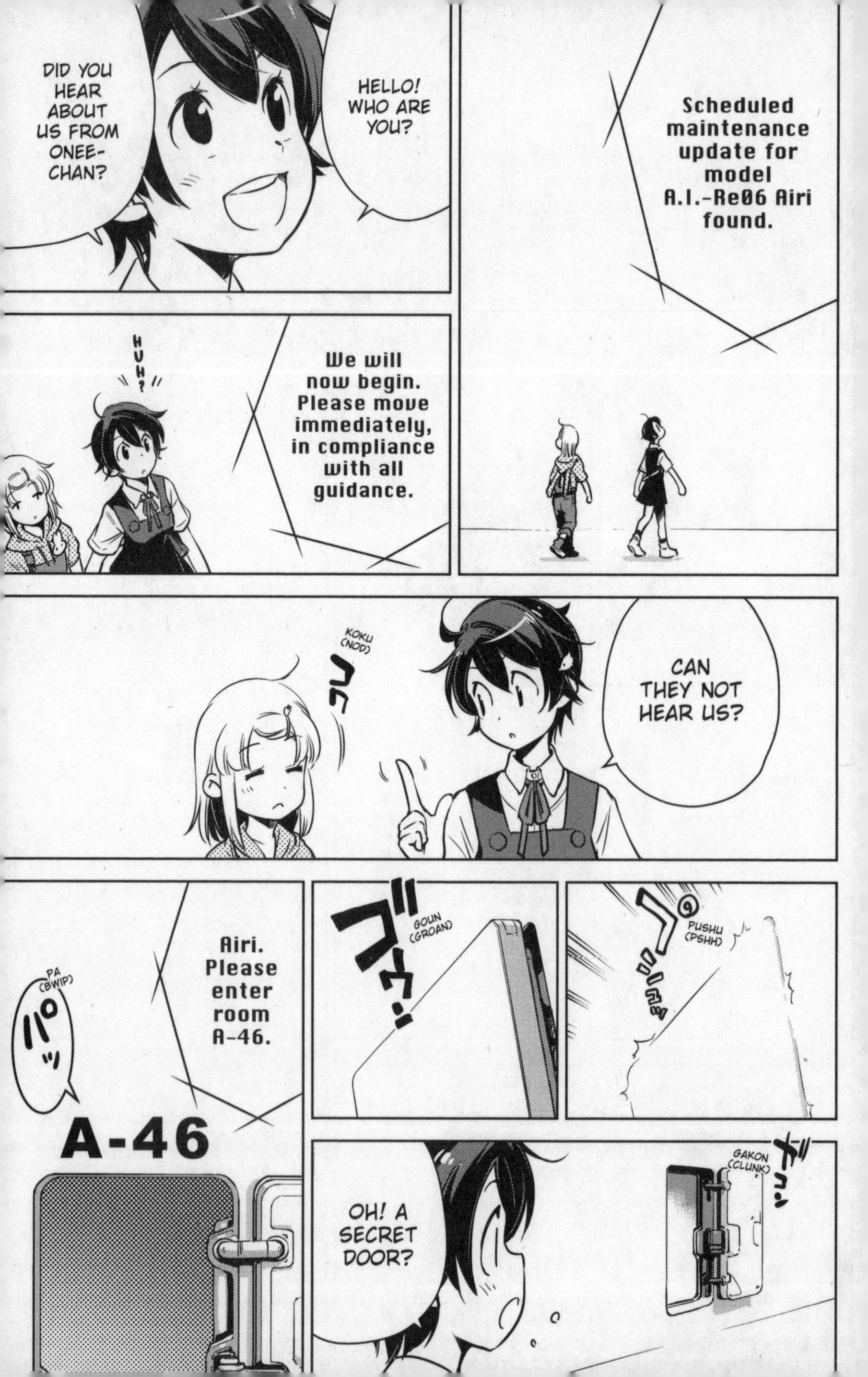
Scheduled maintenance update for model A.I.-Re06 Airi found.
HELLO! WHO ARE YOU?
DID YOU HEAR ABOUT US FROM ONEE-CHAN?
We will now begin. Please move immediately, in compliance with all guidance.
HUH?
CAN THEY NOT HEAR US?
KOKU (NOD)
PUSHU (PSHH)
GOUN (GROAN)
GAKON (CLUNK)
OH! A SECRET DOOR?
Airi. Please enter room A-46.
PA (BWIP)
A-46

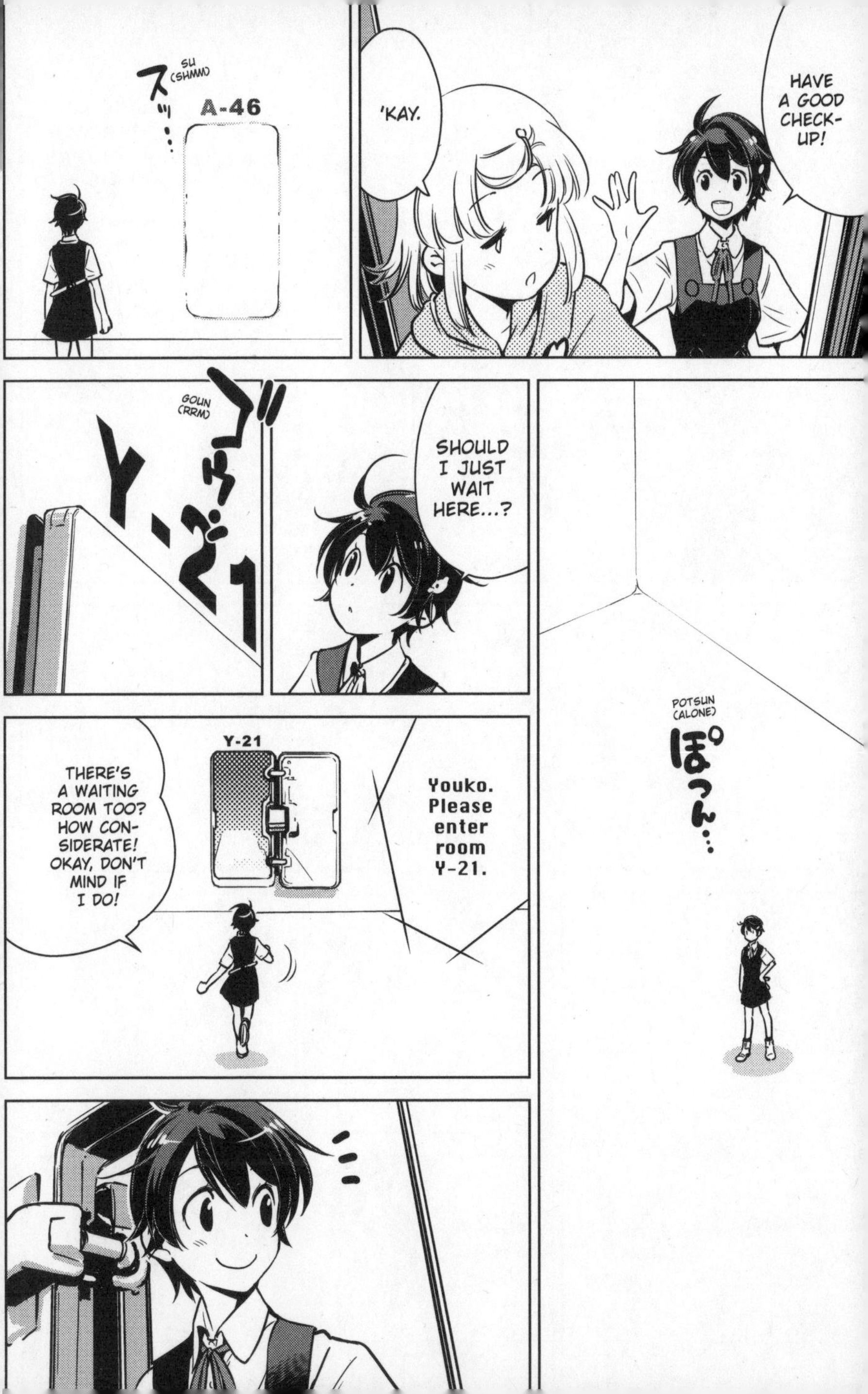
HAVE A GOOD CHECK-UP!
'KAY.
SU (SHMM)
A-46
POTSUN (ALONE)
ぽつん…
SHOULD I JUST WAIT HERE...?
GOUN (RRM)
ゴゥゥ
Y-21
Youko. Please enter room Y-21.
Y-21
THERE'S A WAITING ROOM TOO? HOW CON-SIDERATE! OKAY, DON'T MIND IF I DO!

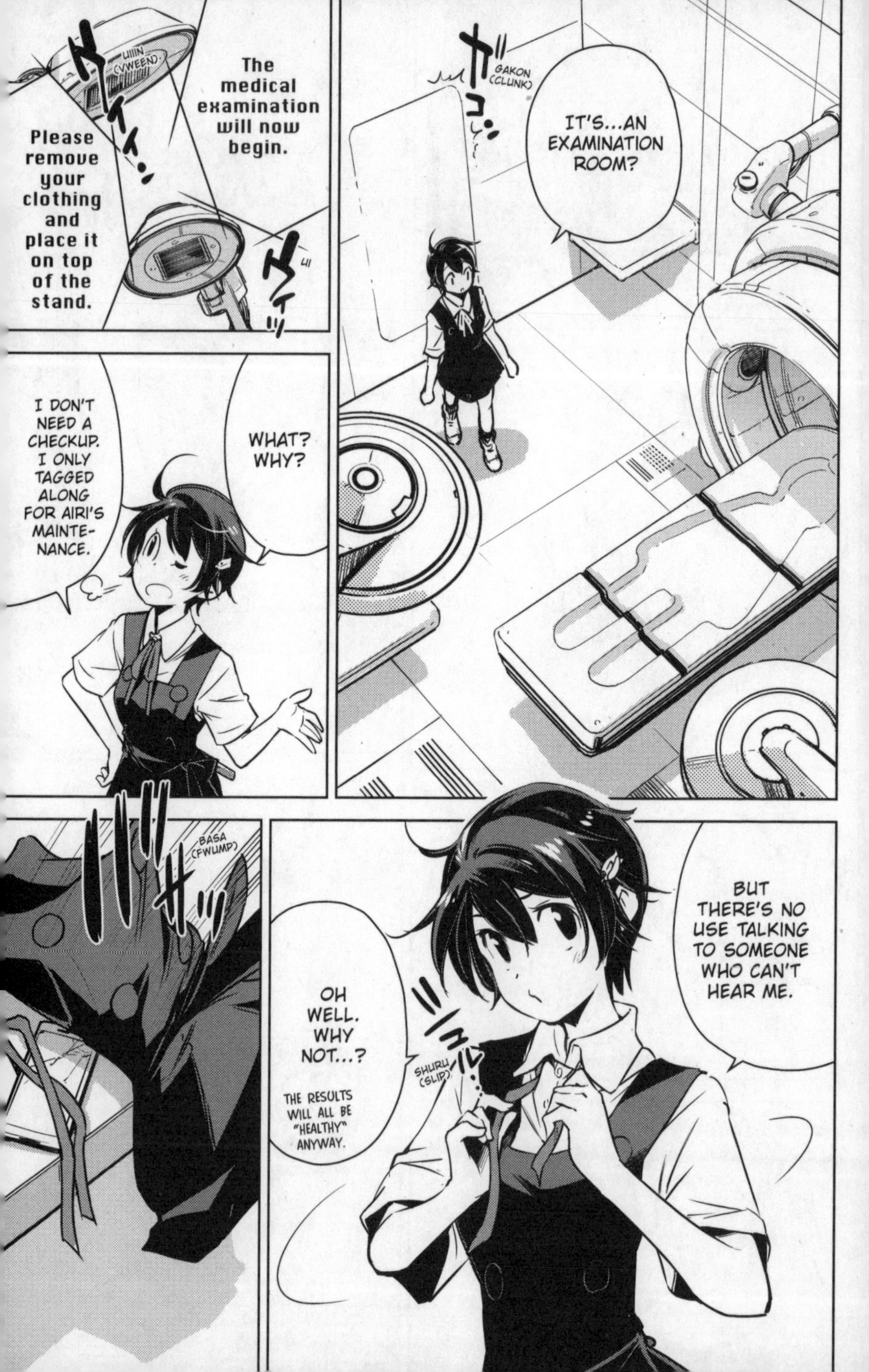
GAKON (CLUNK)
IT'S...AN EXAMINATION ROOM?
UIIIN (VWEEN)
The medical examination will now begin.
Please remove your clothing and place it on top of the stand.
WHAT? WHY?
I DON'T NEED A CHECKUP. I ONLY TAGGED ALONG FOR AIRI'S MAINTE-NANCE.
BUT THERE'S NO USE TALKING TO SOMEONE WHO CAN'T HEAR ME.
OH WELL. WHY NOT...?
SHURU (SLIP)
THE RESULTS WILL ALL BE "HEALTHY" ANYWAY.
BASA (FWUMP)

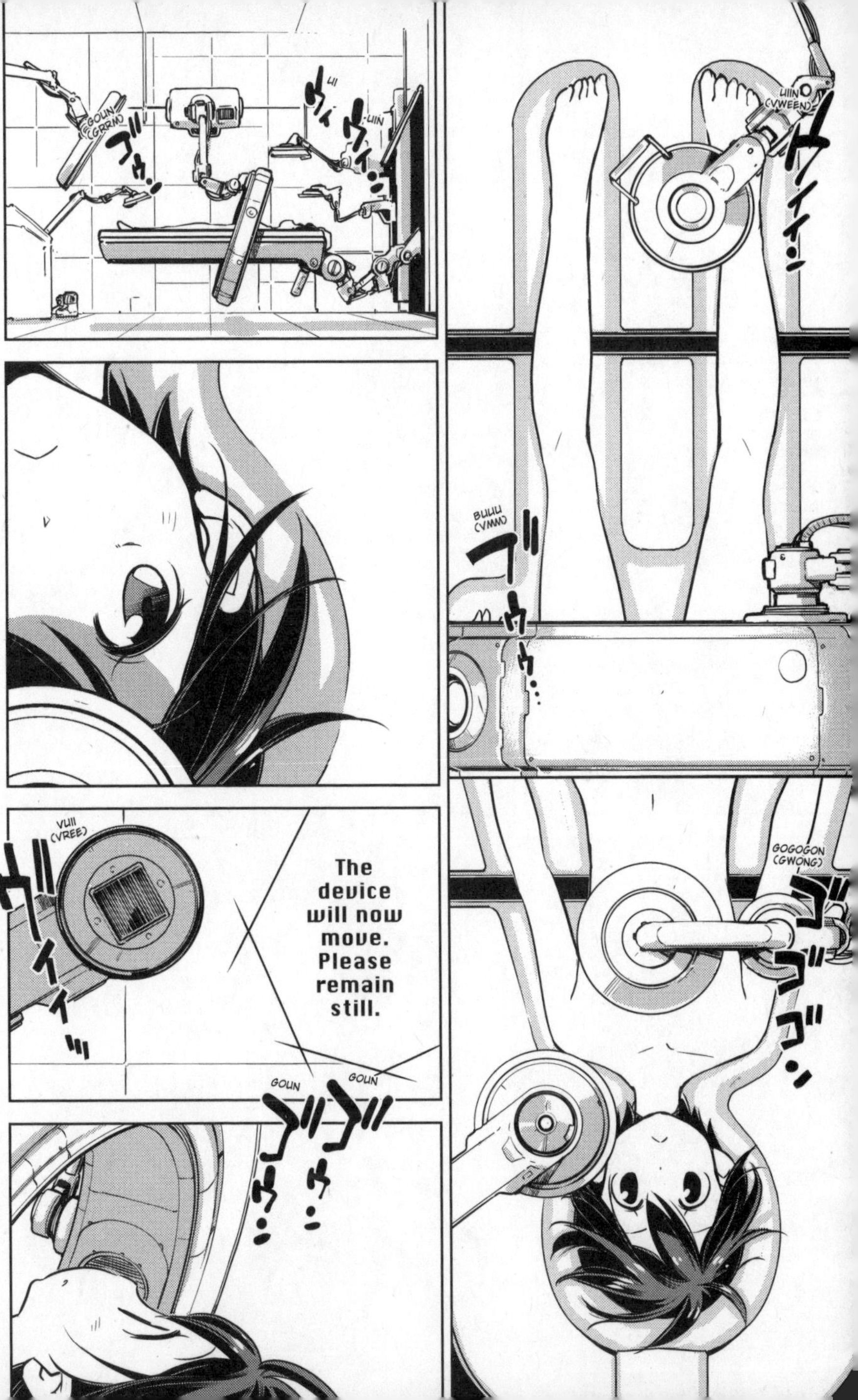
UIIN (VWEEN)
BUUU (VMM)
GOGOGON (GWONG)
UI
UIN
GOUN (GRRN)
The device will now move. Please remain still.
VUII (VREE)
GOUN
GOUN

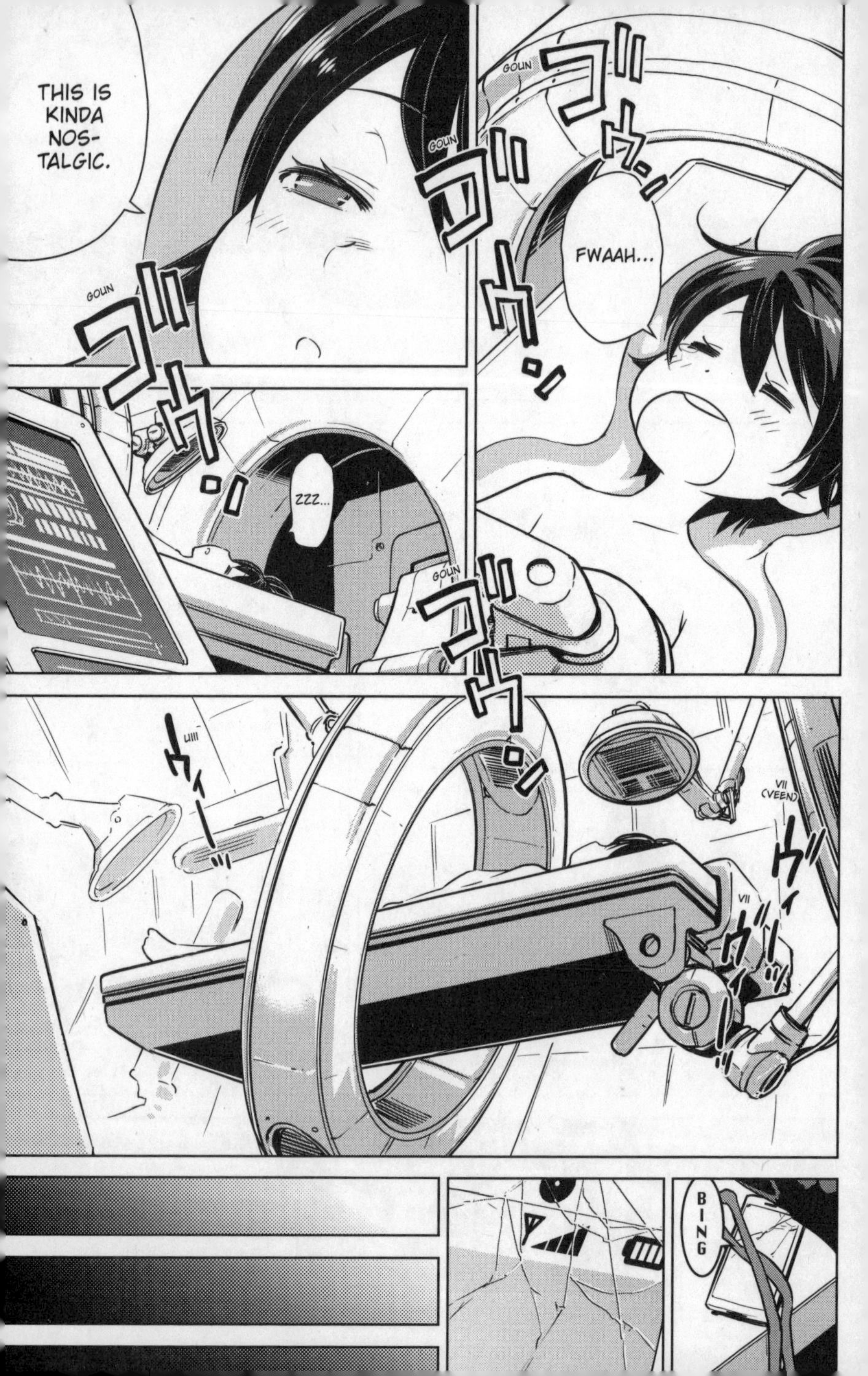
GOUN
GOUN
FWAAH...
THIS IS KINDA NOS-TALGIC.
GOUN
ZZZ...
GOUN
VII (VEEN)
VII
UIII
BING

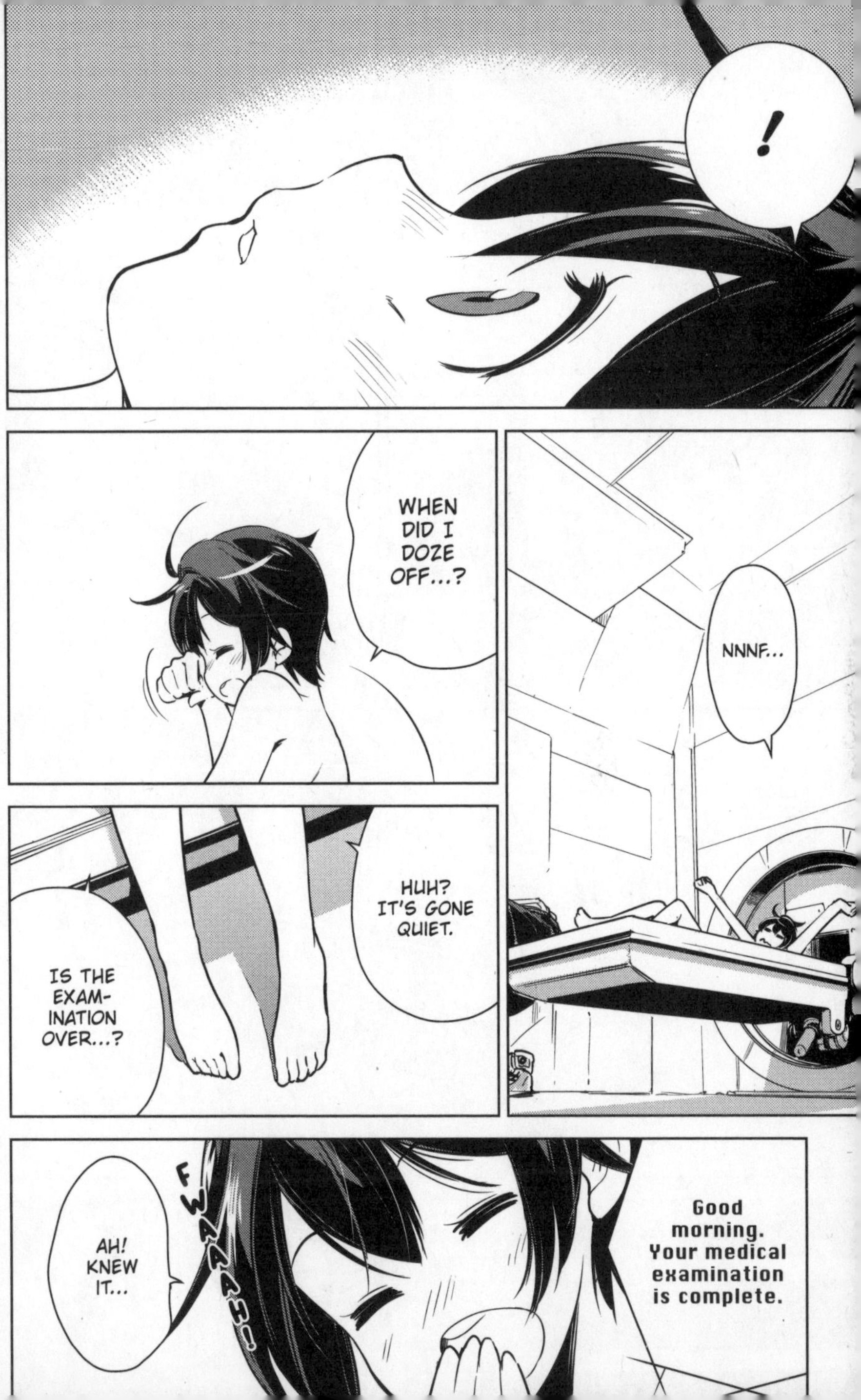
!
NNNF...
WHEN DID I DOZE OFF...?
HUH? IT'S GONE QUIET.
IS THE EXAM-INATION OVER...?
Good morning. Your medical examination is complete.
FWAAAAH!
AH! KNEW IT...

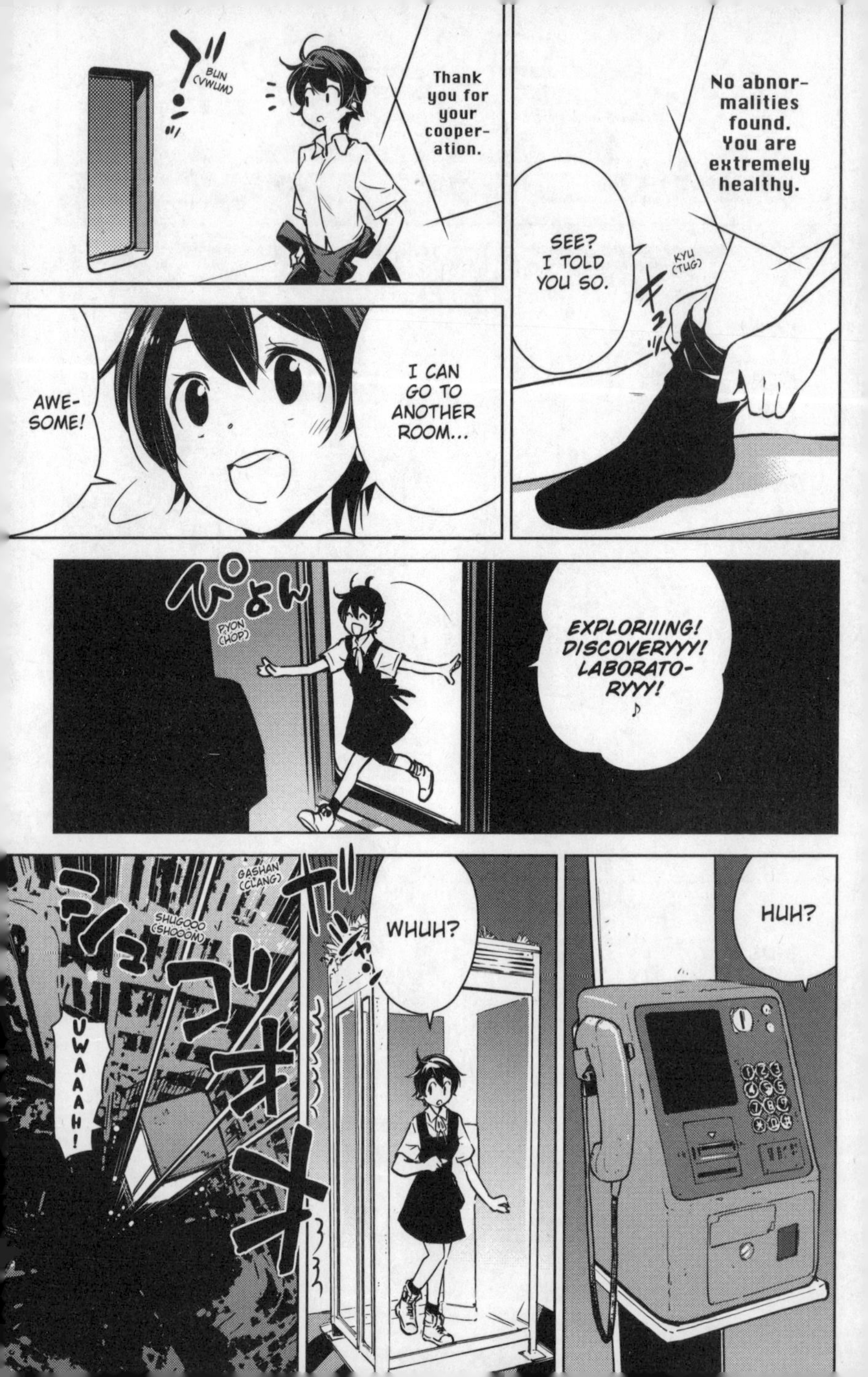
No abnor-
malities
found.
You are
extremely
healthy.
SEE?
I TOLD
YOU SO.
KYU
(TUG)
Thank
you for
your
cooper-
ation.
BUN
(VWUM)
I CAN
GO TO
ANOTHER
ROOM...
AWE-
SOME!
EXPLORIIING!
DISCOVERYYY!
LABORATO-
RYYY!
♪
ぴょん
PYON
(HOP)
HUH?
WHUH?
GASHAN
(CLANG)
SHUGOOO
(SHOOOM)
UWAAAH!

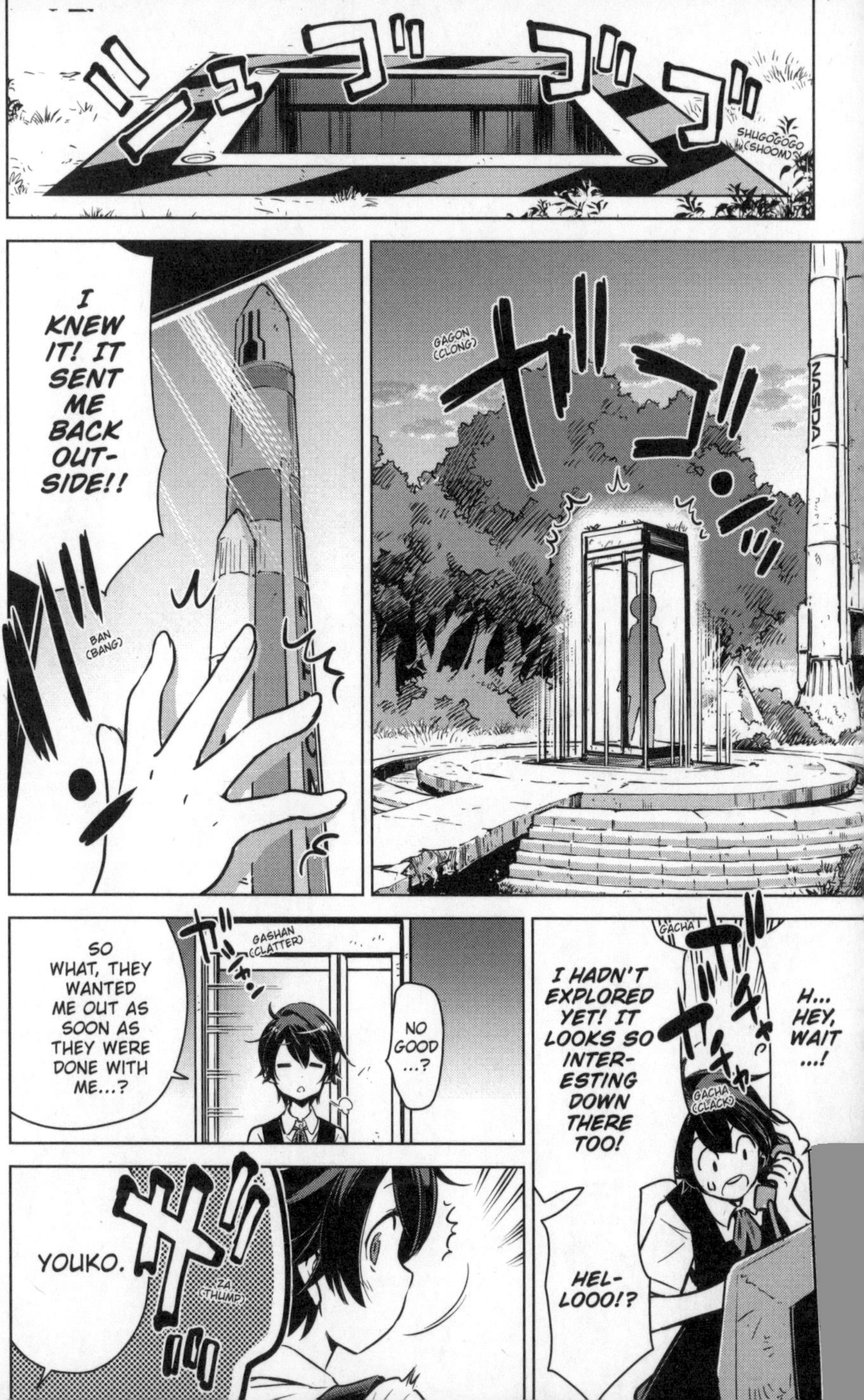
SHUGOGOGO (SHOOM)
GAGON (CLONG)
NASDA
I KNEW IT! IT SENT ME BACK OUTSIDE!!
BAN (BANG)
GACHA
H... HEY, WAIT ...!
I HADN'T EXPLORED YET! IT LOOKS SO INTERESTING DOWN THERE TOO!
GACHA (CLACK)
HEL-LOOO!?
GASHAN (CLATTER)
NO GOOD ...?
SO WHAT, THEY WANTED ME OUT AS SOON AS THEY WERE DONE WITH ME...?
YOUKO.
ZA (THUMP)

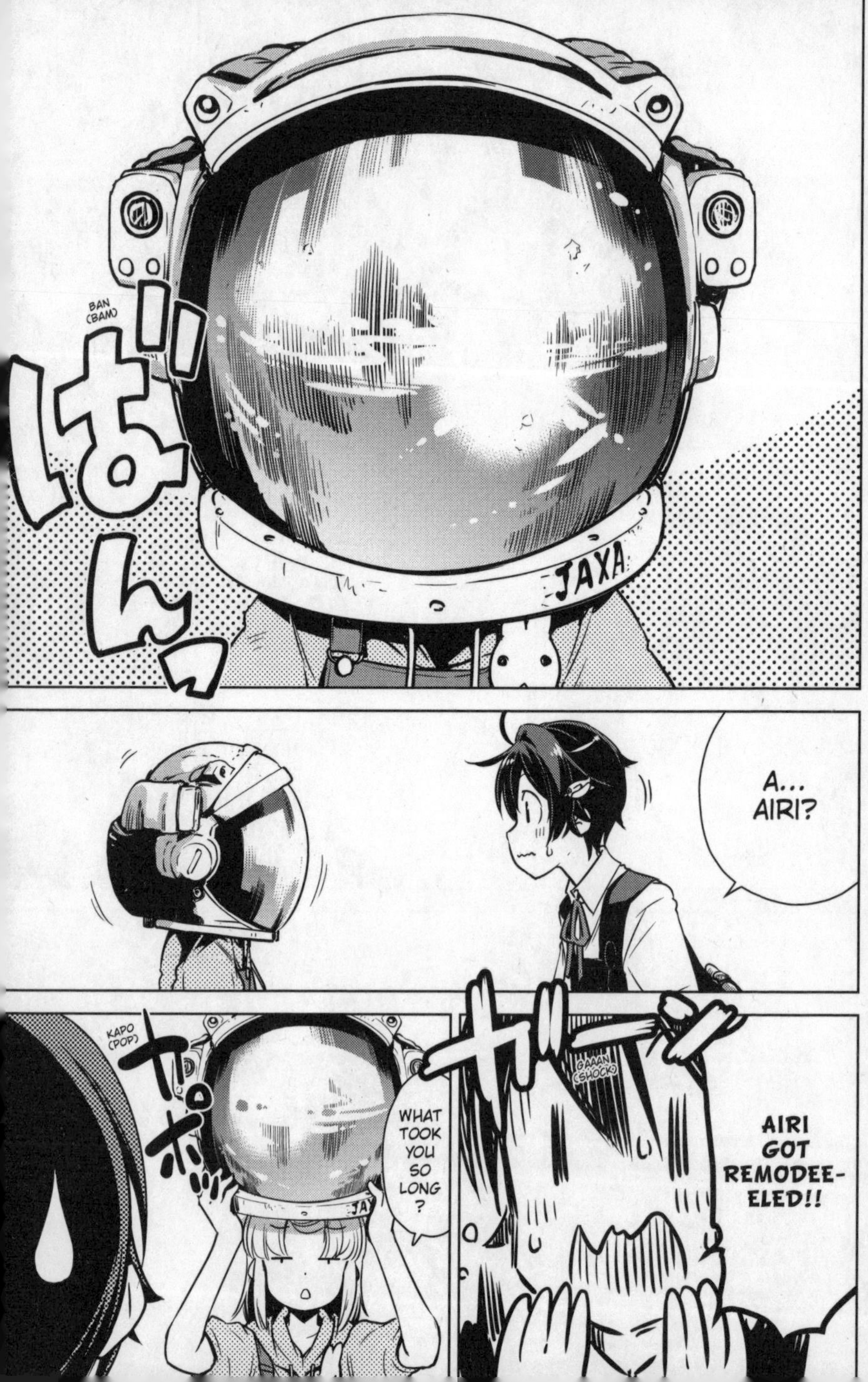
BAN (BAM)
A... AIRI?
GAAAN (SHOCK)
AIRI GOT REMODEE-ELED!!
KAPO (POP)
WHAT TOOK YOU SO LONG?

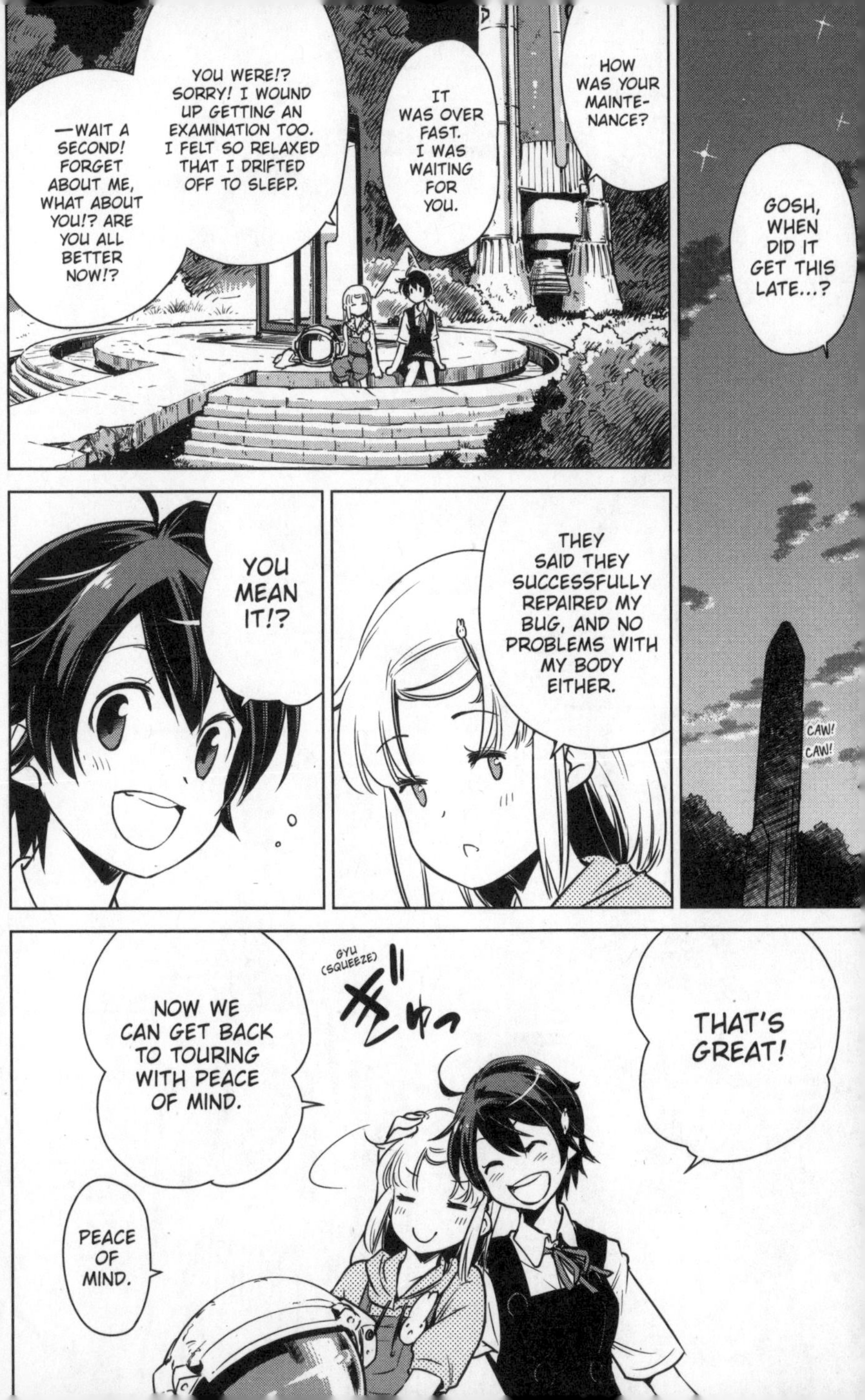
GOSH, WHEN DID IT GET THIS LATE...?
CAW! CAW!
HOW WAS YOUR MAINTE-NANCE?
IT WAS OVER FAST. I WAS WAITING FOR YOU.
YOU WERE!? SORRY! I WOUND UP GETTING AN EXAMINATION TOO. I FELT SO RELAXED THAT I DRIFTED OFF TO SLEEP.
—WAIT A SECOND! FORGET ABOUT ME, WHAT ABOUT YOU!? ARE YOU ALL BETTER NOW!?
THEY SAID THEY SUCCESSFULLY REPAIRED MY BUG, AND NO PROBLEMS WITH MY BODY EITHER.
YOU MEAN IT!?
THAT'S GREAT!
GYU (SQUEEZE)
NOW WE CAN GET BACK TO TOURING WITH PEACE OF MIND.
PEACE OF MIND.

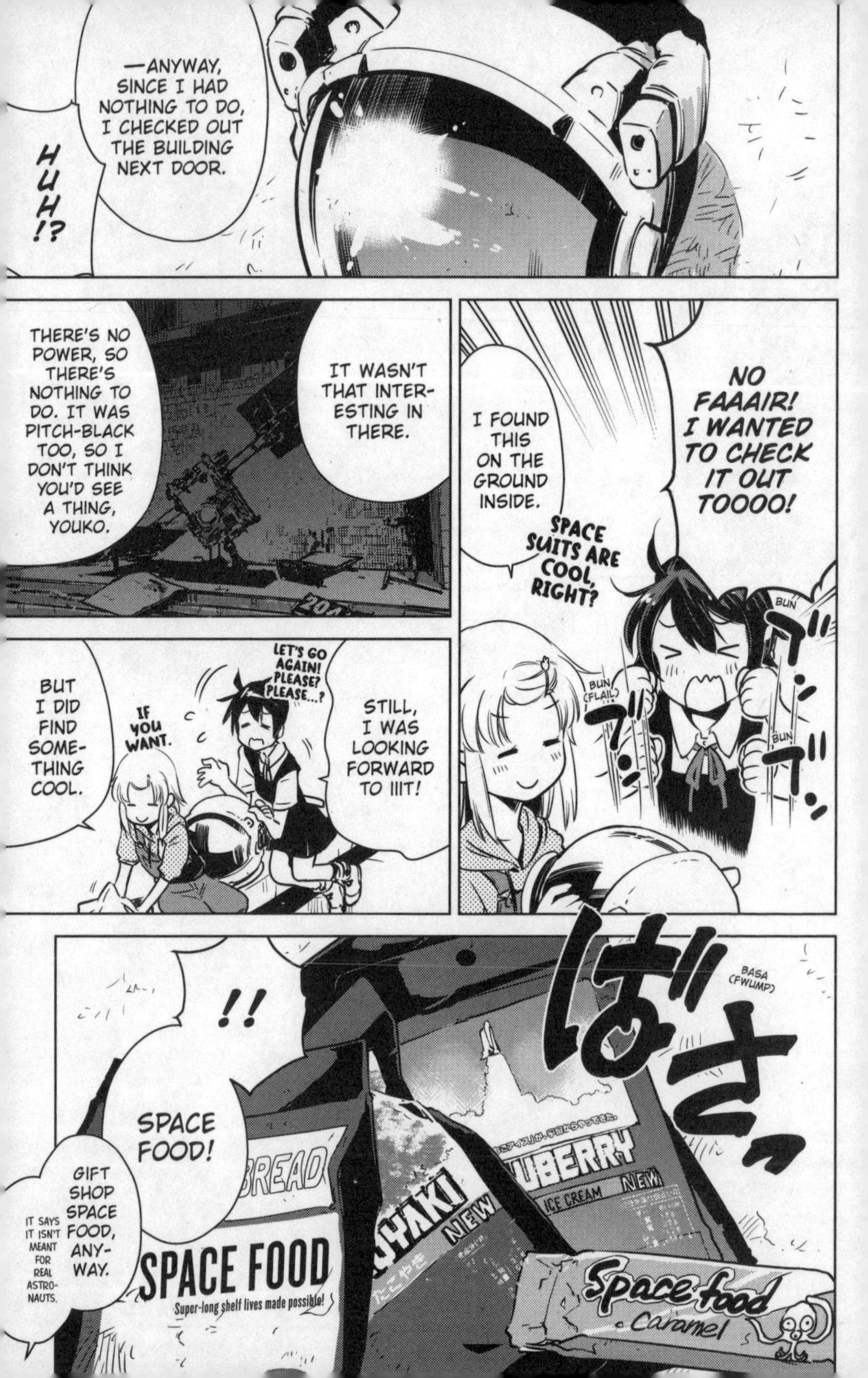
—ANYWAY, SINCE I HAD NOTHING TO DO, I CHECKED OUT THE BUILDING NEXT DOOR.
HUH!?
NO FAAAIR! I WANTED TO CHECK IT OUT TOOOO!
I FOUND THIS ON THE GROUND INSIDE.
SPACE SUITS ARE COOL, RIGHT?
BUN
BUN (FLAIL)
BUN
IT WASN'T THAT INTER-ESTING IN THERE.
THERE'S NO POWER, SO THERE'S NOTHING TO DO. IT WAS PITCH-BLACK TOO, SO I DON'T THINK YOU'D SEE A THING, YOUKO.
STILL, I WAS LOOKING FORWARD TO IIIT!
LET'S GO AGAIN! PLEASE? PLEASE...?
IF YOU WANT.
BUT I DID FIND SOME-THING COOL.
ばさっ
BASA (FWUMP)
!!
SPACE FOOD!
GIFT SHOP SPACE FOOD, ANY-WAY.
IT SAYS IT ISN'T MEANT FOR REAL ASTRO-NAUTS.
BREAD
SPACE FOOD
Super-long shelf lives made possible!
UBERRY
ICE CREAM
NEW
YAKI
NEW
Space food
Caramel

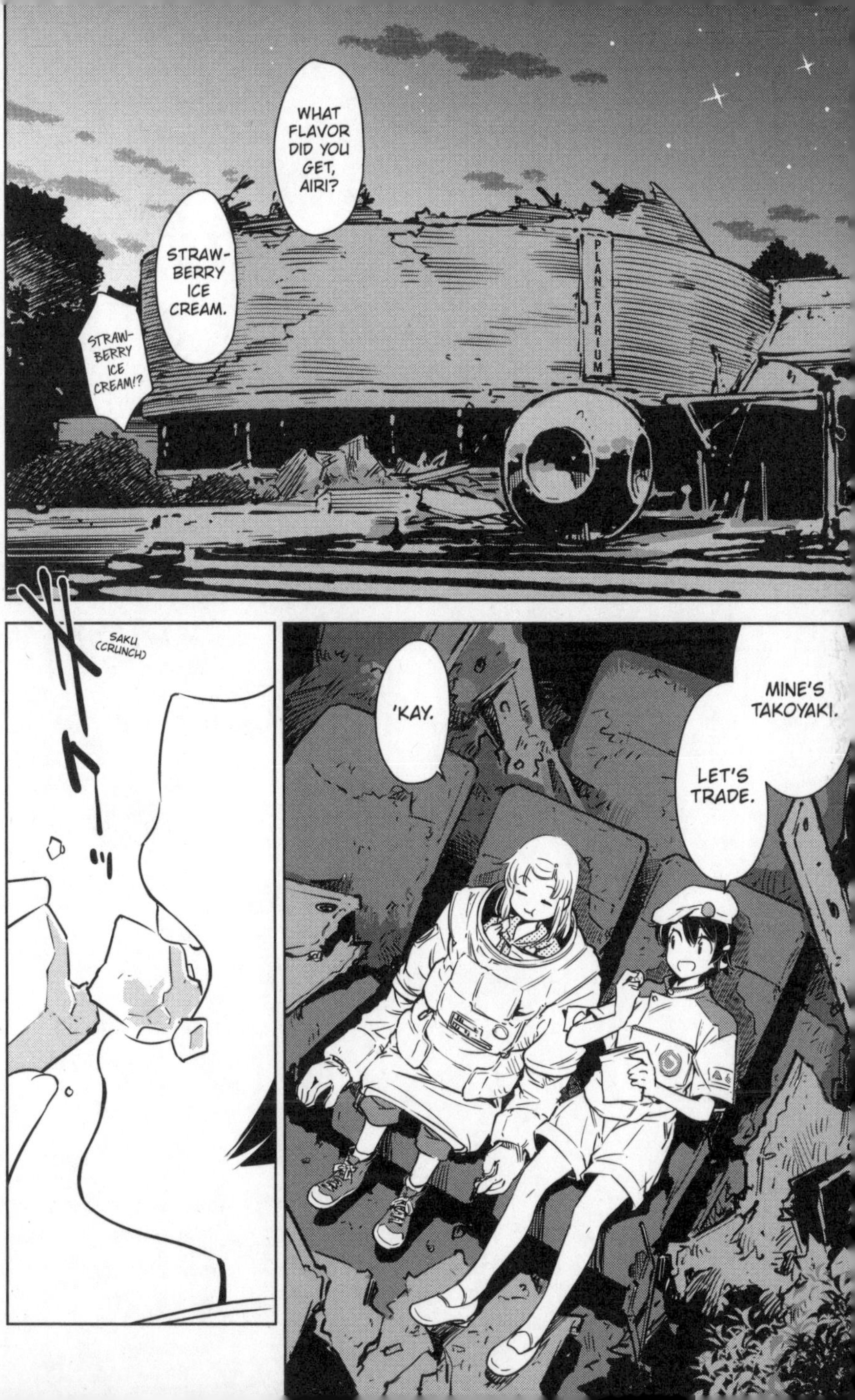
WHAT FLAVOR DID YOU GET, AIRI?
STRAW-BERRY ICE CREAM.
STRAW-BERRY ICE CREAM!?
PLANETARIUM
MINE'S TAKOYAKI.
LET'S TRADE.
'KAY.
SAKU (CRUNCH)

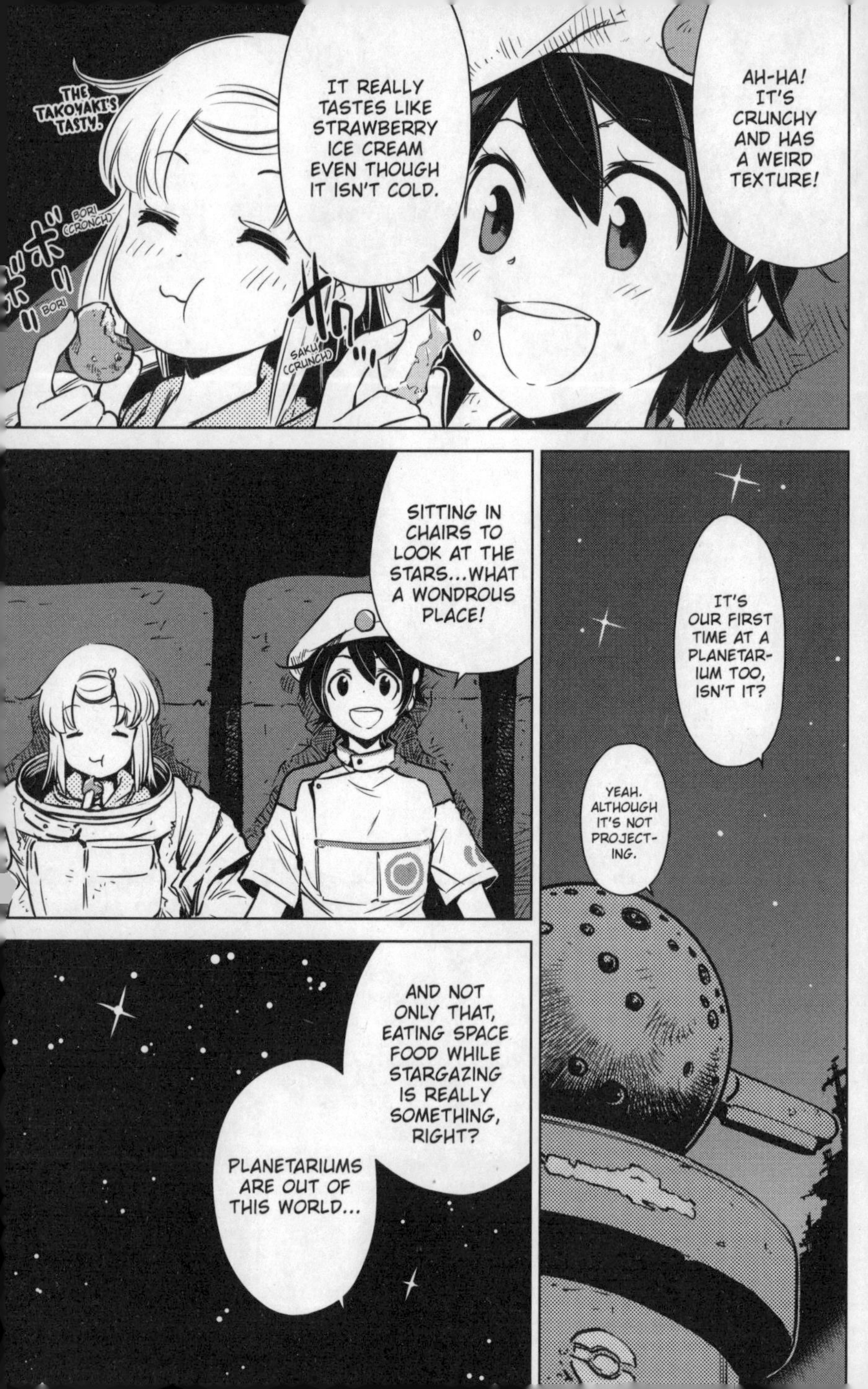
AH-HA! IT'S CRUNCHY AND HAS A WEIRD TEXTURE!
IT REALLY TASTES LIKE STRAWBERRY ICE CREAM EVEN THOUGH IT ISN'T COLD.
SAKU (CRUNCH)
BORI (CRONCH)
BORI
THE TAKOYAKI'S TASTY.
IT'S OUR FIRST TIME AT A PLANETARIUM TOO, ISN'T IT?
YEAH. ALTHOUGH IT'S NOT PROJECTING.
SITTING IN CHAIRS TO LOOK AT THE STARS...WHAT A WONDROUS PLACE!
AND NOT ONLY THAT, EATING SPACE FOOD WHILE STARGAZING IS REALLY SOMETHING, RIGHT?
PLANETARIUMS ARE OUT OF THIS WORLD...

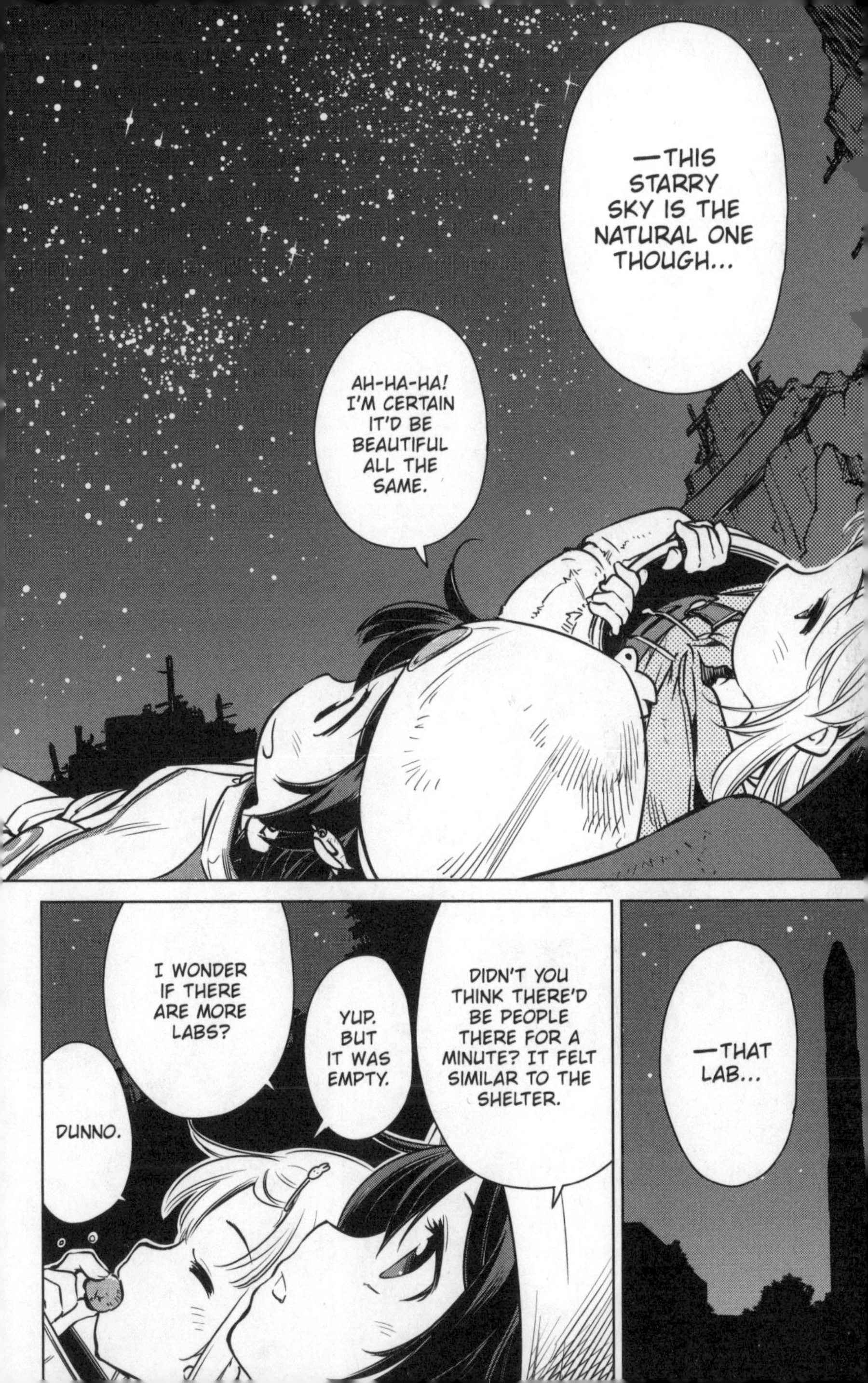
—THIS STARRY SKY IS THE NATURAL ONE THOUGH...
AH-HA-HA! I'M CERTAIN IT'D BE BEAUTIFUL ALL THE SAME.
—THAT LAB...
DIDN'T YOU THINK THERE'D BE PEOPLE THERE FOR A MINUTE? IT FELT SIMILAR TO THE SHELTER.
YUP. BUT IT WAS EMPTY.
I WONDER IF THERE ARE MORE LABS?
DUNNO.

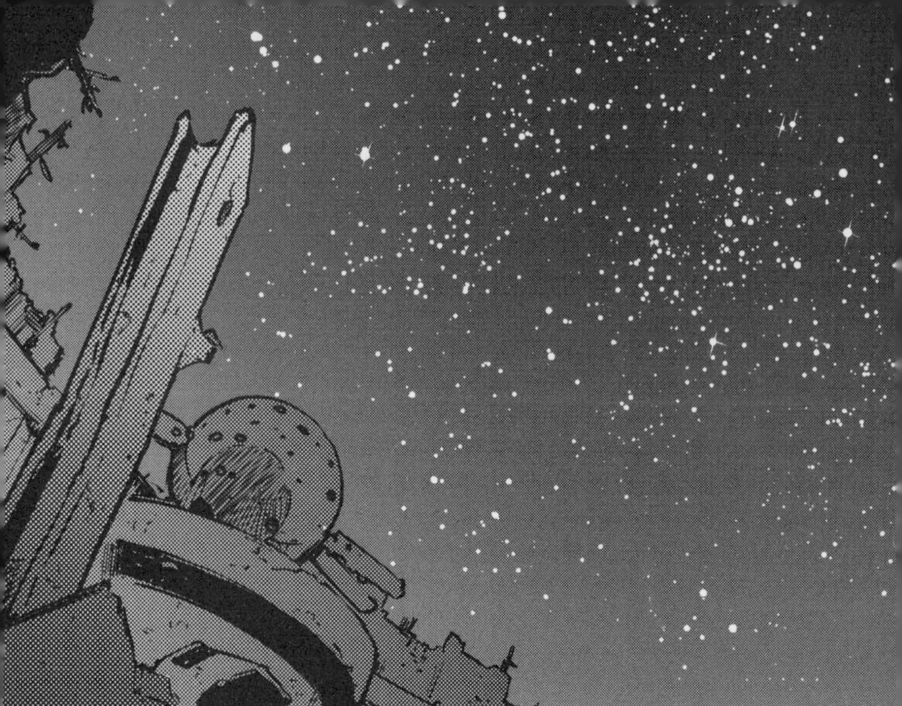
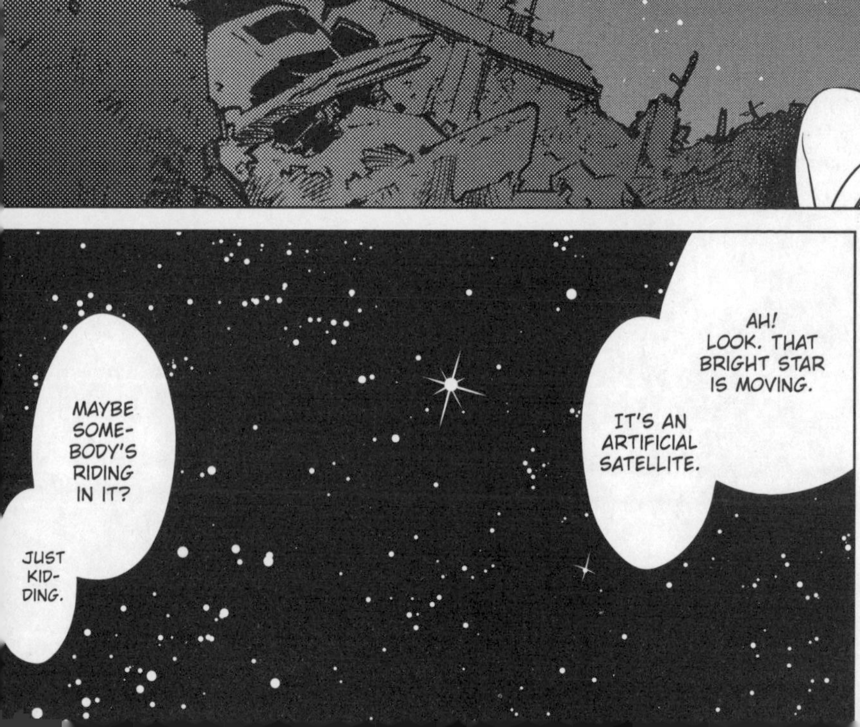
AH! LOOK. THAT BRIGHT STAR IS MOVING.
IT'S AN ARTIFICIAL SATELLITE.
MAYBE SOMEBODY'S RIDING IN IT?
JUST KIDDING.

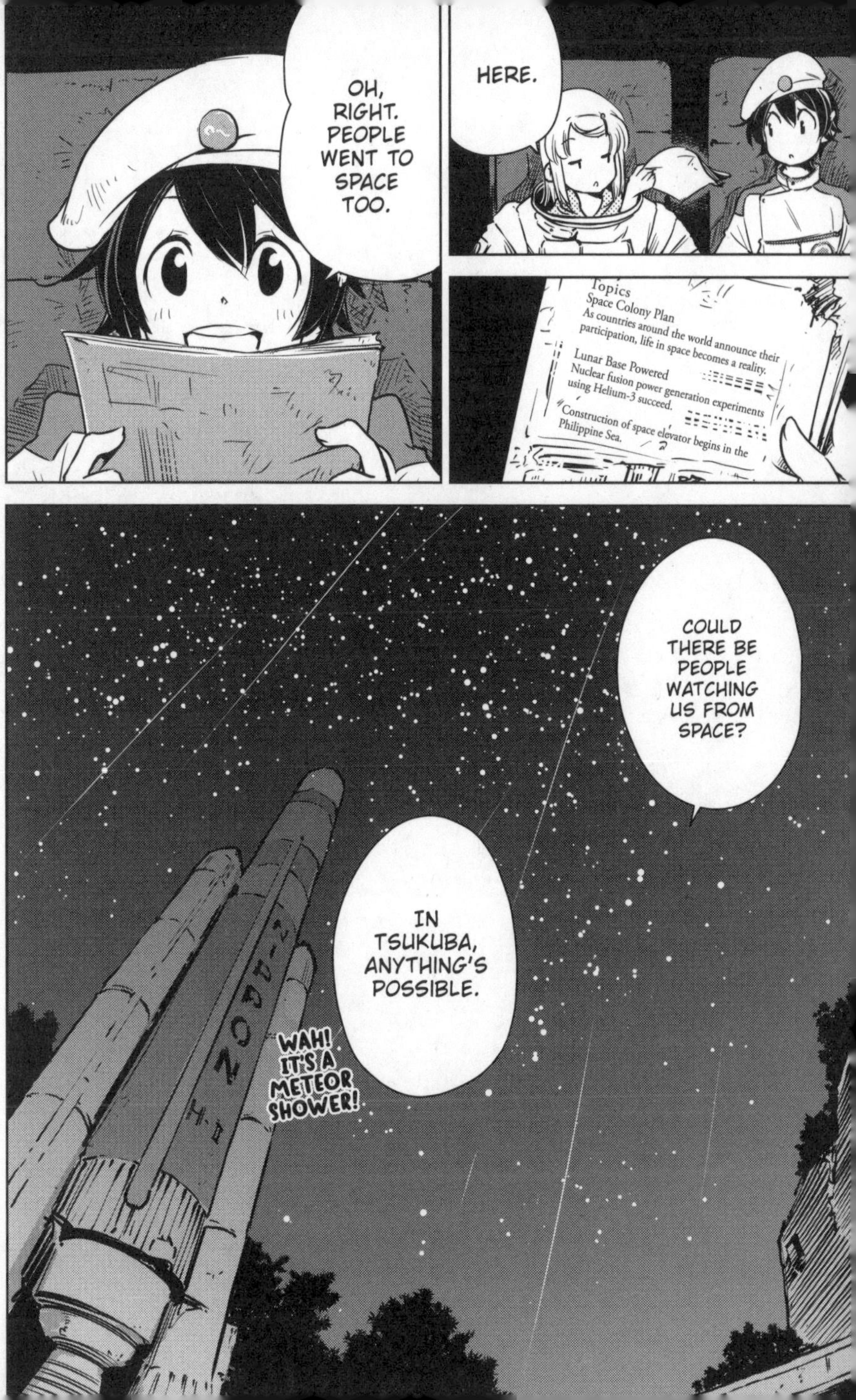
HERE.
Topics
Space Colony Plan
As countries around the world announce their participation, life in space becomes a reality.
Lunar Base Powered
Nuclear fusion power generation experiments using Helium-3 succeed.
Construction of space elevator begins in the Philippine Sea.
OH, RIGHT. PEOPLE WENT TO SPACE TOO.
COULD THERE BE PEOPLE WATCHING US FROM SPACE?
IN TSUKUBA, ANYTHING'S POSSIBLE.
WAH! IT'S A METEOR SHOWER!

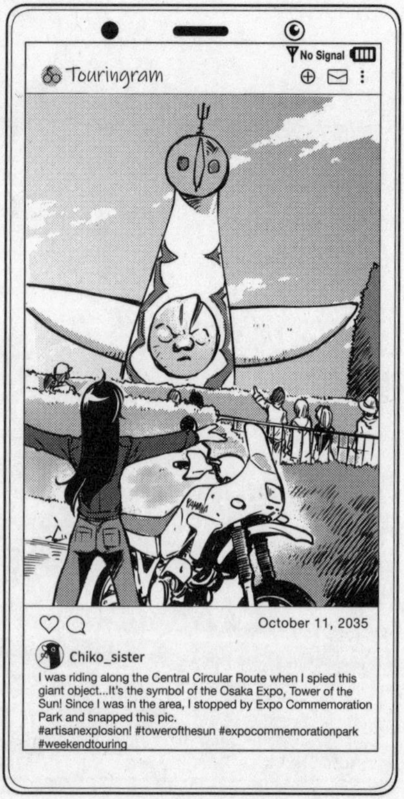
No Signal
Touringram
October 11, 2035
Chiko_sister
I was riding along the Central Circular Route when I spied this giant object...It's the symbol of the Osaka Expo, Tower of the Sun! Since I was in the area, I stopped by Expo Commemoration Park and snapped this pic.
#artisanexplosion! #towerofthesun #expocommemorationpark #weekendtouring

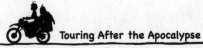
Touring After the Apocalypse

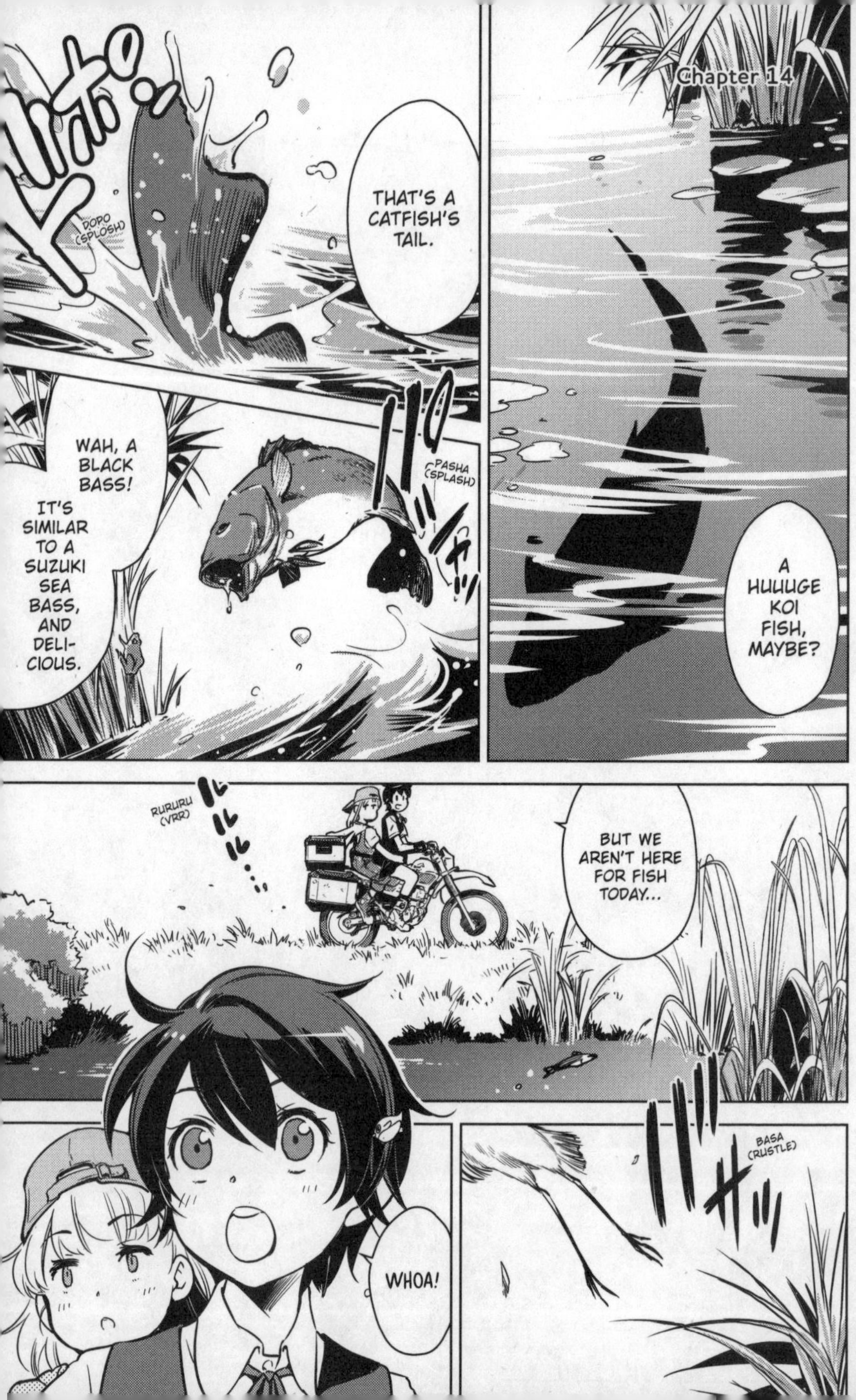
Chapter 14
A HUUUGE KOI FISH, MAYBE?
DOPO (SPLOSH)
THAT'S A CATFISH'S TAIL.
PASHA (SPLASH)
WAH, A BLACK BASS!
IT'S SIMILAR TO A SUZUKI SEA BASS, AND DELICIOUS.
BUT WE AREN'T HERE FOR FISH TODAY...
RURURU (VRR)
BASA (RUSTLE)
WHOA!

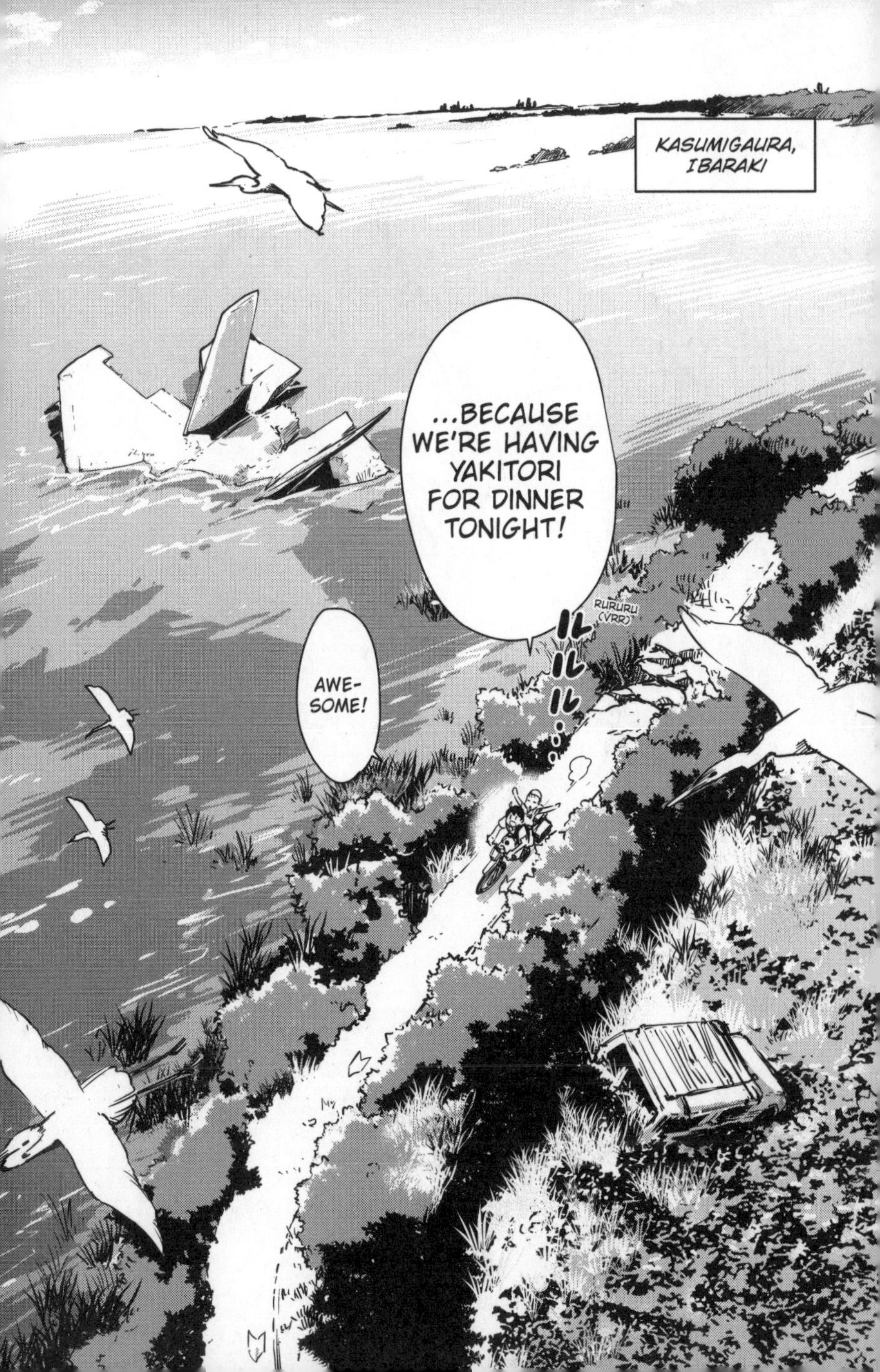
KASUMIGAURA, IBARAKI
...BECAUSE WE'RE HAVING YAKITORI FOR DINNER TONIGHT!
RURURU (VRR)
AWE-SOME!

|Chapter 14| Kasumigaura

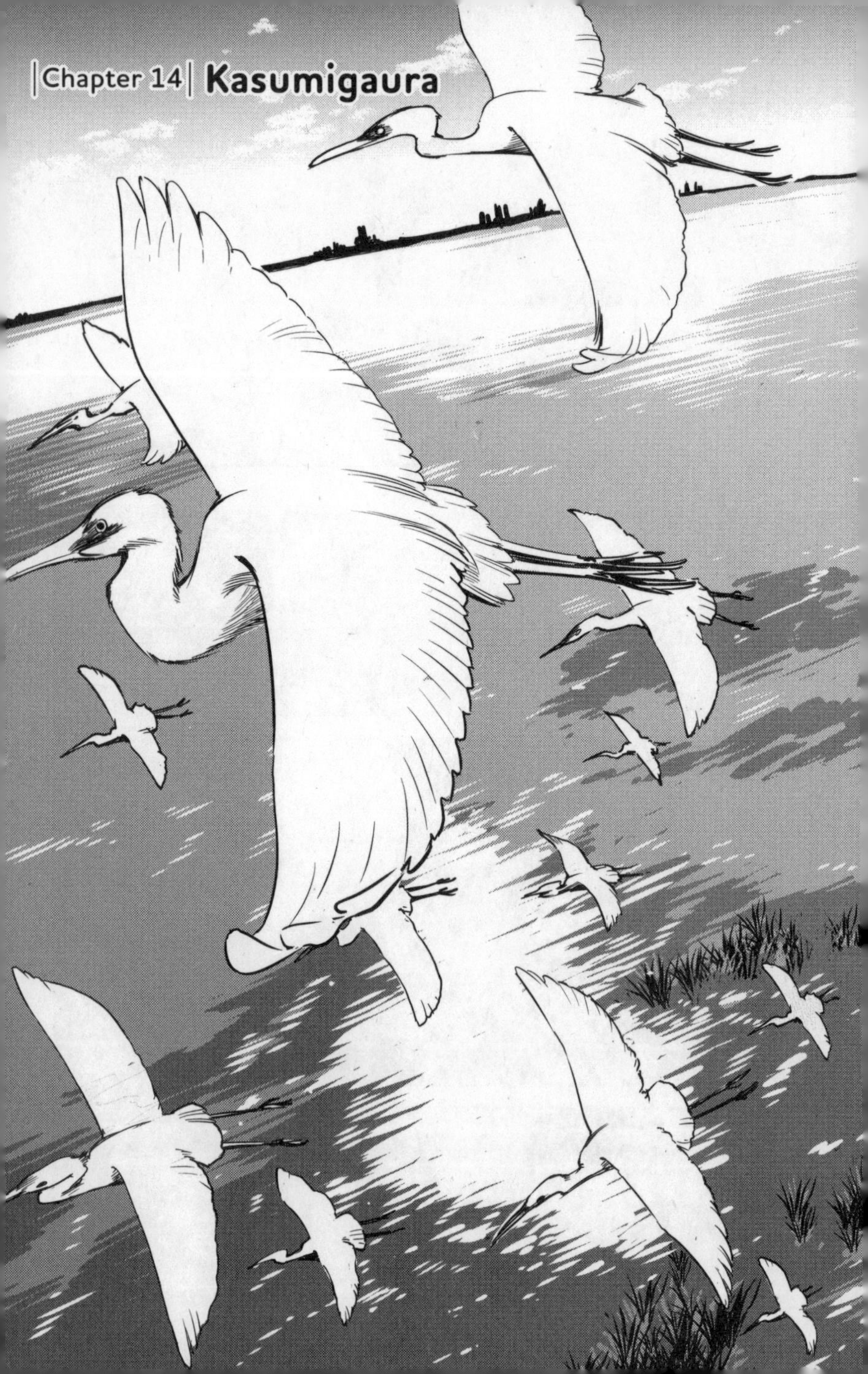

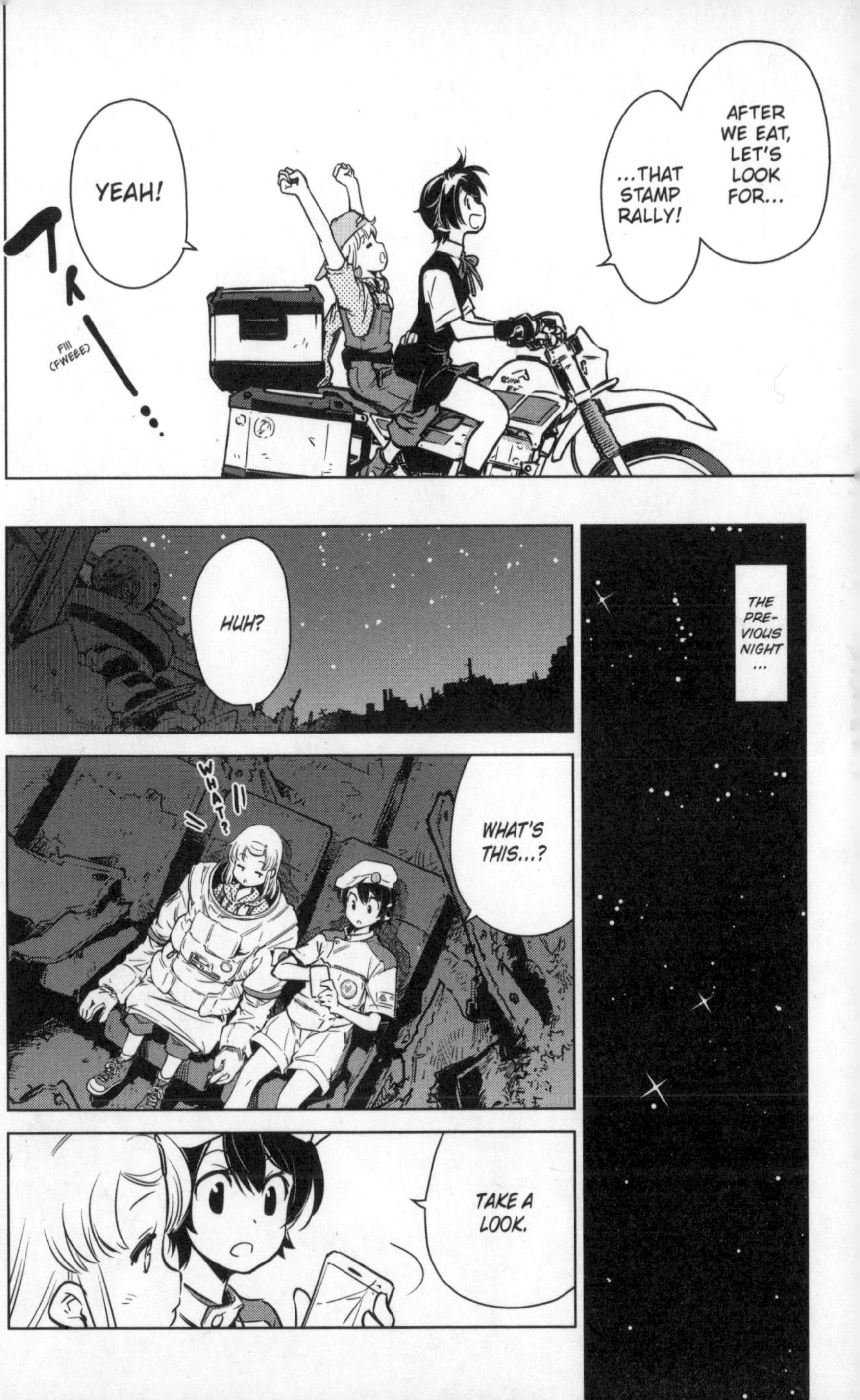
AFTER WE EAT, LET'S LOOK FOR...
...THAT STAMP RALLY!
YEAH!
FIII (FWEEE)
THE PRE-VIOUS NIGHT...
HUH?
WHAT'S THIS...?
WHAT?!
TAKE A LOOK.

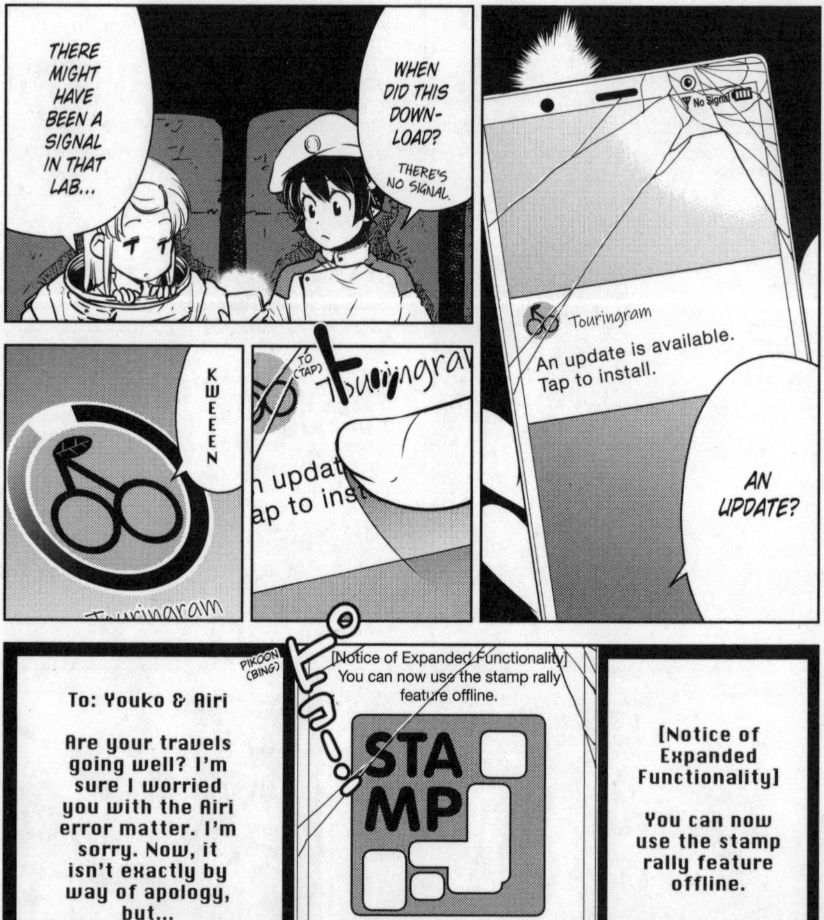

No Signal
Touringram
An update is available. Tap to install.
AN UPDATE?
WHEN DID THIS DOWNLOAD?
THERE'S NO SIGNAL.
THERE MIGHT HAVE BEEN A SIGNAL IN THAT LAB...
TO (TAP)
Touringram
An updat
ap to inst
KWEEEEN
Touringram
[Notice of Expanded Functionality] You can now use the stamp rally feature offline.
PIKOON (BING)
[Notice of Expanded Functionality] You can now use the stamp rally feature offline.
STAMP
To: Youko & Airi
Are your travels going well?
I'm sure I worried you with the Airi error matter.
To: Youko & Airi
Are your travels going well? I'm sure I worried you with the Airi error matter. I'm sorry. Now, it isn't exactly by way of apology, but...
...I upgraded one of Touringram's features. Try it out!
From: Onee-chan
ONEE-CHAN!

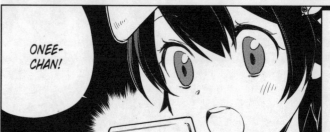

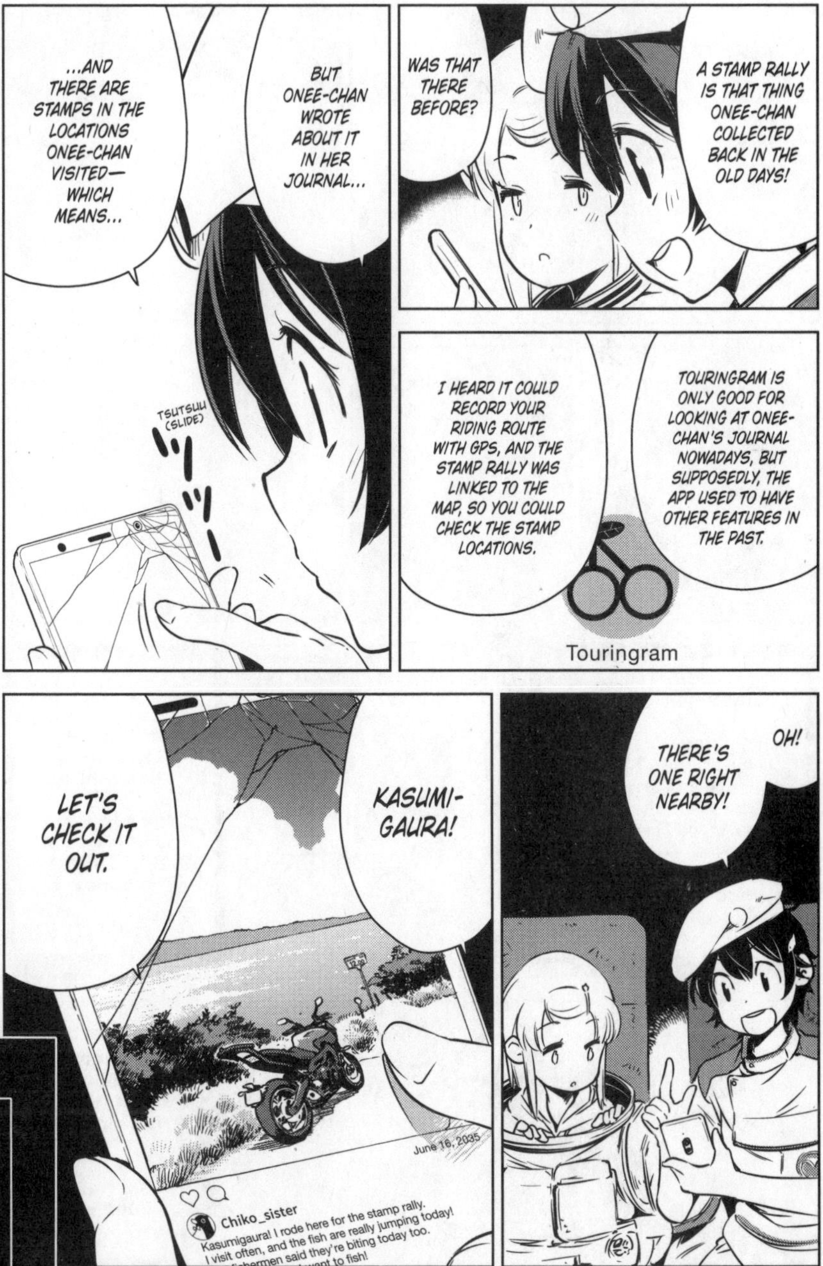
A STAMP RALLY IS THAT THING ONEE-CHAN COLLECTED BACK IN THE OLD DAYS!
WAS THAT THERE BEFORE?
TOURINGRAM IS ONLY GOOD FOR LOOKING AT ONEE-CHAN'S JOURNAL NOWADAYS, BUT SUPPOSEDLY, THE APP USED TO HAVE OTHER FEATURES IN THE PAST.
I HEARD IT COULD RECORD YOUR RIDING ROUTE WITH GPS, AND THE STAMP RALLY WAS LINKED TO THE MAP, SO YOU COULD CHECK THE STAMP LOCATIONS.
Touringram
BUT ONEE-CHAN WROTE ABOUT IT IN HER JOURNAL...
...AND THERE ARE STAMPS IN THE LOCATIONS ONEE-CHAN VISITED—WHICH MEANS...
TSUTSUU (SLIDE)
OH!
THERE'S ONE RIGHT NEARBY!
KASUMI-GAURA!
LET'S CHECK IT OUT.
June 16, 2035
Chiko_sister
Kasumigaura! I rode here for the stamp rally.
I visit often, and the fish are really jumping today!
said they're biting today too.
to fish!

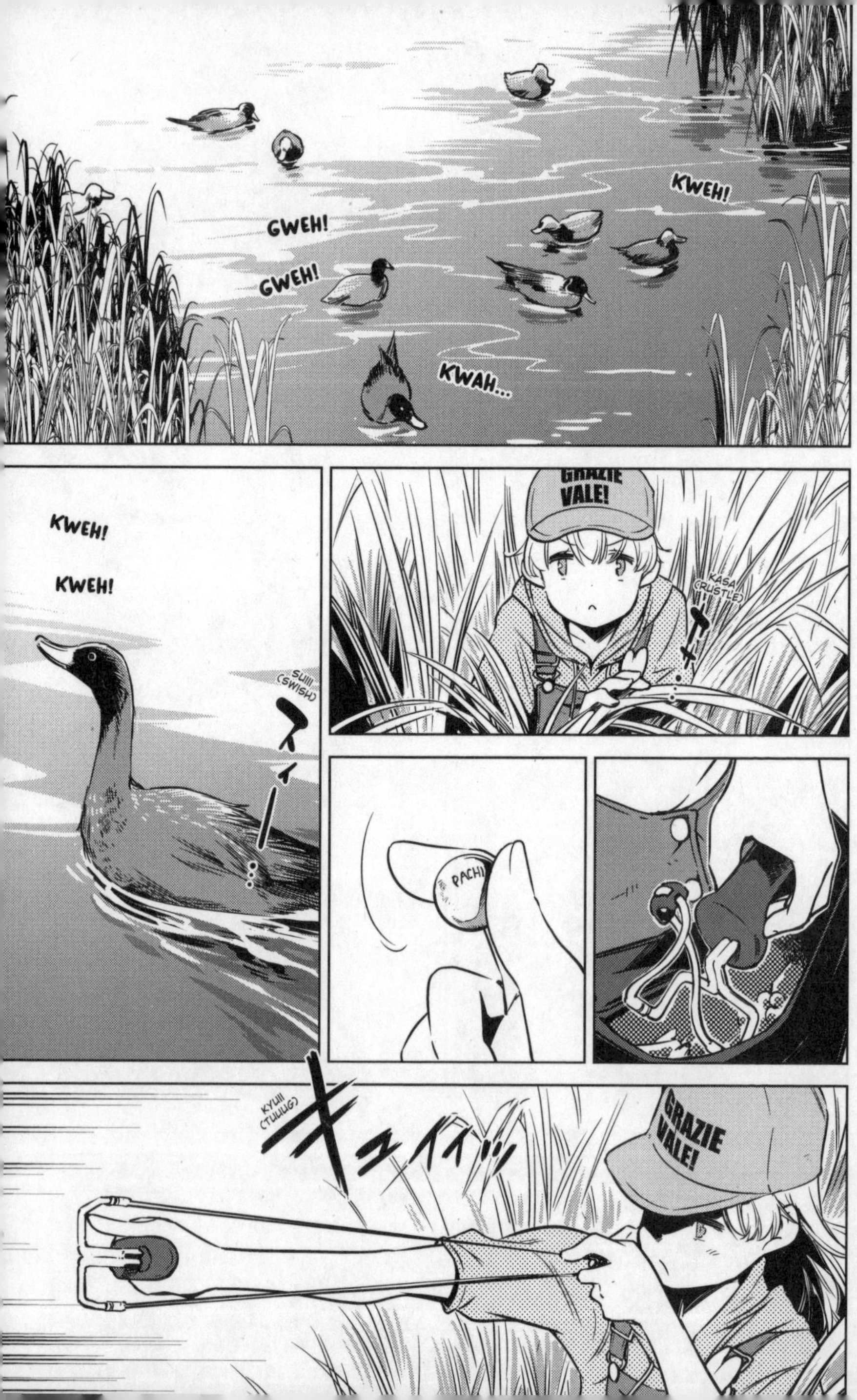
KWEH!
GWEH!
GWEH!
KWAH...
GRAZIE VALE!
KASA (RUSTLE)
PACHI
KWEH!
KWEH!
SUIII (SWISH)
GRAZIE VALE!
KYUIII (TUUUG)

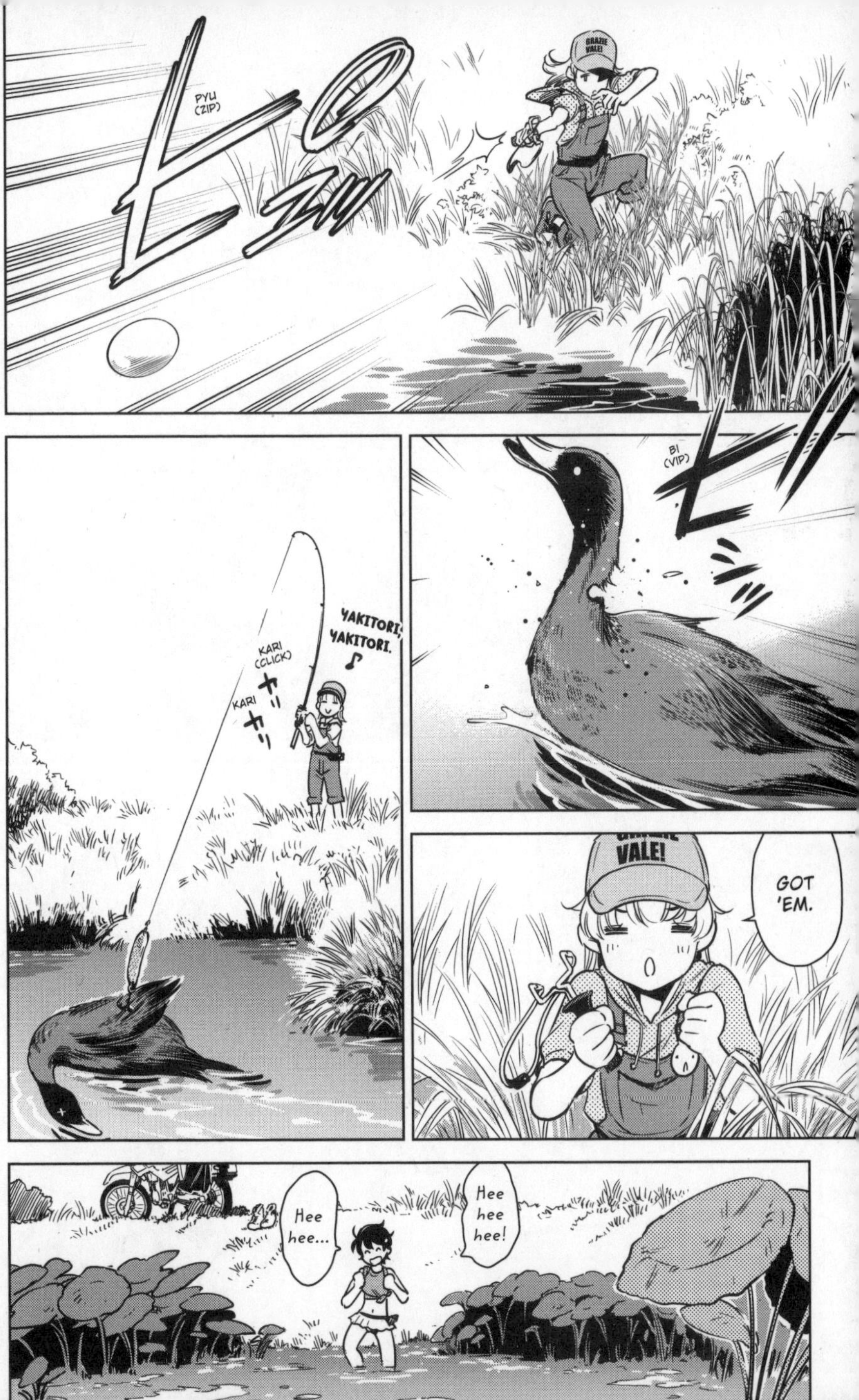

PYU (ZIP)
GRAZIE VALE!
BI (VIP)
GRAZIE VALE!
GOT 'EM.
YAKITORI, YAKITORI.
KARI (CLICK)
カリ
KARI
カリ
Hee hee hee!
Hee hee...

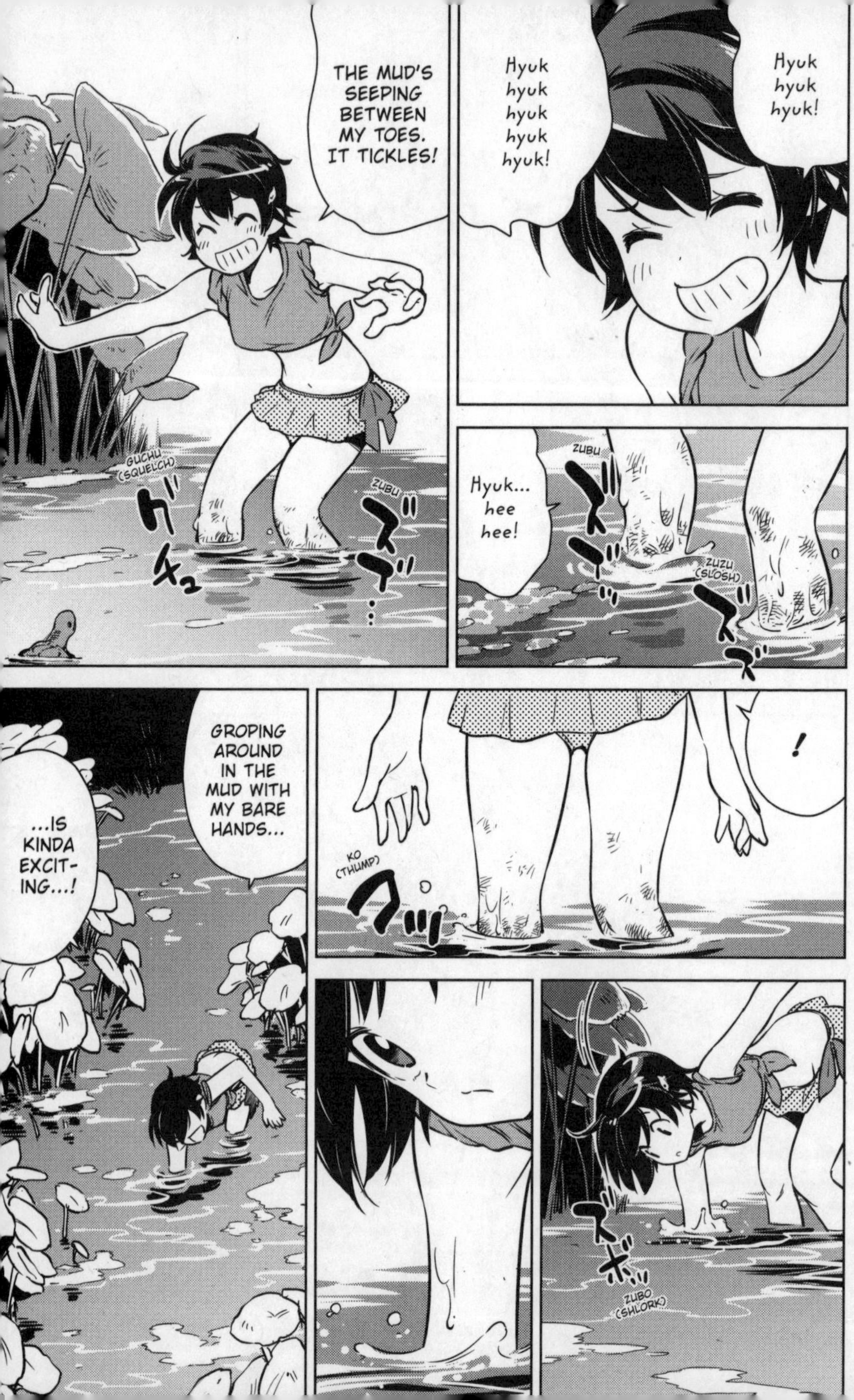
Hyuk hyuk hyuk!
Hyuk hyuk hyuk hyuk hyuk!
ZUBU
Hyuk... hee hee!
ZUZU (SLOSH)
THE MUD'S SEEPING BETWEEN MY TOES. IT TICKLES!
GUCHU (SQUELCH)
ZUBU
!
KO (THUMP)
ZUBO (SHLORK)
GROPING AROUND IN THE MUD WITH MY BARE HANDS...
...IS KINDA EXCIT-ING...!

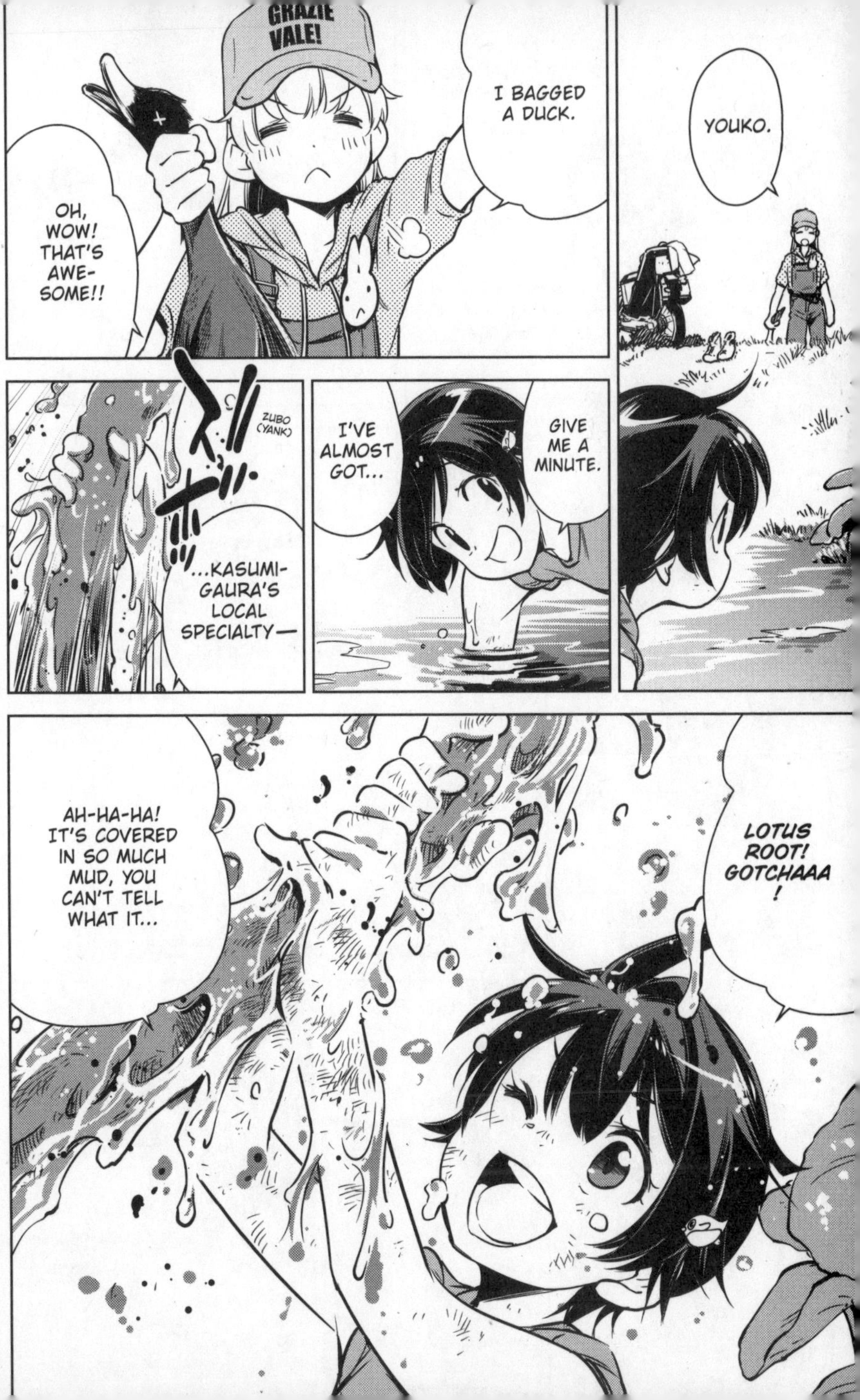
YOUKO.
GRAZIE VALE!
I BAGGED A DUCK.
OH, WOW! THAT'S AWE-SOME!!
GIVE ME A MINUTE.
I'VE ALMOST GOT...
ZUBO (YANK)
...KASUMI-GAURA'S LOCAL SPECIALTY—
LOTUS ROOT! GOTCHAAA!
AH-HA-HA! IT'S COVERED IN SO MUCH MUD, YOU CAN'T TELL WHAT IT...

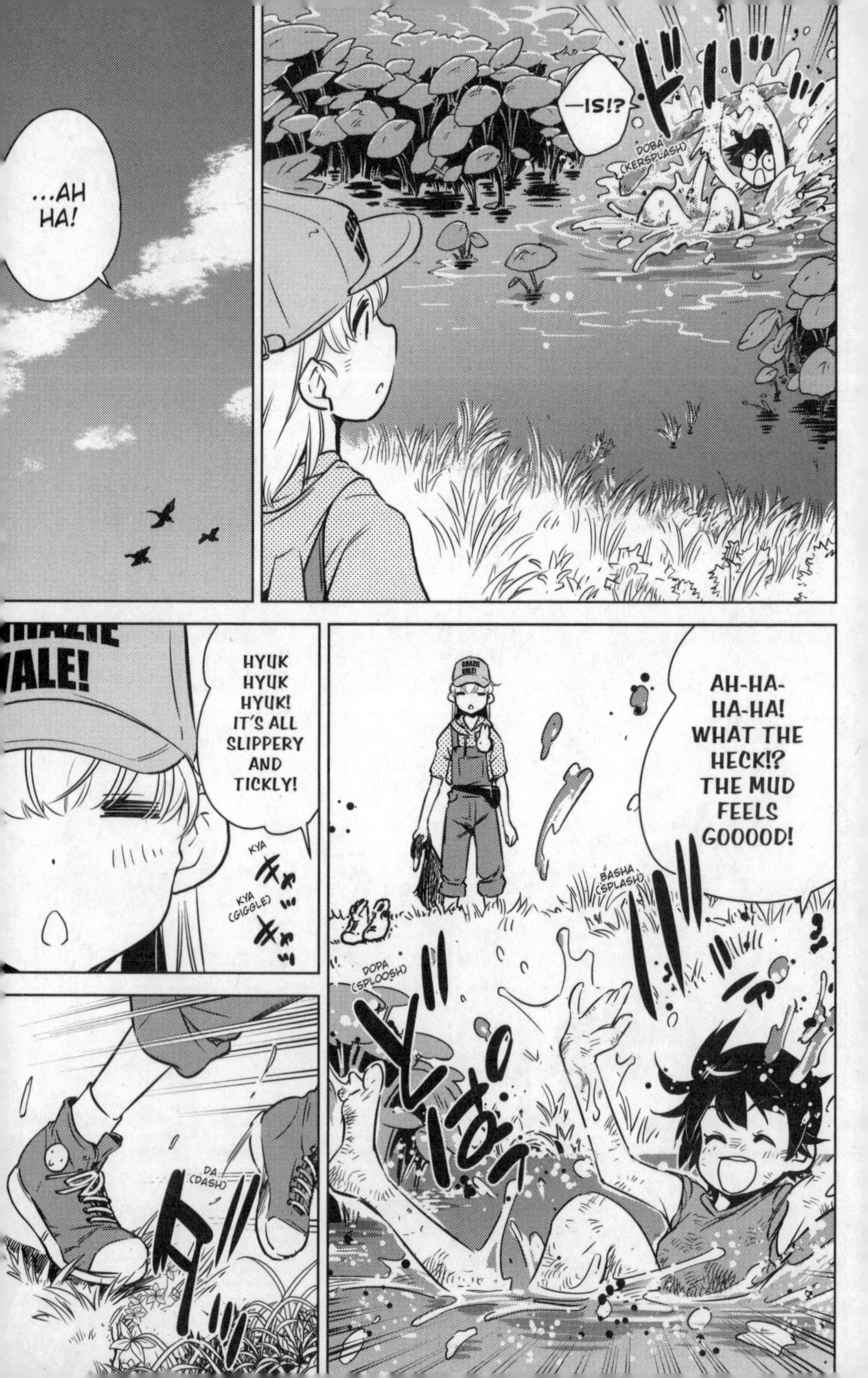
—IS!?
DOBA (KERSPLASH)
...AH HA!
AH-HA-HA-HA! WHAT THE HECK!? THE MUD FEELS GOOOOD!
BASHA (SPLASH)
DOPA (SPLOOSH)
HYUK HYUK HYUK! IT'S ALL SLIPPERY AND TICKLY!
KYA KYA (GIGGLE)
DA (DASH)

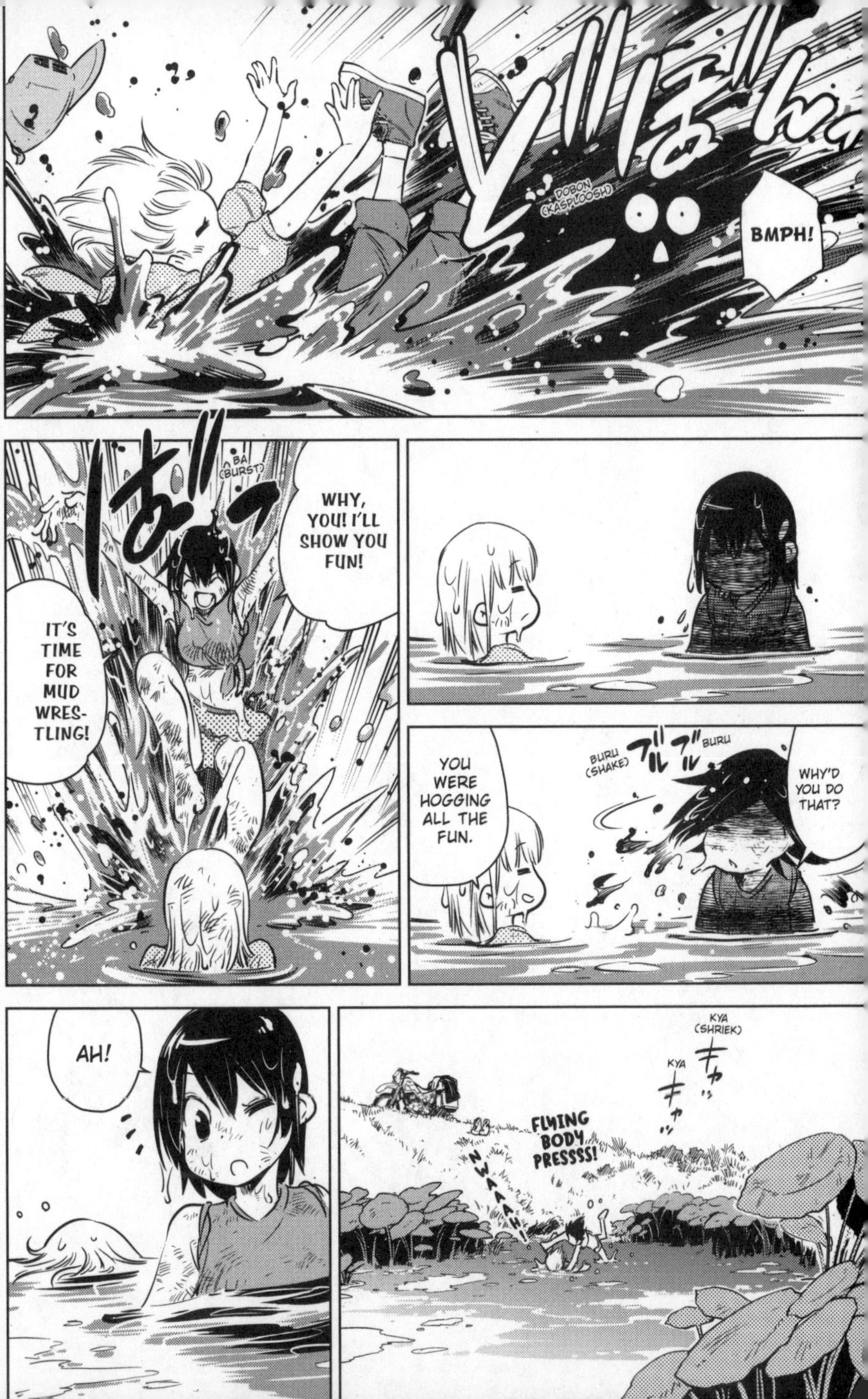
BMPH!
DOBON (KASPLOOSH)
WHY'D YOU DO THAT?
BURU (SHAKE) BURU
YOU WERE HOGGING ALL THE FUN.
WHY, YOU! I'LL SHOW YOU FUN!
BA (BURST)
IT'S TIME FOR MUD WRES-TLING!
KYA (SHRIEK)
KYA
FLYING BODY PRESSSS!
NWAAAAH!
AH!

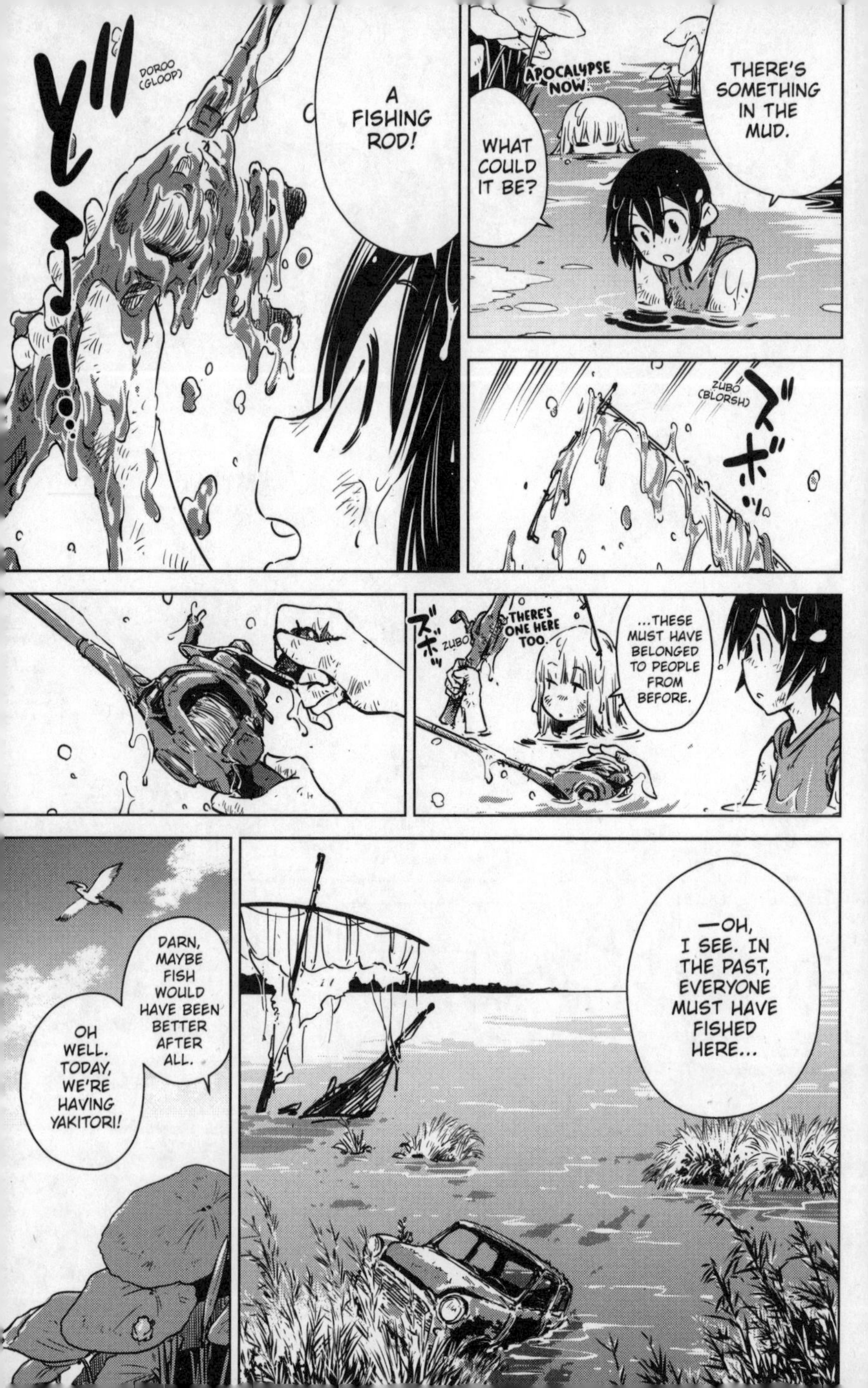
THERE'S SOMETHING IN THE MUD.
APOCALYPSE NOW.
WHAT COULD IT BE?
ZUBO (BLORSH)
ズボッ
A FISHING ROD!
DOROO (GLOOP)
どろー…
...THESE MUST HAVE BELONGED TO PEOPLE FROM BEFORE.
THERE'S ONE HERE TOO.
ズボッ
ZUBO
—OH, I SEE. IN THE PAST, EVERYONE MUST HAVE FISHED HERE...
DARN, MAYBE FISH WOULD HAVE BEEN BETTER AFTER ALL.
OH WELL. TODAY, WE'RE HAVING YAKITORI!

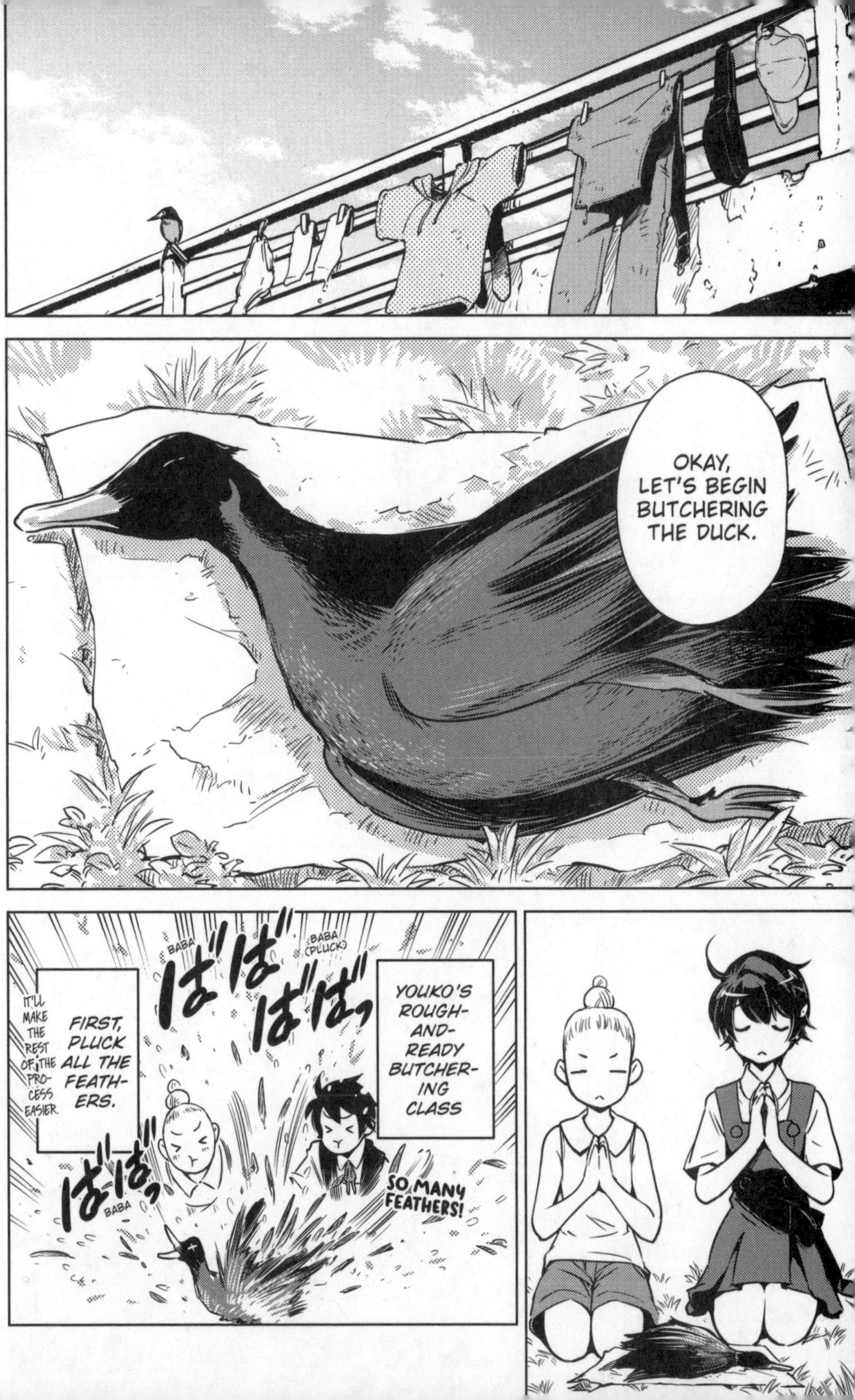
OKAY, LET'S BEGIN BUTCHERING THE DUCK.
YOUKO'S ROUGH-AND-READY BUTCHERING CLASS
ばばっ
BABA (PLUCK)
ばばっ
BABA
FIRST, PLUCK ALL THE FEATHERS.
IT'LL MAKE THE REST OF THE PROCESS EASIER.
SO MANY FEATHERS!
ばばっ
BABA

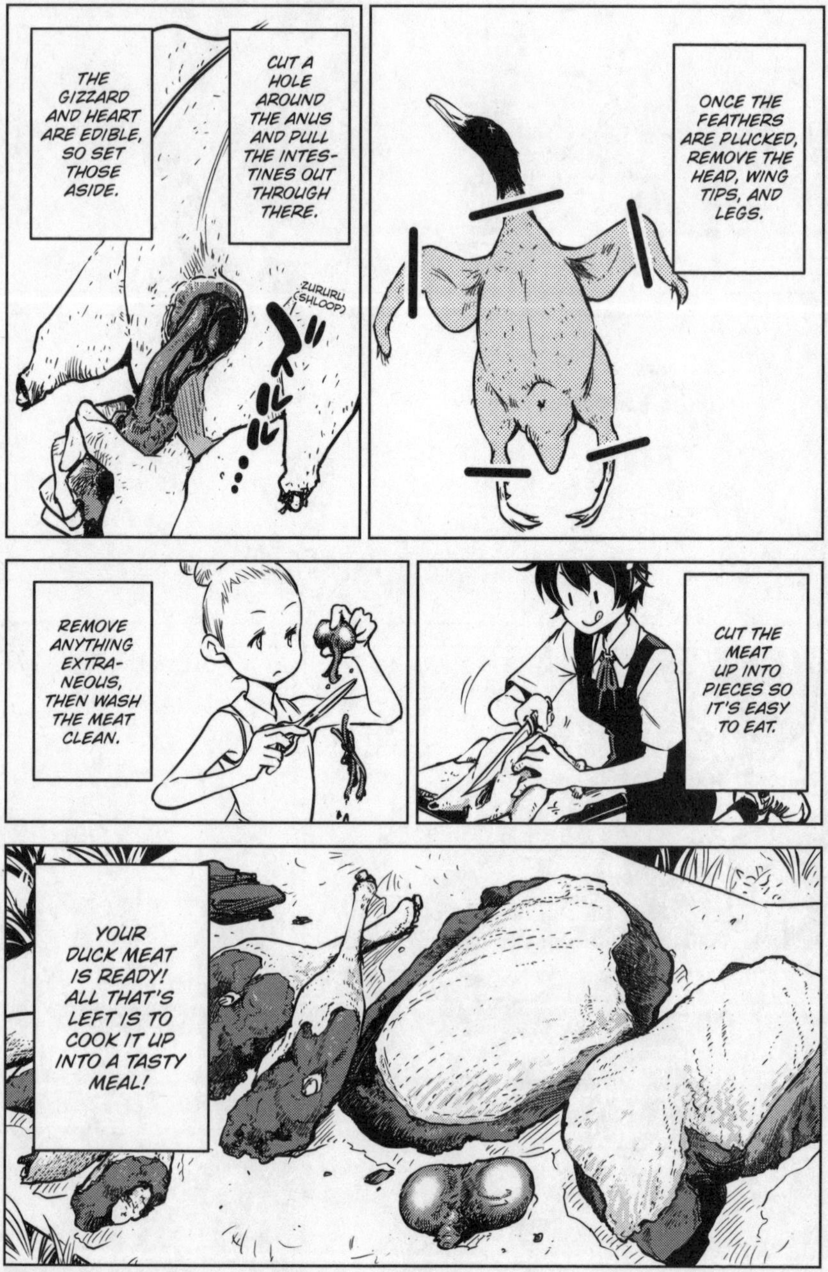
ONCE THE FEATHERS ARE PLUCKED, REMOVE THE HEAD, WING TIPS, AND LEGS.
CUT A HOLE AROUND THE ANUS AND PULL THE INTES-TINES OUT THROUGH THERE.
THE GIZZARD AND HEART ARE EDIBLE, SO SET THOSE ASIDE.
ZURURU (SHLOOP)
CUT THE MEAT UP INTO PIECES SO IT'S EASY TO EAT.
REMOVE ANYTHING EXTRA-NEOUS, THEN WASH THE MEAT CLEAN.
YOUR DUCK MEAT IS READY! ALL THAT'S LEFT IS TO COOK IT UP INTO A TASTY MEAL!

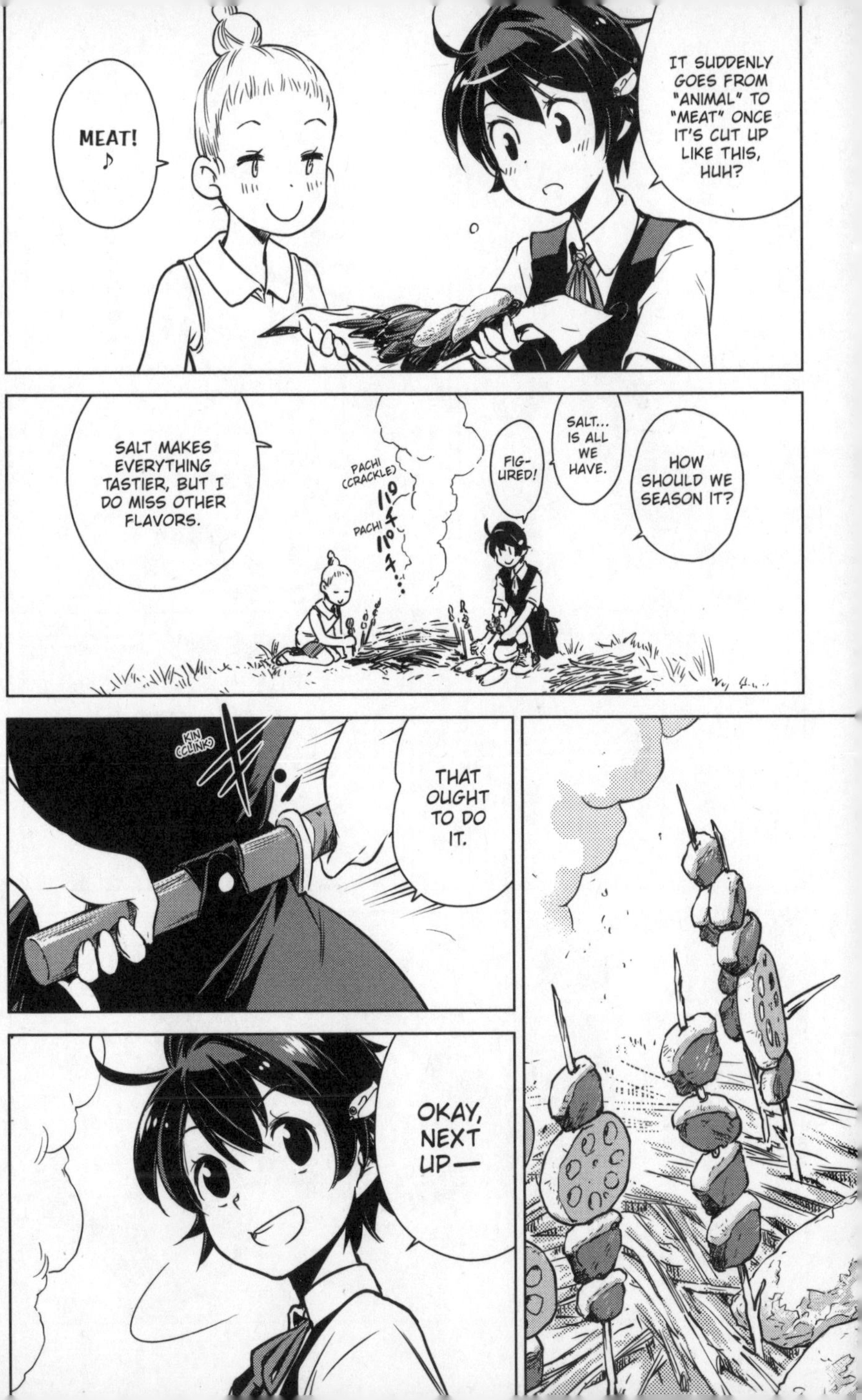
IT SUDDENLY GOES FROM "ANIMAL" TO "MEAT" ONCE IT'S CUT UP LIKE THIS, HUH?
MEAT! ♪
HOW SHOULD WE SEASON IT?
SALT... IS ALL WE HAVE.
FIG-URED!
PACHI (CRACKLE)
PACHI
SALT MAKES EVERYTHING TASTIER, BUT I DO MISS OTHER FLAVORS.
KIN (CLINK)
THAT OUGHT TO DO IT.
OKAY, NEXT UP—

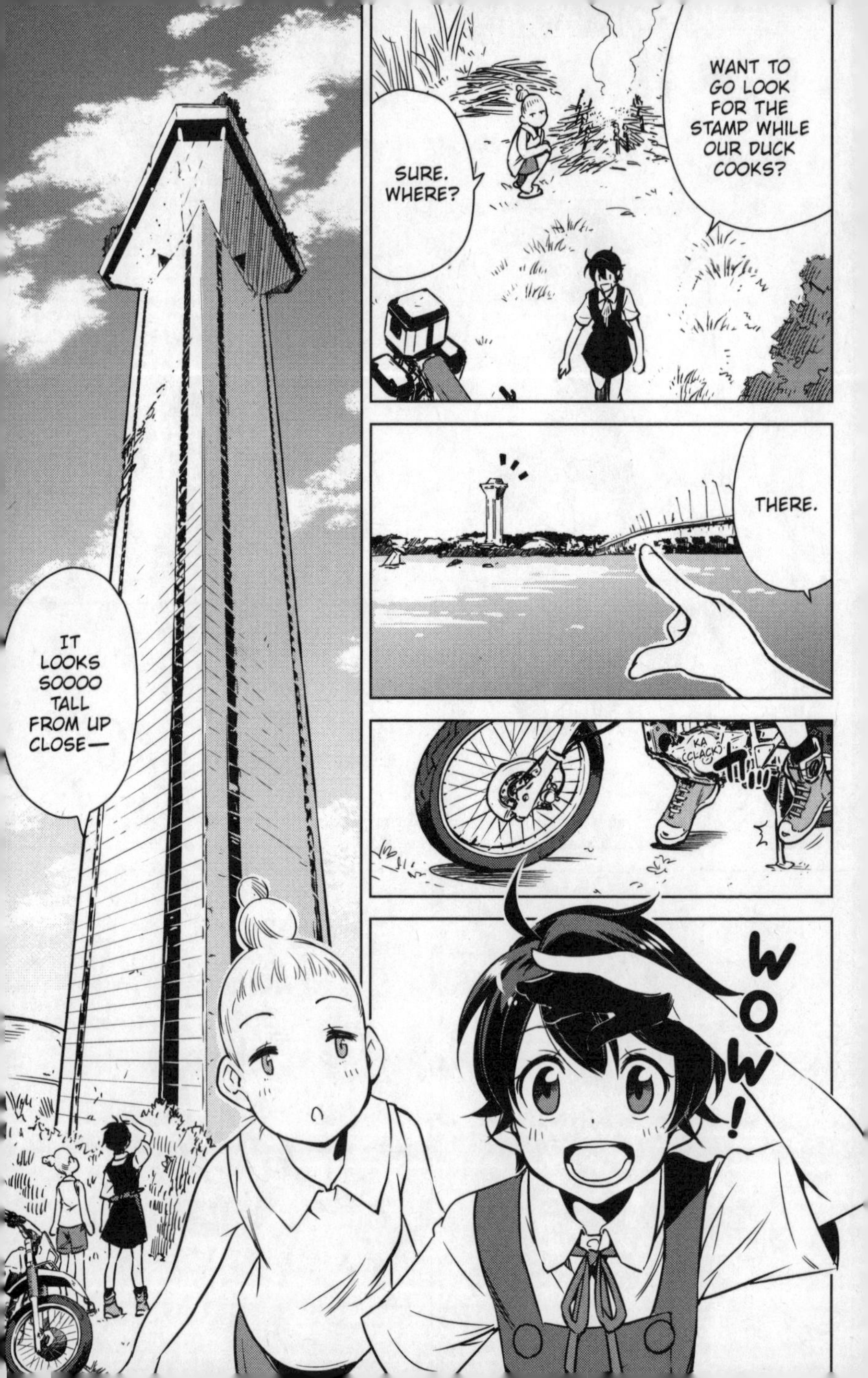
WANT TO GO LOOK FOR THE STAMP WHILE OUR DUCK COOKS?
SURE. WHERE?
THERE.
KA CLACK
WOW!
IT LOOKS SOOOO TALL FROM UP CLOSE—

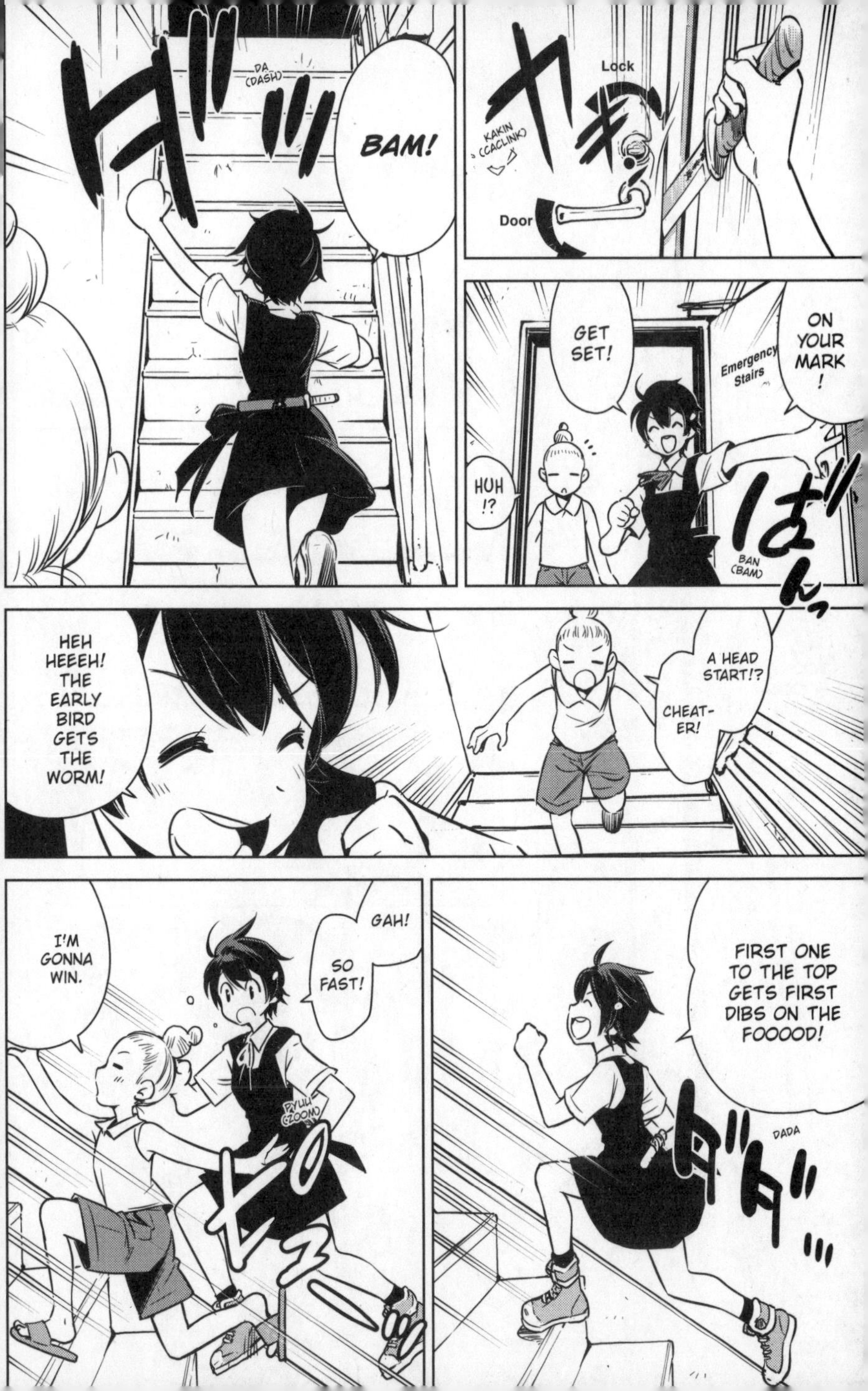
Lock
KAKIN (CACLINK)
Door
ON YOUR MARK!
Emergency Stairs
GET SET!
HUH!?
BAN (BAM)
BAM!
DA (DASH)
A HEAD START!?
CHEATER!
HEH HEEEH! THE EARLY BIRD GETS THE WORM!
FIRST ONE TO THE TOP GETS FIRST DIBS ON THE FOOOOD!
DADA
GAH!
SO FAST!
I'M GONNA WIN.
PYUU (ZOOM)

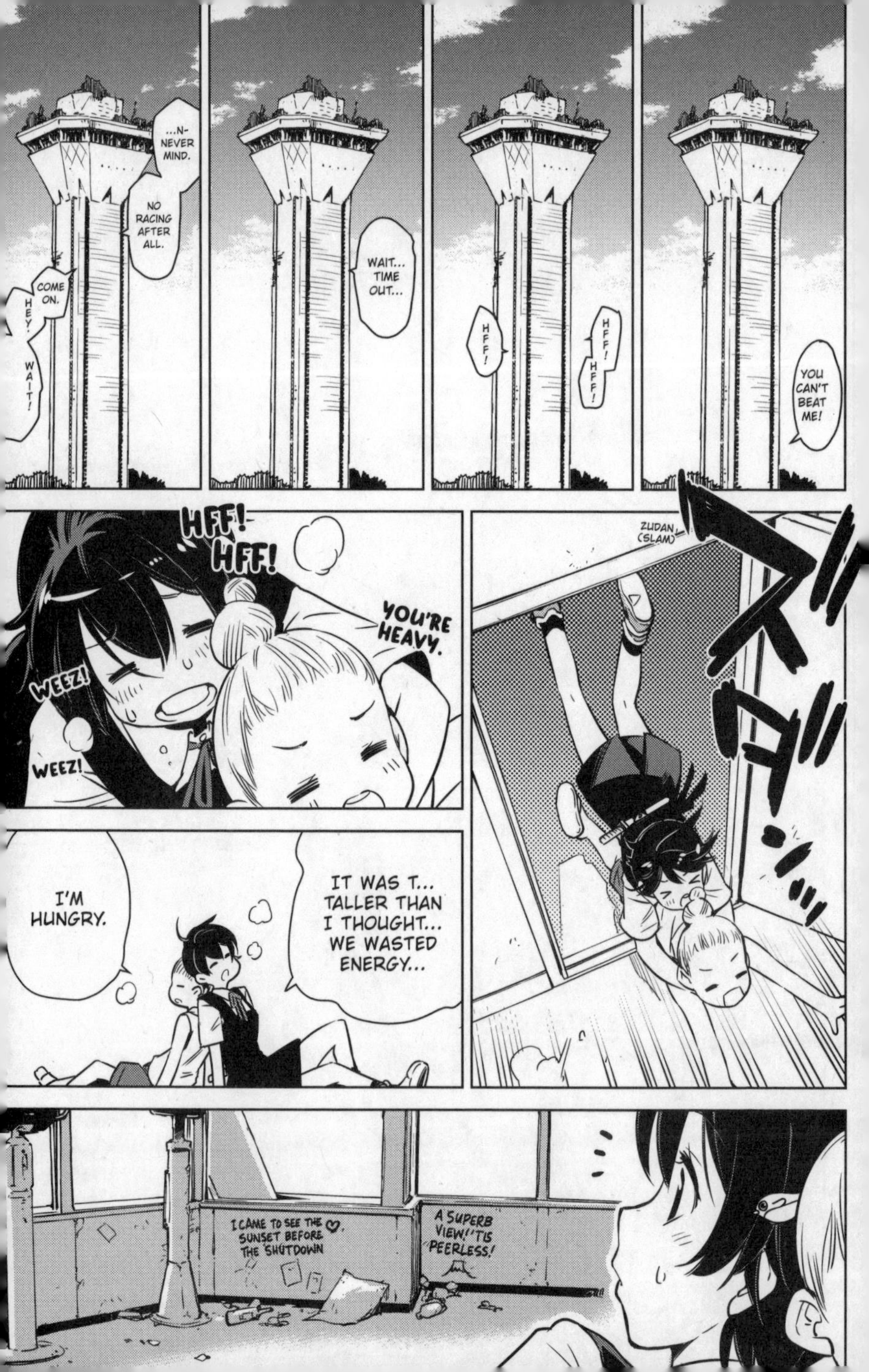
YOU CAN'T BEAT ME!
HFF! HFF!
HFF!
WAIT... TIME OUT...
...N-NEVER MIND.
NO RACING AFTER ALL.
COME ON.
HEY. WAIT!
ZUDAN (SLAM)
HFF! HFF!
YOU'RE HEAVY.
WEEZ!
WEEZ!
IT WAS T... TALLER THAN I THOUGHT... WE WASTED ENERGY...
I'M HUNGRY.
A SUPERB VIEW! 'TIS PEERLESS!
I CAME TO SEE THE SUNSET BEFORE THE SHUTDOWN

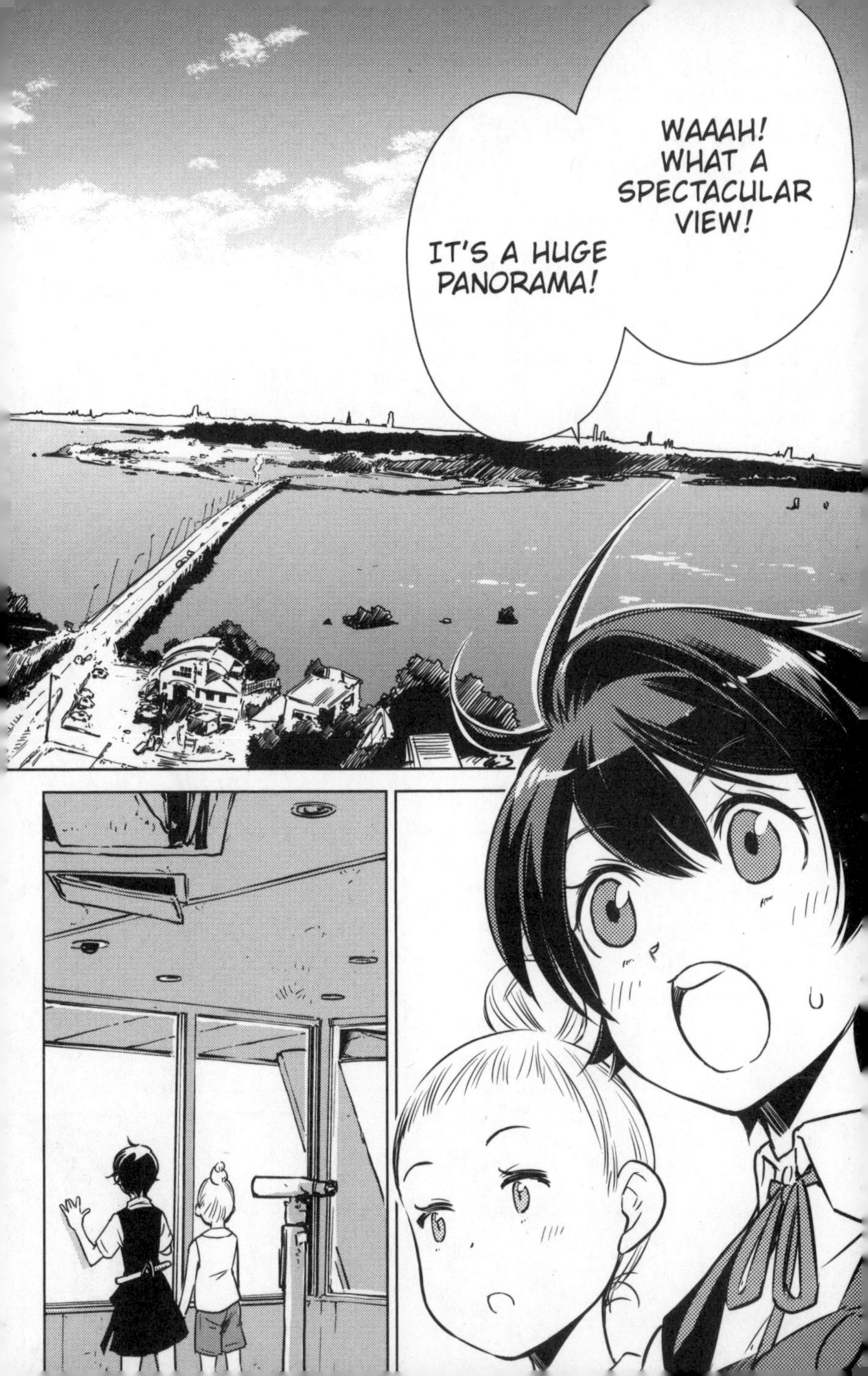
WAAAH! WHAT A SPECTACULAR VIEW!
IT'S A HUGE PANORAMA!

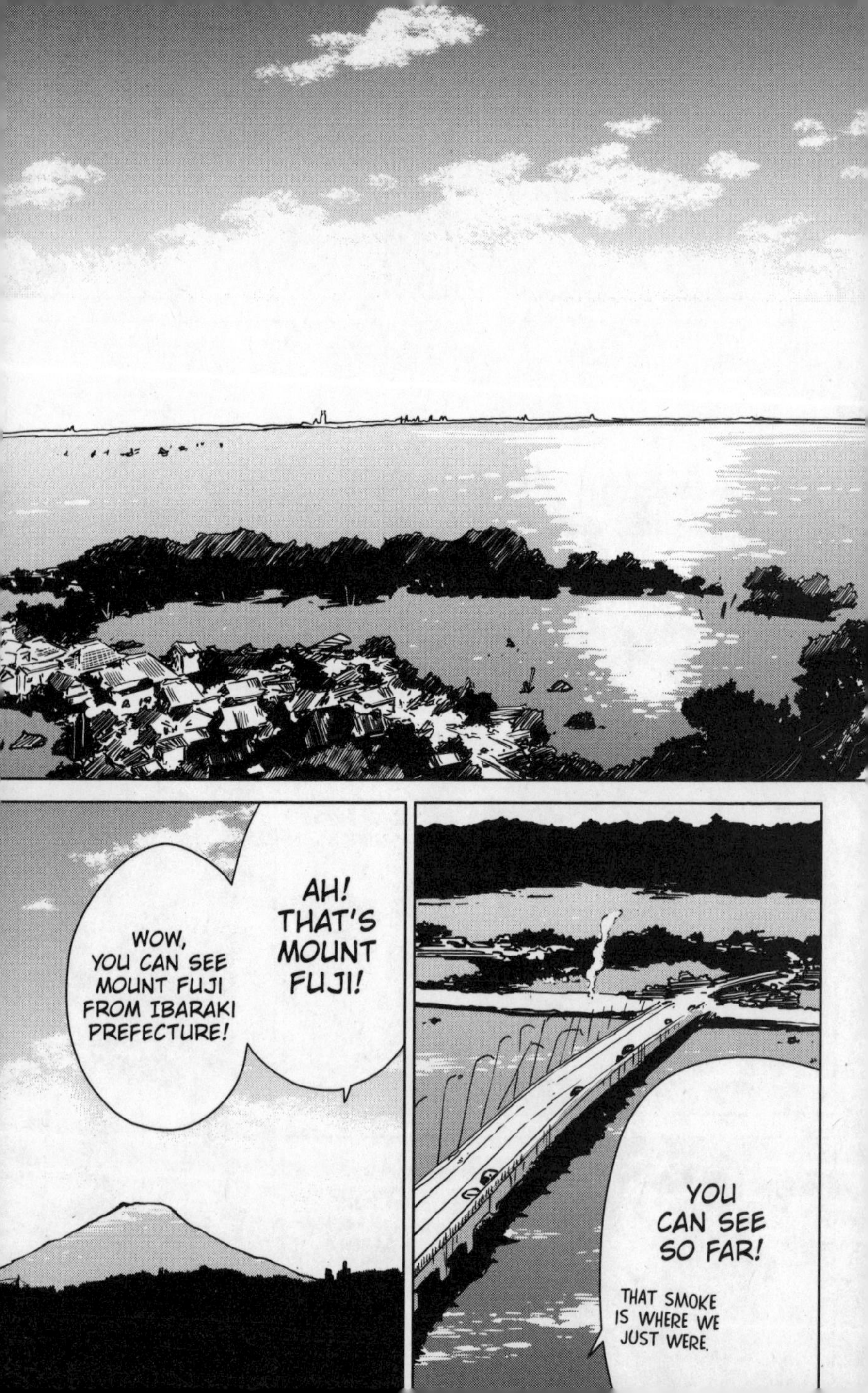
YOU CAN SEE SO FAR!
THAT SMOKE IS WHERE WE JUST WERE.
AH! THAT'S MOUNT FUJI!
WOW, YOU CAN SEE MOUNT FUJI FROM IBARAKI PREFECTURE!

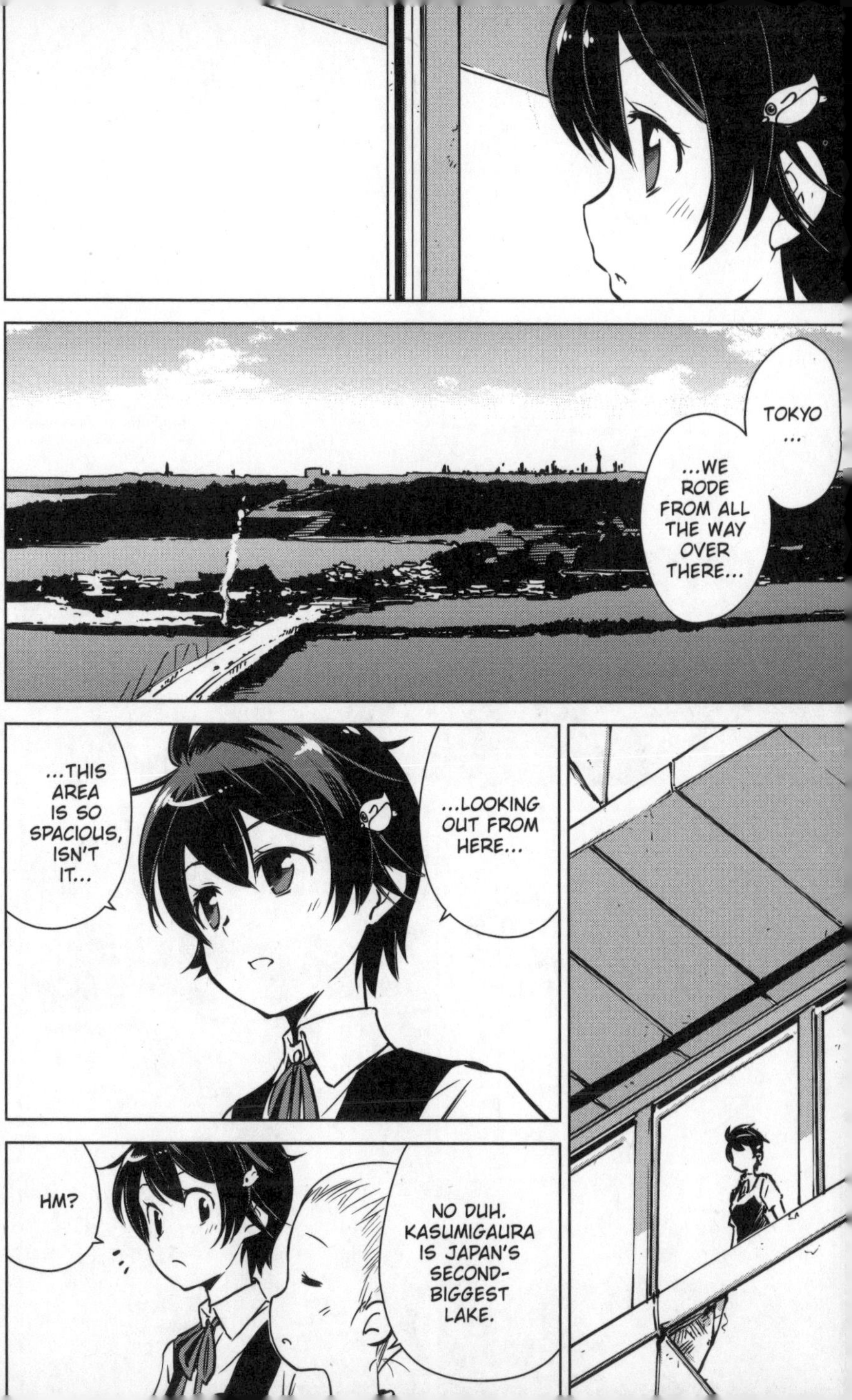
TOKYO ...
...WE RODE FROM ALL THE WAY OVER THERE...
...LOOKING OUT FROM HERE...
...THIS AREA IS SO SPACIOUS, ISN'T IT...
NO DUH. KASUMIGAURA IS JAPAN'S SECOND-BIGGEST LAKE.
HM?

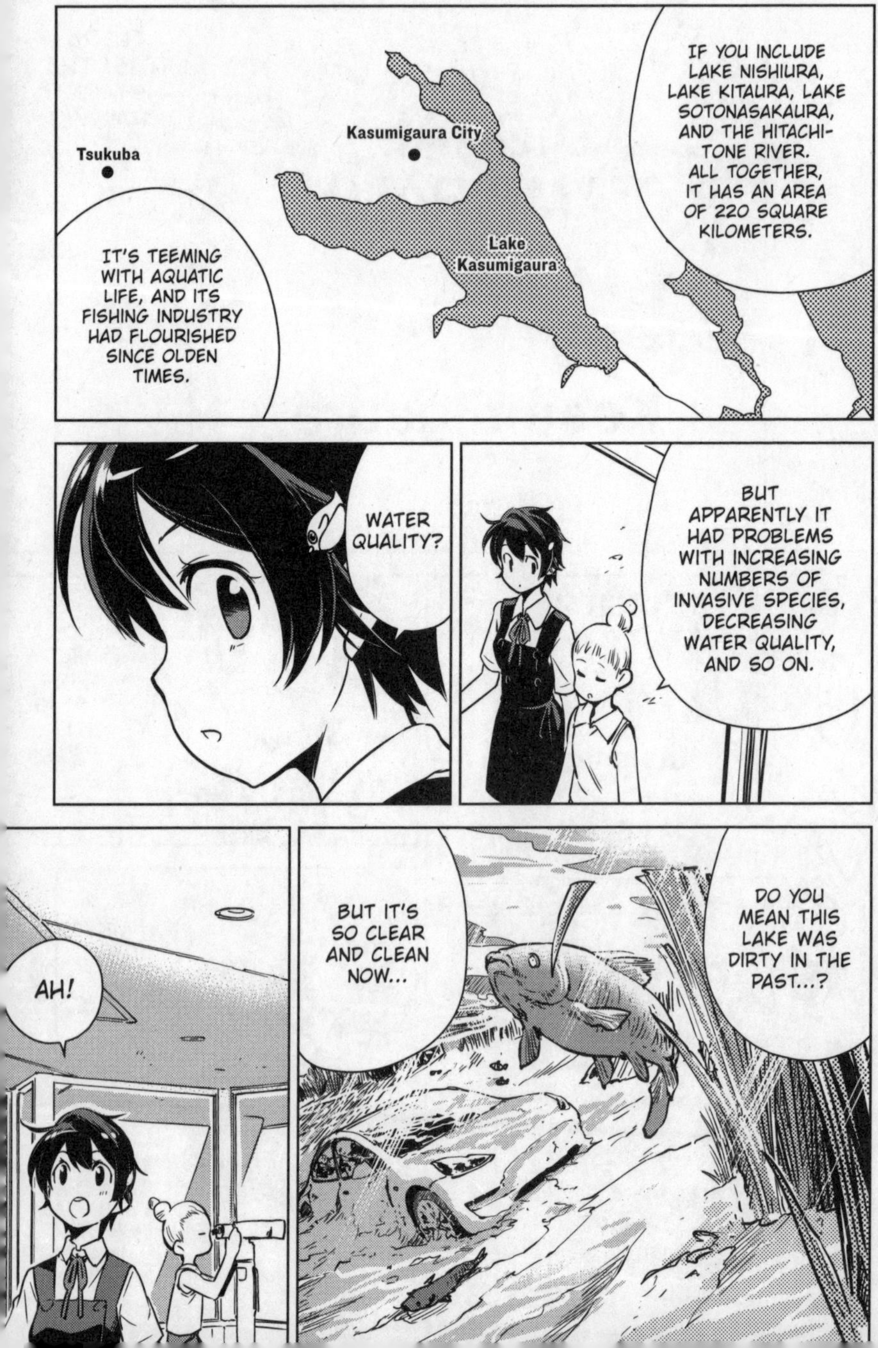
IF YOU INCLUDE LAKE NISHIURA, LAKE KITAURA, LAKE SOTONASAKAURA, AND THE HITACHI-TONE RIVER. ALL TOGETHER, IT HAS AN AREA OF 220 SQUARE KILOMETERS.
Kasumigaura City
Tsukuba
Lake Kasumigaura
IT'S TEEMING WITH AQUATIC LIFE, AND ITS FISHING INDUSTRY HAD FLOURISHED SINCE OLDEN TIMES.
BUT APPARENTLY IT HAD PROBLEMS WITH INCREASING NUMBERS OF INVASIVE SPECIES, DECREASING WATER QUALITY, AND SO ON.
WATER QUALITY?
DO YOU MEAN THIS LAKE WAS DIRTY IN THE PAST...?
BUT IT'S SO CLEAR AND CLEAN NOW...
AH!

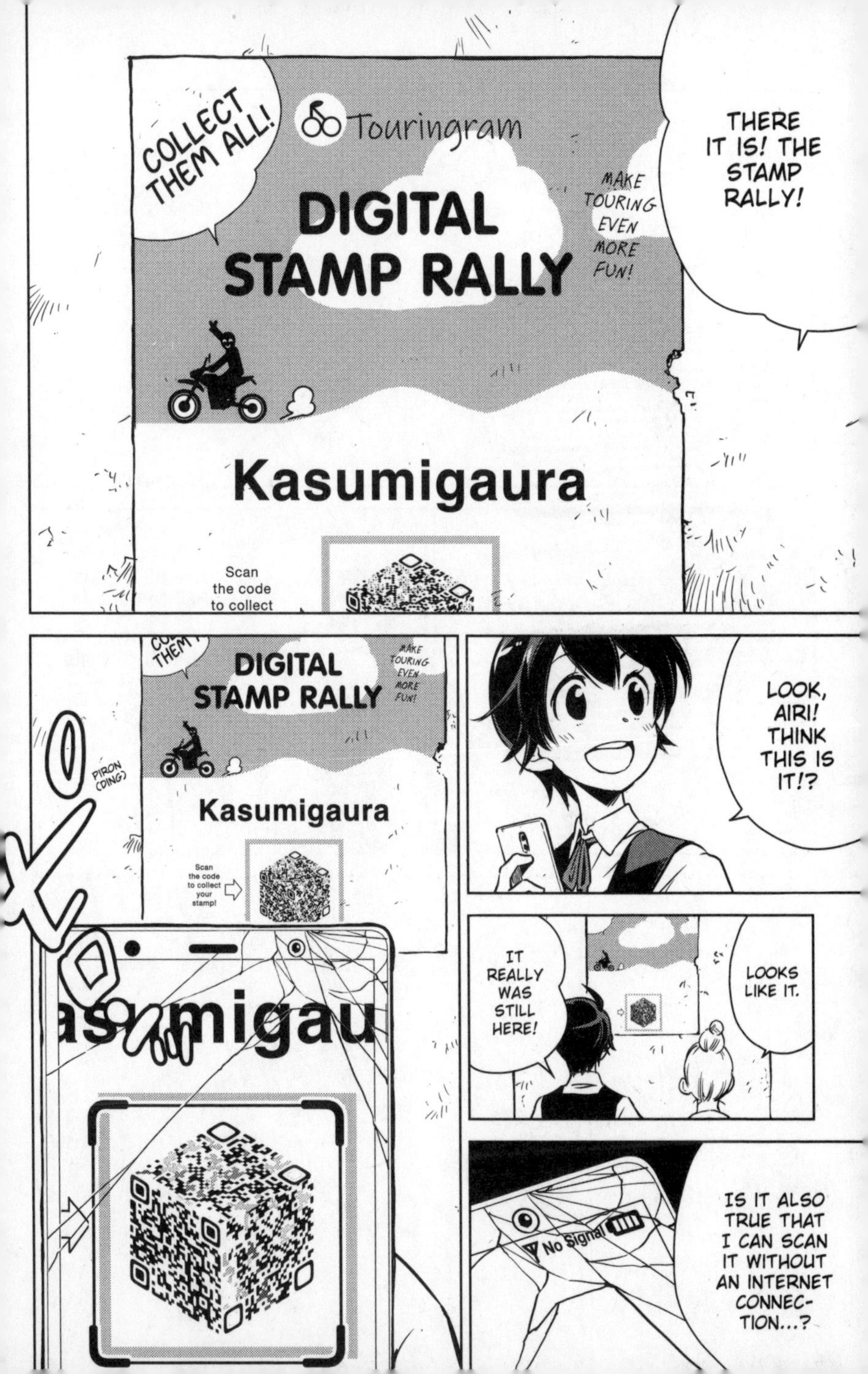
THERE IT IS! THE STAMP RALLY!
COLLECT THEM ALL!
Touringram
DIGITAL STAMP RALLY
MAKE TOURING EVEN MORE FUN!
Kasumigaura
Scan the code to collect
LOOK, AIRI! THINK THIS IS IT!?
LOOKS LIKE IT.
IT REALLY WAS STILL HERE!
No Signal
IS IT ALSO TRUE THAT I CAN SCAN IT WITHOUT AN INTERNET CONNEC- TION...?
DIGITAL STAMP RALLY
MAKE TOURING EVEN MORE FUN!
Kasumigaura
Scan the code to collect your stamp!
PIRON (DING)

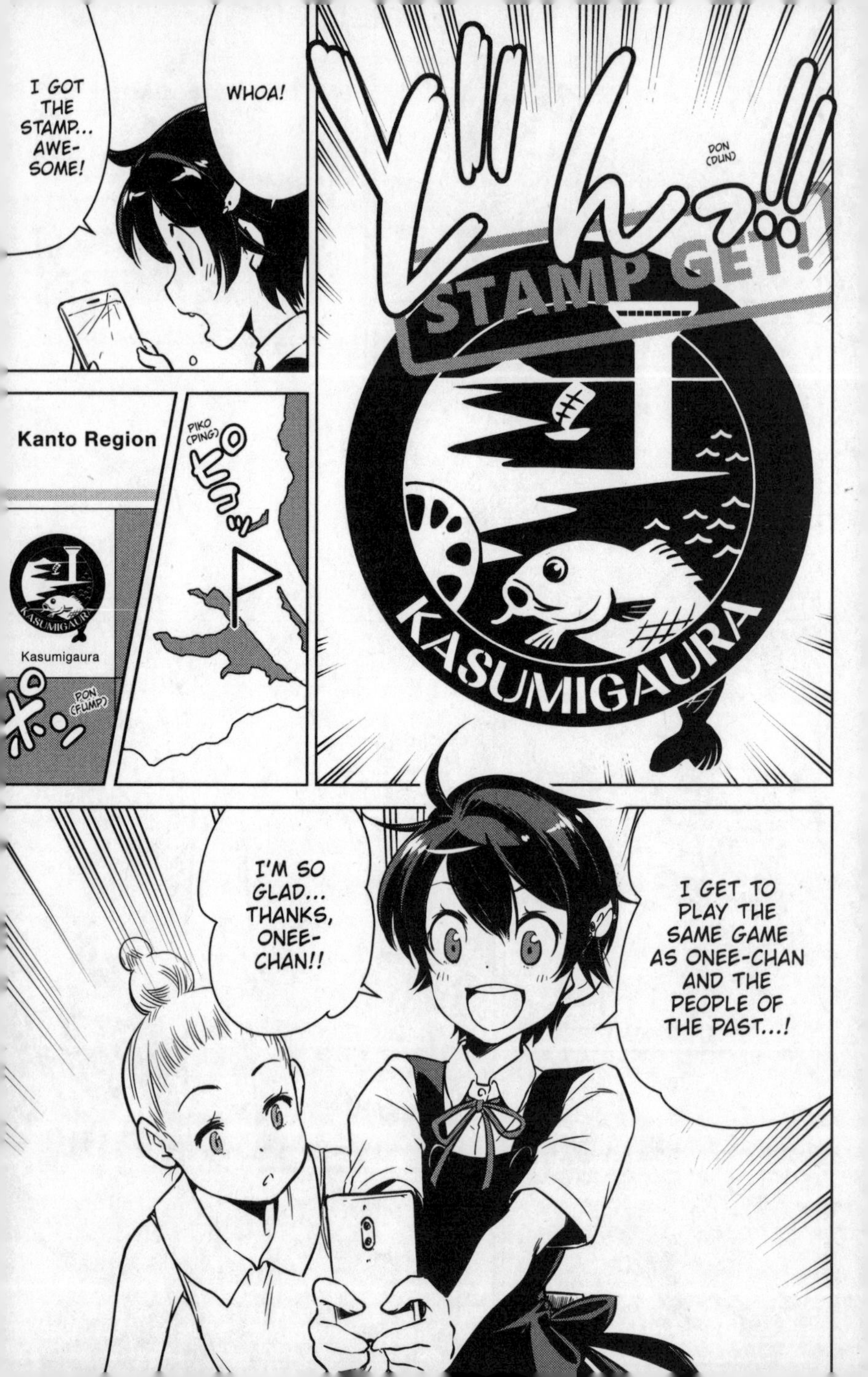
DON (DUND)
STAMP GET!
KASUMIGAURA
WHOA!
I GOT THE STAMP... AWESOME!
PIKO (PING)
Kanto Region
KASUMIGAURA
Kasumigaura
PON (FUMP)
I GET TO PLAY THE SAME GAME AS ONEE-CHAN AND THE PEOPLE OF THE PAST...!
I'M SO GLAD... THANKS, ONEE-CHAN!!

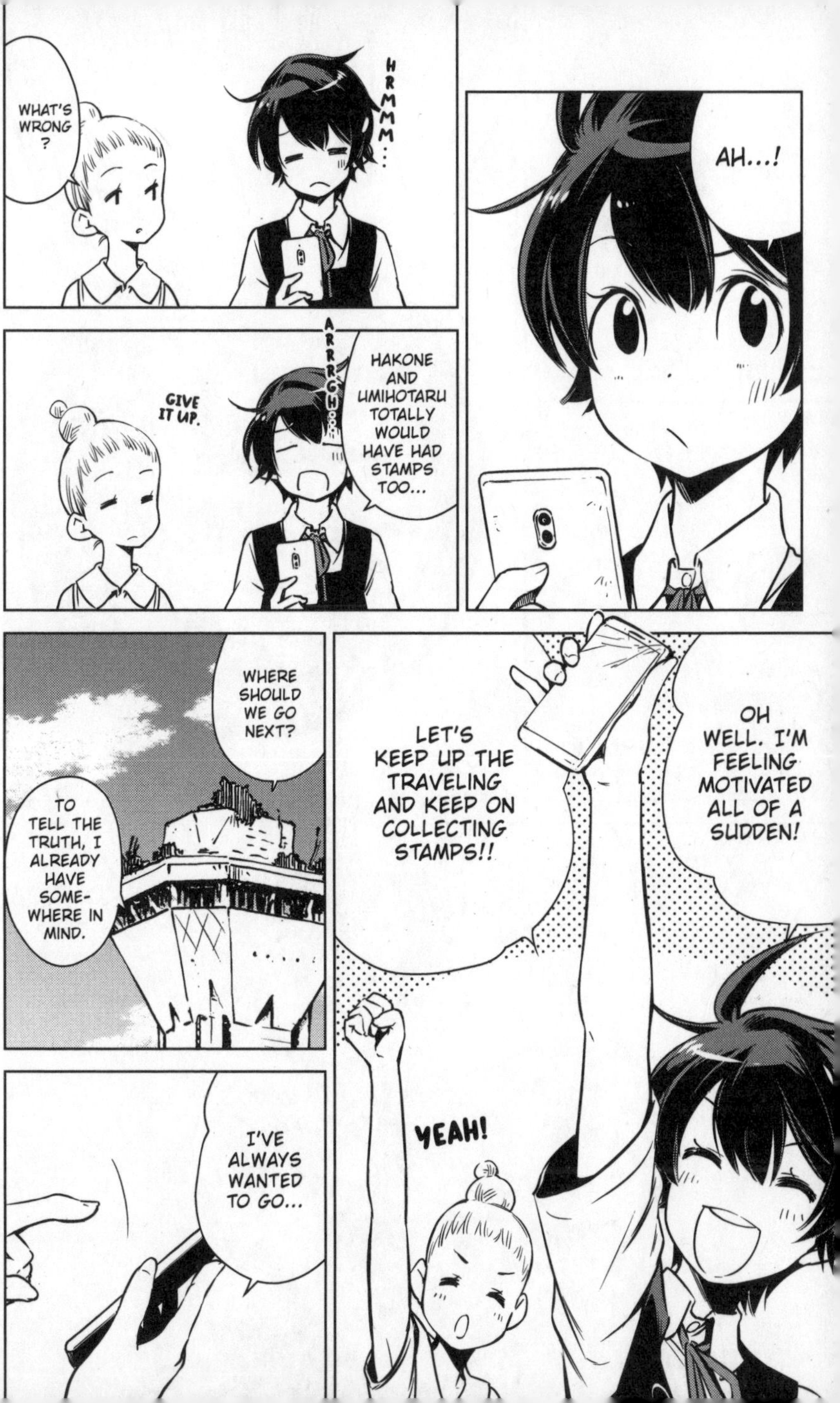
AH...!
HRMMM...
WHAT'S WRONG?
HAKONE AND UMIHOTARU TOTALLY WOULD HAVE HAD STAMPS TOO...
ARRRGH...
GIVE IT UP.
OH WELL. I'M FEELING MOTIVATED ALL OF A SUDDEN!
LET'S KEEP UP THE TRAVELING AND KEEP ON COLLECTING STAMPS!!
YEAH!
WHERE SHOULD WE GO NEXT?
TO TELL THE TRUTH, I ALREADY HAVE SOMEWHERE IN MIND.
I'VE ALWAYS WANTED TO GO...

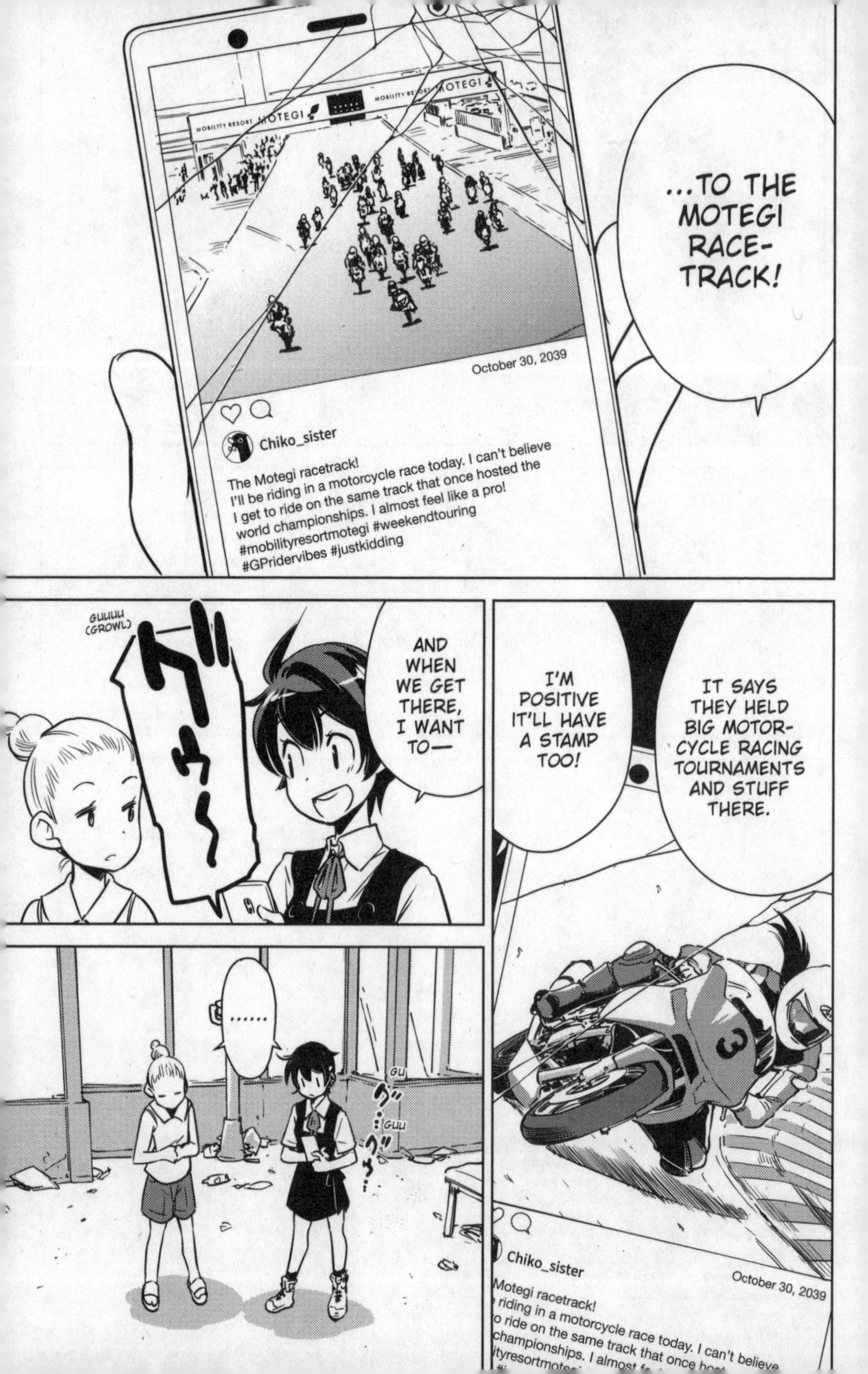
MOBILITY RESORT MOTEGI
October 30, 2039
Chiko_sister
The Motegi racetrack! The Motegi racetrack! I'll be riding in a motorcycle race today. I can't believe I get to ride on the same track that once hosted the world championships. I almost feel like a pro! #mobilityresortmotegi #weekendtouring #GPridervibes #justkidding
...TO THE MOTEGI RACE-TRACK!
IT SAYS THEY HELD BIG MOTOR-CYCLE RACING TOURNAMENTS AND STUFF THERE.
I'M POSITIVE IT'LL HAVE A STAMP TOO!
Chiko_sister
October 30, 2039
AND WHEN WE GET THERE, I WANT TO—
GUUUU (GROWL)
......
GU
GUU

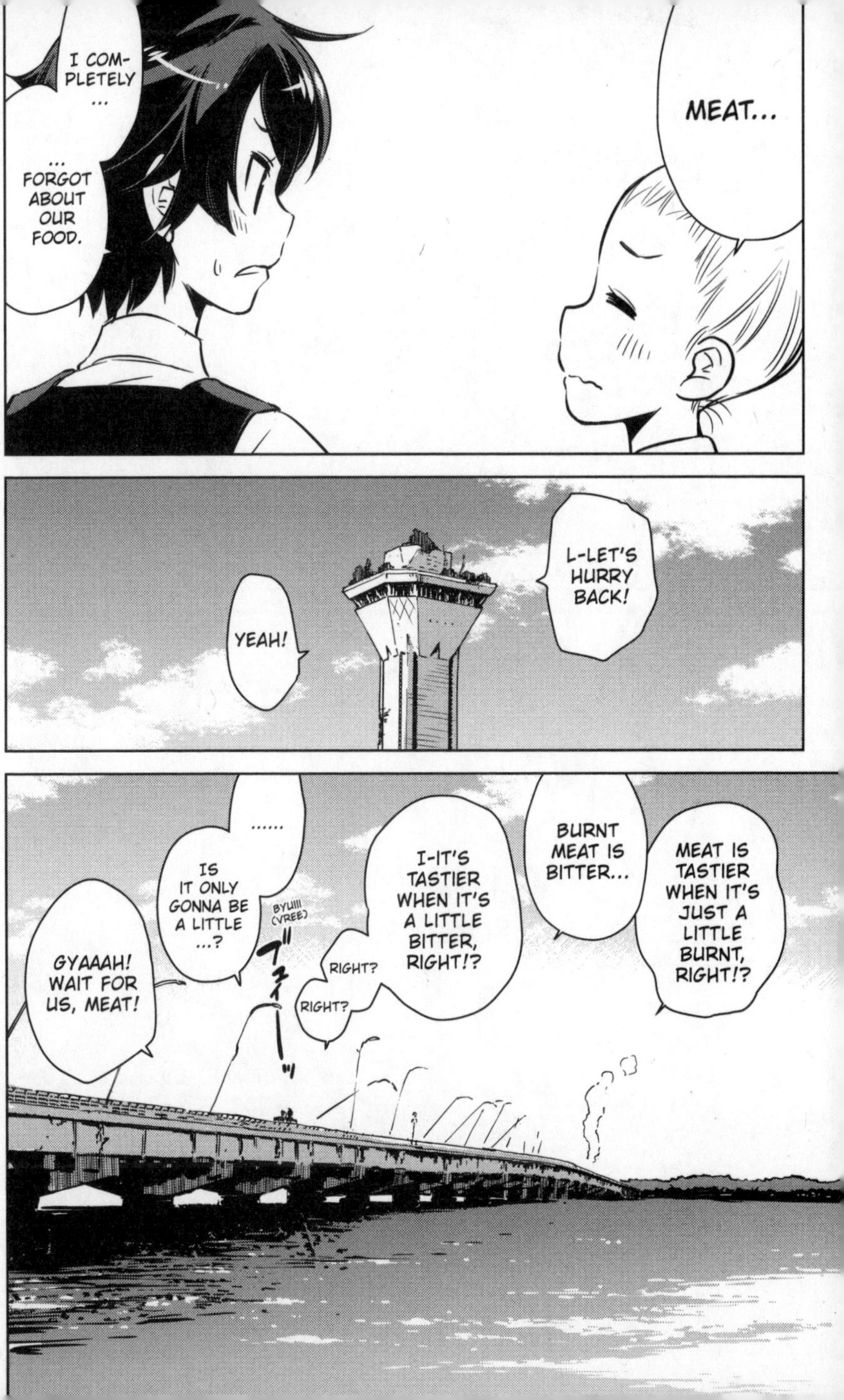
MEAT...
I COMPLETELY ...
... FORGOT ABOUT OUR FOOD.
L-LET'S HURRY BACK!
YEAH!
MEAT IS TASTIER WHEN IT'S JUST A LITTLE BURNT, RIGHT!?
BURNT MEAT IS BITTER...
I-IT'S TASTIER WHEN IT'S A LITTLE BITTER, RIGHT!?
RIGHT?
RIGHT?
BYUIII (VREE)
......
IS IT ONLY GONNA BE A LITTLE ...?
GYAAAH! WAIT FOR US, MEAT!

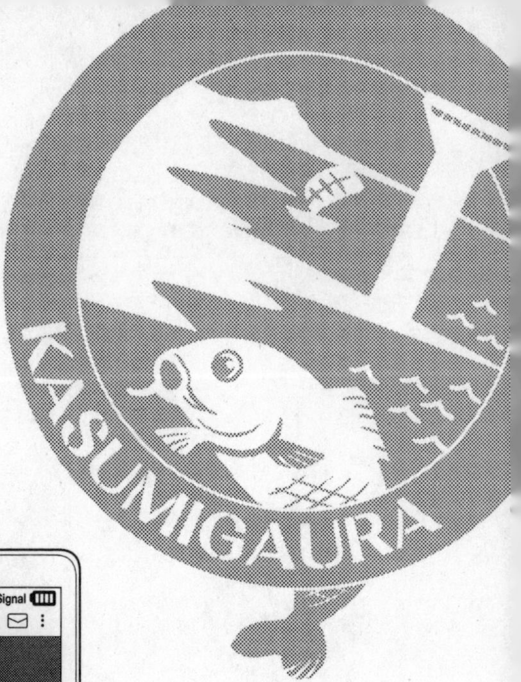
KASUMIGAURA

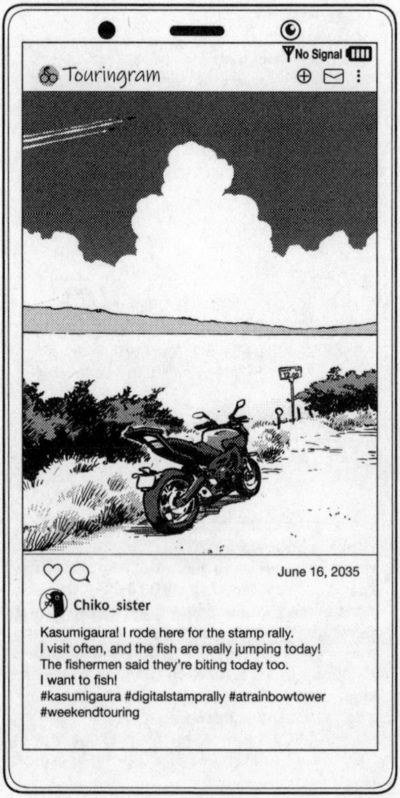
No Signal
Touringram
June 16, 2035
Chiko_sister
Kasumigaura! I rode here for the stamp rally.
I visit often, and the fish are really jumping today!
The fishermen said they're biting today too.
I want to fish!
#kasumigaura #digitalstamprally #atrainbowtower
#weekendtouring

Gadget Explanation

Touringram

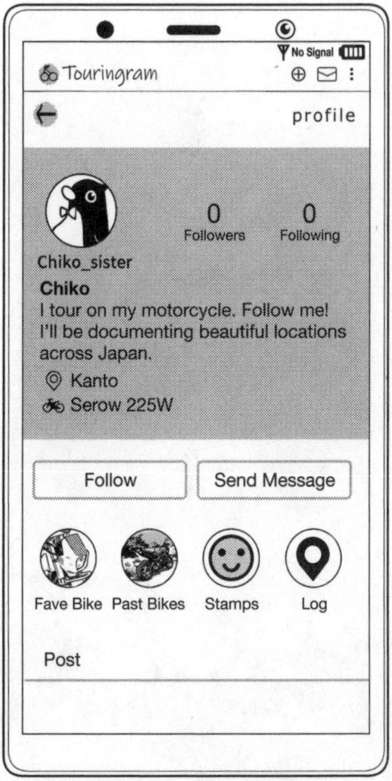
No Signal
Touringram
profile
0
Followers
0
Following
Chiko_sister
Chiko
I tour on my motorcycle. Follow me!
I'll be documenting beautiful locations across Japan.
Kanto
Serow 225W
Follow
Send Message
Fave Bike
Past Bikes
Stamps
Log
Post

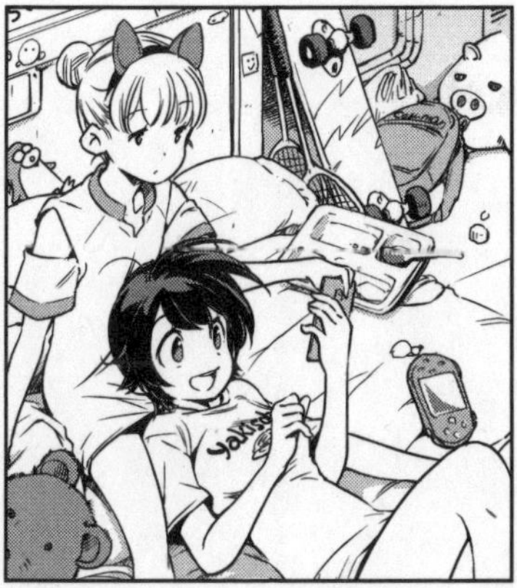

What is Touringram?

A social media app aimed at motorcyclists that was popular in the 2030s. Focused on photo- and video-posting features, it was developed mainly as an app for journaling motorcycle touring. In its heyday, users could link their GPS with the map to record their routes, look back on their old trips, and check for sightseeing spots and digital stamp rally locations. In the present, it can only view the archives of a journal saved on one's device.

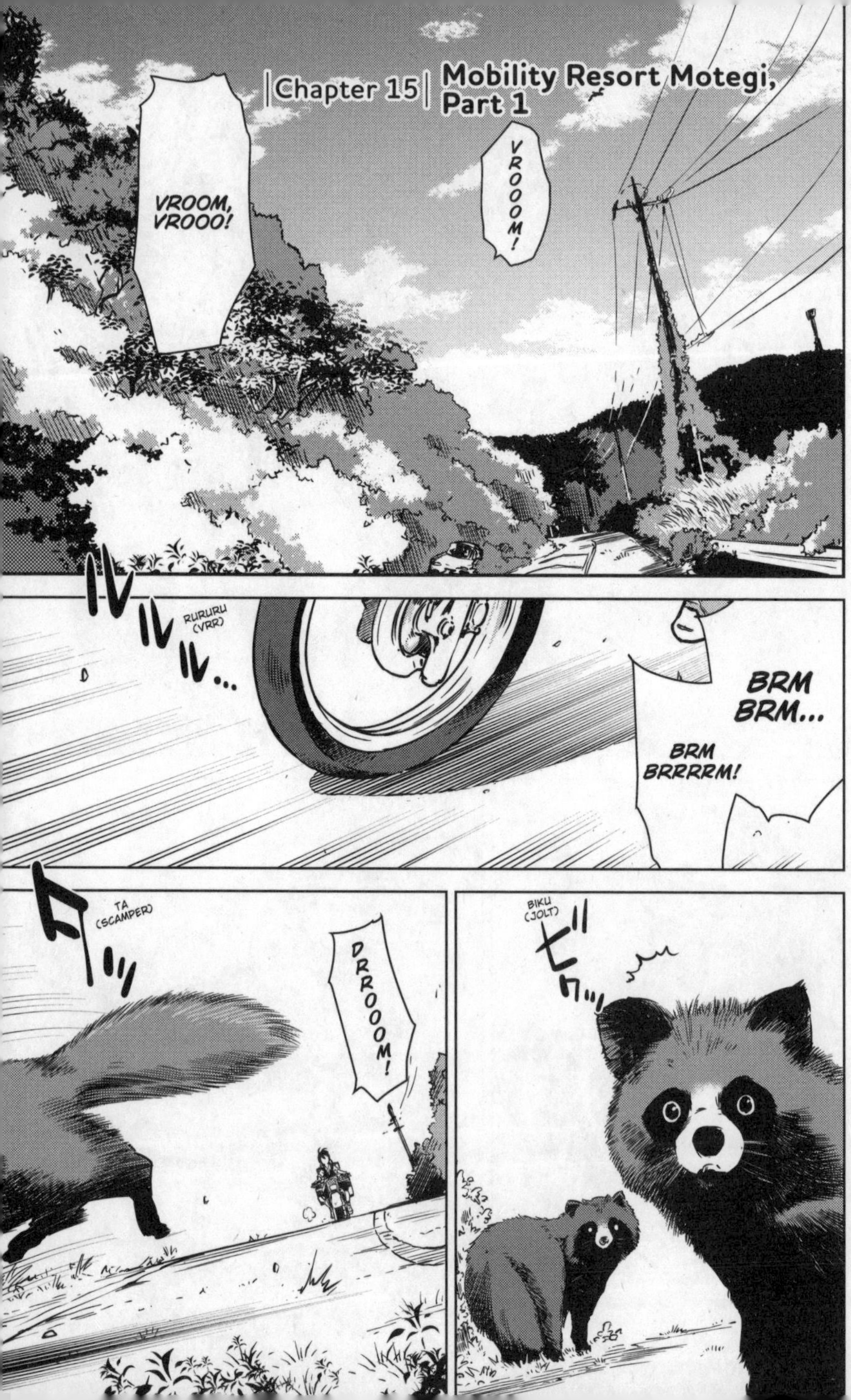
Chapter 15 Mobility Resort Motegi, Part 1
VROOOOM!
VROOM, VROOO!
BRM BRM...
BRM BRRRRM!
RURURU (VRR)
BIKU (JOLT)
DRROOOOM!
TA (SCAMPER)

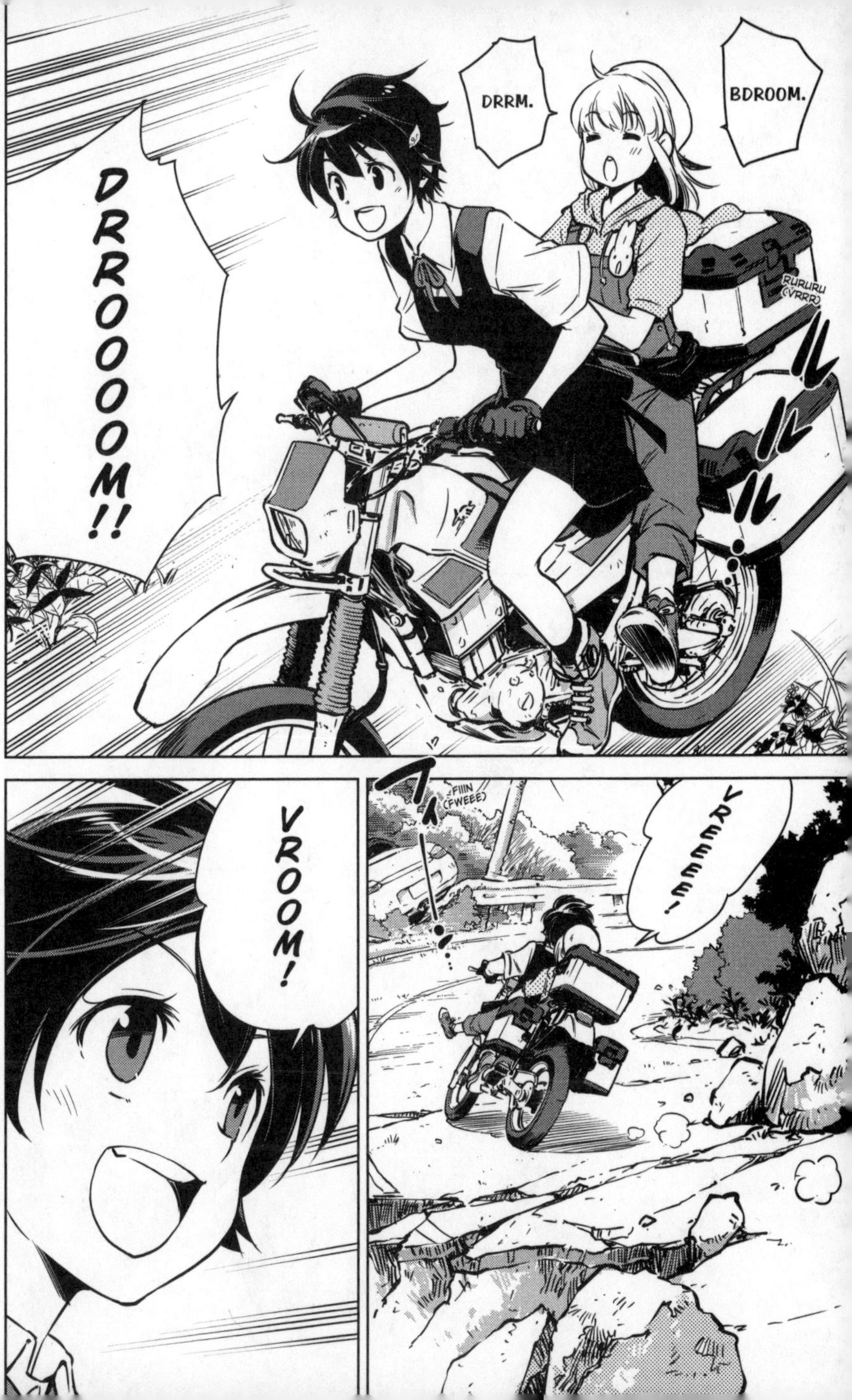
BDROOM.
DRRM.
DRROOOOOM!!
RURURU (VRRR)
VREEEE!
FIIIN (FWEEE)
VROOOM!

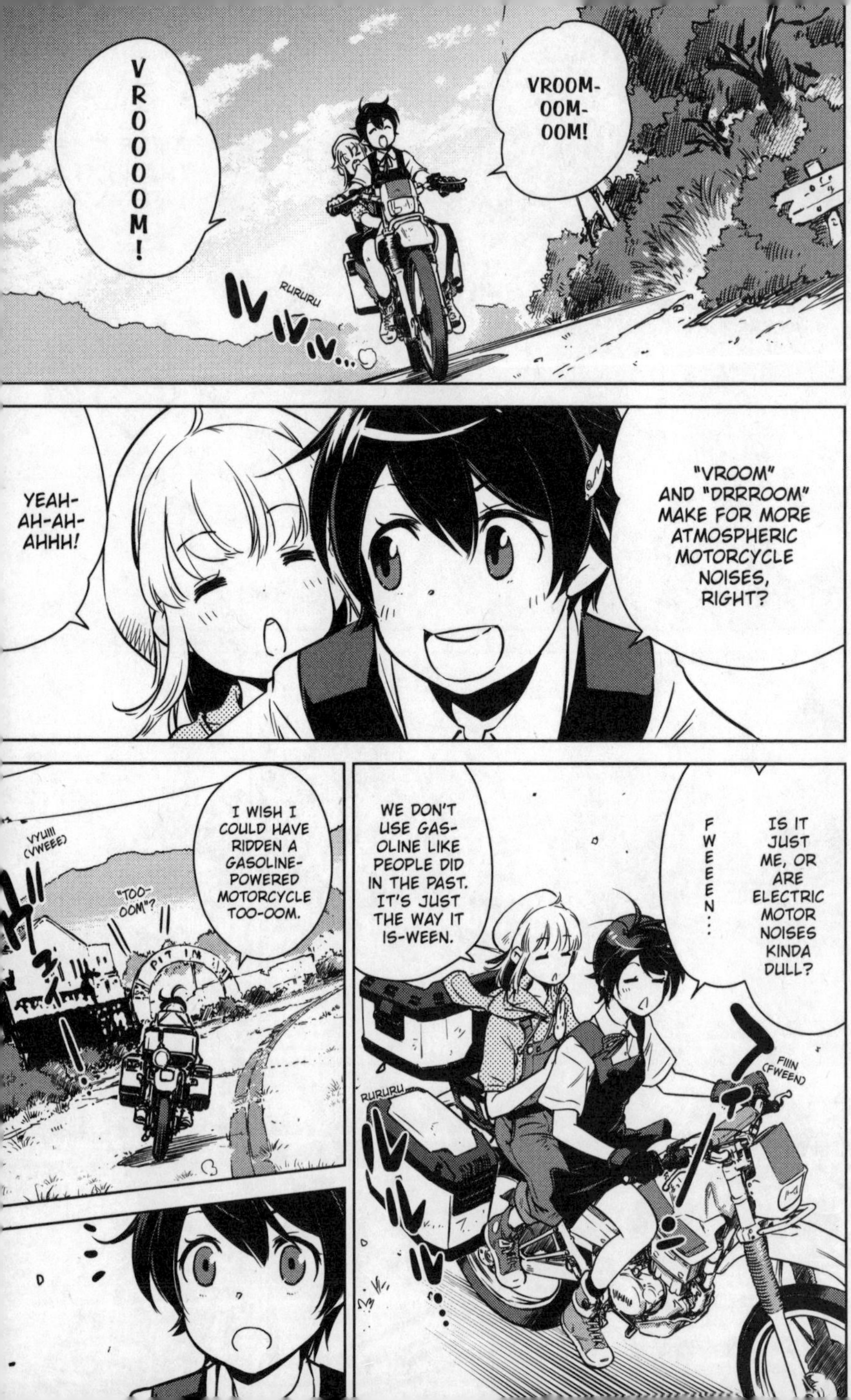
VROOM-OOM-OOM!
VROOOOOM!
RURURU
"VROOM" AND "DRRROOM" MAKE FOR MORE ATMOSPHERIC MOTORCYCLE NOISES, RIGHT?
YEAH-AH-AH-AHHH!
IS IT JUST ME, OR ARE ELECTRIC MOTOR NOISES KINDA DULL?
FWEEN...
WE DON'T USE GAS-OLINE LIKE PEOPLE DID IN THE PAST. IT'S JUST THE WAY IT IS-WEEN.
FIIIN (FWEEND)
RURURU
I WISH I COULD HAVE RIDDEN A GASOLINE-POWERED MOTORCYCLE TOO-OOM.
VYUIII (VWEEE)
"TOO-OOM"?
PIT IN

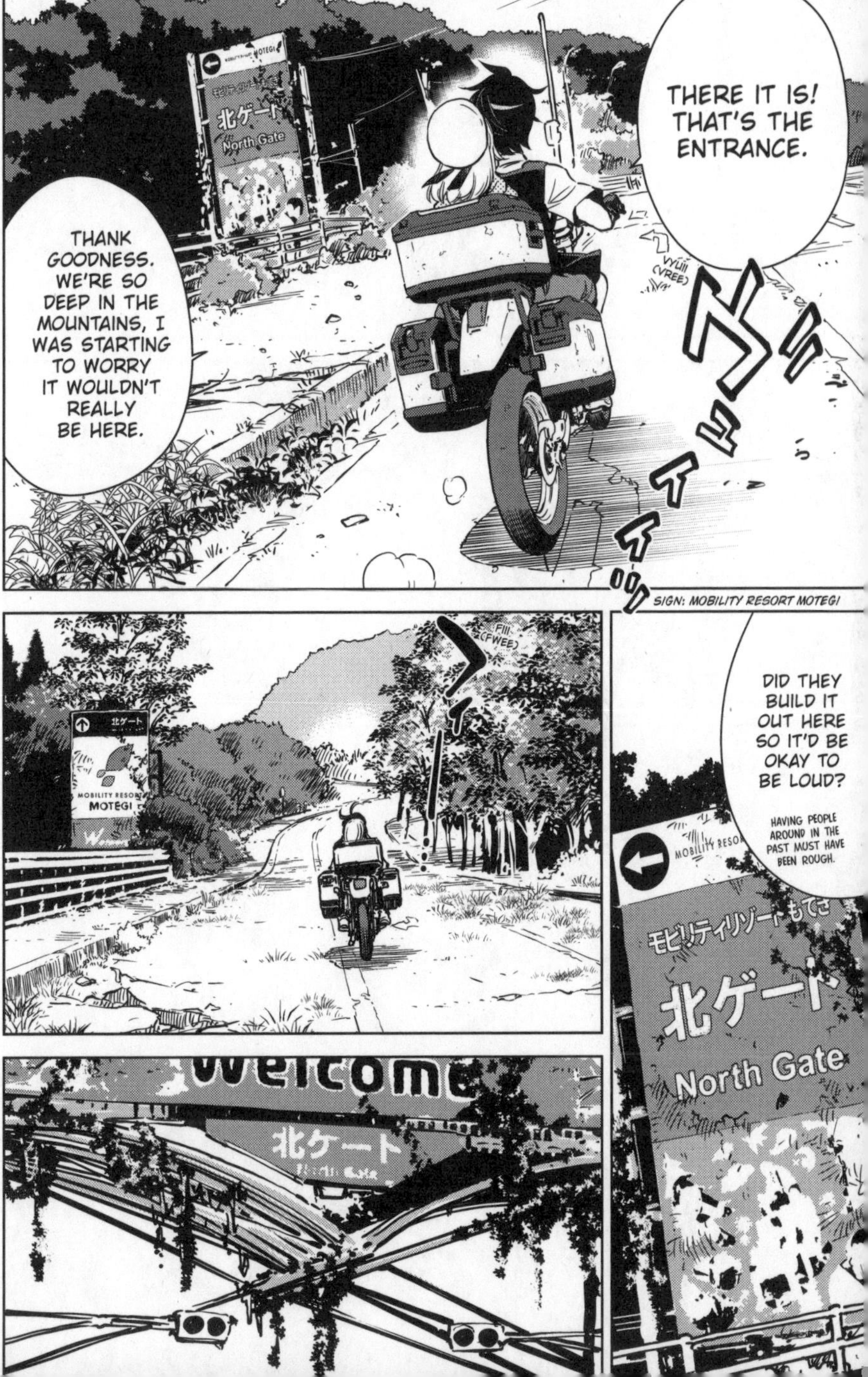
THERE IT IS! THAT'S THE ENTRANCE.
THANK GOODNESS. WE'RE SO DEEP IN THE MOUNTAINS, I WAS STARTING TO WORRY IT WOULDN'T REALLY BE HERE.
MOTEGI
北ゲート
North Gate
VYUII (VREE)
SIGN: MOBILITY RESORT MOTEGI
DID THEY BUILD IT OUT HERE SO IT'D BE OKAY TO BE LOUD?
HAVING PEOPLE AROUND IN THE PAST MUST HAVE BEEN ROUGH.
MOBILITY RESORT
モビリティリゾートもてぎ
北ゲート
North Gate
FIII (FWEE)
北ゲート
MOBILITY RESORT MOTEGI
Welcome
北ゲート

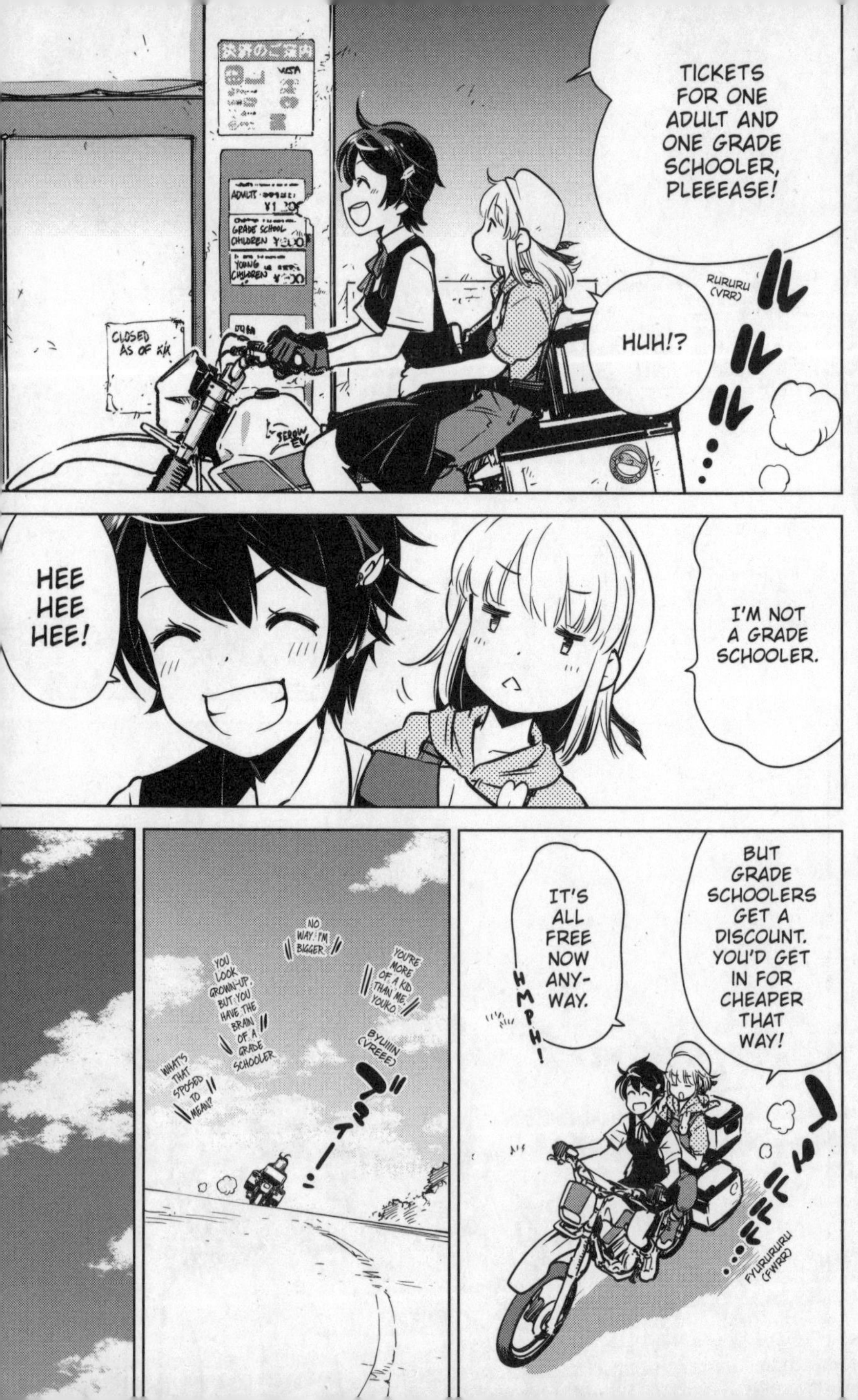
TICKETS FOR ONE ADULT AND ONE GRADE SCHOOLER, PLEEEASE!
HUH!?
RURURU (VRR)
ADULT
GRADE SCHOOL CHILDREN
YOUNG CHILDREN
CLOSED AS OF X/X
SEROW EV
I'M NOT A GRADE SCHOOLER.
HEE HEE HEE!
BUT GRADE SCHOOLERS GET A DISCOUNT. YOU'D GET IN FOR CHEAPER THAT WAY!
IT'S ALL FREE NOW ANYWAY.
HMPH!
FYURURURU (FWRR)
YOU'RE MORE OF A KID THAN ME, YOUKO.
NO WAY. I'M BIGGER.
YOU LOOK GROWN-UP, BUT YOU HAVE THE BRAIN OF A GRADE SCHOOLER.
WHAT'S THAT SPOSED TO MEAN?
BYUIIIN (VREEE)

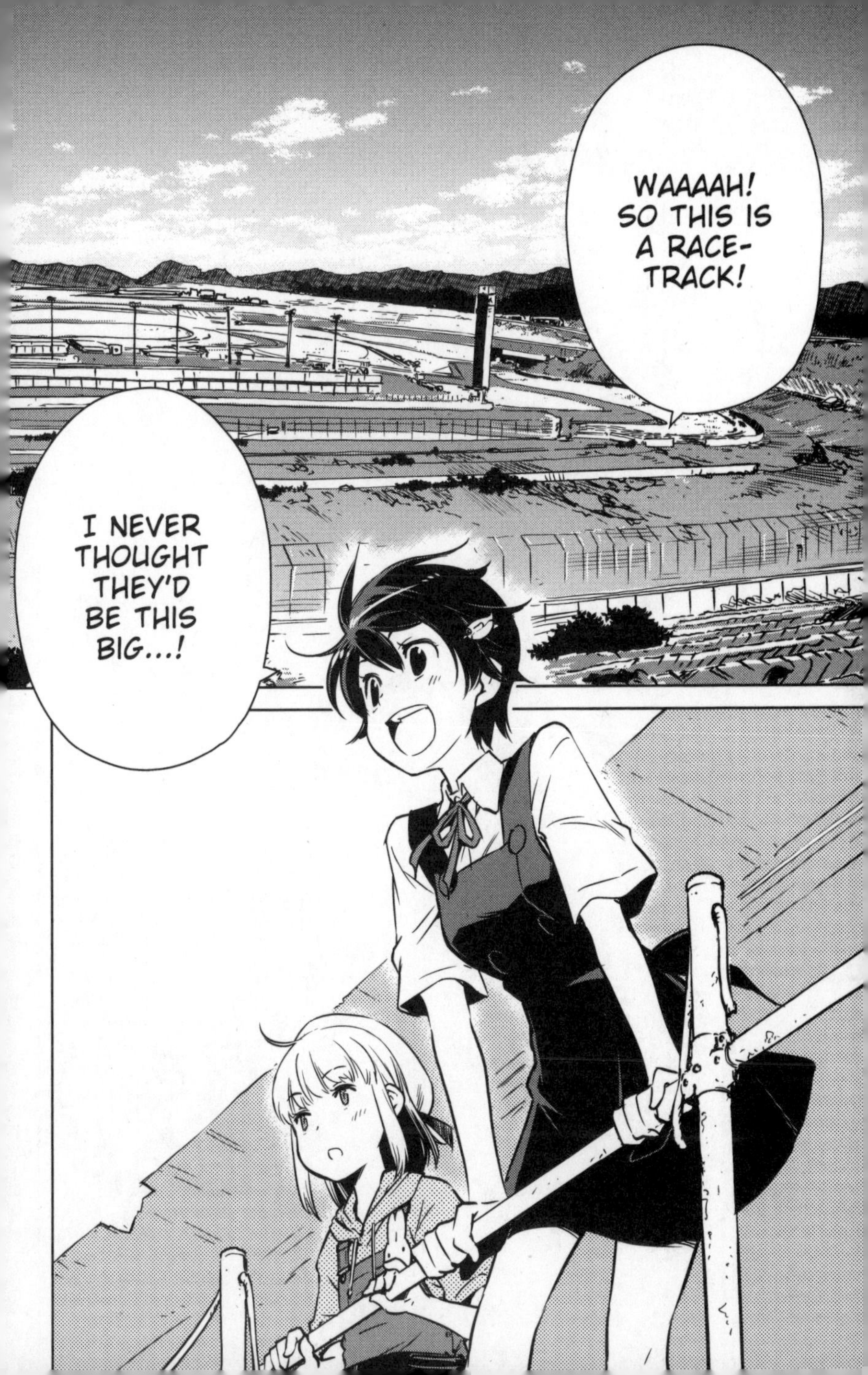
WAAAAH! SO THIS IS A RACE-TRACK!
I NEVER THOUGHT THEY'D BE THIS BIG...!

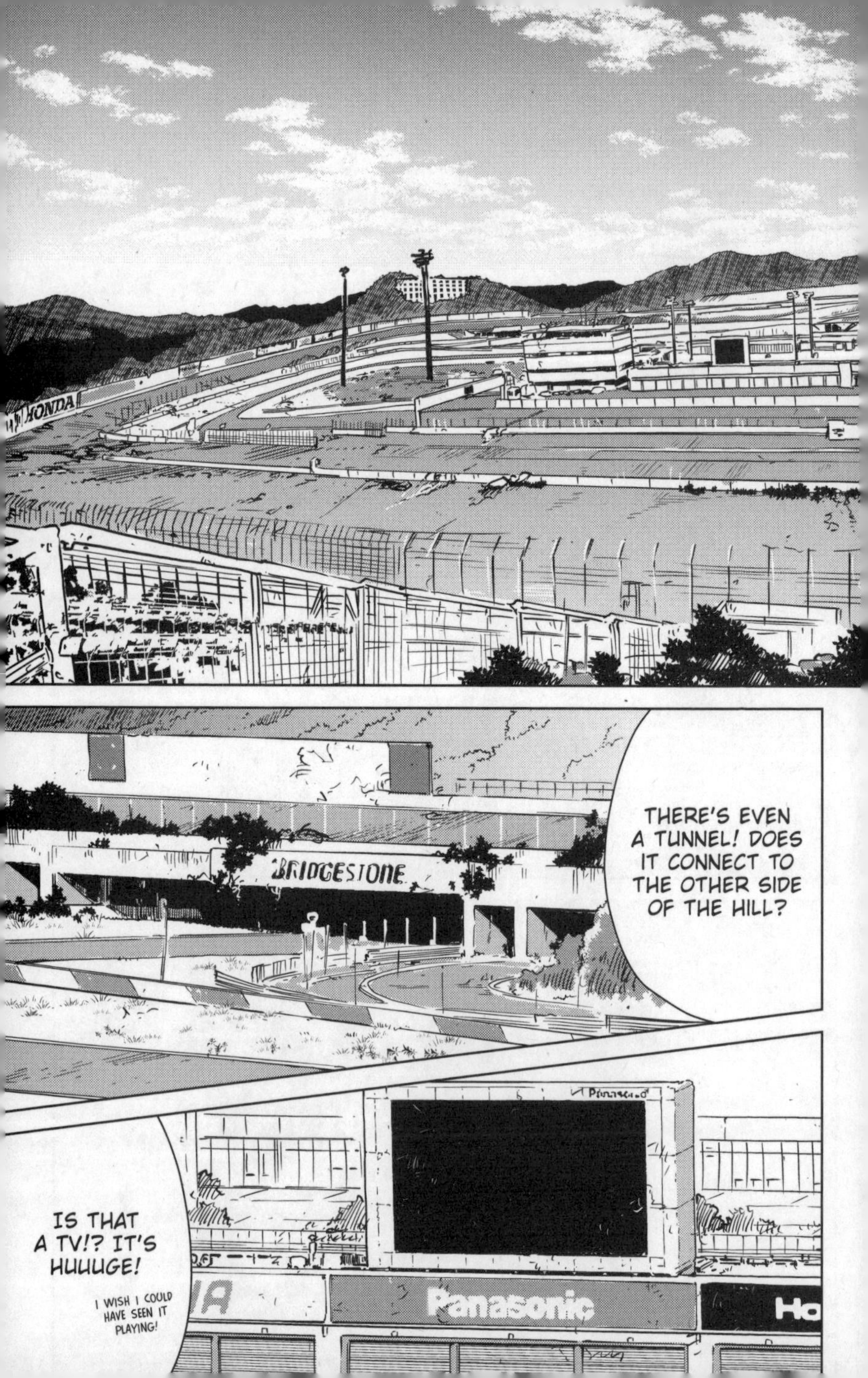
HONDA
THERE'S EVEN A TUNNEL! DOES IT CONNECT TO THE OTHER SIDE OF THE HILL?
BRIDGESTONE
IS THAT A TV!? IT'S HUUUGE!
I WISH I COULD HAVE SEEN IT PLAYING!
Panasonic

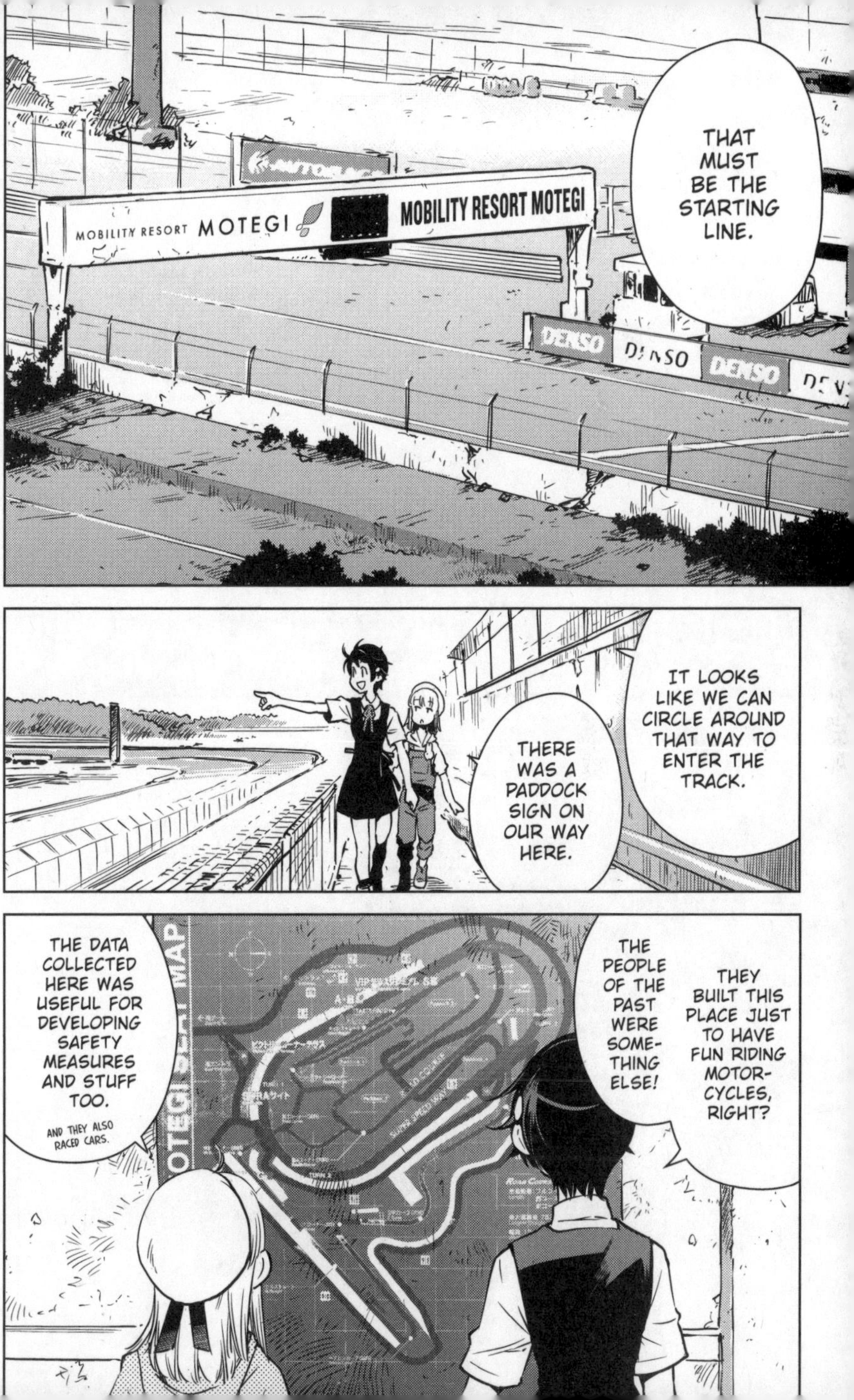
MOBILITY RESORT MOTEGI
MOBILITY RESORT MOTEGI
DENSO
THAT MUST BE THE STARTING LINE.
IT LOOKS LIKE WE CAN CIRCLE AROUND THAT WAY TO ENTER THE TRACK.
THERE WAS A PADDOCK SIGN ON OUR WAY HERE.
THEY BUILT THIS PLACE JUST TO HAVE FUN RIDING MOTOR-CYCLES, RIGHT?
THE PEOPLE OF THE PAST WERE SOME-THING ELSE!
THE DATA COLLECTED HERE WAS USEFUL FOR DEVELOPING SAFETY MEASURES AND STUFF TOO.
AND THEY ALSO RACED CARS.

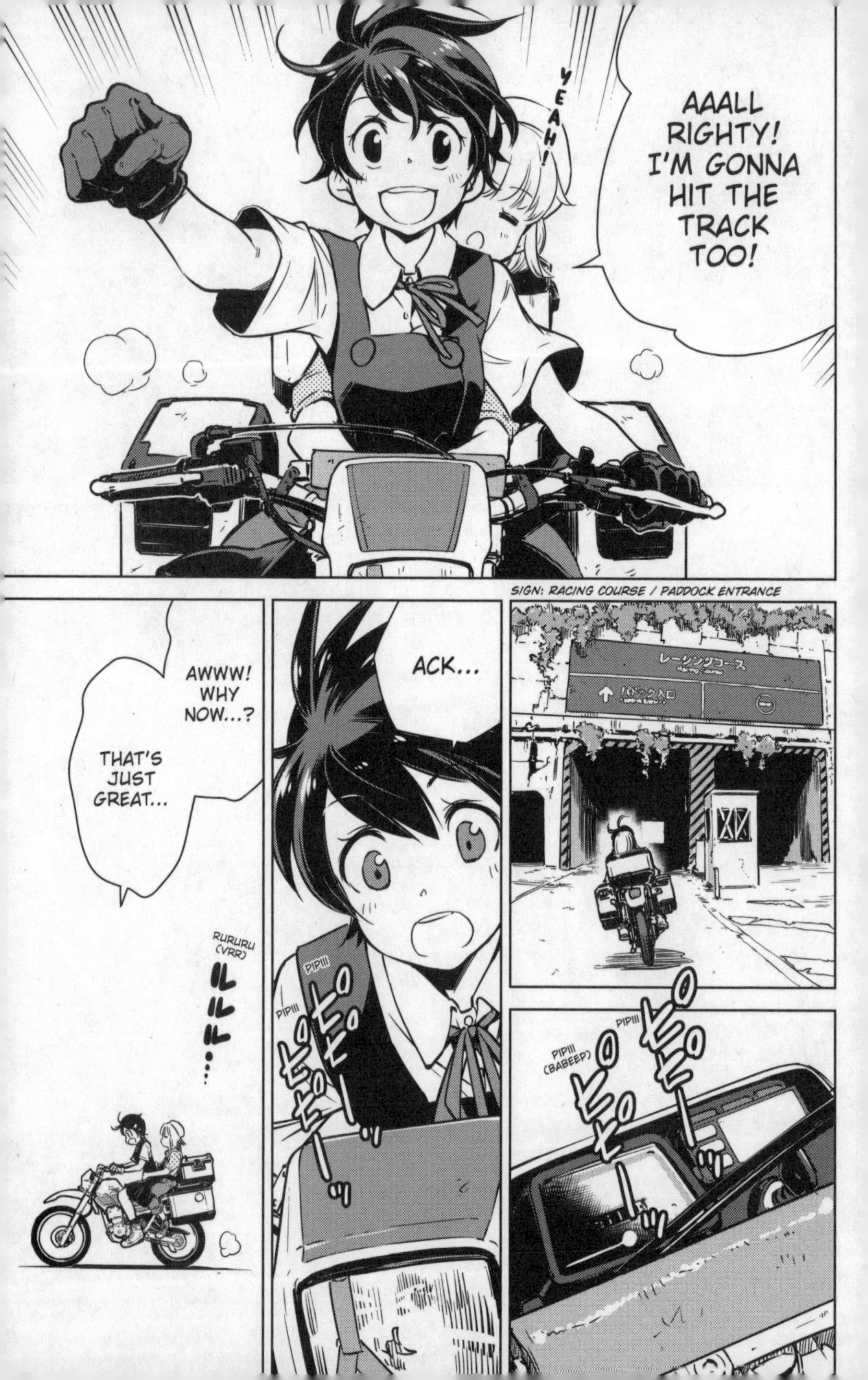
AAALL RIGHTY! I'M GONNA HIT THE TRACK TOO!
YEAH!
SIGN: RACING COURSE / PADDOCK ENTRANCE
レーシングコース
パドック入口
PIPIII
PIPIII (BABEEP)
ACK...
PIPIII
PIPIII
AWWW! WHY NOW...?
THAT'S JUST GREAT...
RURURU (VRR)

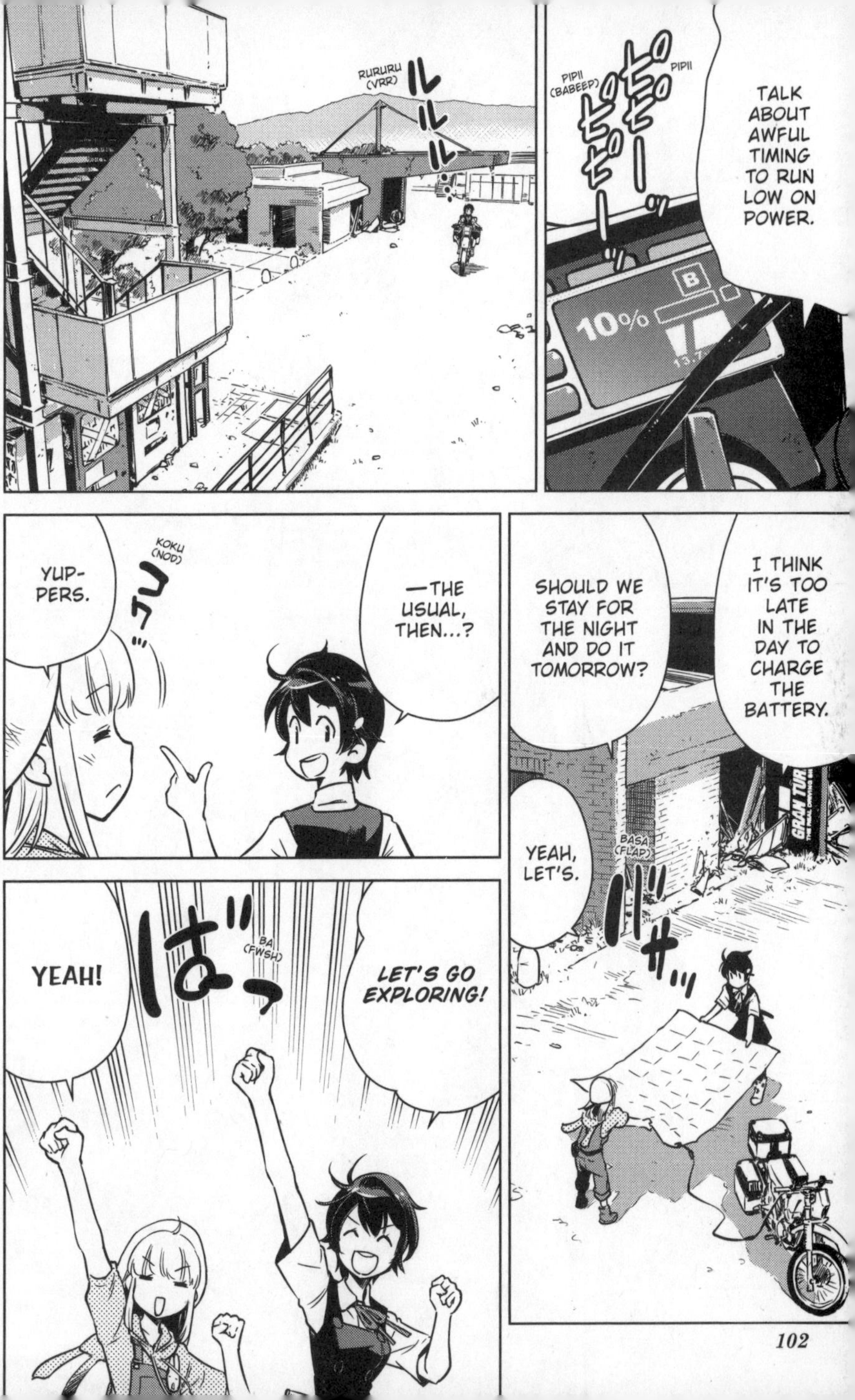
PIPII
PIPII (BABEEP)
TALK ABOUT AWFUL TIMING TO RUN LOW ON POWER.
10%
RURURU (VRR)
I THINK IT'S TOO LATE IN THE DAY TO CHARGE THE BATTERY.
SHOULD WE STAY FOR THE NIGHT AND DO IT TOMORROW?
YEAH, LET'S.
BASA (FLAP)
—THE USUAL, THEN...?
KOKU (NOD)
YUP-PERS.
LET'S GO EXPLORING!
BA (FWSH)
YEAH!

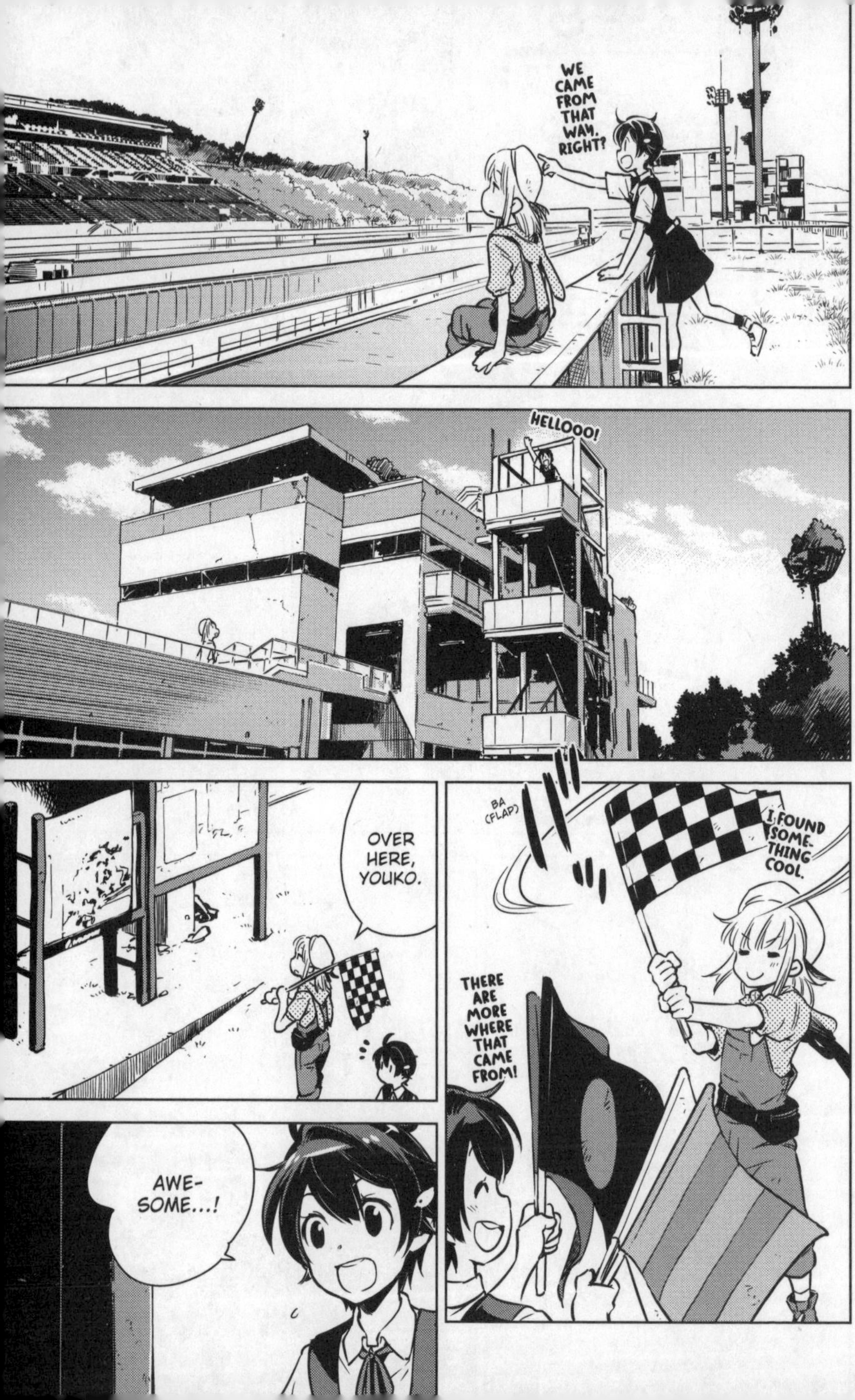
WE CAME FROM THAT WAY, RIGHT?
HELLOOO!
BA (FLAP)
I FOUND SOME-THING COOL.
THERE ARE MORE WHERE THAT CAME FROM!
OVER HERE, YOUKO.
AWE-SOME...!

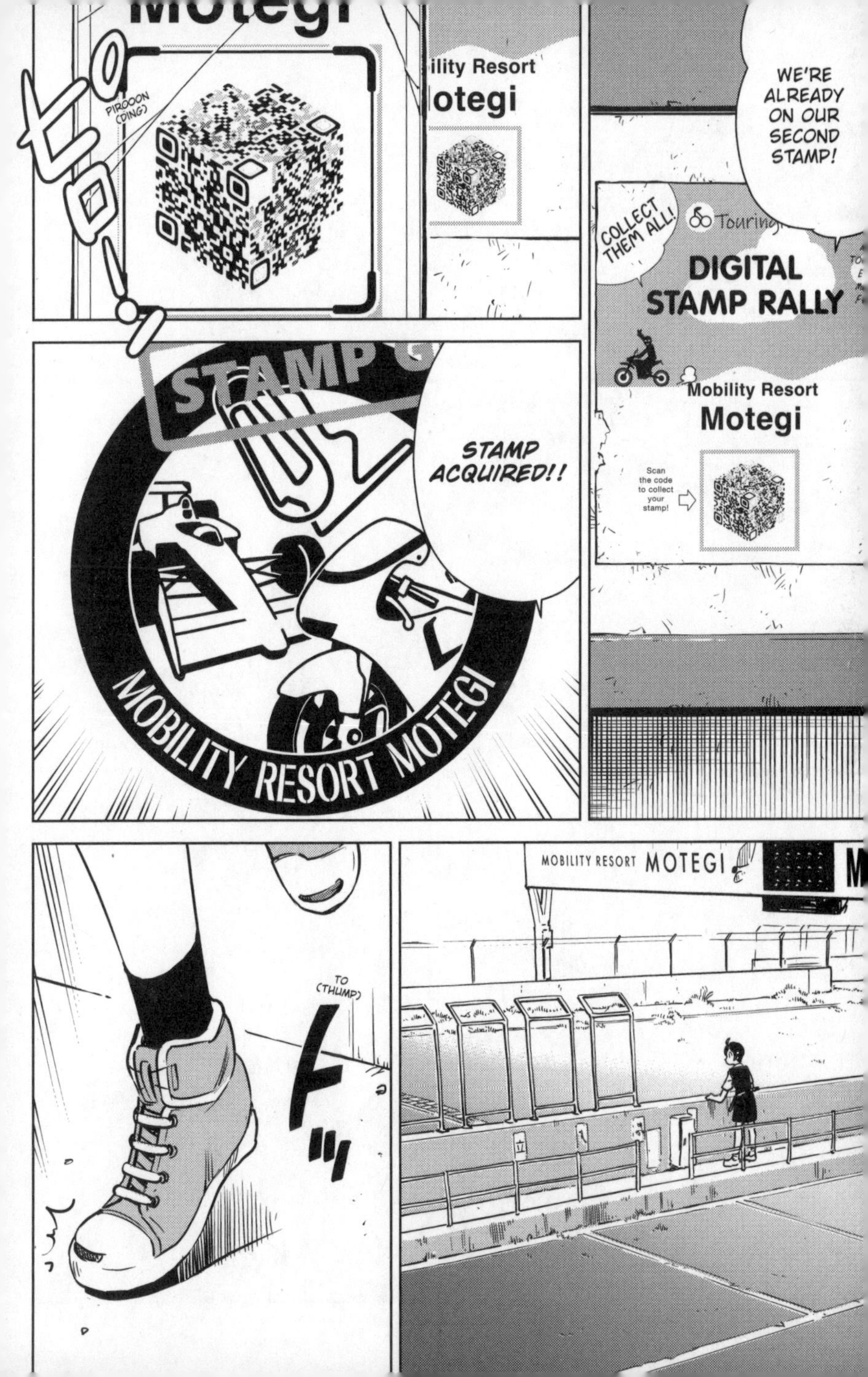

WE'RE ALREADY ON OUR SECOND STAMP!
COLLECT THEM ALL!
Touring
DIGITAL STAMP RALLY
Mobility Resort
Motegi
Scan the code to collect your stamp!
ility Resort
otegi
Motegi
PIROOON (DING)
STAMP ACQUIRED!!
STAMP G
MOBILITY RESORT MOTEGI
MOBILITY RESORT MOTEGI
TO (THUMP)

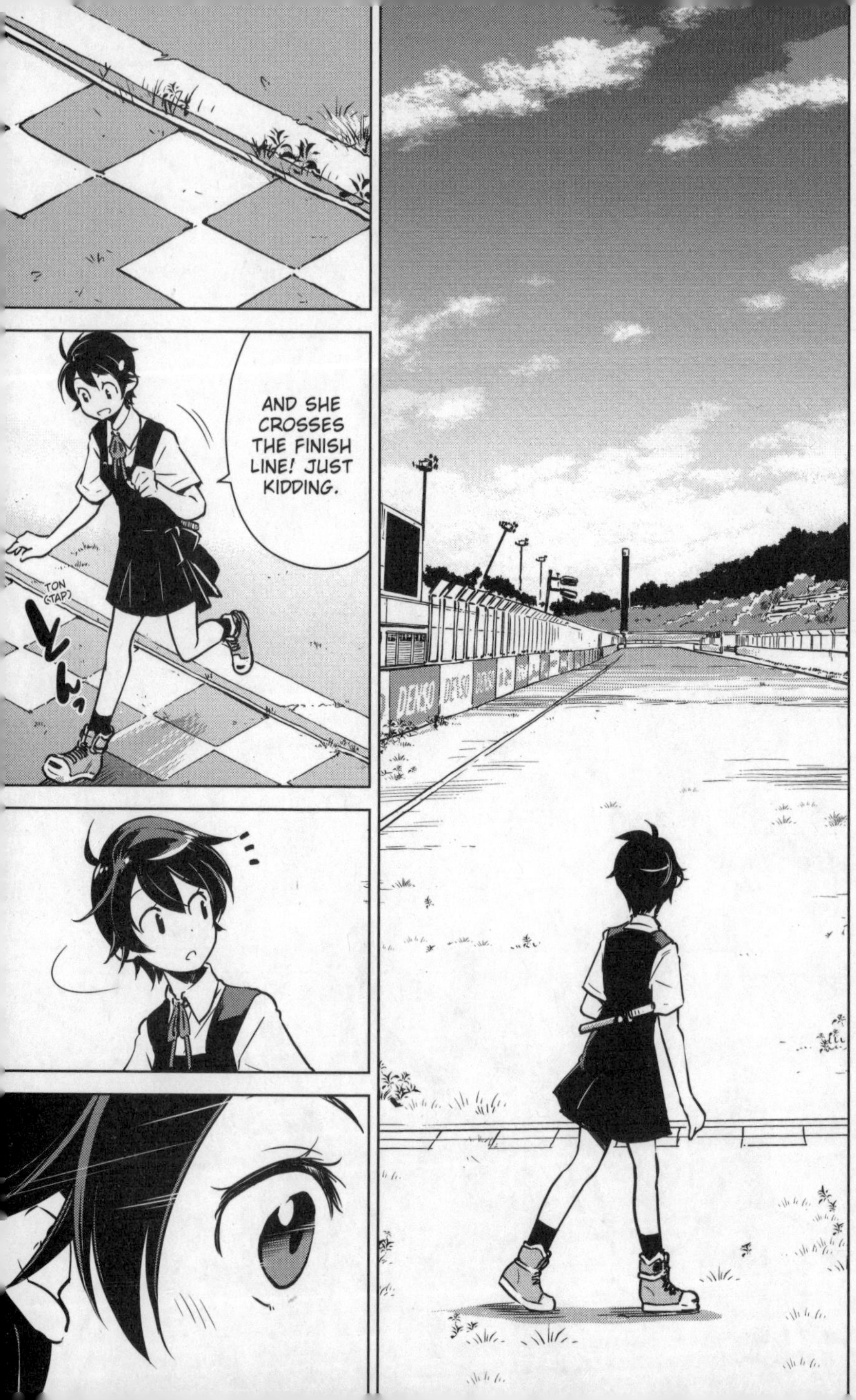
AND SHE CROSSES THE FINISH LINE! JUST KIDDING.
TON (TAP)

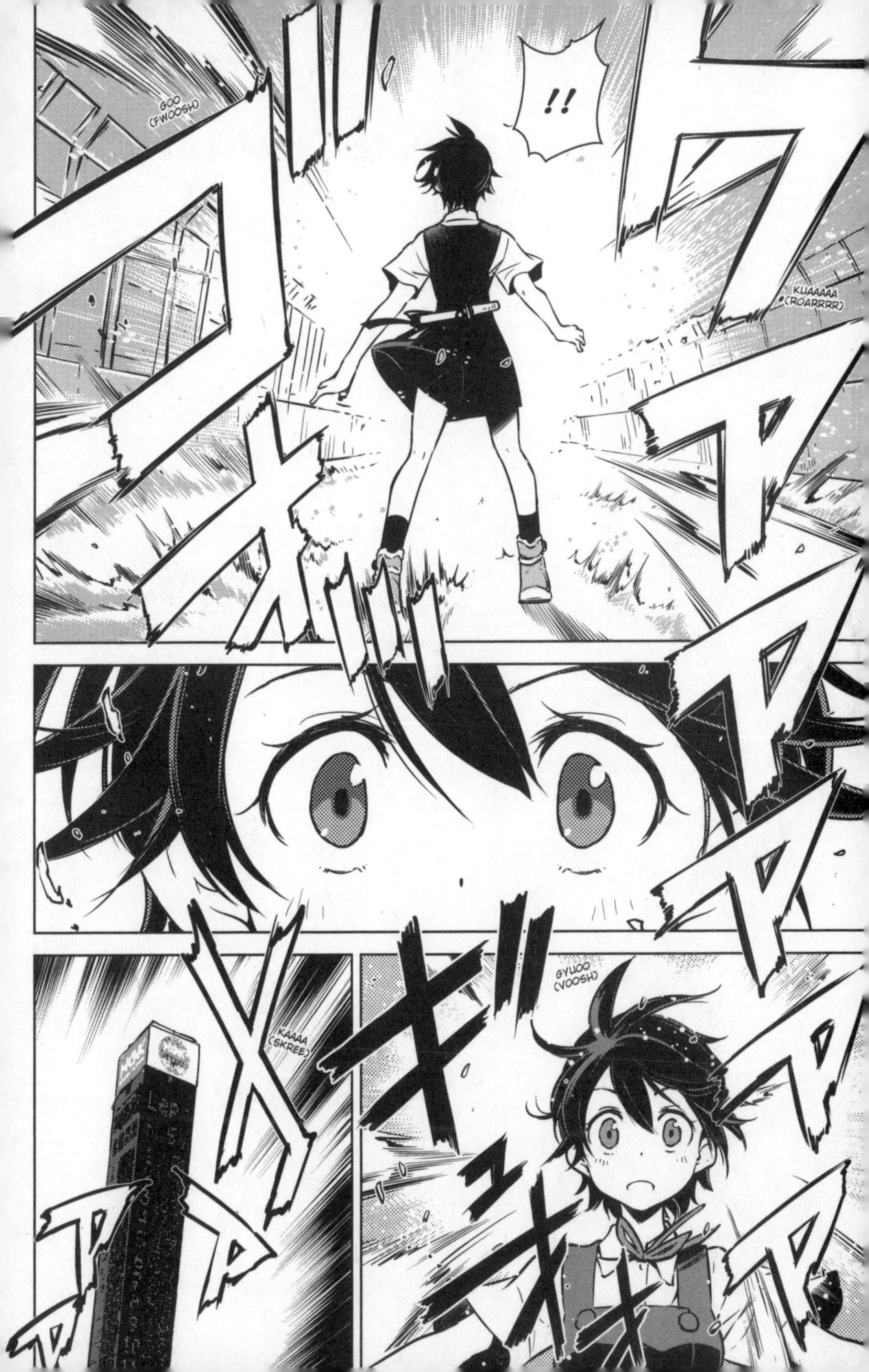
!!
KUAAAAA (ROARRRR)
GOO (FWOOSH)
GYUOO (VOOSH)
KAAAA (SKREE)

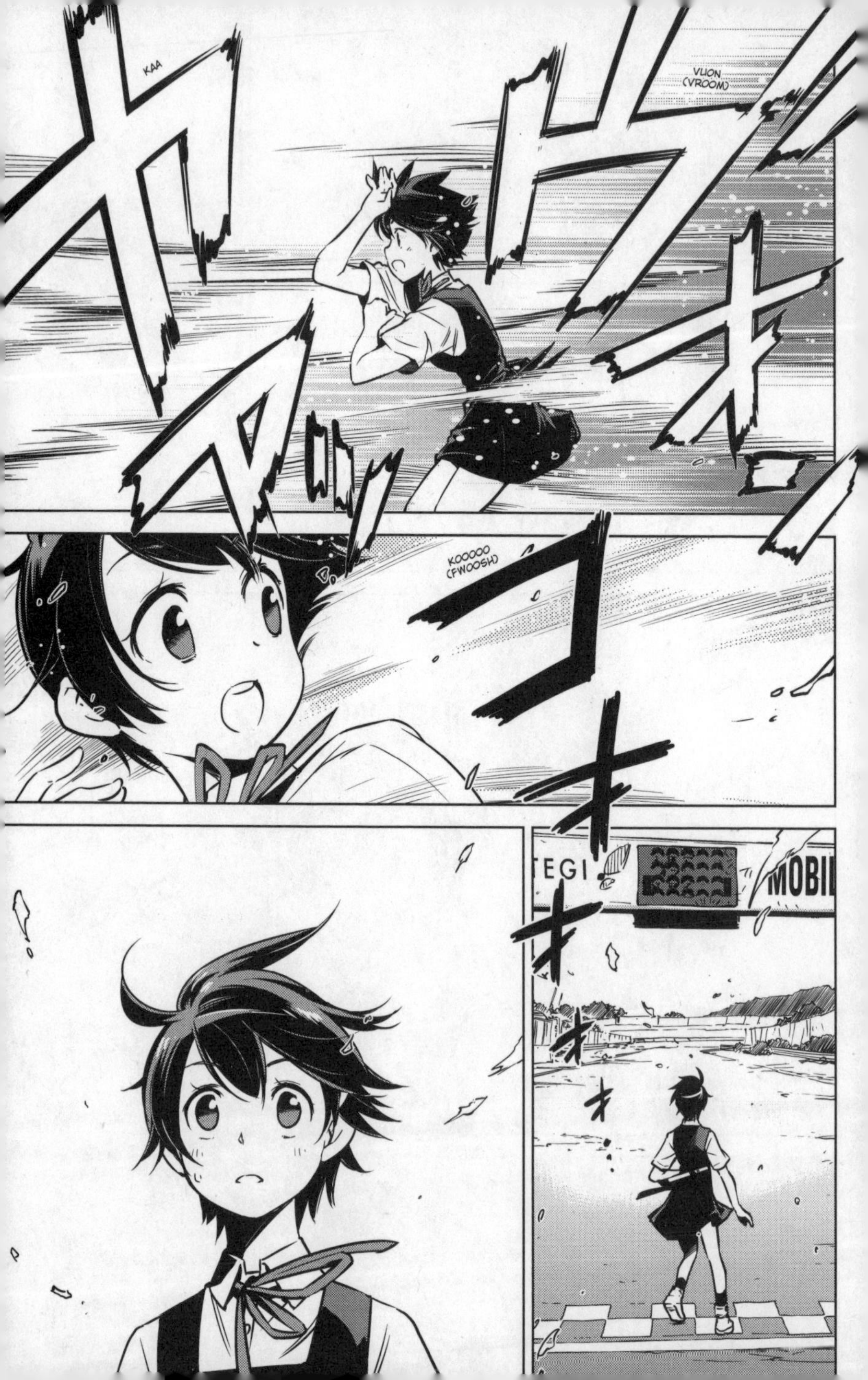
VUON
(VROOM)
KAA
KOOOOO
(FWOOSH)
TEGI
MOBIL

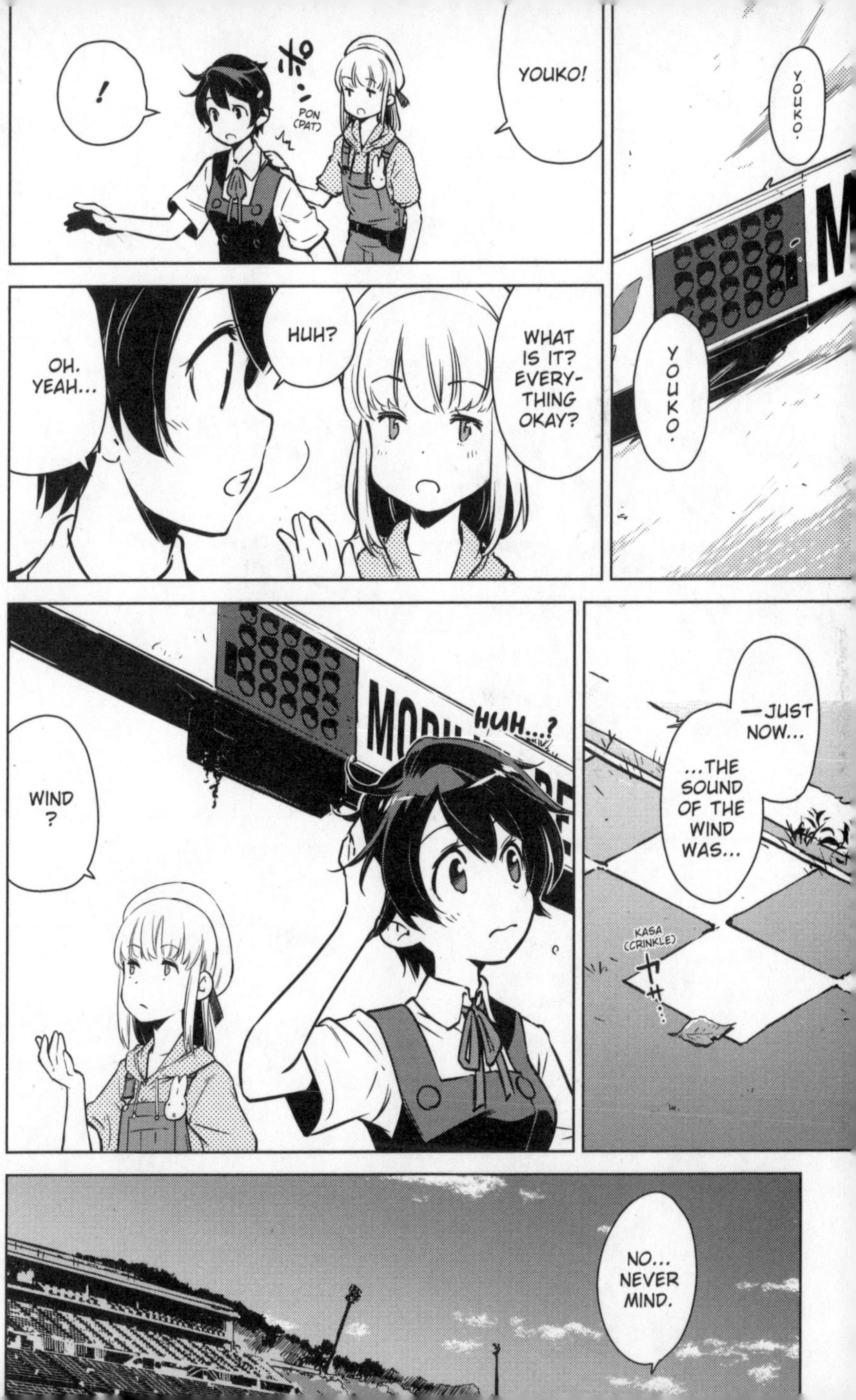
YOUKO.
YOUKO.
YOUKO!
PON (PAT)
!
WHAT IS IT? EVERY-THING OKAY?
HUH?
OH. YEAH...
—JUST NOW...
...THE SOUND OF THE WIND WAS...
KASA (CRINKLE)
HUH...?
WIND?
NO... NEVER MIND.

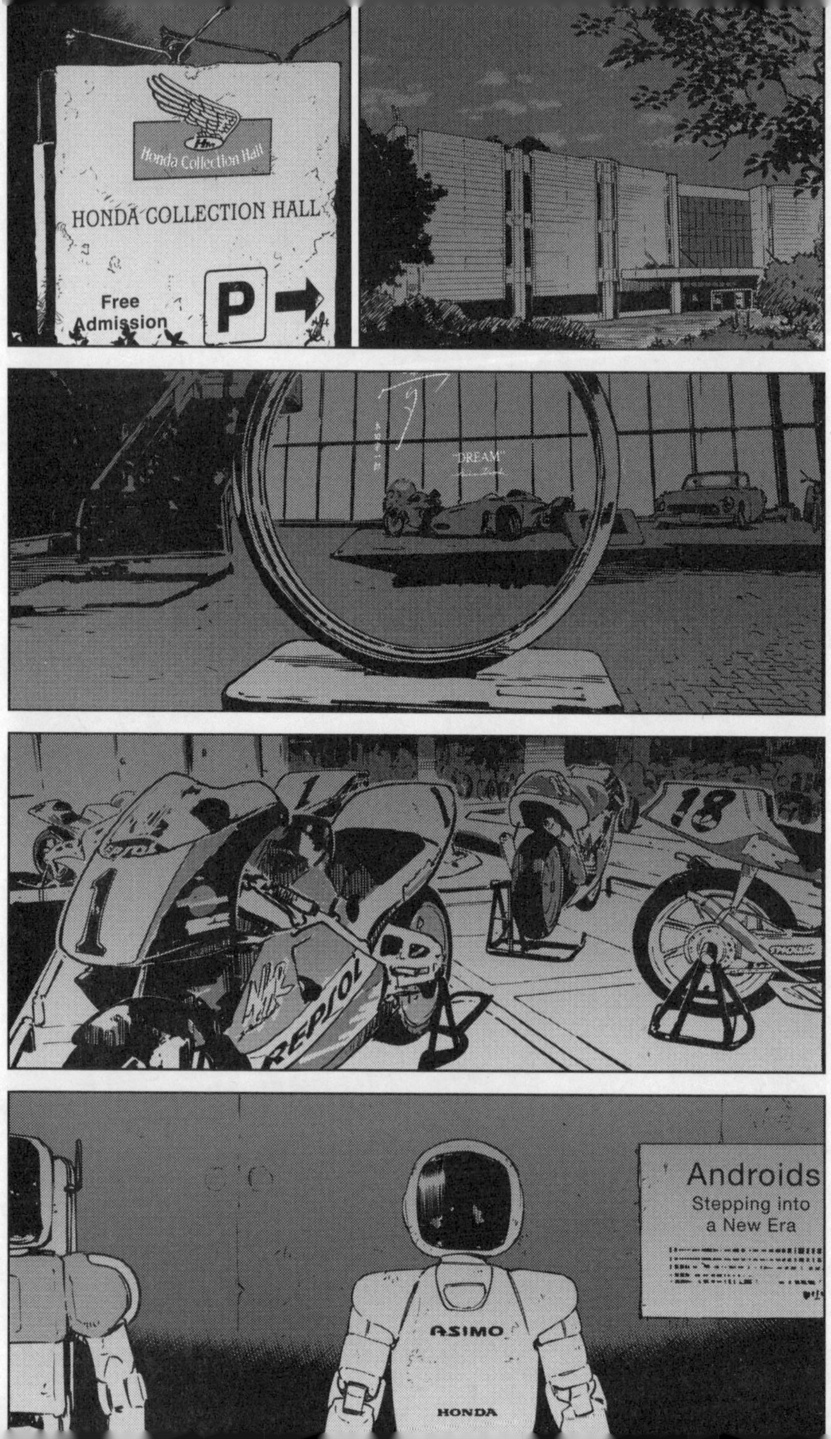
Honda Collection Hall
HONDA COLLECTION HALL
Free Admission
P
"DREAM"
REPSOL
Androids
Stepping into
a New Era
ASIMO
HONDA

ポ
PO
(GLOW)
PO
ポ
Androids
Stepping into
a New Era
ASIMO
HONDA

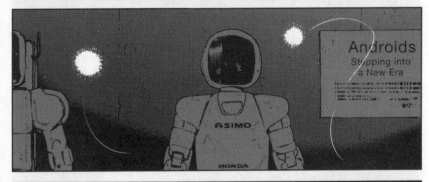

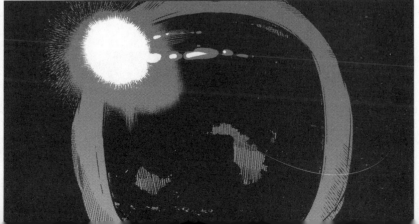

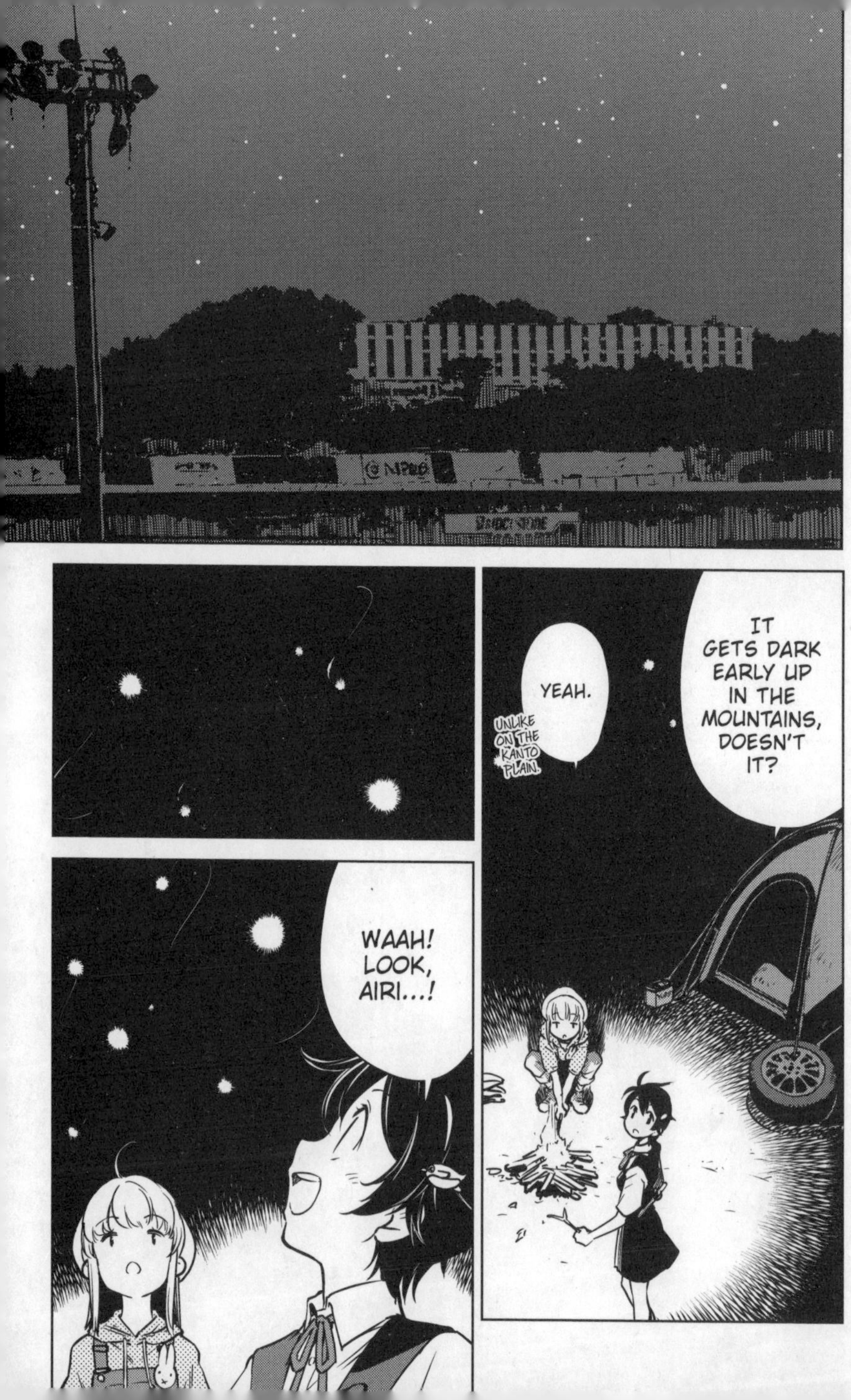
IT GETS DARK EARLY UP IN THE MOUNTAINS, DOESN'T IT?
YEAH.
UNLIKE ON THE KANTO PLAIN.
WAAH! LOOK, AIRI...!

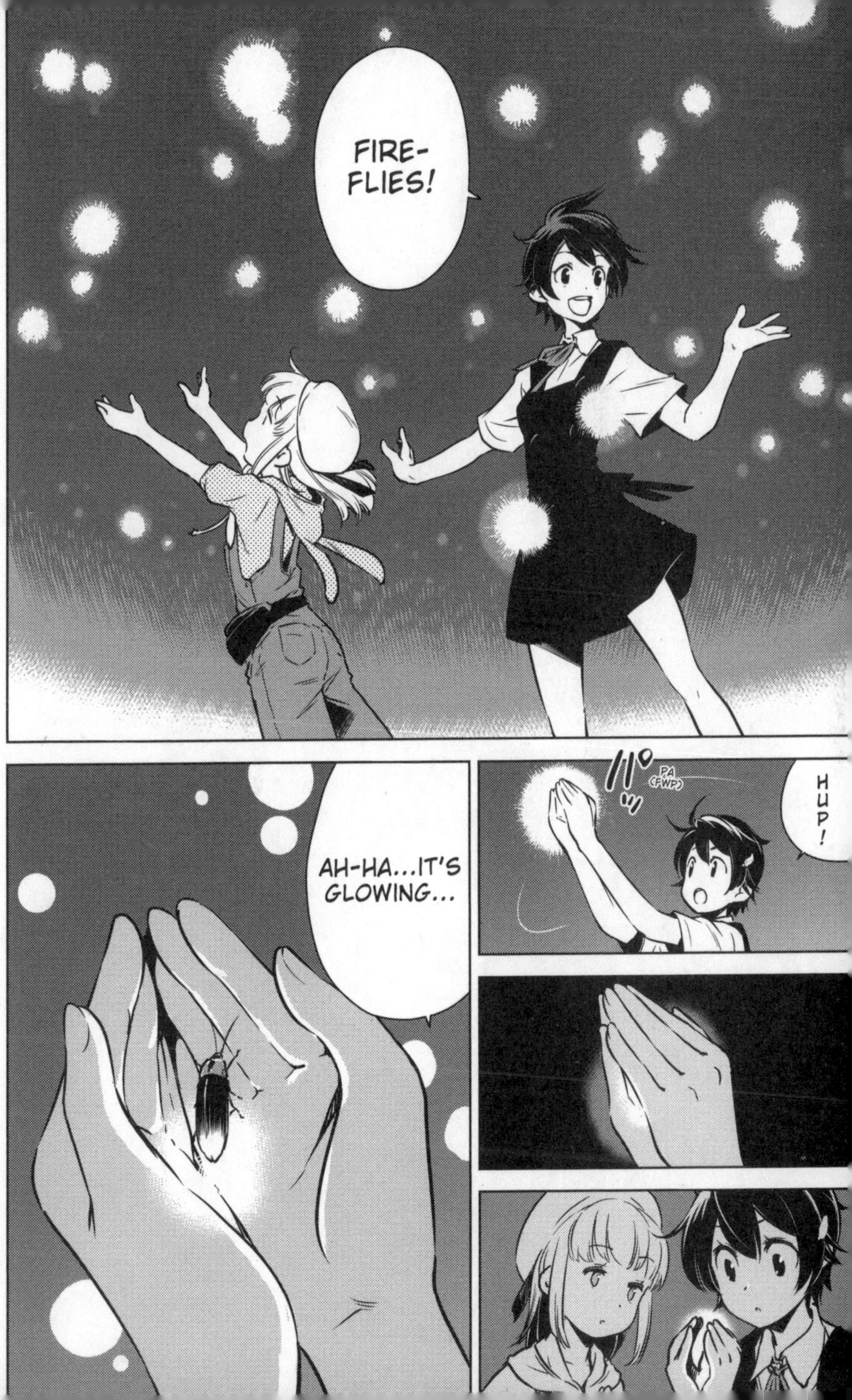
FIRE-FLIES!
HUP!
パッ
PA (FWP)
AH-HA...IT'S GLOWING...

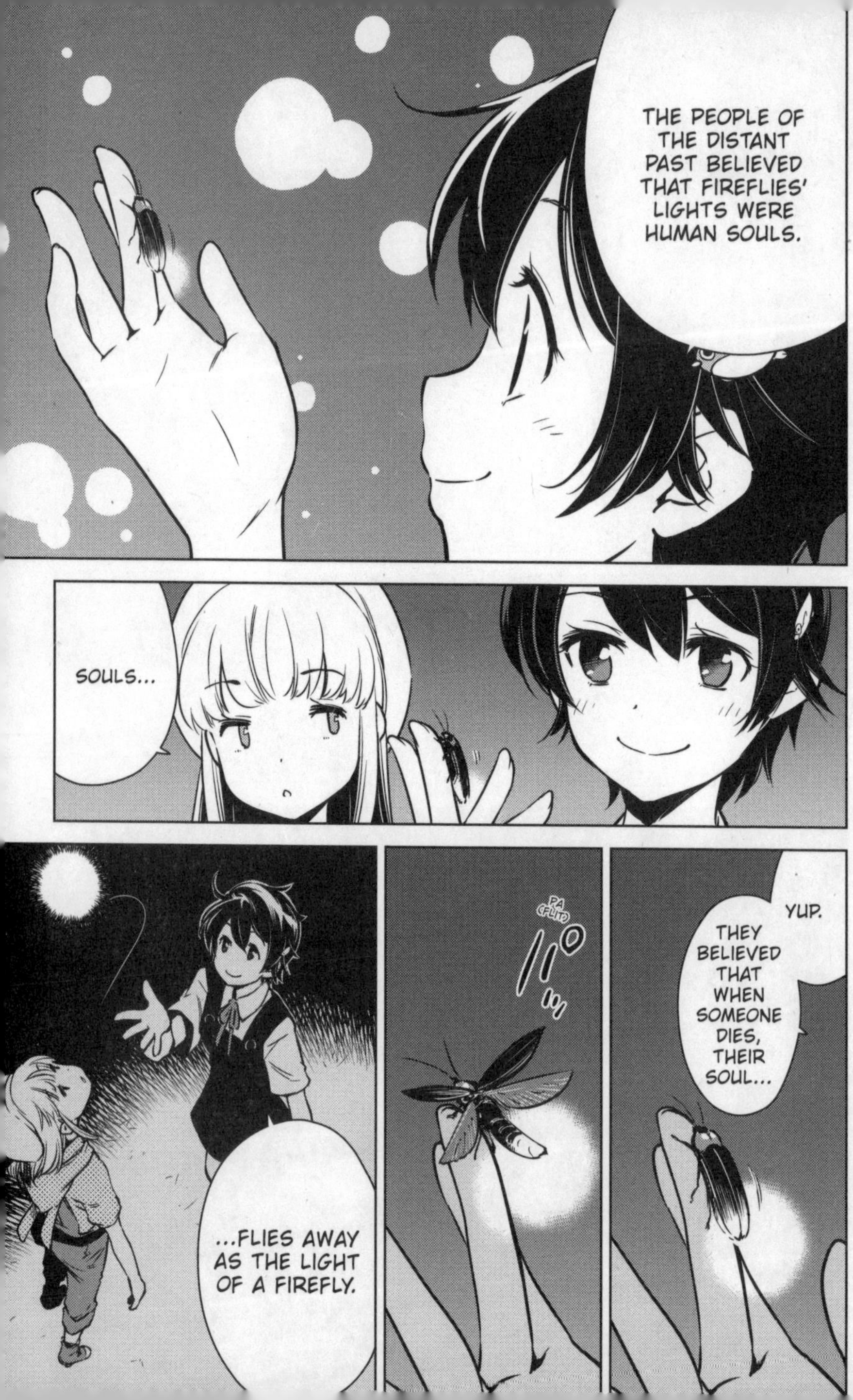
THE PEOPLE OF THE DISTANT PAST BELIEVED THAT FIREFLIES' LIGHTS WERE HUMAN SOULS.
SOULS...
YUP.
THEY BELIEVED THAT WHEN SOMEONE DIES, THEIR SOUL...
PA (FLIT)
...FLIES AWAY AS THE LIGHT OF A FIREFLY.

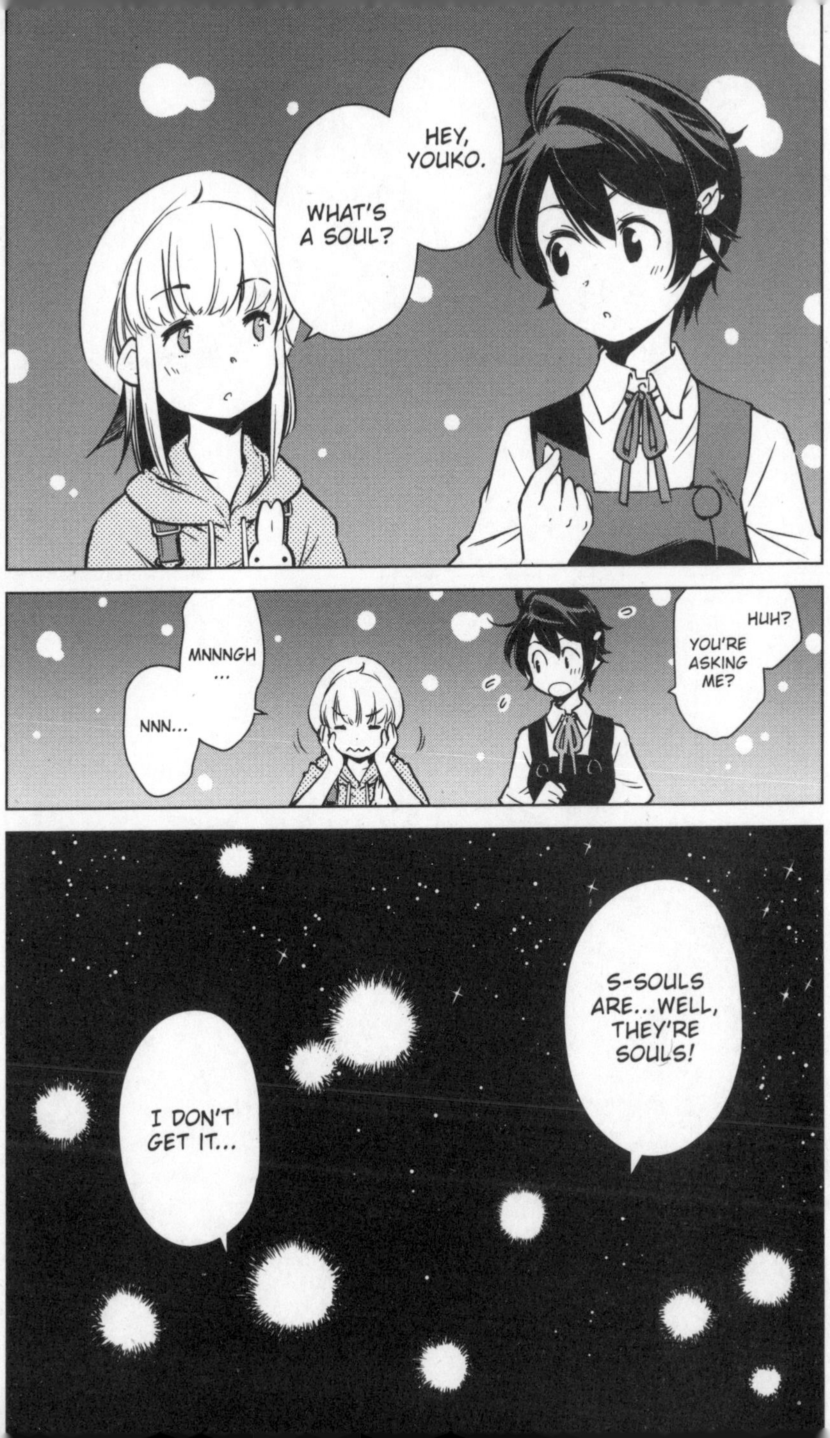
HEY, YOUKO. WHAT'S A SOUL?
HUH? YOU'RE ASKING ME?
MNNNGH... NNN...
S-SOULS ARE...WELL, THEY'RE SOULS!
I DON'T GET IT...

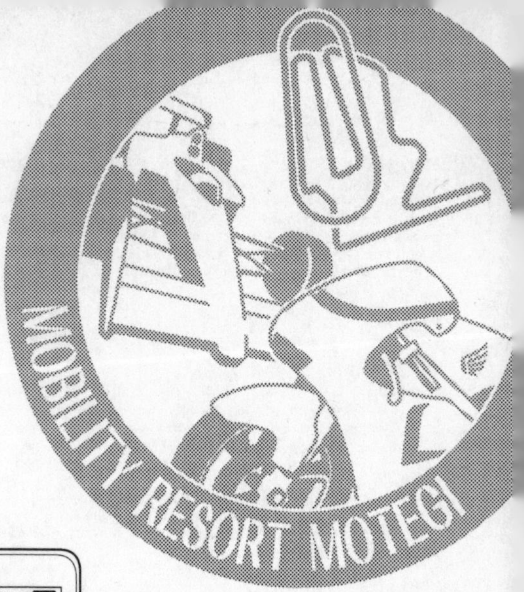
MOBILITY RESORT MOTEGI

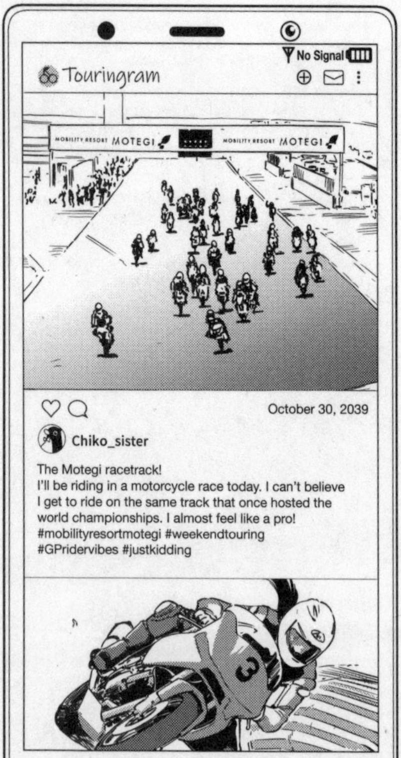
No Signal
Touringram
MOBILITY RESORT MOTEGI
MOBILITY RESORT MOTEGI
October 30, 2039
Chiko_sister
The Motegi racetrack!
I'll be riding in a motorcycle race today. I can't believe I get to ride on the same track that once hosted the world championships. I almost feel like a pro!
#mobilityresortmotegi #weekendtouring
#GPridervibes #justkidding
3

Translation Notes

Page 13

Tsukuba is a planned city developed by the Japanese government in the 1960s with the intention of promoting scientific research and expanding the university system in an easier area to build in than overcrowded Tokyo. Built in a rural area about an hour away from the city by train, its campuses were inspired by Western colleges such as the University of California.

Page 16

Airi is referring to the Japanese **saying** that "fools don't catch colds."

Page 28

Youko's knife is inscribed with the characters for "fold" (*ori*), "spring" (*haru*), and "soul" (*kon*), which when read together becomes *orichalcum*, the legendary ancient metal.

Page 29

There are more than sixteen locations in Japan with Japan Motorcycle Association–sanctioned **motorcycle shrines**. This one is on the campus of BDS, a company that runs the largest motorbike auction in Japan.

Page 31

The **Tone River** is the second longest river in Japan, running north of Tokyo.

Tsukune are ground meatballs fried on skewers in a manner similar to yakitori.

Battera is a type of sushi originating from Osaka. The name comes from *bateira*, a portuguese word meaning "small boat."

Page 33

Airi's retort to Youko is in the *Kansai* dialect native to Osaka, and imitating the city's famous *manzai* comedy duos.

Page 34

Taro Okamoto's **sculpture** in Tsukuba is a butterfly-like statue titled *Looking at the Future*, and is located in front of the Expo Memorial Park train station.

The Tsukuba **High Energy Accelerator Research Organization**, which Youko and Airi are likely looking at the ruins of, is the largest particle physics laboratory in Japan.

Page 38

The **H-II rocket** was a 1990s-era satellite launch system, the first one Japan developped fully domestically.

Page 69

Grazie Vale, on Airi's hat, is the Italian message used by fans to congratulate motorcycle racing legend Valentino Rossi upon his retirement in 2021.

Page 75

Apocalypse Now is a 1979 Vietnam War epic directed by Francis Ford Coppola, which is itself loosely based on Joseph Conrad's *Heart of Darkness* novella. Airi's emergence from the muddy water mirrors one of the film's more iconic shots.

Page 79

The building Youko and Airi climb is the Rainbow Tower at Kasumigaura Fureai Land, a science museum and theme park devoted to water.

Page 81

The graffiti about the **superb view** is specifically a line from the *Kabuki* play *The Golden Gate and the Paulownia Crest*, telling the life of folk outlaw hero Goemon Ishikawa. The line comes from Goemon's introduction, as he gazes down upon Kyoto before learning of his father's death.

Page 83

Mount Fuji is located on the border of Shizuoka and Yamanashi Prefectures, an entire two prefectures away from Youko and Airi's position in Ibaraki Prefecture. That's more than a hundred miles!

Page 89

The **Motegi racetrack** was built in 1997 by the Honda Motor Company under the name Twin Ring Motegi, referring to its two separate circuits—one road course and one oval ring. Operating today as Mobility Resort Motegi, the surrounding area has several family-focused tourism destinations, such as the Honda Collection Hall.

Page 109

ASIMO is a bipedal robot developed in 2000 by Honda as a test bed for a number of technologies. The name is both an acronym (Advanced Step in Innovative Mobility) as well as a reference to sci-fi writer Isaac Asimov.

Page 119

Ayrton Senna was a Brazilian Formula One racer who won championships in 1988, 1990, and 1991 before tragically dying in an accident during the 1994 San Marino Grand Prix.

Page 146

Takaaki Nakagami is a Japanese Grand Prix motorcycle racer on the LCR Honda Idemitsu team.

The Honda NXR750 picked up the nickname "**The Desert Queen**" after scoring consecutive wins in the Dakar Rally across the Sahara Desert in the 1980s.

Page 181

The **lemon milk** on Youko's shirt is a local specialty of Tochigi Prefecture, where Motegi is located, and a popular souvenir for tourists. Despite the name, it contains no lemon.

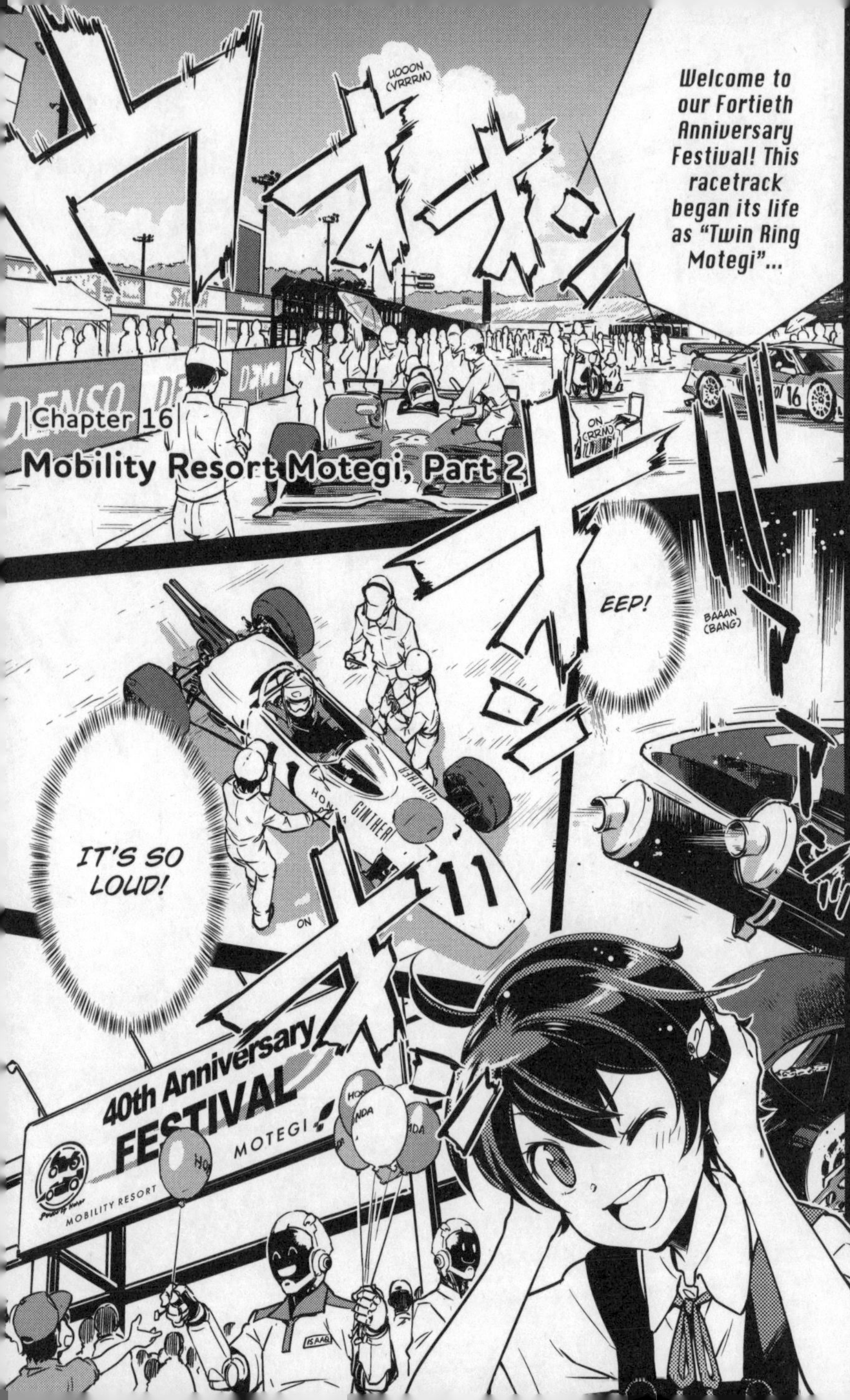
Welcome to our Fortieth Anniversary Festival! This racetrack began its life as "Twin Ring Motegi"...
HOOON (VRRRM)
ON (RRRM)
Chapter 16
Mobility Resort Motegi, Part 2
BAAAN (BANG)
EEP!
IT'S SO LOUD!
ON
40th Anniversary FESTIVAL
MOTEGI
MOBILITY RESORT

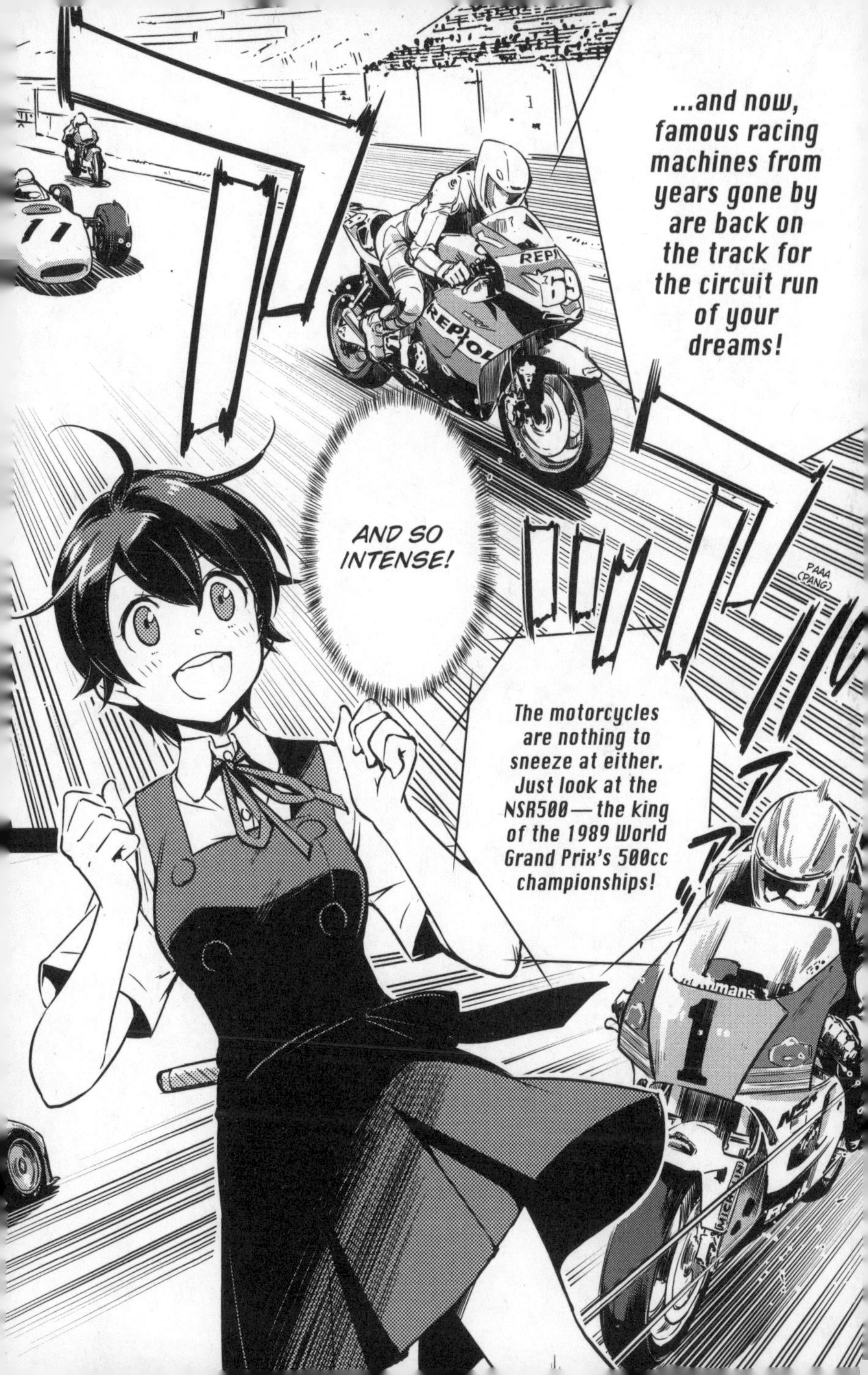
...and now, famous racing machines from years gone by are back on the track for the circuit run of your dreams!
PAAA (PANG)
AND SO INTENSE!
The motorcycles are nothing to sneeze at either. Just look at the NSR500— the king of the 1989 World Grand Prix's 500cc championships!

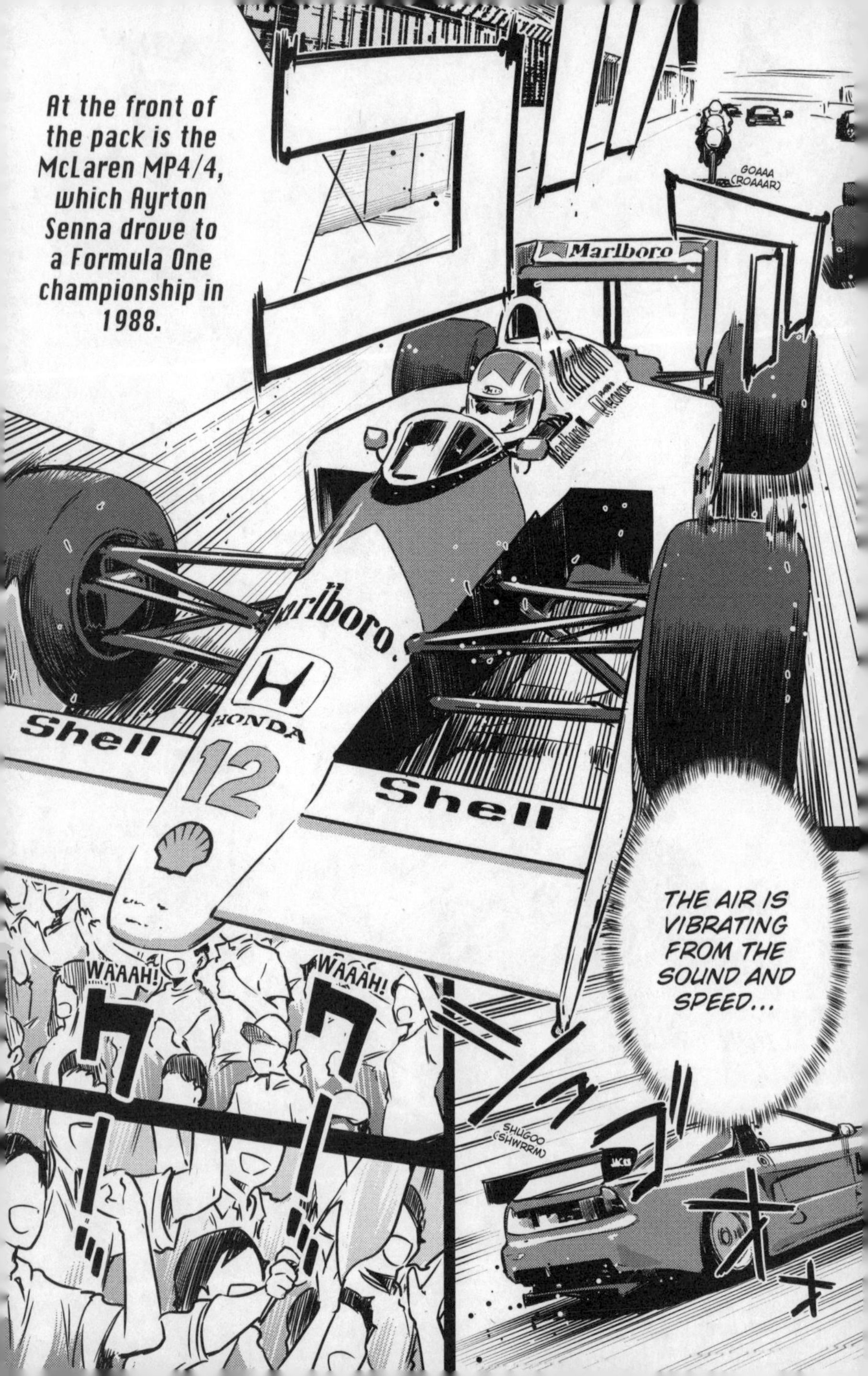
GOAAA (ROAAAR)
At the front of the pack is the McLaren MP4/4, which Ayrton Senna drove to a Formula One championship in 1988.
Marlboro
Marlboro
HONDA
12
Shell
Shell
THE AIR IS VIBRATING FROM THE SOUND AND SPEED...
SHUGOO (SHWRRM)
WAAAH!
WAAAH!

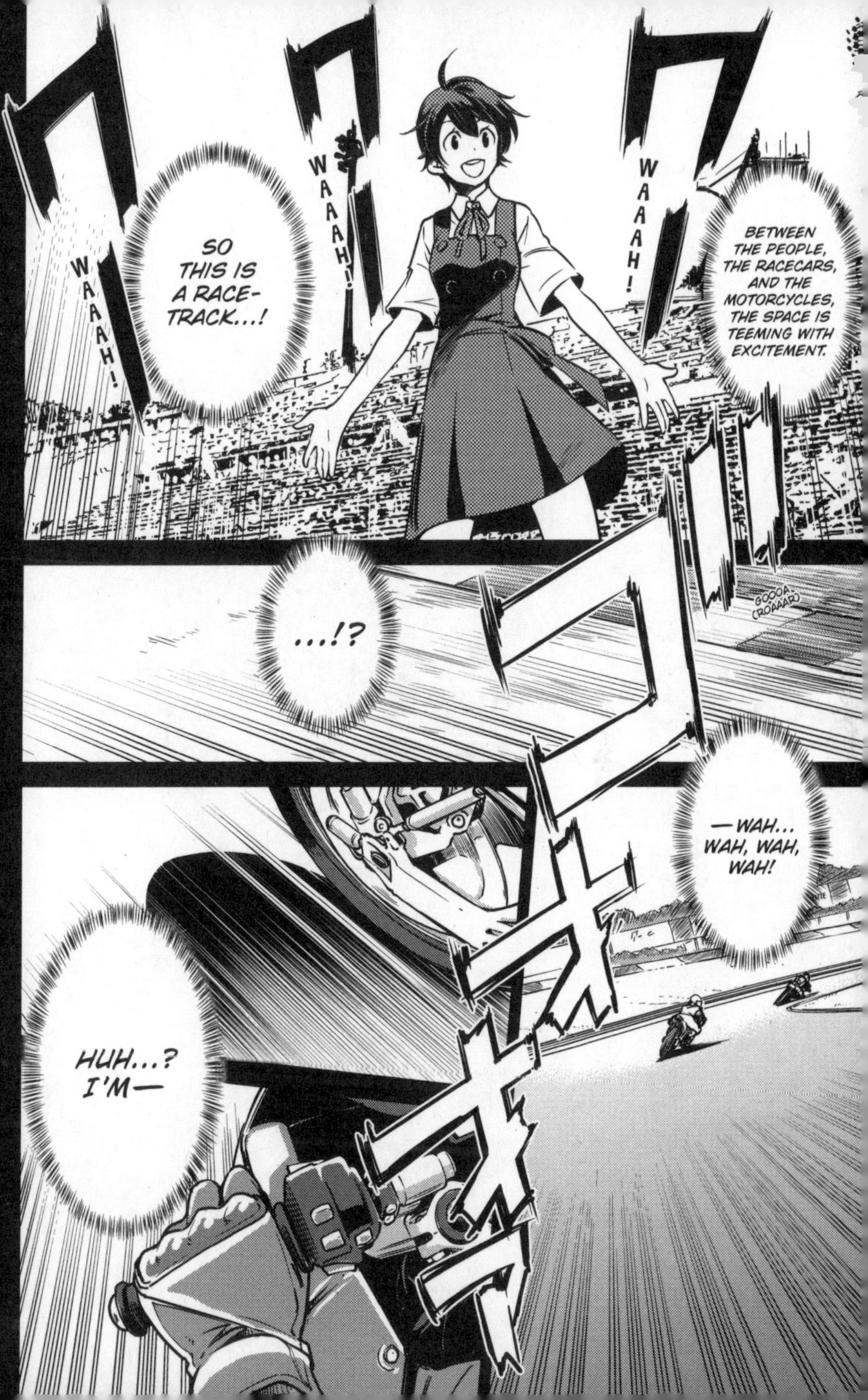
WAAAAH!
BETWEEN THE PEOPLE, THE RACECARS, AND THE MOTORCYCLES, THE SPACE IS TEEMING WITH EXCITEMENT.
WAAAAH!
SO THIS IS A RACE-TRACK...!
WAAAAH!
GOOOA (ROAAAR)
...!?
—WAH... WAH, WAH, WAH!
HUH...? I'M—

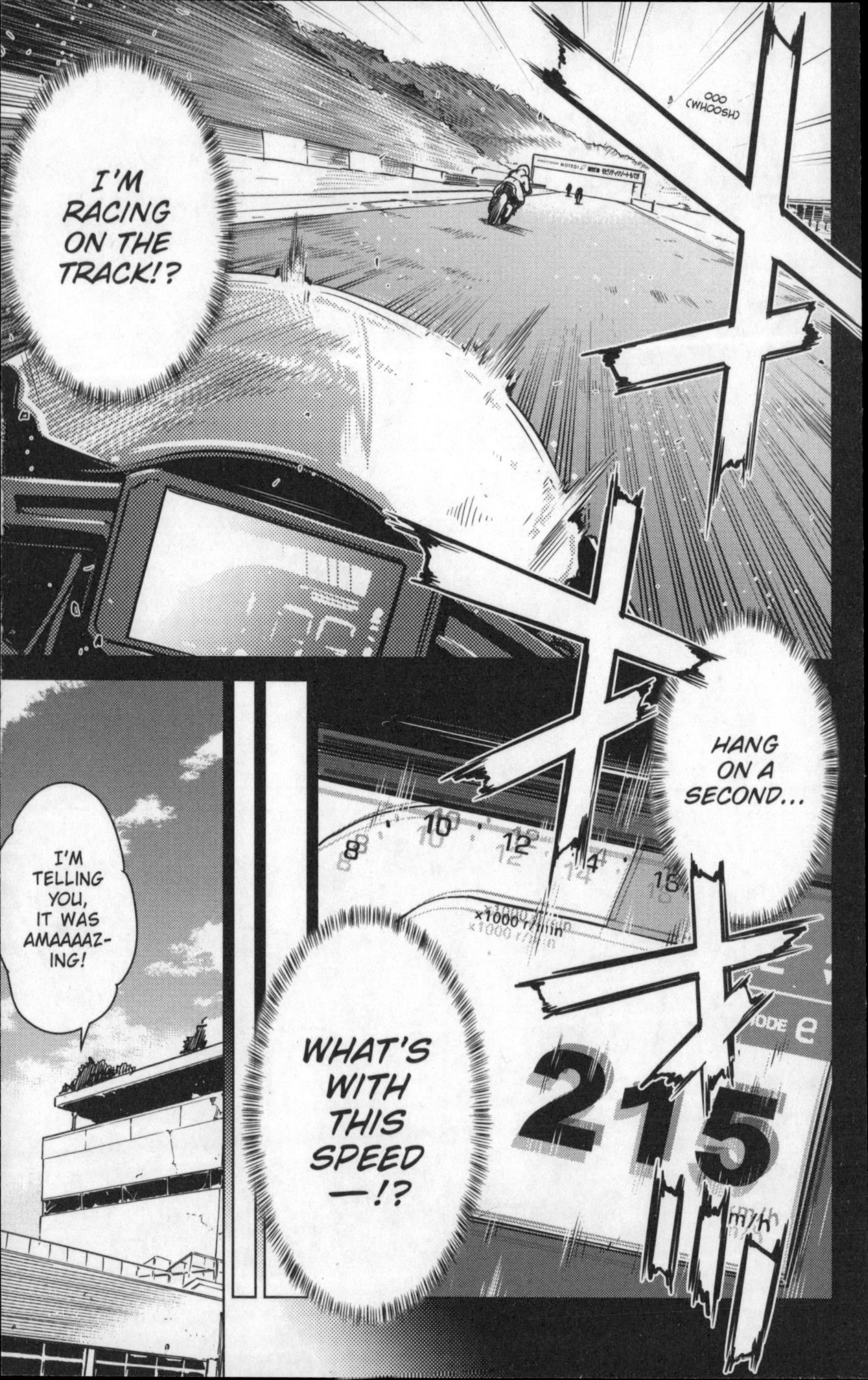
OOO (WHOOSH)
I'M RACING ON THE TRACK!?
HANG ON A SECOND...
WHAT'S WITH THIS SPEED—!?
I'M TELLING YOU, IT WAS AMAAAAZ-ING!

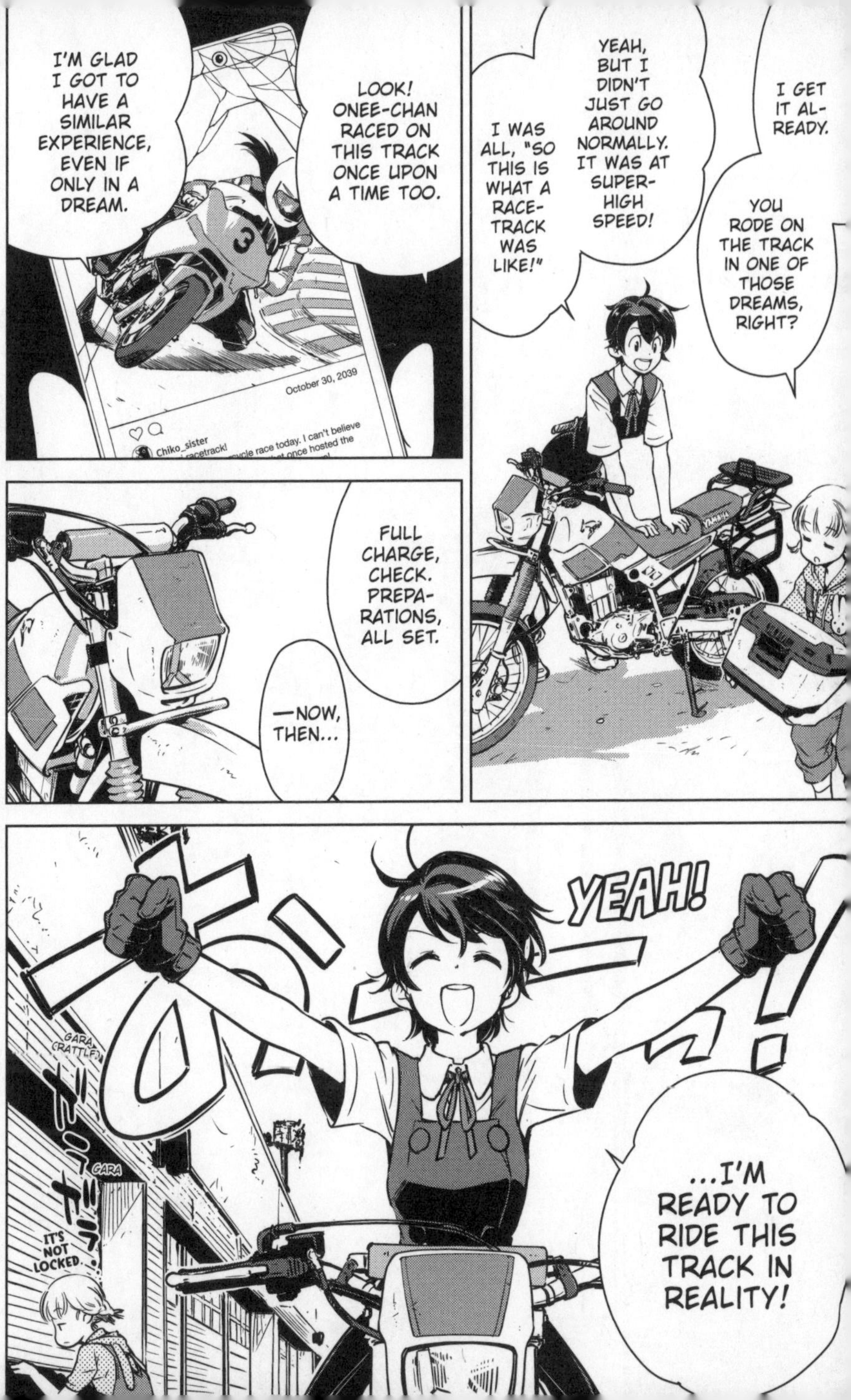
I GET IT ALREADY.
YOU RODE ON THE TRACK IN ONE OF THOSE DREAMS, RIGHT?
YEAH, BUT I DIDN'T JUST GO AROUND NORMALLY. IT WAS AT SUPER-HIGH SPEED!
I WAS ALL, "SO THIS IS WHAT A RACETRACK WAS LIKE!"
LOOK! ONEE-CHAN RACED ON THIS TRACK ONCE UPON A TIME TOO.
I'M GLAD I GOT TO HAVE A SIMILAR EXPERIENCE, EVEN IF ONLY IN A DREAM.
October 30, 2039
Chiko_sister
FULL CHARGE, CHECK. PREPARATIONS, ALL SET.
—NOW, THEN...
YEAH!
...I'M READY TO RIDE THIS TRACK IN REALITY!
GARA (RATTLE)
GARA
IT'S NOT LOCKED.

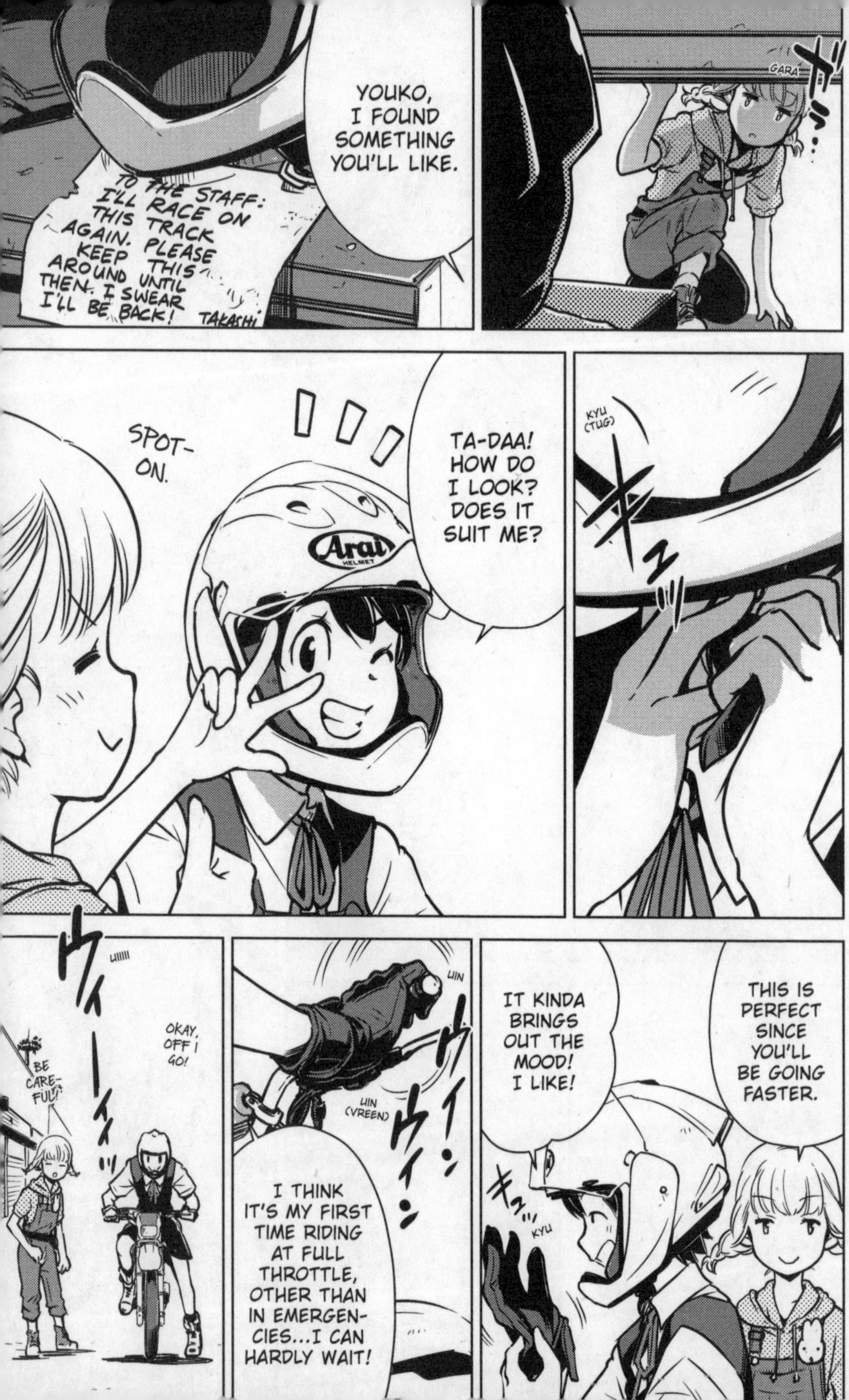
GARA
YOUKO, I FOUND SOMETHING YOU'LL LIKE.
TO THE STAFF: I'LL RACE ON THIS TRACK AGAIN. PLEASE KEEP THIS AROUND UNTIL THEN. I SWEAR I'LL BE BACK!
TAKASHI
KYU (TUG)
TA-DAA! HOW DO I LOOK? DOES IT SUIT ME?
SPOT-ON.
THIS IS PERFECT SINCE YOU'LL BE GOING FASTER.
IT KINDA BRINGS OUT THE MOOD! I LIKE!
KYU
UIN
UIN (VREEN)
I THINK IT'S MY FIRST TIME RIDING AT FULL THROTTLE, OTHER THAN IN EMERGENCIES...I CAN HARDLY WAIT!
UIIIII
OKAY, OFF I GO!
BE CAREFUL!

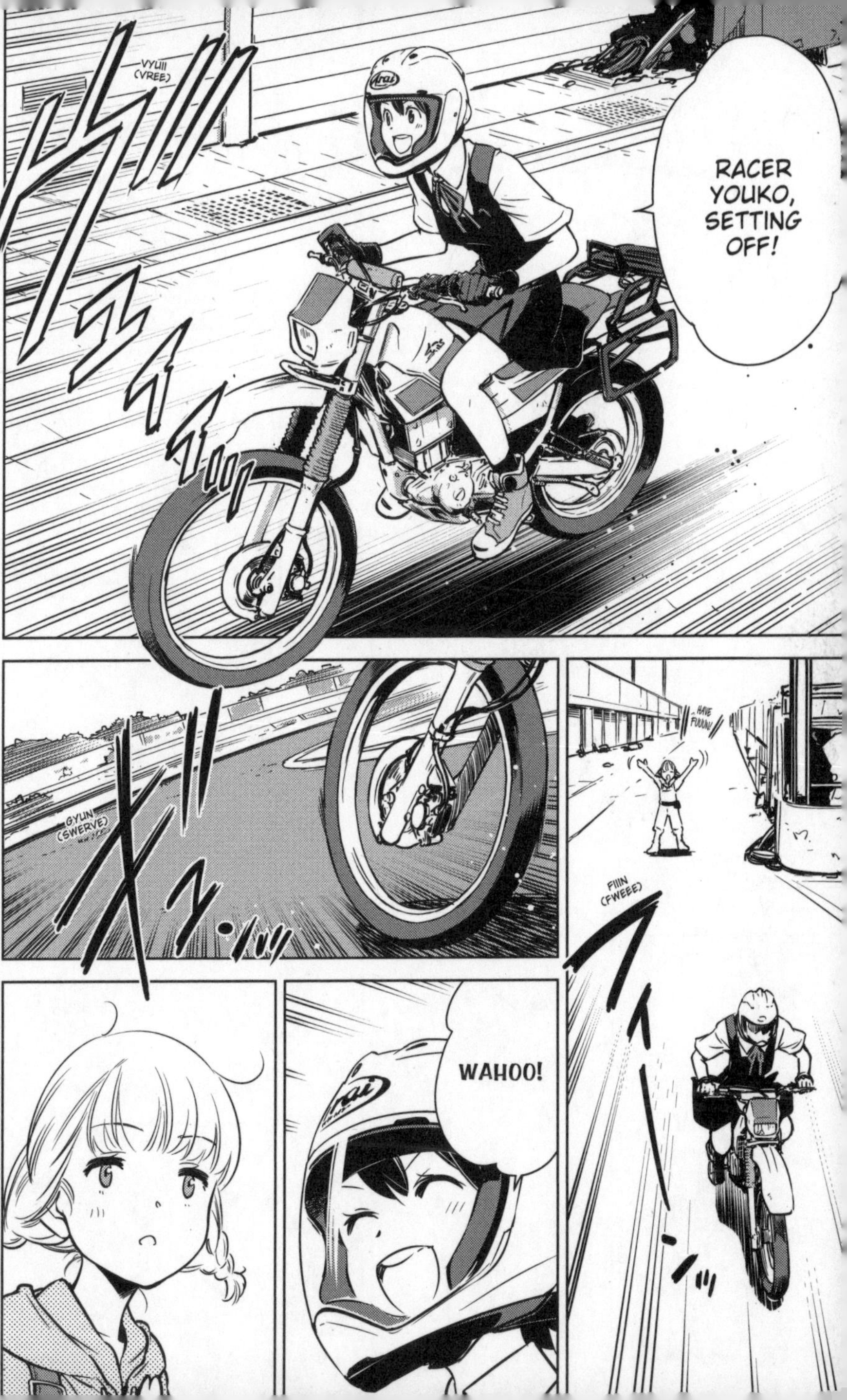
RACER YOUKO, SETTING OFF!
VYUII (VREE)
...HAVE FUUUN!
FIIN (FWEEE)
GYUN (SWERVE)
WAHOO!

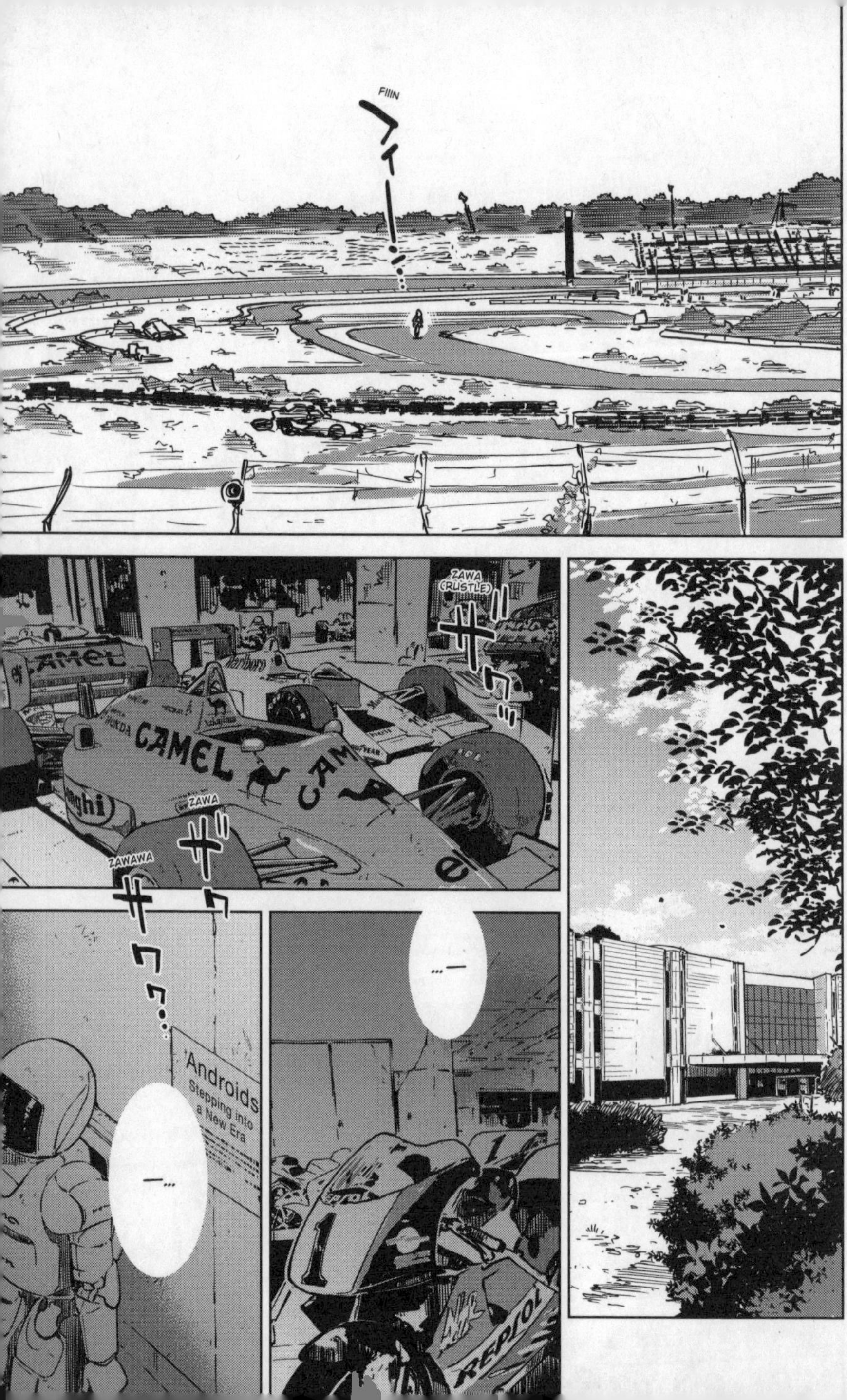
FIIN
ZAWA (RUSTLE)
ZAWA
ZAWAWA
...—
—...
'Androids Stepping into a New Era

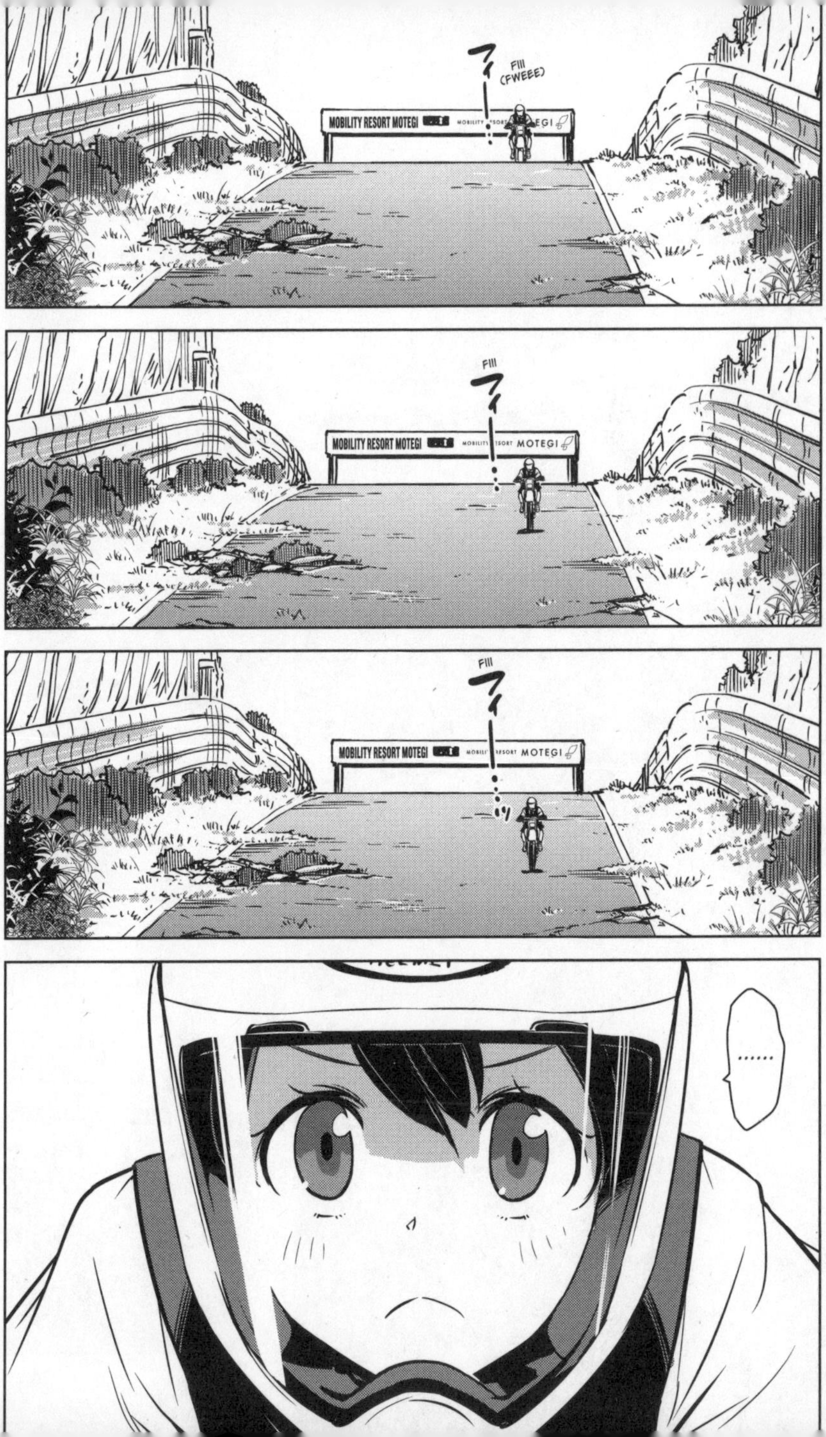

フィー…
FIII
(FWEEE)
MOBILITY RESORT MOTEGI
フィー…
FIII
MOBILITY RESORT MOTEGI
フィー…ッ
FIII
MOBILITY RESORT MOTEGI
......

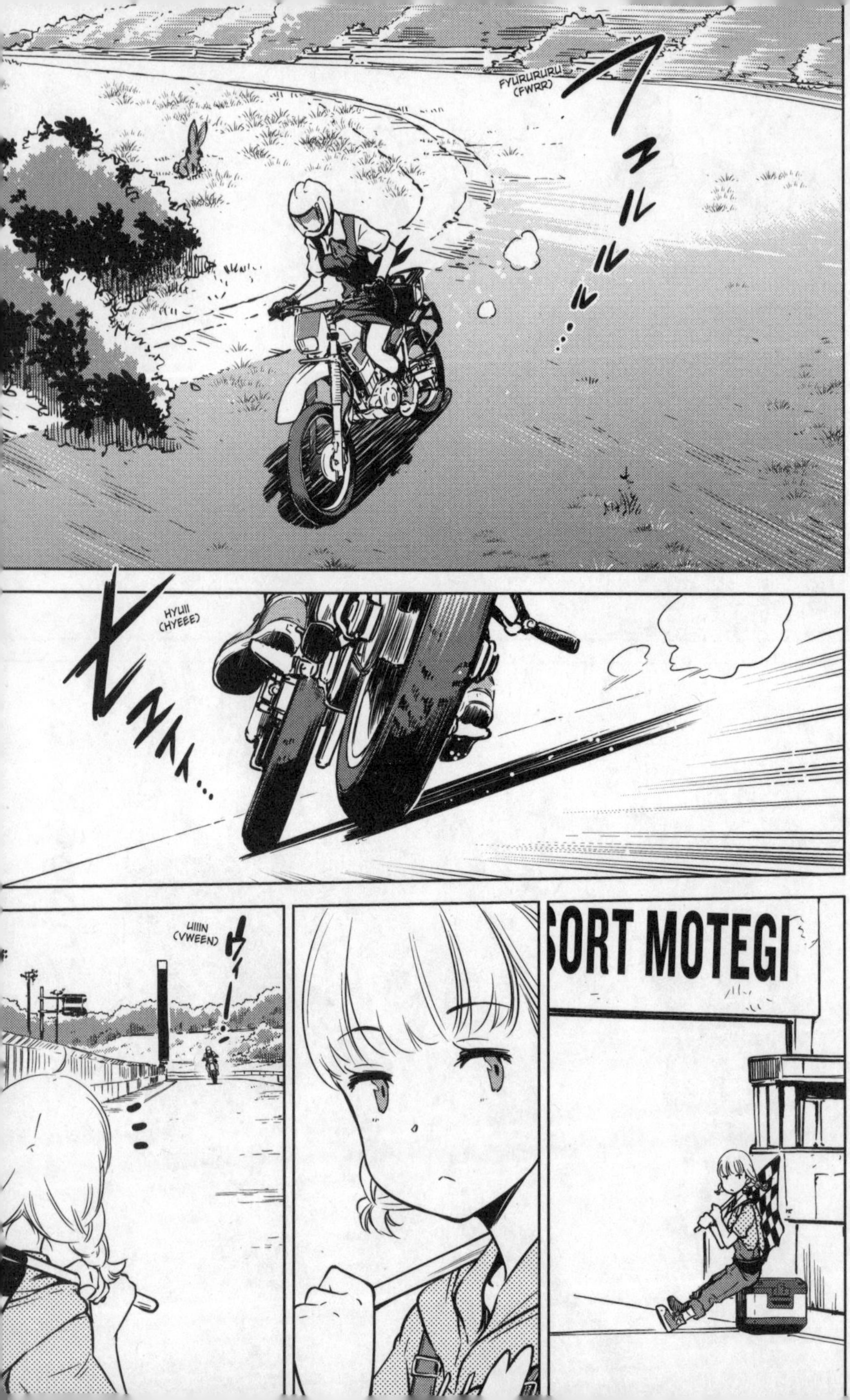
FYURURURU
(FWRR)
HYUII
(HYEEE)
SORT MOTEGI
UIIIN
(VWEEN)

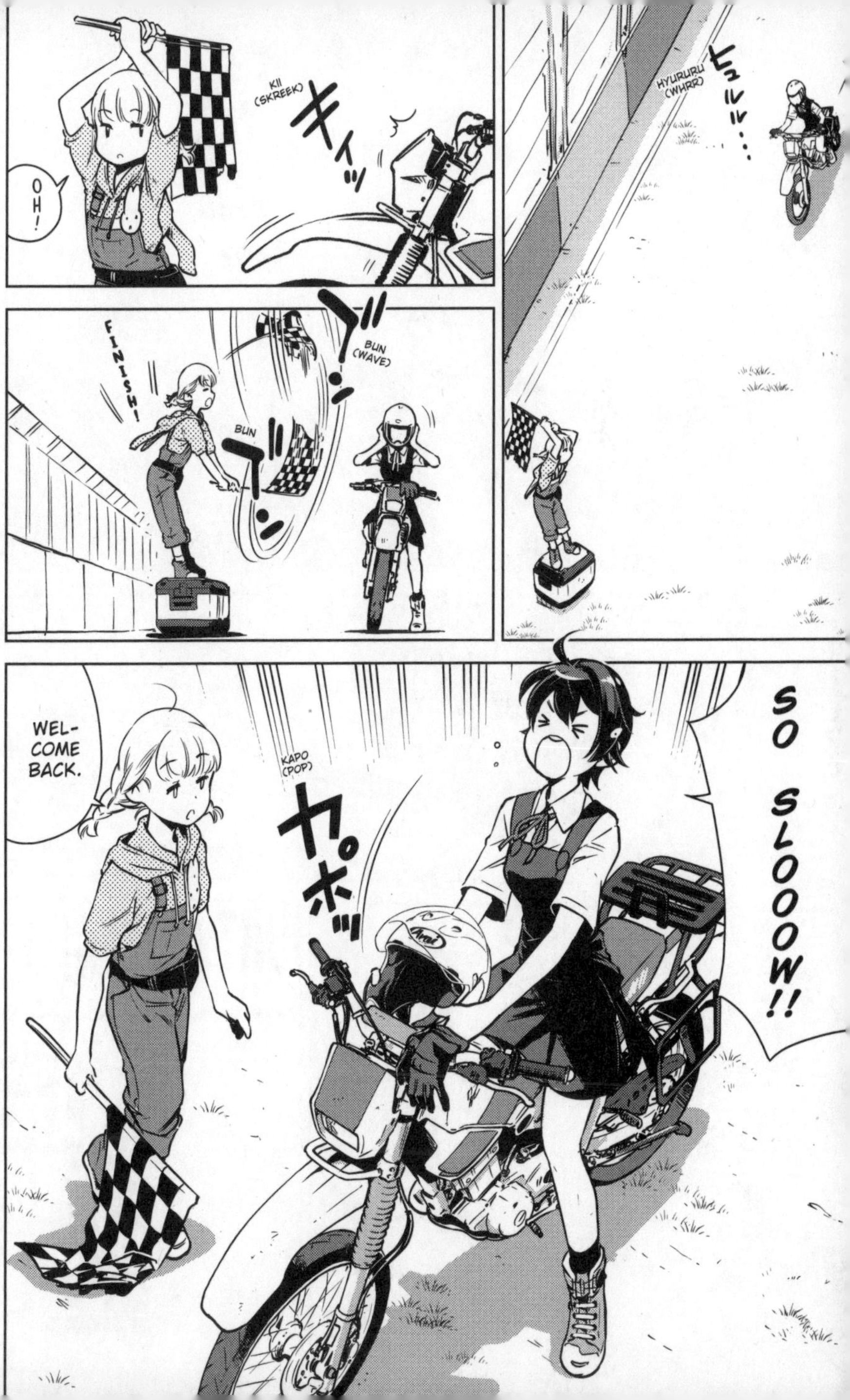
ヒュルル…
HYURURU (WHRR)
KII (SKREEK)
キィッ
OH!
ブンッ
BUN (WAVE)
FINISH!
BUN
ブンッ
SO SLOOOOW!!
KAPO (POP)
カポッ
WEL-COME BACK.

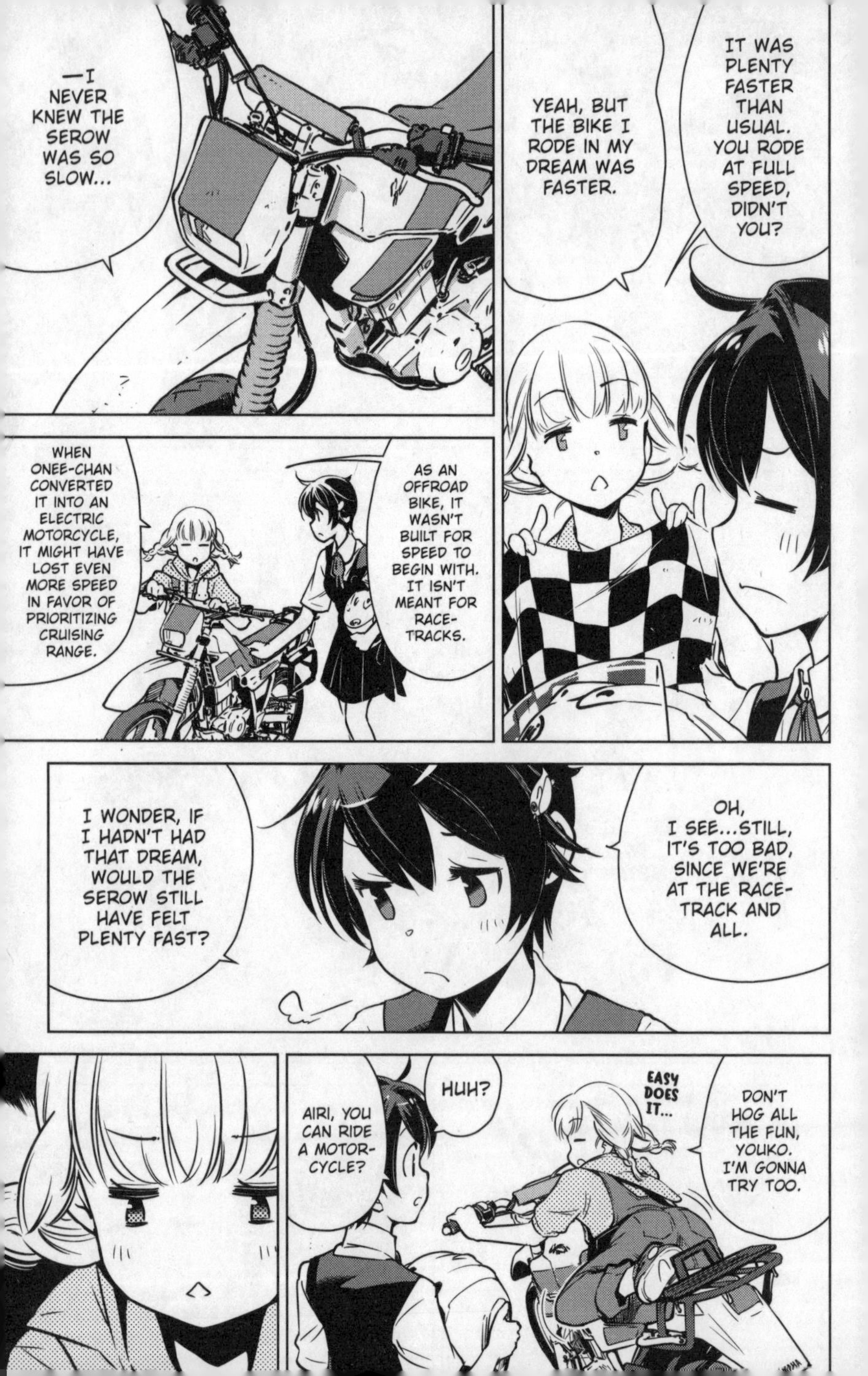
IT WAS PLENTY FASTER THAN USUAL. YOU RODE AT FULL SPEED, DIDN'T YOU?
YEAH, BUT THE BIKE I RODE IN MY DREAM WAS FASTER.
—I NEVER KNEW THE SEROW WAS SO SLOW...
AS AN OFFROAD BIKE, IT WASN'T BUILT FOR SPEED TO BEGIN WITH. IT ISN'T MEANT FOR RACE-TRACKS.
WHEN ONEE-CHAN CONVERTED IT INTO AN ELECTRIC MOTORCYCLE, IT MIGHT HAVE LOST EVEN MORE SPEED IN FAVOR OF PRIORITIZING CRUISING RANGE.
OH, I SEE...STILL, IT'S TOO BAD, SINCE WE'RE AT THE RACE-TRACK AND ALL.
I WONDER, IF I HADN'T HAD THAT DREAM, WOULD THE SEROW STILL HAVE FELT PLENTY FAST?
DON'T HOG ALL THE FUN, YOUKO. I'M GONNA TRY TOO.
EASY DOES IT...
HUH?
AIRI, YOU CAN RIDE A MOTOR-CYCLE?

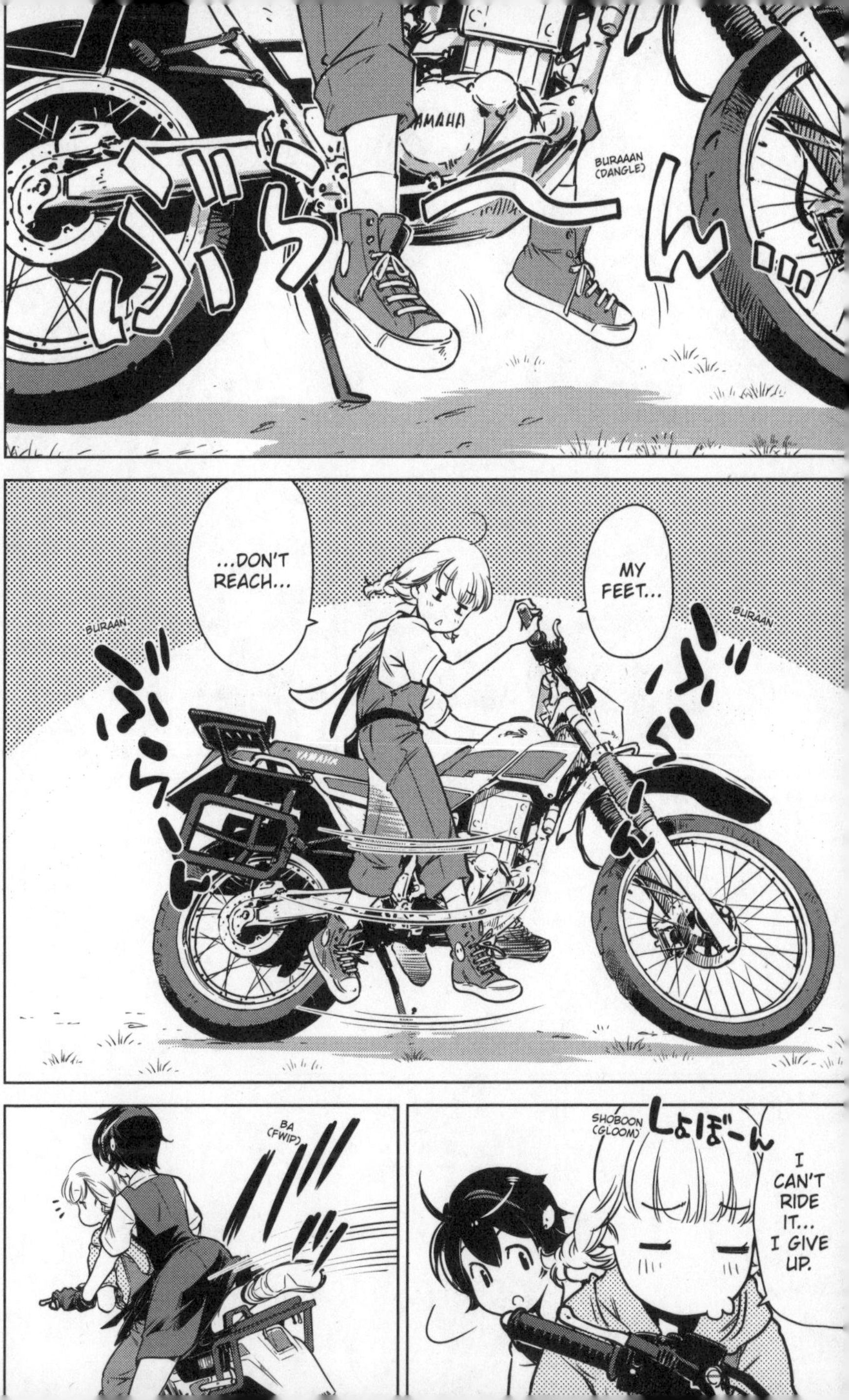
BURAAAN (DANGLE)
BURAAN
MY FEET...
...DON'T REACH...
BURAAN
SHOBOON (GLOOM)
しょぼーん
I CAN'T RIDE IT... I GIVE UP.
BA (FWIP)

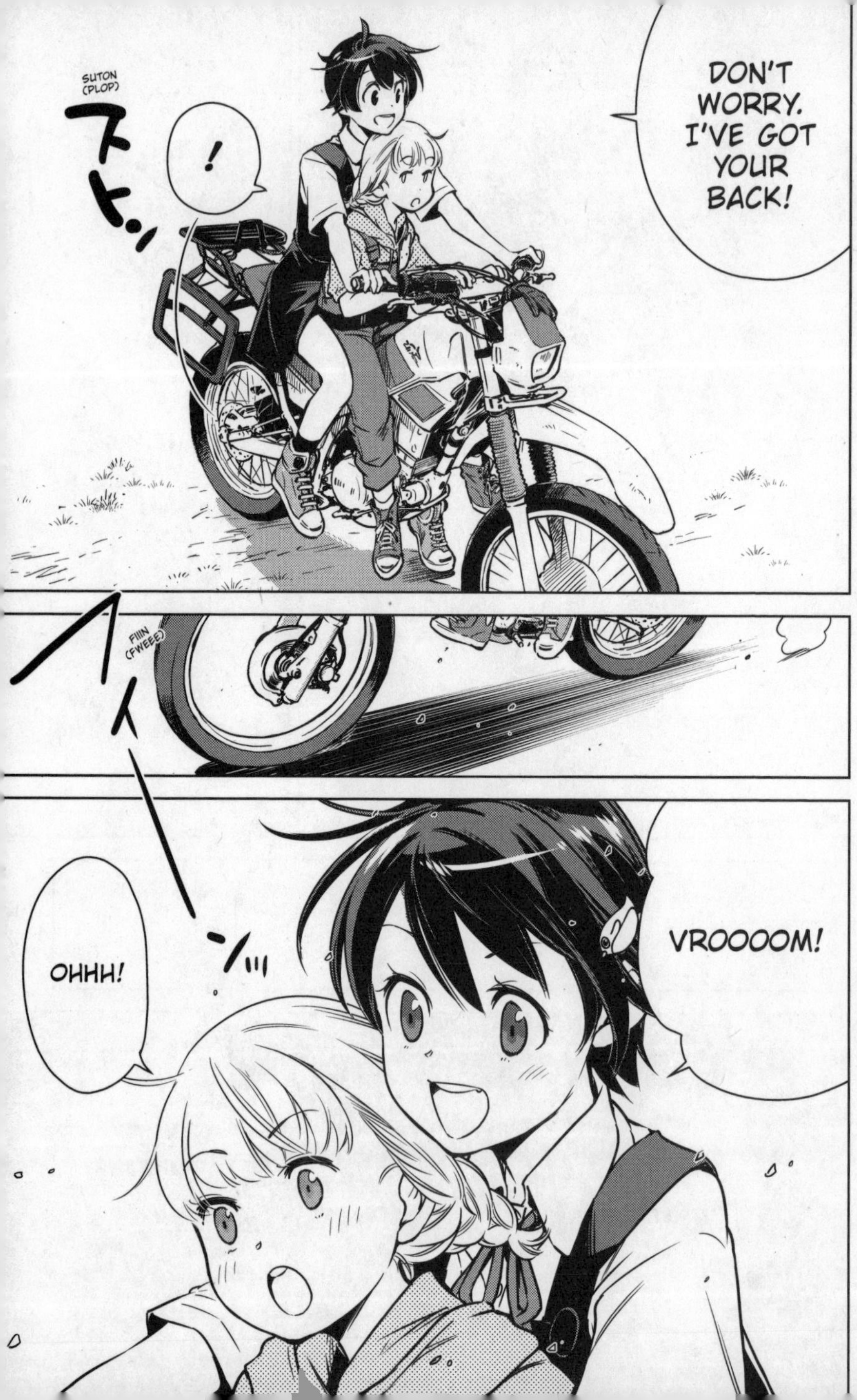
DON'T WORRY. I'VE GOT YOUR BACK!
!
SUTON (PLOP)
FIIIN (FWEEE)
VROOOOM!
OHHH!

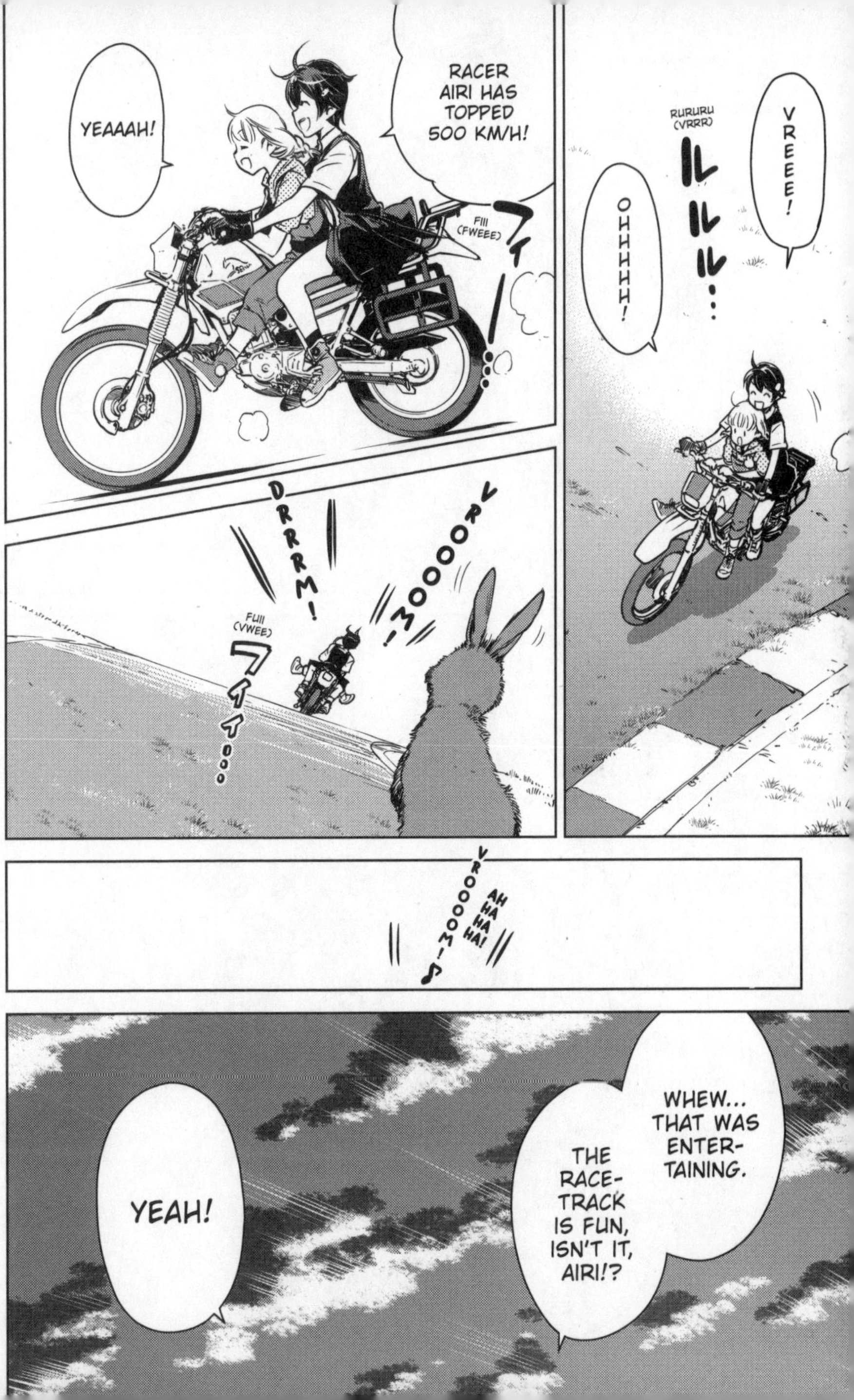
VREEE!
RURURU (VRRR)
OHHHHH!
RACER AIRI HAS TOPPED 500 KM/H!
YEAAAH!
FIII (FWEEE)
VROOOOOM!
DRRRRM!
FUII (VWEE)
VROOOOOM!♪
AH HA HA HA!
WHEW... THAT WAS ENTER-TAINING.
THE RACE-TRACK IS FUN, ISN'T IT, AIRI!?
YEAH!

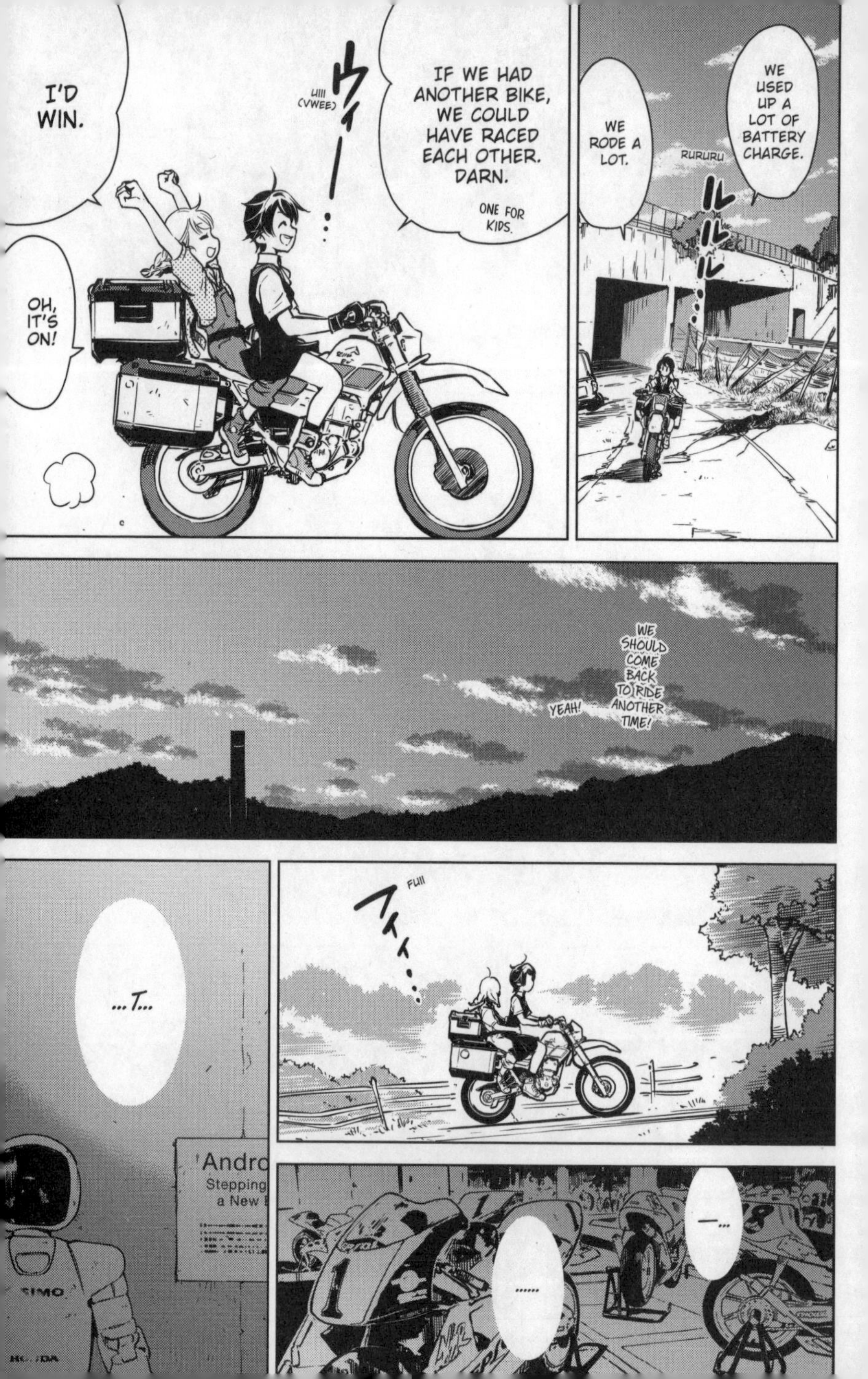
WE USED UP A LOT OF BATTERY CHARGE.
RURURU
WE RODE A LOT.
IF WE HAD ANOTHER BIKE, WE COULD HAVE RACED EACH OTHER. DARN.
ONE FOR KIDS.
UIII (VWEE)
I'D WIN.
OH, IT'S ON!
WE SHOULD COME BACK TO RIDE ANOTHER TIME!
YEAH!
FUIII
—...
......
...T...
Andro
Stepping
a New

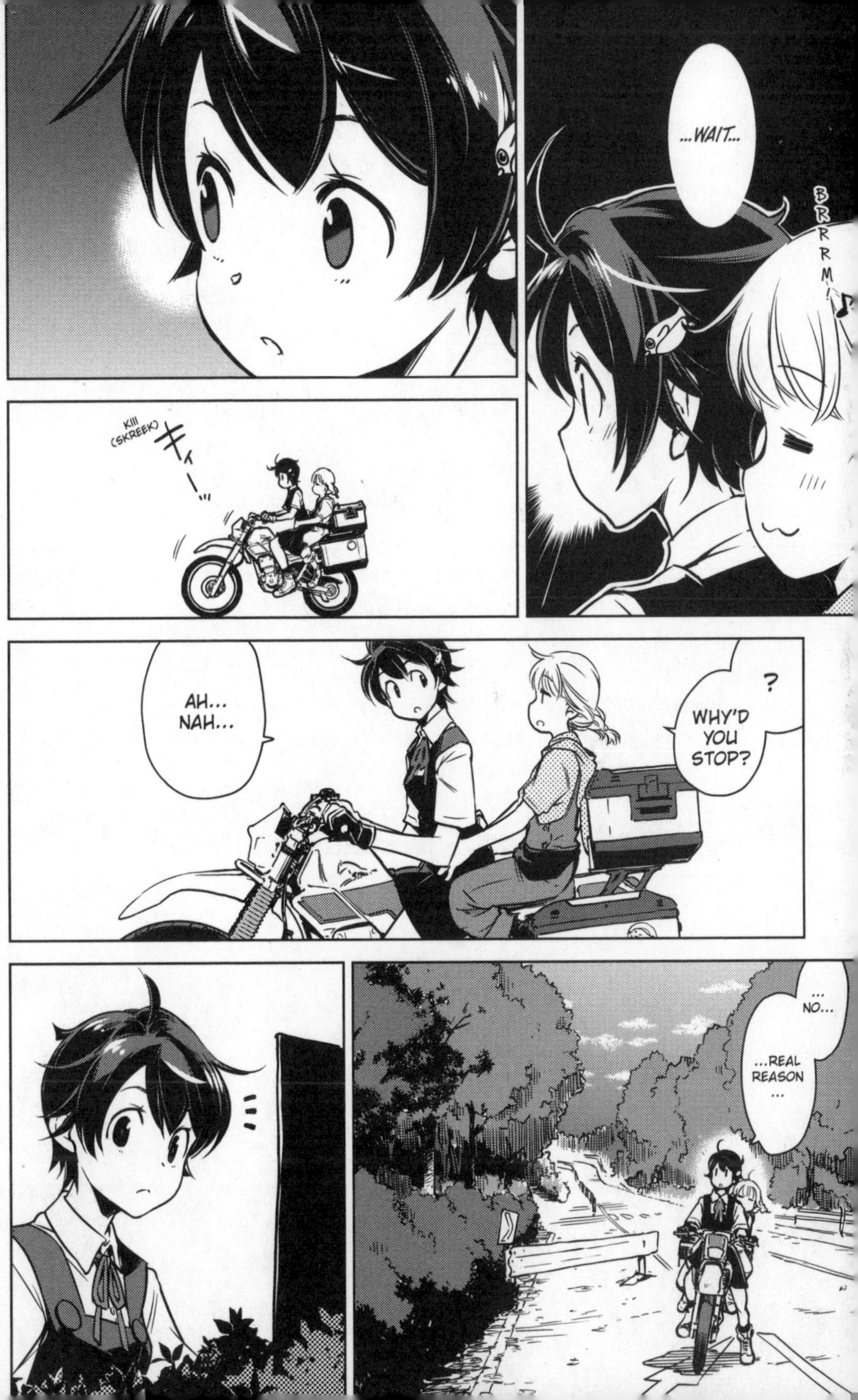
...WAIT...
BRRRM!
KIII (SKREEK)
?
WHY'D YOU STOP?
AH... NAH...
... NO...
...REAL REASON ...

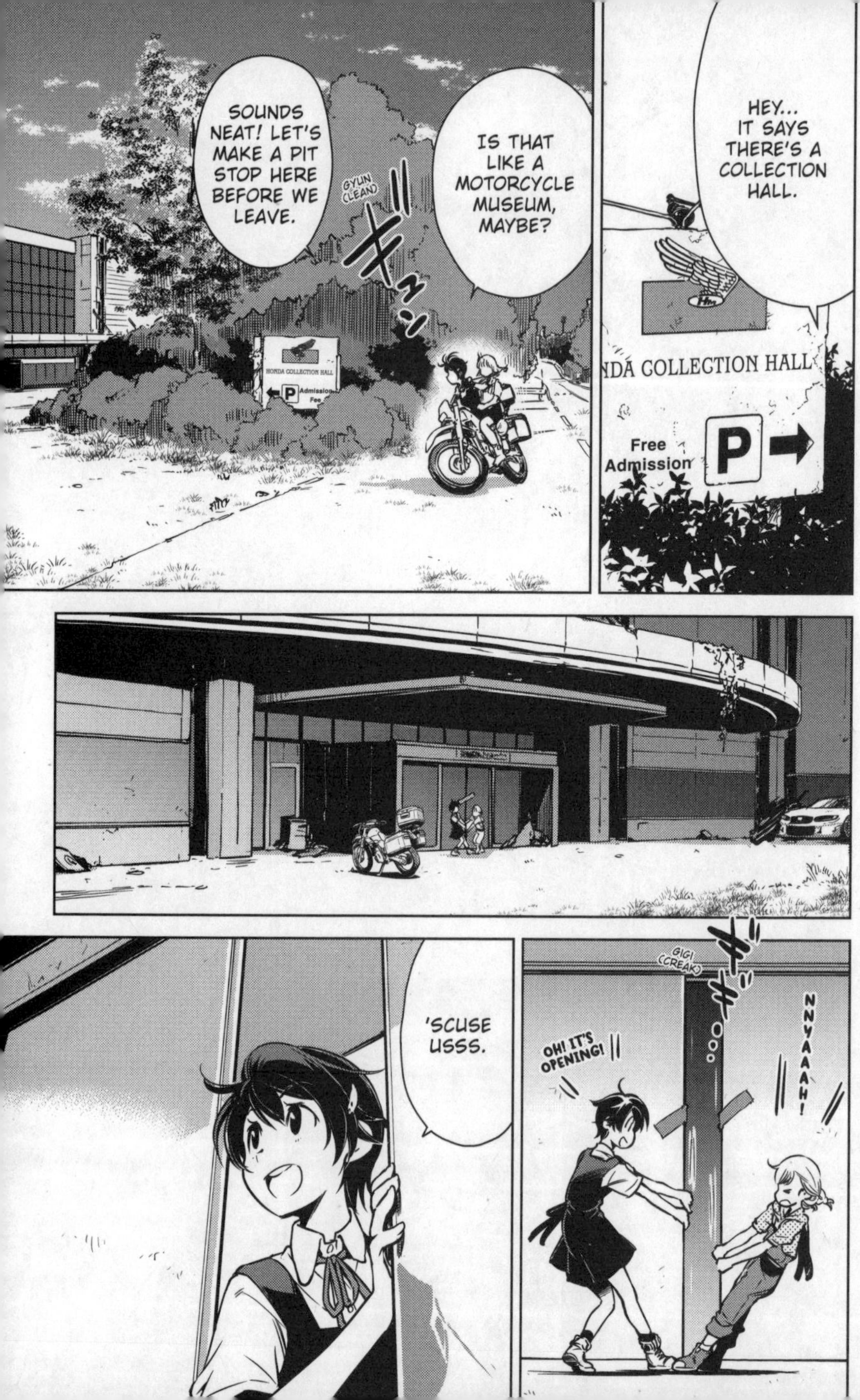
HEY... IT SAYS THERE'S A COLLECTION HALL.
NDA COLLECTION HALL
Free Admission
P
IS THAT LIKE A MOTORCYCLE MUSEUM, MAYBE?
SOUNDS NEAT! LET'S MAKE A PIT STOP HERE BEFORE WE LEAVE.
GYUN (CLEAN)
HONDA COLLECTION HALL
P Admission Fee
GIGI (CREAK)
NNYAAAAH!
OH! IT'S OPENING!
'SCUSE USSS.

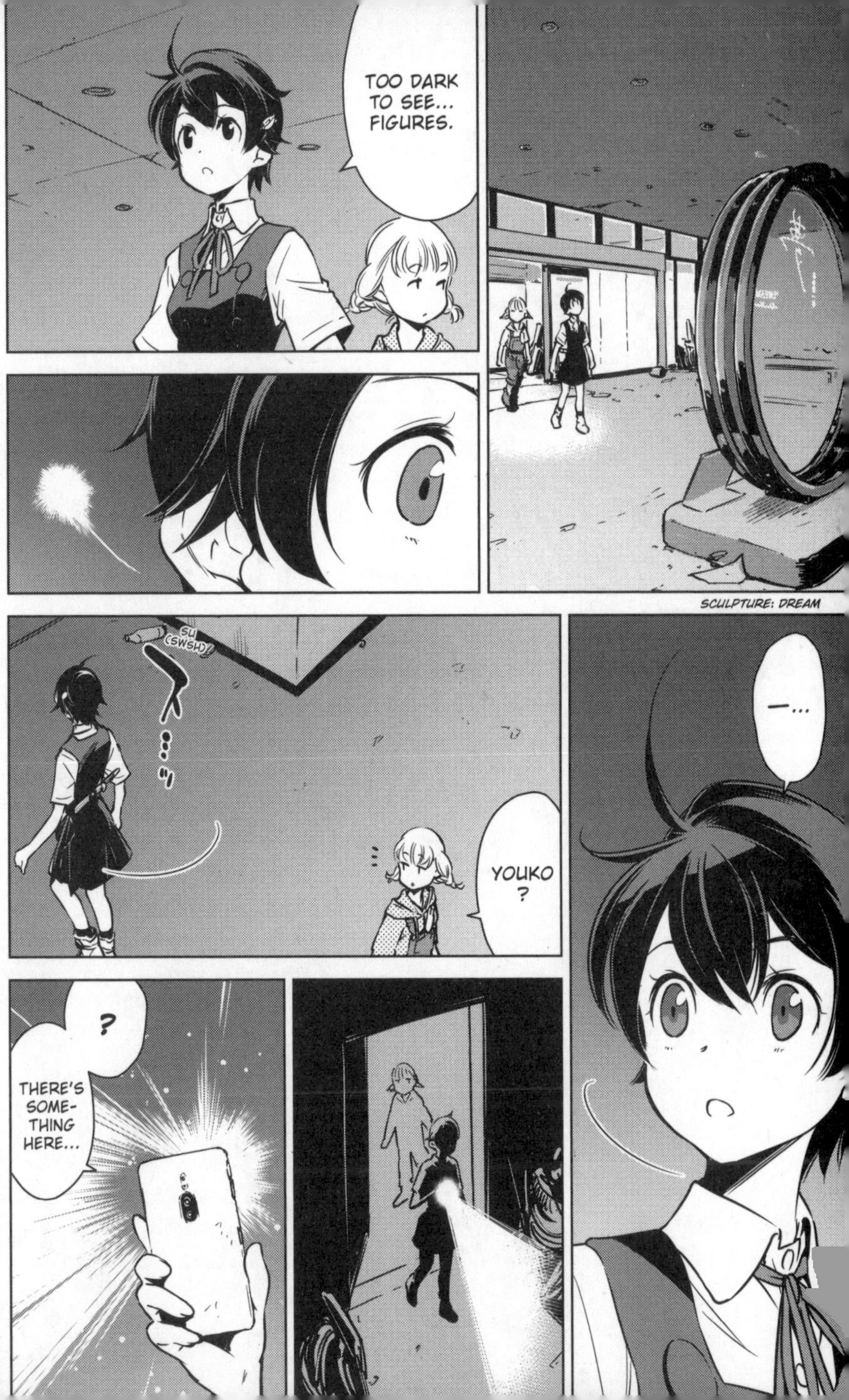
SCULPTURE: DREAM
TOO DARK TO SEE... FIGURES.
—...
SU (SWSH)
YOUKO?
?
THERE'S SOME-THING HERE...

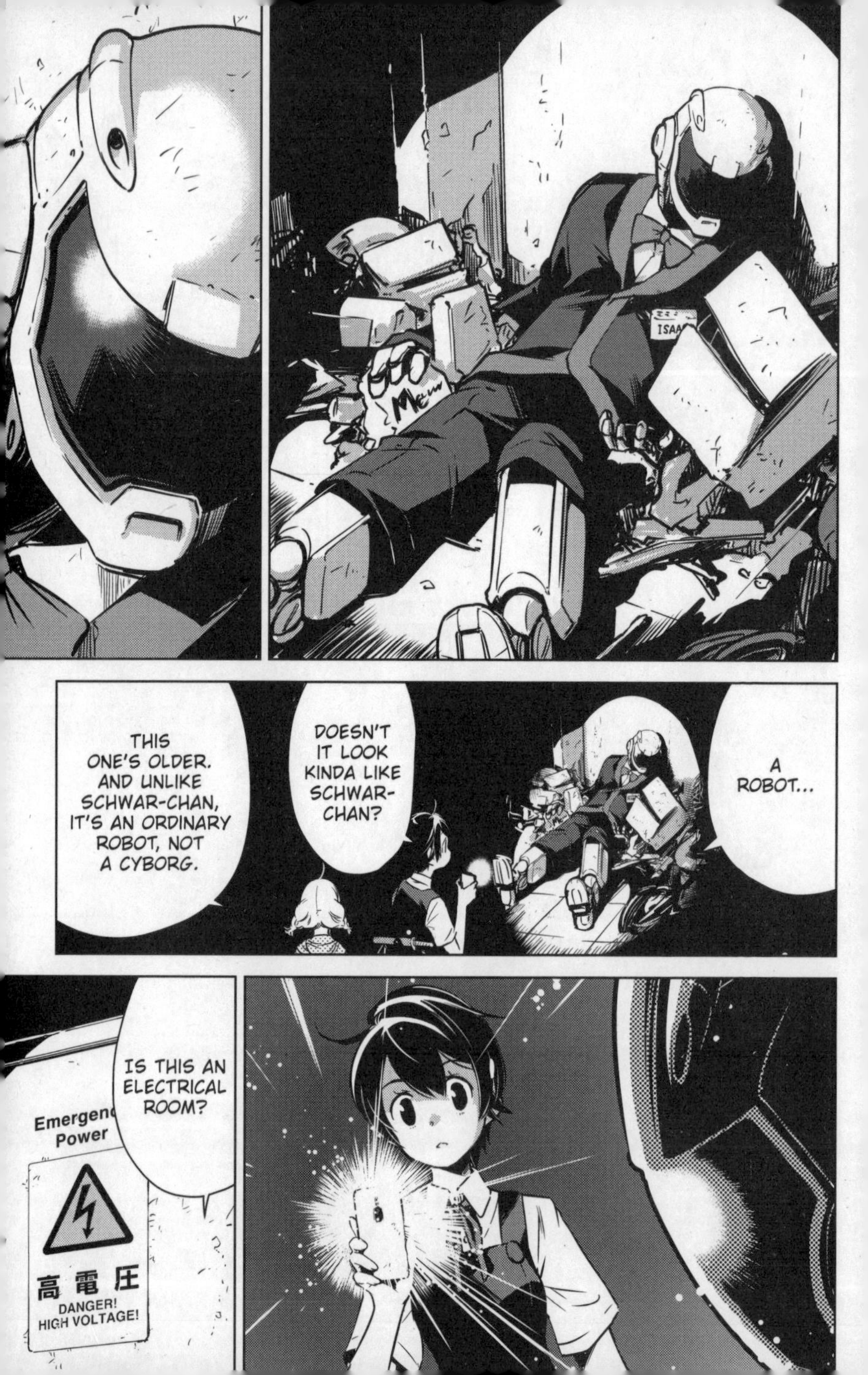
A ROBOT...
DOESN'T IT LOOK KINDA LIKE SCHWAR-CHAN?
THIS ONE'S OLDER. AND UNLIKE SCHWAR-CHAN, IT'S AN ORDINARY ROBOT, NOT A CYBORG.
IS THIS AN ELECTRICAL ROOM?
Emergenc Power
高電圧
DANGER! HIGH VOLTAGE!

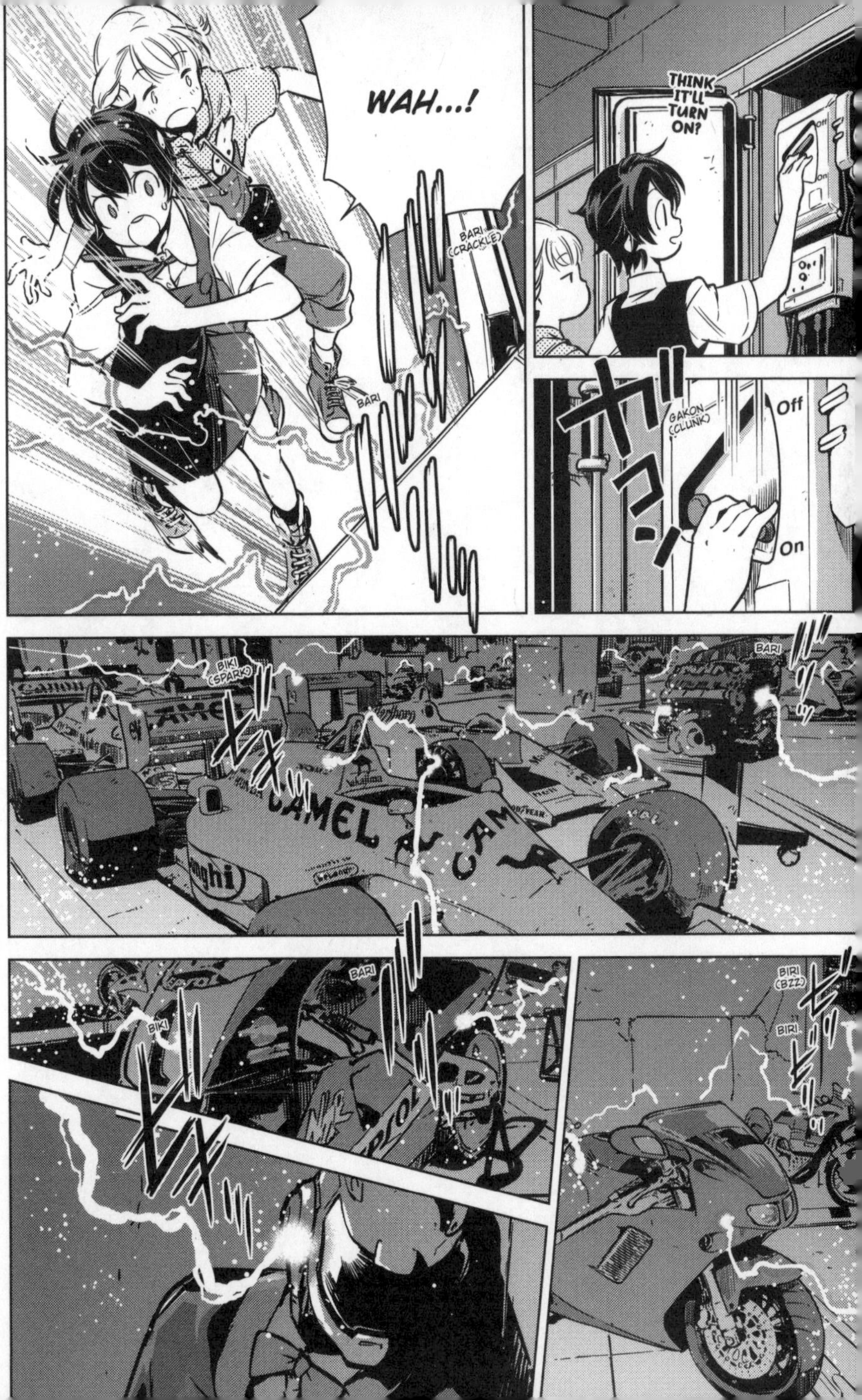
THINK IT'LL TURN ON?
Off
On
GAKON (CLUNK)
Off
On
WAH...!
BARI (CRACKLE)
BARI
BARI
BIKI (SPARK)
BIRI (BZZ)
BIRI
BARI
BIKI

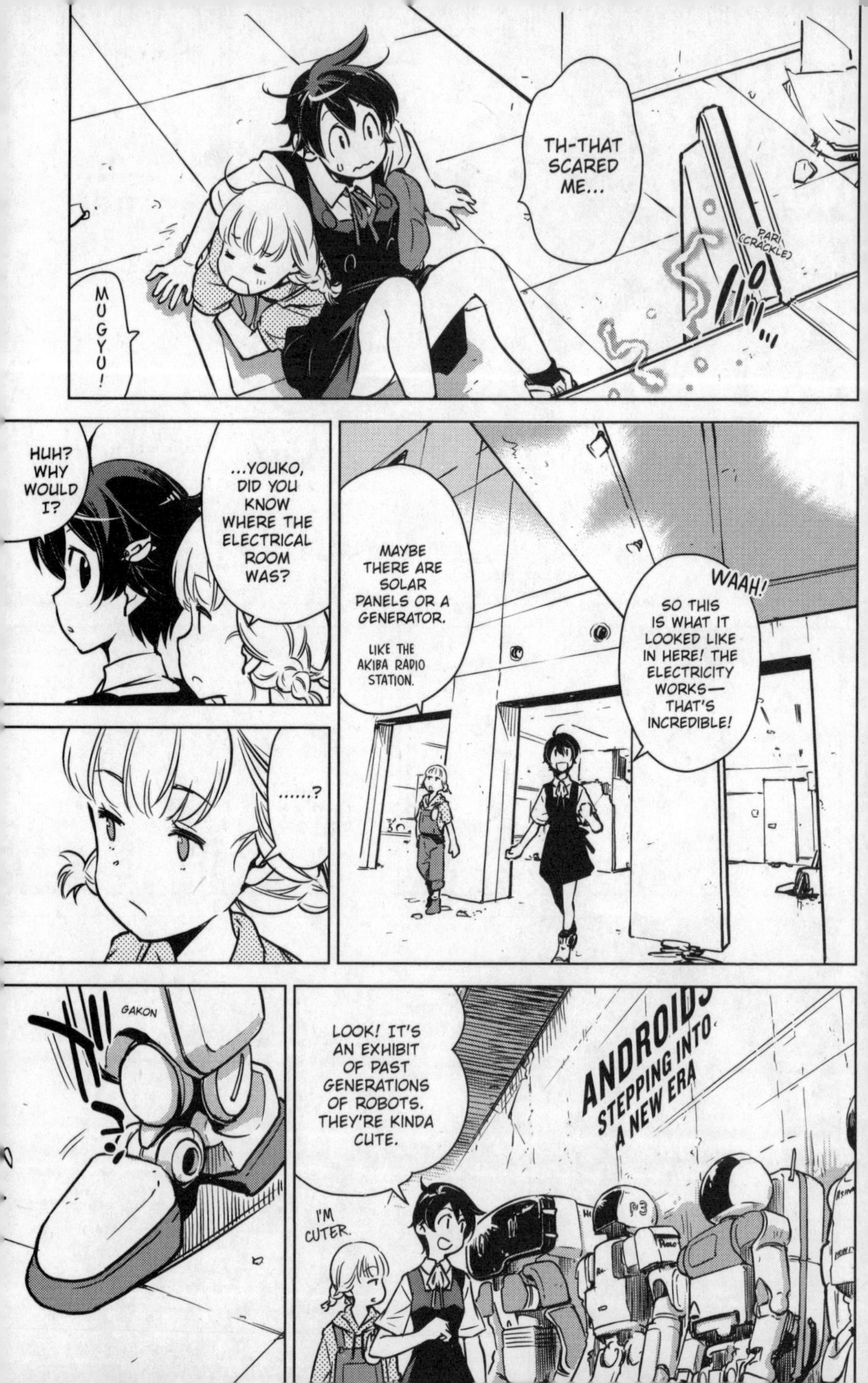
TH-THAT SCARED ME...
PARI (CRACKLE)
MUGYU!
WAAH!
SO THIS IS WHAT IT LOOKED LIKE IN HERE! THE ELECTRICITY WORKS— THAT'S INCREDIBLE!
MAYBE THERE ARE SOLAR PANELS OR A GENERATOR.
LIKE THE AKIBA RADIO STATION.
...YOUKO, DID YOU KNOW WHERE THE ELECTRICAL ROOM WAS?
HUH? WHY WOULD I?
......?
ANDROIDS STEPPING INTO A NEW ERA
LOOK! IT'S AN EXHIBIT OF PAST GENERATIONS OF ROBOTS. THEY'RE KINDA CUTE.
I'M CUTER.
GAKON

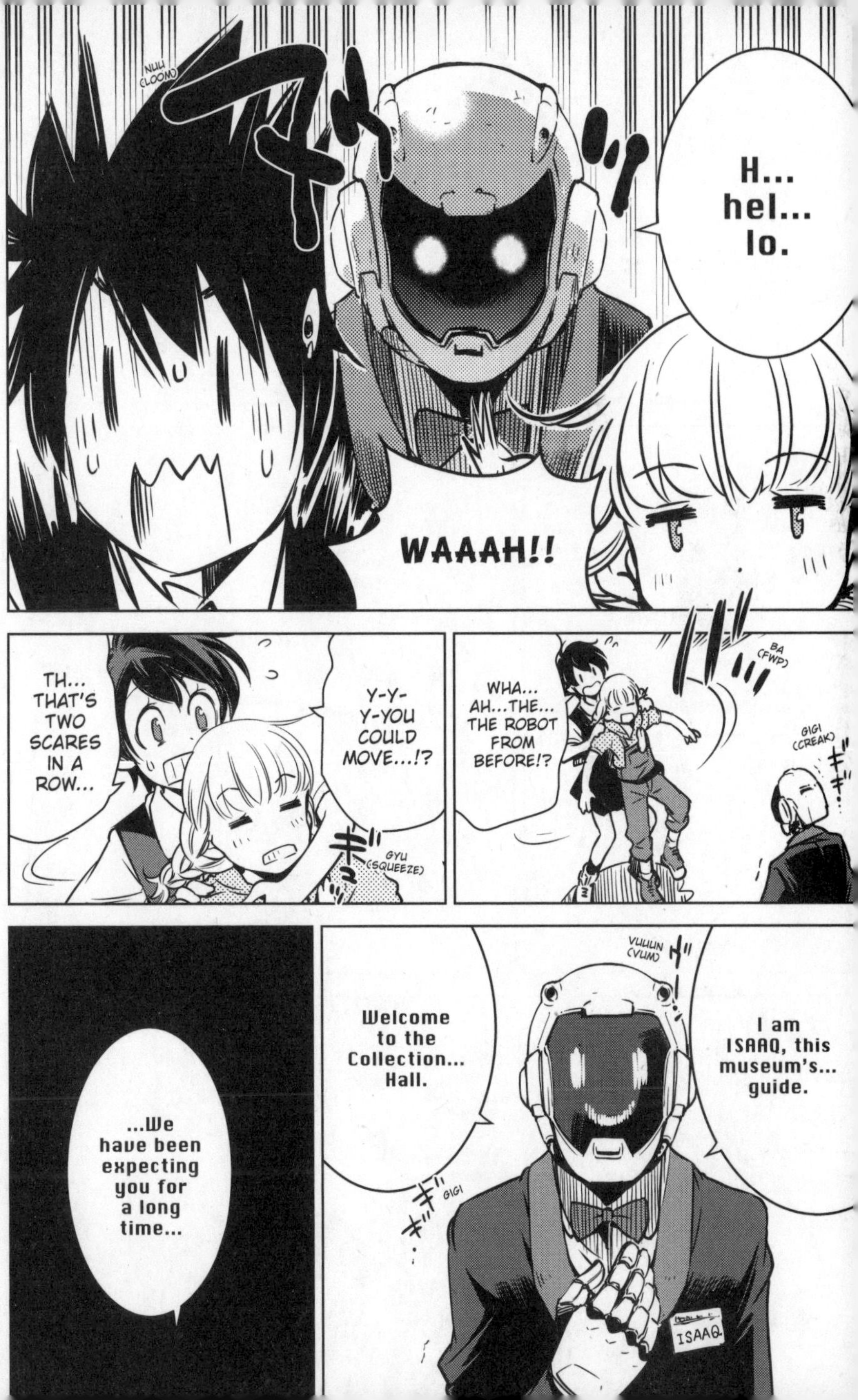

H... hel... lo.
NUU (LOOM)
WAAAH!!
BA (FWP)
GIGI (CREAK)
WHA... AH...THE... THE ROBOT FROM BEFORE!?
Y-Y-Y-YOU COULD MOVE...!?
TH... THAT'S TWO SCARES IN A ROW...
GYU (SQUEEZE)
VUUUN (VUM)
I am ISAAQ, this museum's... guide.
Welcome to the Collection... Hall.
GIGI
ISAAQ
...We have been expecting you for a long time...

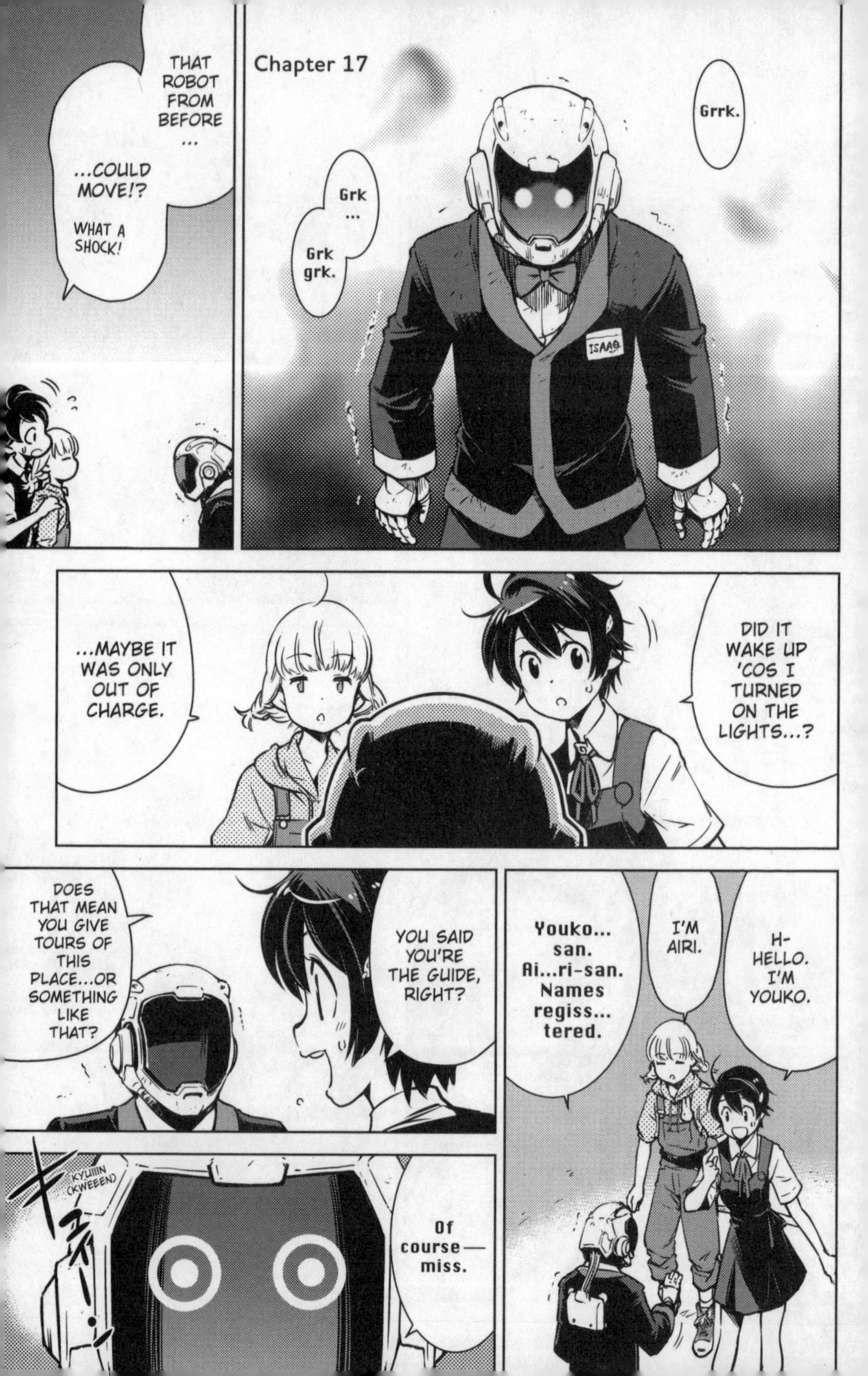
Chapter 17
Grrk.
Grk ... Grk grk.
THAT ROBOT FROM BEFORE ... ...COULD MOVE!?
WHAT A SHOCK!
DID IT WAKE UP 'COS I TURNED ON THE LIGHTS...?
...MAYBE IT WAS ONLY OUT OF CHARGE.
H- HELLO. I'M YOUKO.
I'M AIRI.
Youko... san. Ai...ri-san. Names regiss... tered.
YOU SAID YOU'RE THE GUIDE, RIGHT?
DOES THAT MEAN YOU GIVE TOURS OF THIS PLACE...OR SOMETHING LIKE THAT?
Of course—miss.
KYUIIIN (KWEEEN)

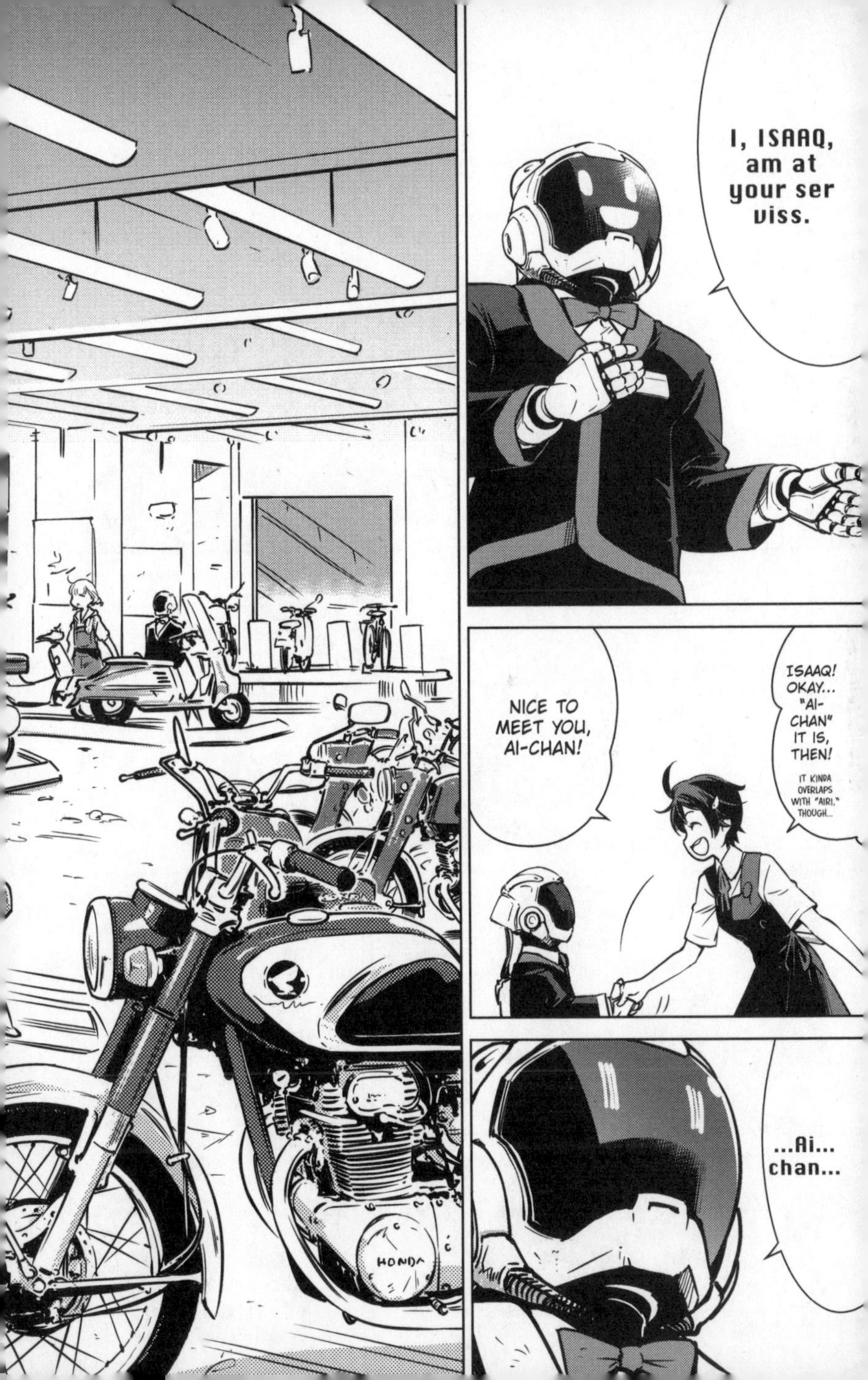
I, ISAAQ, am at your ser viss.
ISAAQ! OKAY... "AI-CHAN" IT IS, THEN!
IT KINDA OVERLAPS WITH "AIRI," THOUGH...
NICE TO MEET YOU, AI-CHAN!
...Ai... chan...
HONDA

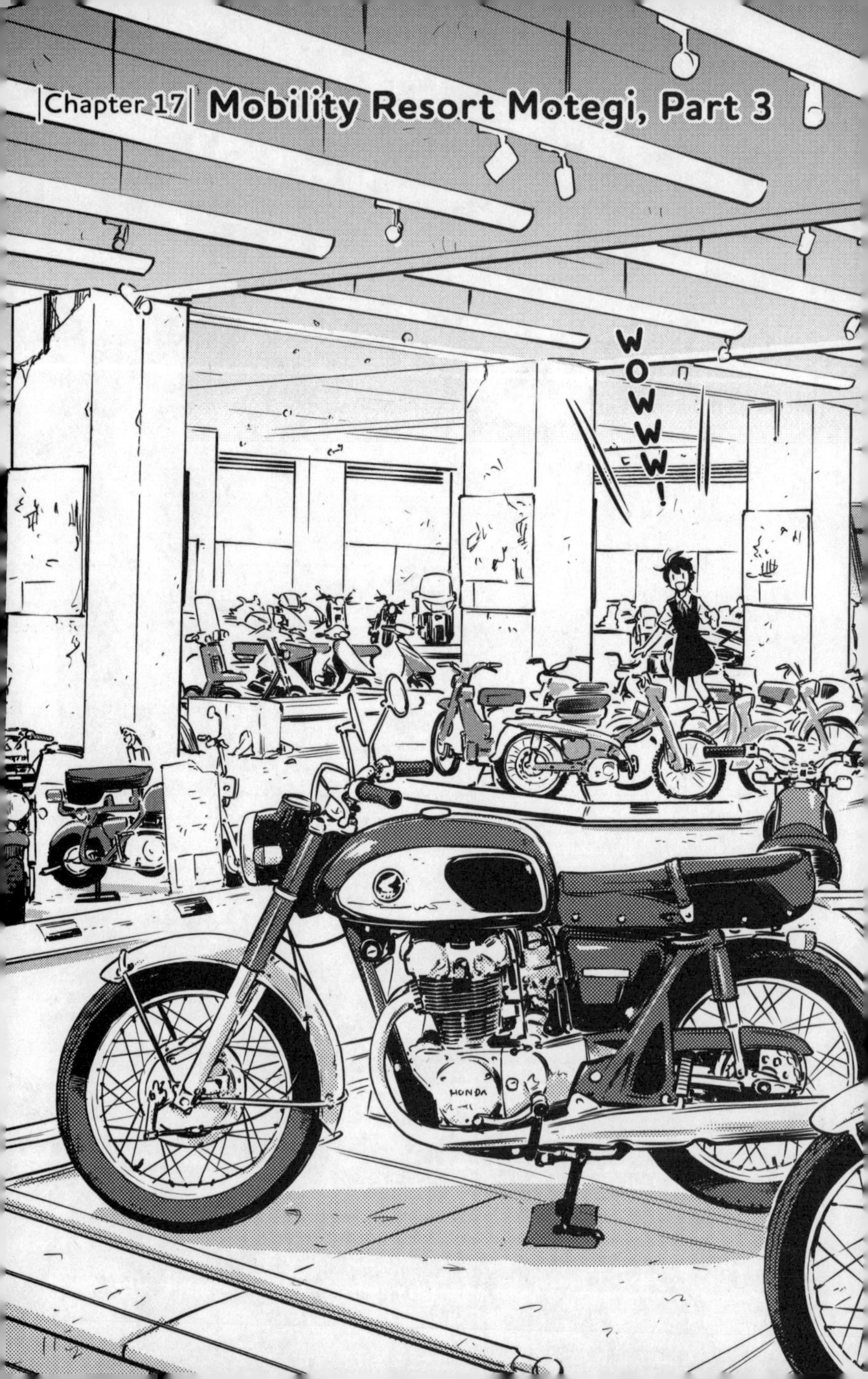
Chapter 17 Mobility Resort Motegi, Part 3
WOWWWW!
HONDA

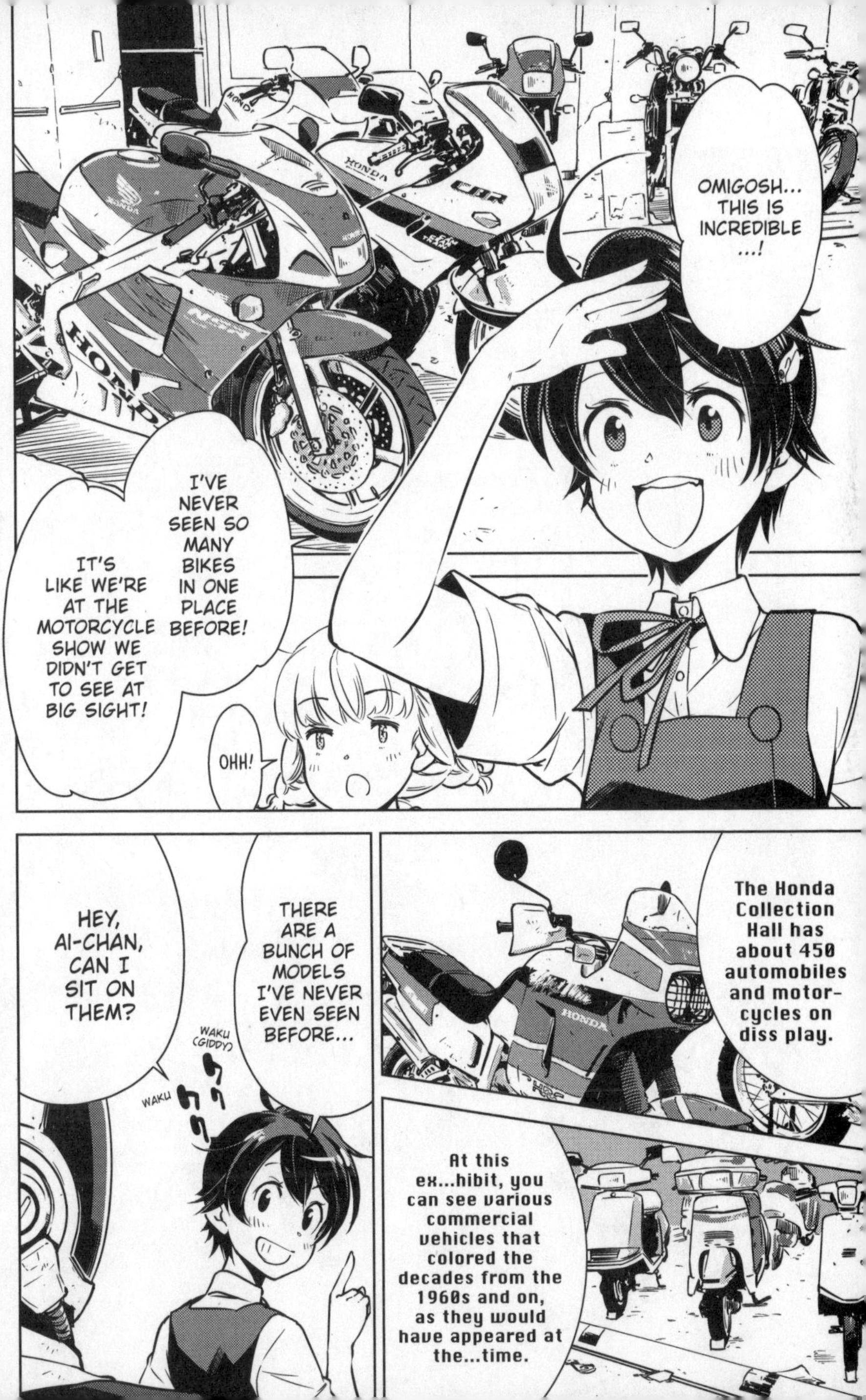
OMIGOSH... THIS IS INCREDIBLE ...!
I'VE NEVER SEEN SO MANY BIKES IN ONE PLACE BEFORE!
IT'S LIKE WE'RE AT THE MOTORCYCLE SHOW WE DIDN'T GET TO SEE AT BIG SIGHT!
OHH!
The Honda Collection Hall has about 450 automobiles and motor-cycles on diss play.
At this ex...hibit, you can see various commercial vehicles that colored the decades from the 1960s and on, as they would have appeared at the...time.
THERE ARE A BUNCH OF MODELS I'VE NEVER EVEN SEEN BEFORE...
HEY, AI-CHAN, CAN I SIT ON THEM?
WAKU (GIDDY)
WAKU

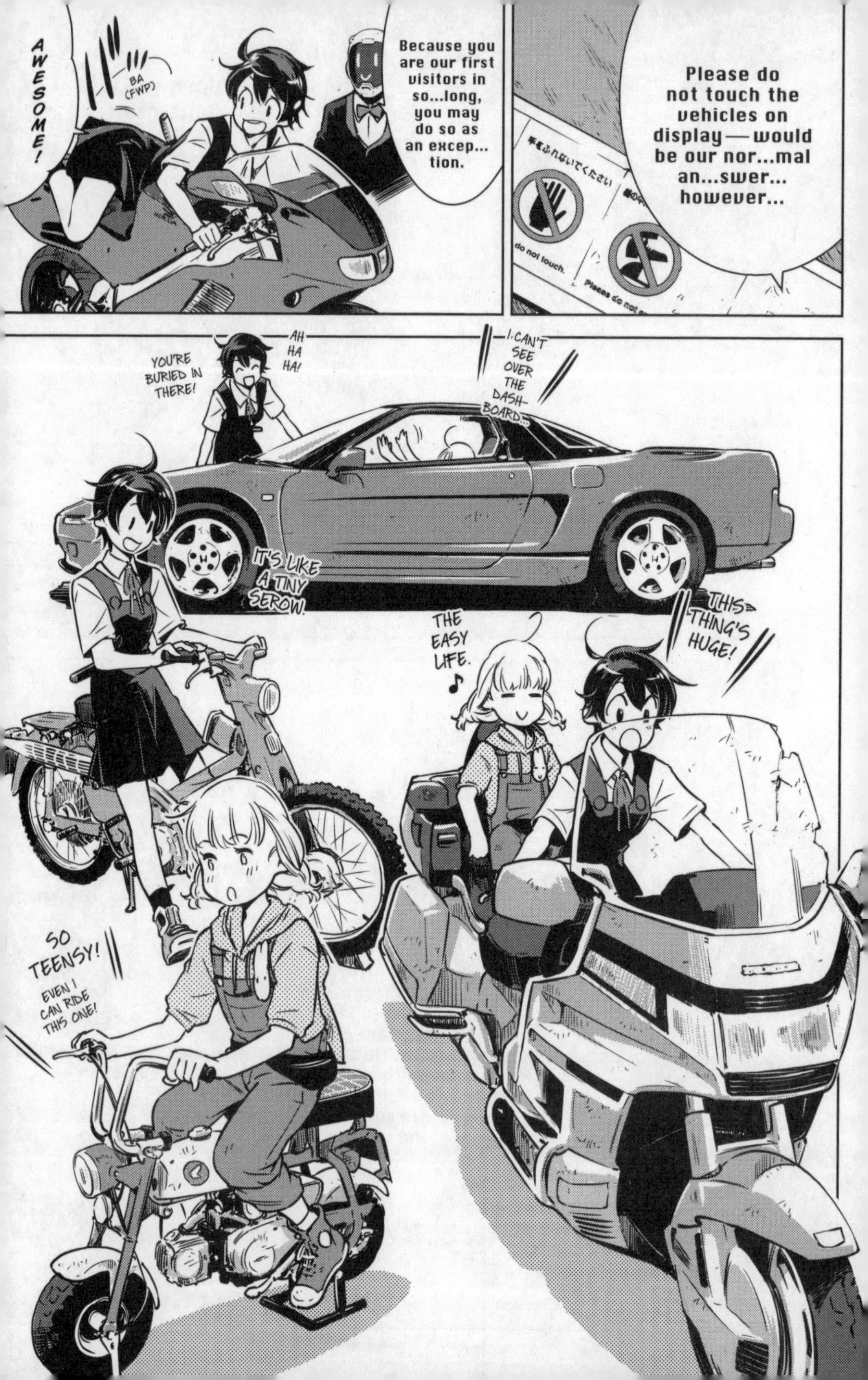
Please do not touch the vehicles on display — would be our nor...mal an...swer... however...
手をふれないでください
do not touch.
Because you are our first visitors in so...long, you may do so as an excep... tion.
AWESOME!
BA (FWP)
I.CAN'T SEE OVER THE DASHBOARD...
AH HA HA!
YOU'RE BURIED IN THERE!
THIS THING'S HUGE!
THE EASY LIFE. ♪
IT'S LIKE A TINY SEROW.
SO TEENSY!
EVEN I CAN RIDE THIS ONE!

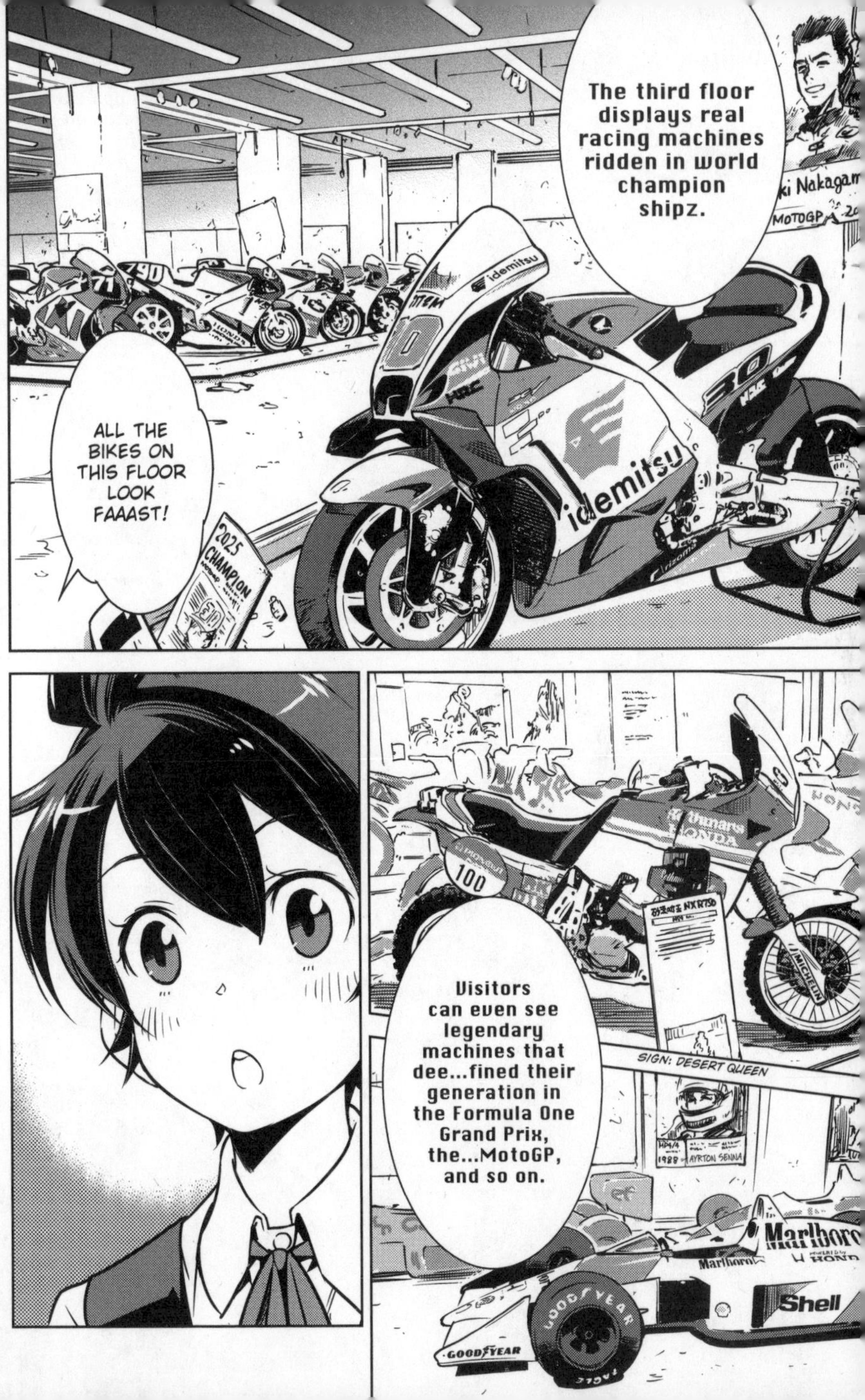
The third floor displays real racing machines ridden in world champion shipz.
ALL THE BIKES ON THIS FLOOR LOOK FAAAST!
2025 CHAMPION
Visitors can even see legendary machines that dee...fined their generation in the Formula One Grand Prix, the...MotoGP, and so on.
SIGN: DESERT QUEEN
1988 AYRTON SENNA

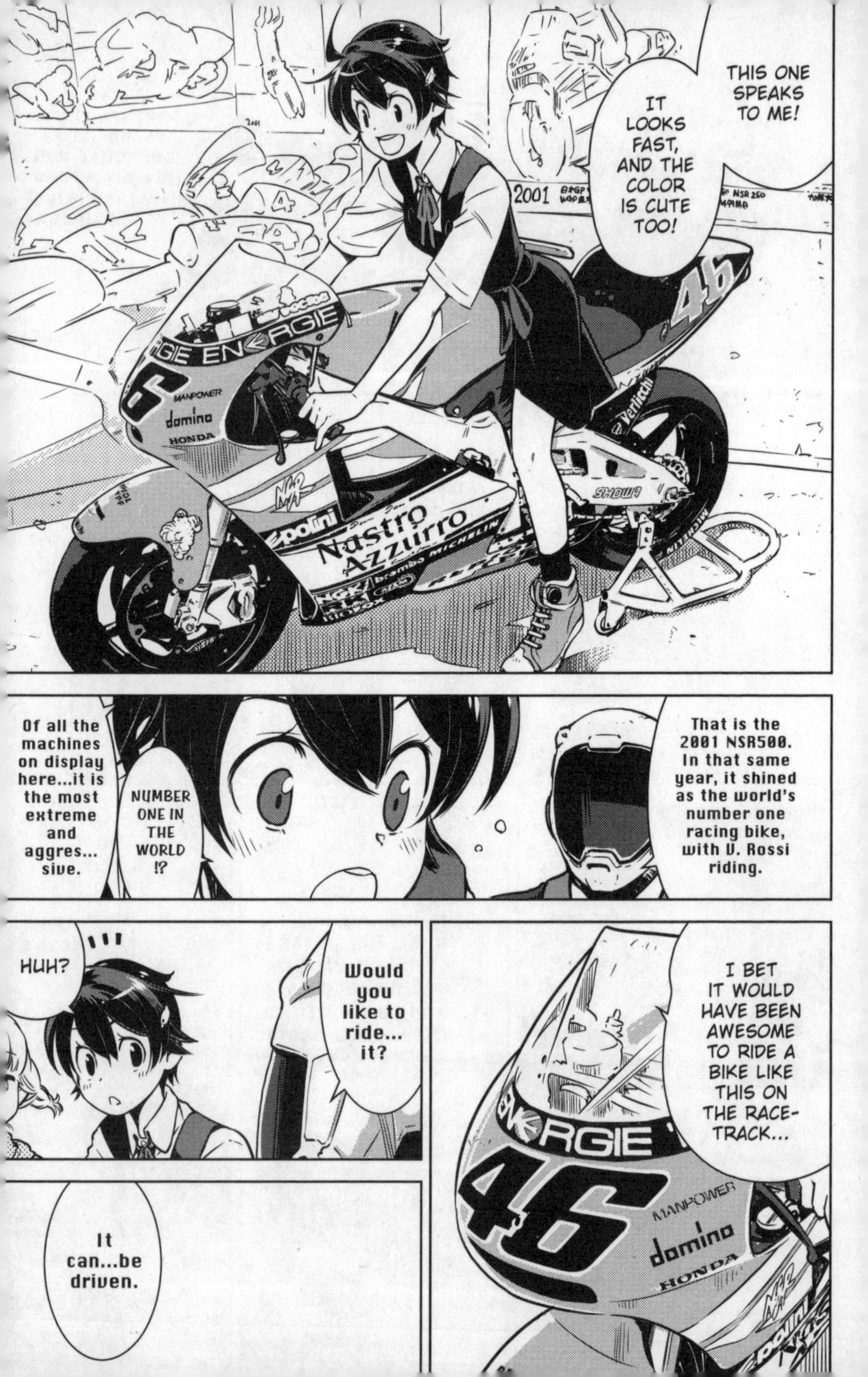
THIS ONE SPEAKS TO ME!
IT LOOKS FAST, AND THE COLOR IS CUTE TOO!
That is the 2001 NSR500. In that same year, it shined as the world's number one racing bike, with V. Rossi riding.
NUMBER ONE IN THE WORLD !?
Of all the machines on display here...it is the most extreme and aggres... sive.
I BET IT WOULD HAVE BEEN AWESOME TO RIDE A BIKE LIKE THIS ON THE RACE-TRACK...
Would you like to ride... it?
HUH?
It can...be driven.

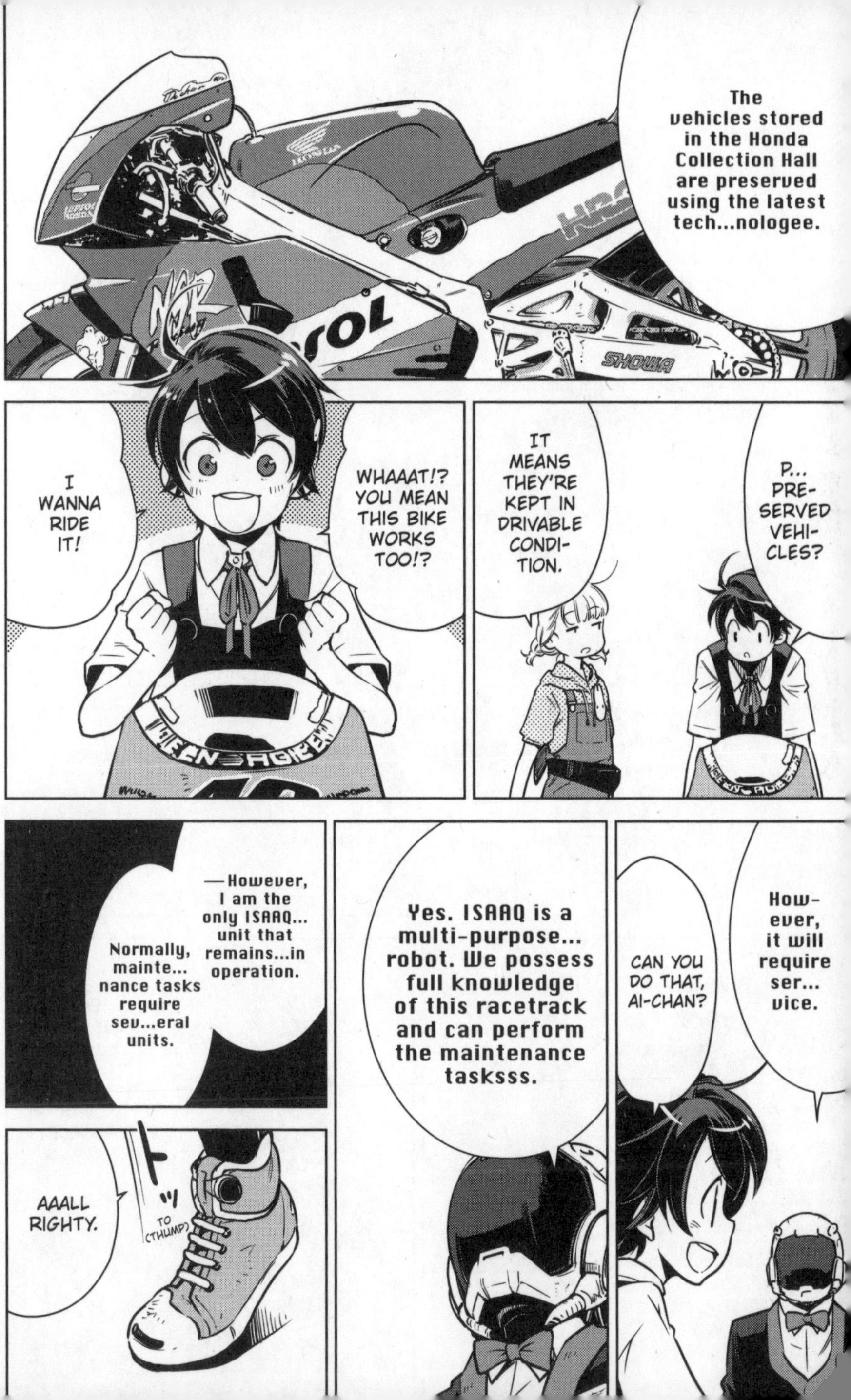
The vehicles stored in the Honda Collection Hall are preserved using the latest tech...nologee.
P... PRE-SERVED VEHI-CLES?
IT MEANS THEY'RE KEPT IN DRIVABLE CONDI-TION.
WHAAAT!? YOU MEAN THIS BIKE WORKS TOO!?
I WANNA RIDE IT!
How-ever, it will require ser... vice.
CAN YOU DO THAT, AI-CHAN?
Yes. ISAAQ is a multi-purpose... robot. We possess full knowledge of this racetrack and can perform the maintenance tasksss.
—However, I am the only ISAAQ... unit that remains...in operation.
Normally, mainte... nance tasks require sev...eral units.
ッ TO (THUMP)
AAALL RIGHTY.

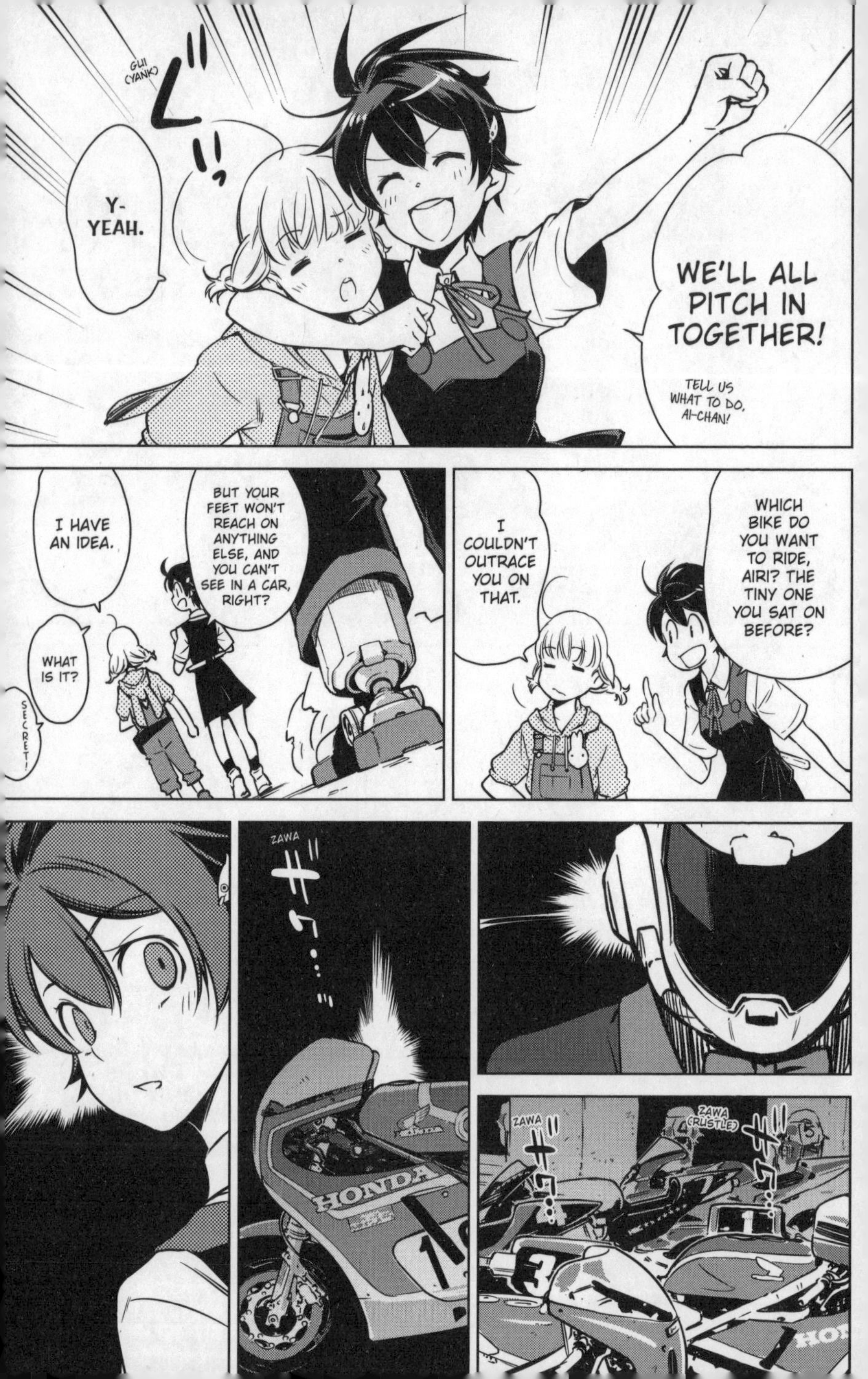
WE'LL ALL PITCH IN TOGETHER!
TELL US WHAT TO DO, AI-CHAN!
GUI (YANK)
Y-YEAH.
WHICH BIKE DO YOU WANT TO RIDE, AIRI? THE TINY ONE YOU SAT ON BEFORE?
I COULDN'T OUTRACE YOU ON THAT.
BUT YOUR FEET WON'T REACH ON ANYTHING ELSE, AND YOU CAN'T SEE IN A CAR, RIGHT?
I HAVE AN IDEA.
WHAT IS IT?
SECRET!
ZAWA (RUSTLE)
ZAWA
ZAWA
HONDA

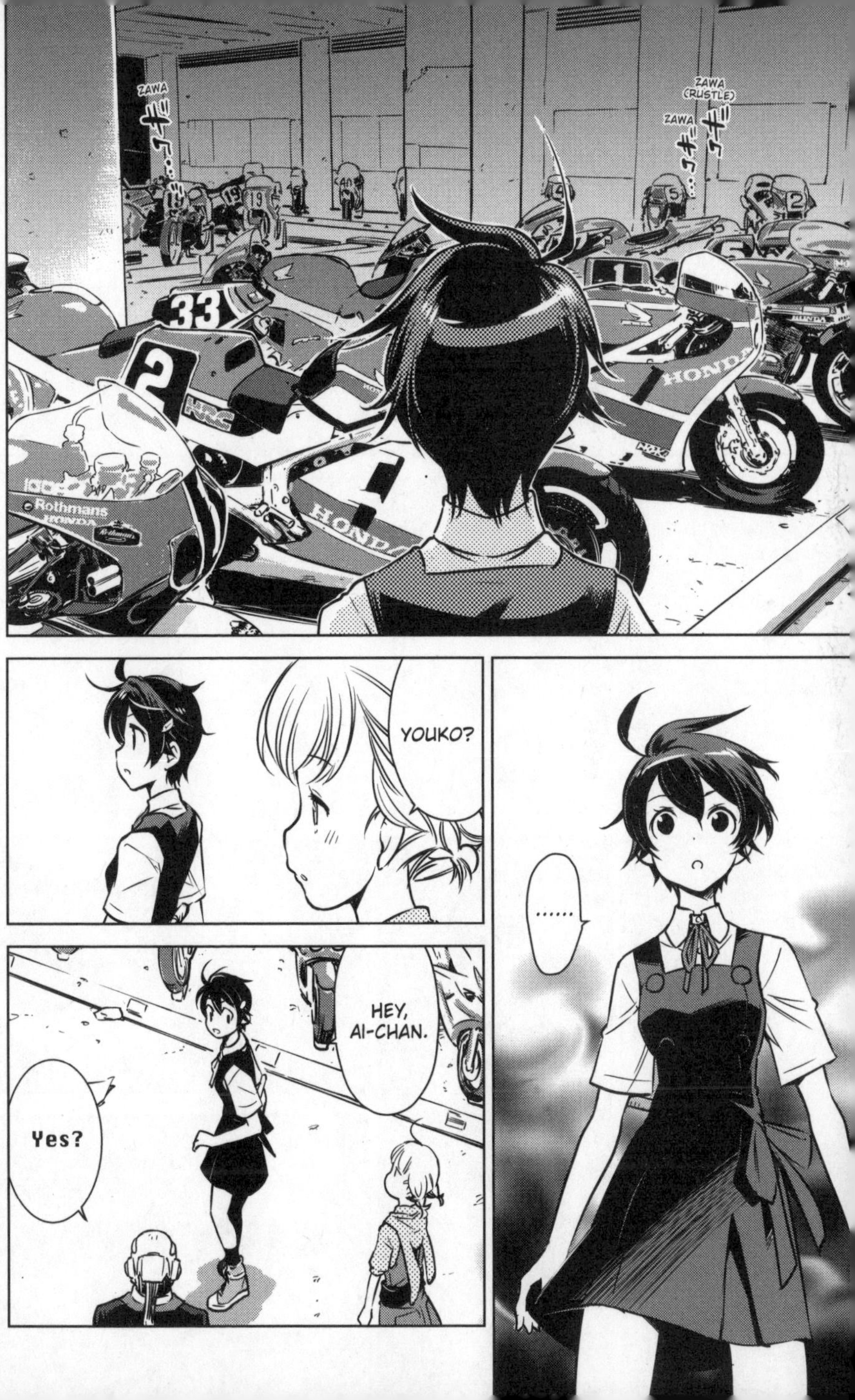
ZAWA
(RUSTLE)
ZAWA
ZAWA
......
YOUKO?
HEY, AI-CHAN.
Yes?

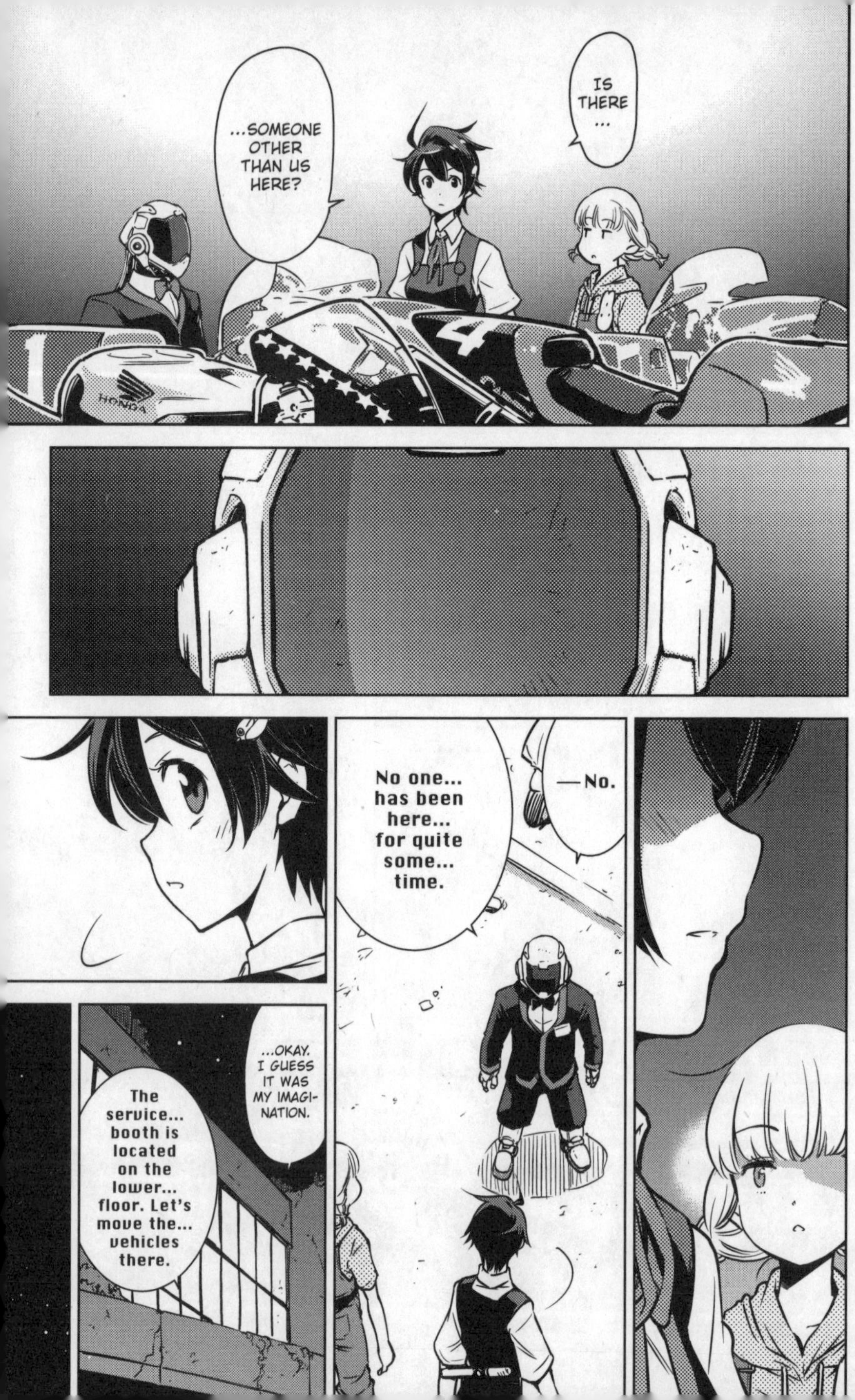
IS THERE ...
...SOMEONE OTHER THAN US HERE?
—No.
No one... has been here... for quite some... time.
...OKAY. I GUESS IT WAS MY IMAGI-NATION.
The service... booth is located on the lower... floor. Let's move the... vehicles there.

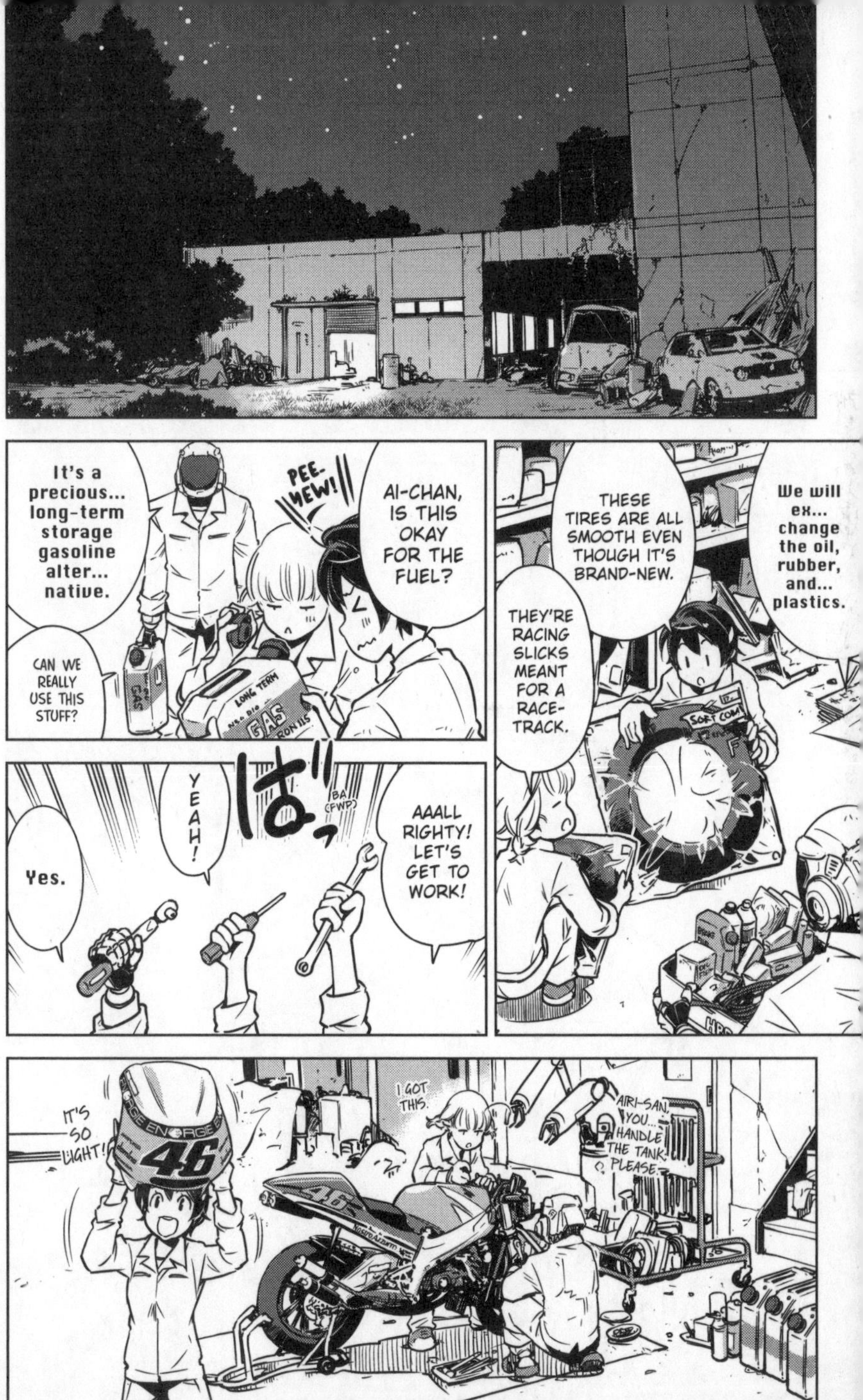

We will ex... change the oil, rubber, and... plastics.
THESE TIRES ARE ALL SMOOTH EVEN THOUGH IT'S BRAND-NEW.
THEY'RE RACING SLICKS MEANT FOR A RACE-TRACK.
AI-CHAN, IS THIS OKAY FOR THE FUEL?
PEE-NEW!
It's a precious... long-term storage gasoline alter... native.
CAN WE REALLY USE THIS STUFF?
AAALL RIGHTY! LET'S GET TO WORK!
ばっ
BA (FWP)
YEAH!
Yes.
AIRI-SAN, YOU... HANDLE THE TANK, PLEASE.
I GOT THIS.
IT'S SO LIGHT!

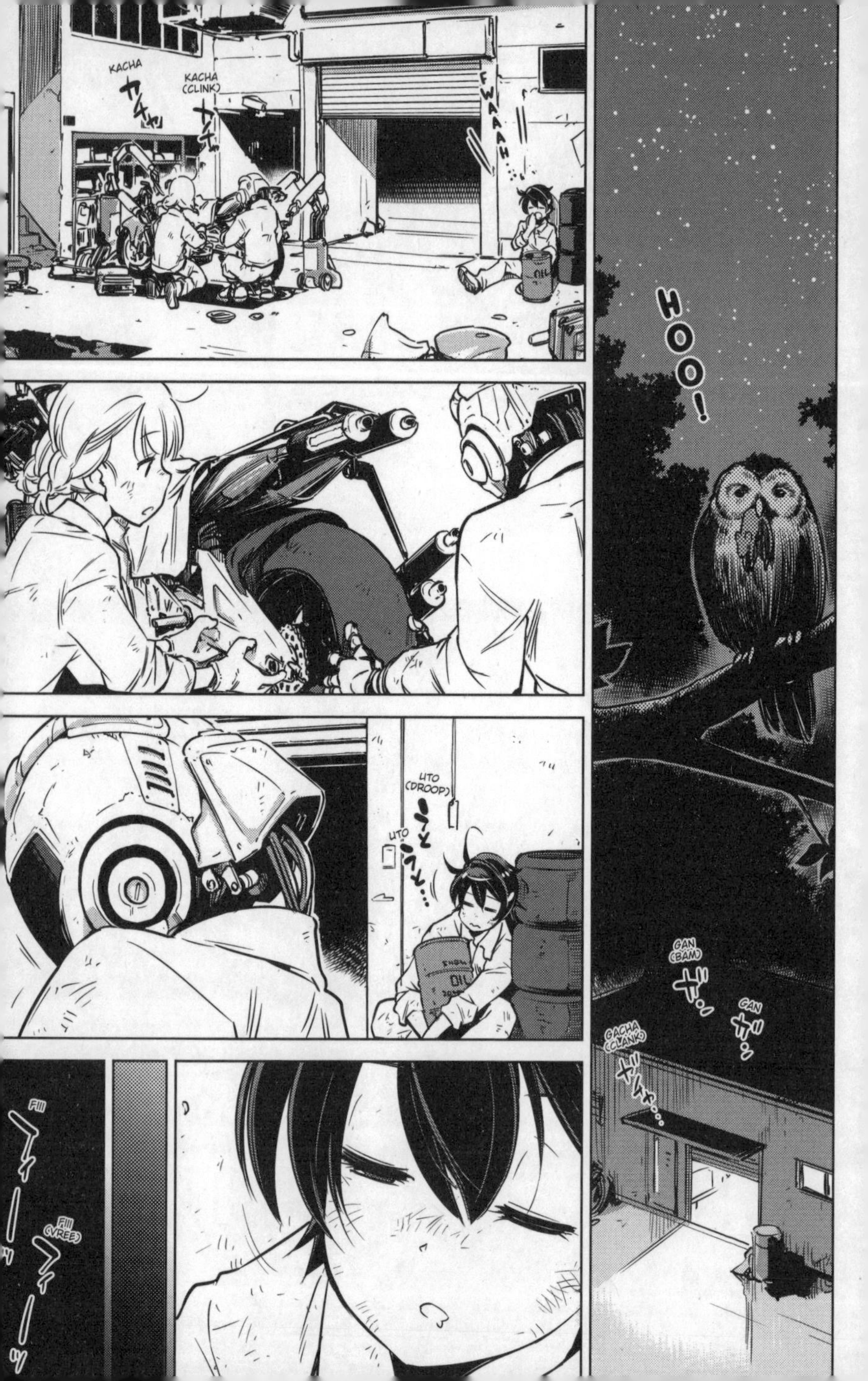
HOO!
GAN (BAM)
GAN
GACHA (CLANK)
FWAAAH
KACHA (CLINK)
KACHA
UTO (DROOP)
UTO
FIII (VREE)
FIII

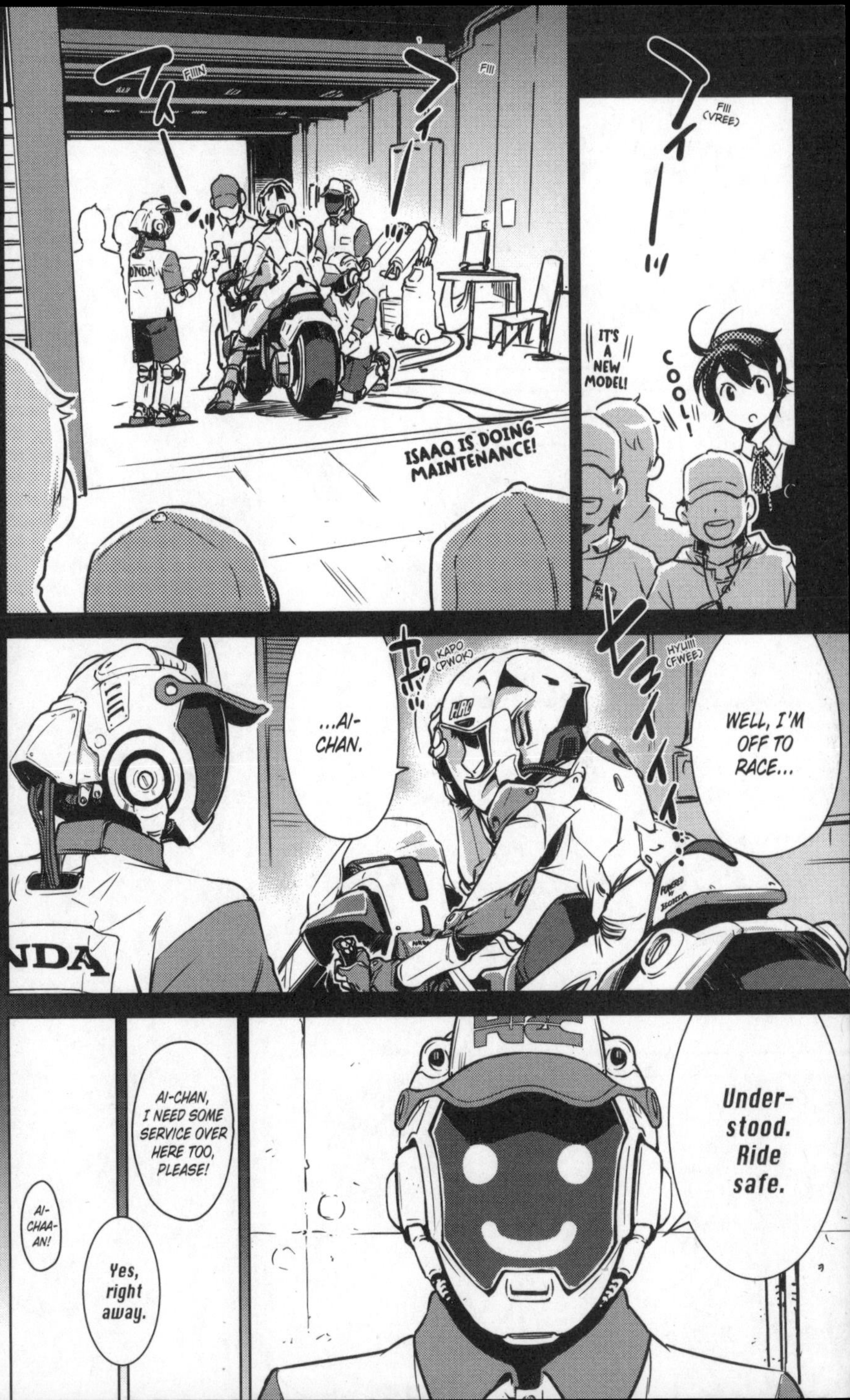
FIII (VREE)
IT'S A NEW MODEL!
COOL!
FIII
FIIIN
ISAAQ IS DOING MAINTENANCE!
HYUIII (FWEE)
WELL, I'M OFF TO RACE...
KAPO (PWOK)
...AI-CHAN.
Under-stood. Ride safe.
AI-CHAN, I NEED SOME SERVICE OVER HERE TOO, PLEASE!
AI-CHAA-AN!
Yes, right away.

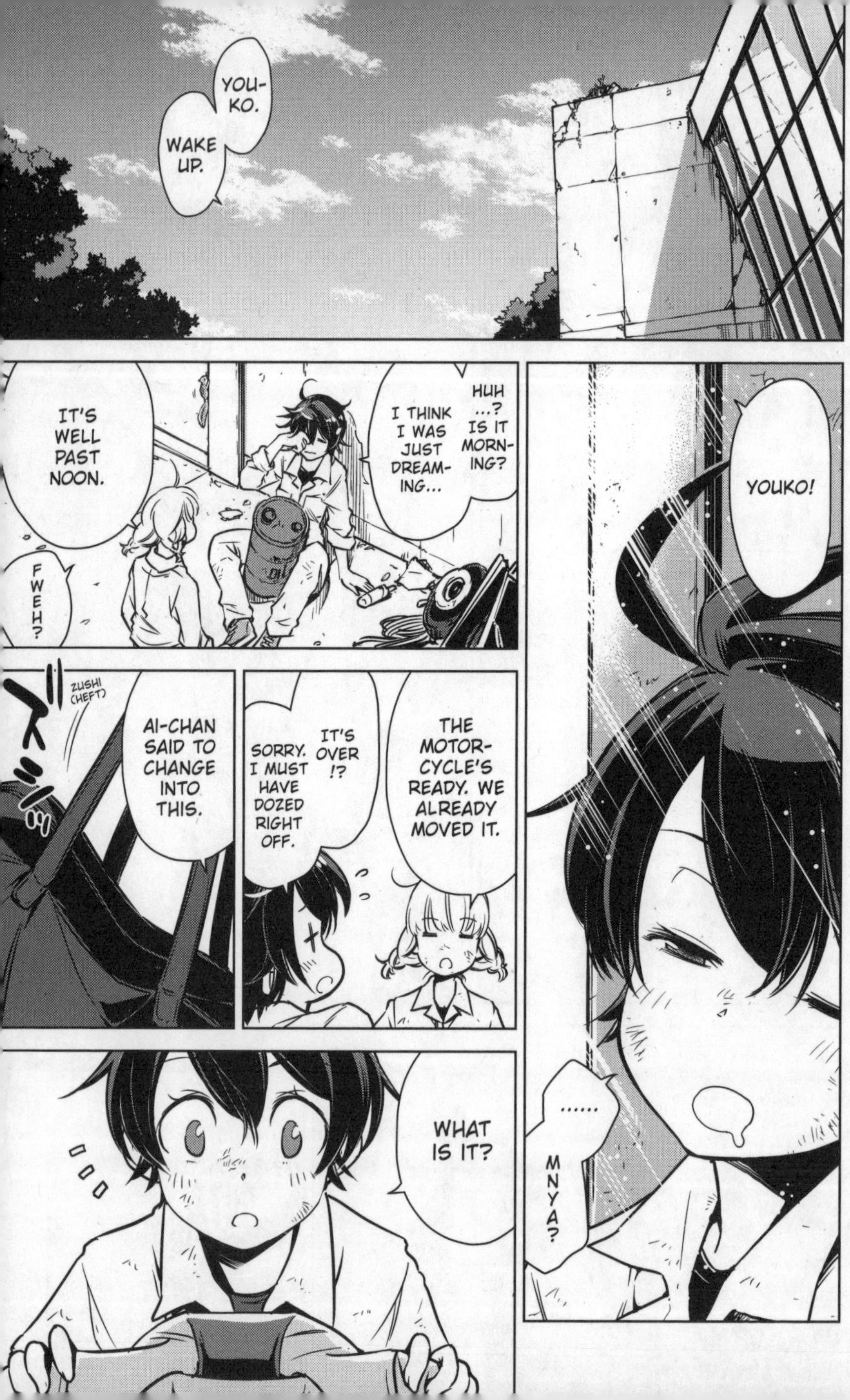
YOUKO.
WAKE UP.
YOUKO!
......
MNYA?
HUH ...? IS IT MORNING?
I THINK I WAS JUST DREAMING...
IT'S WELL PAST NOON.
FWEH?
THE MOTORCYCLE'S READY. WE ALREADY MOVED IT.
IT'S OVER !?
SORRY. I MUST HAVE DOZED RIGHT OFF.
AI-CHAN SAID TO CHANGE INTO THIS.
ZUSHI (HEFT)
WHAT IS IT?

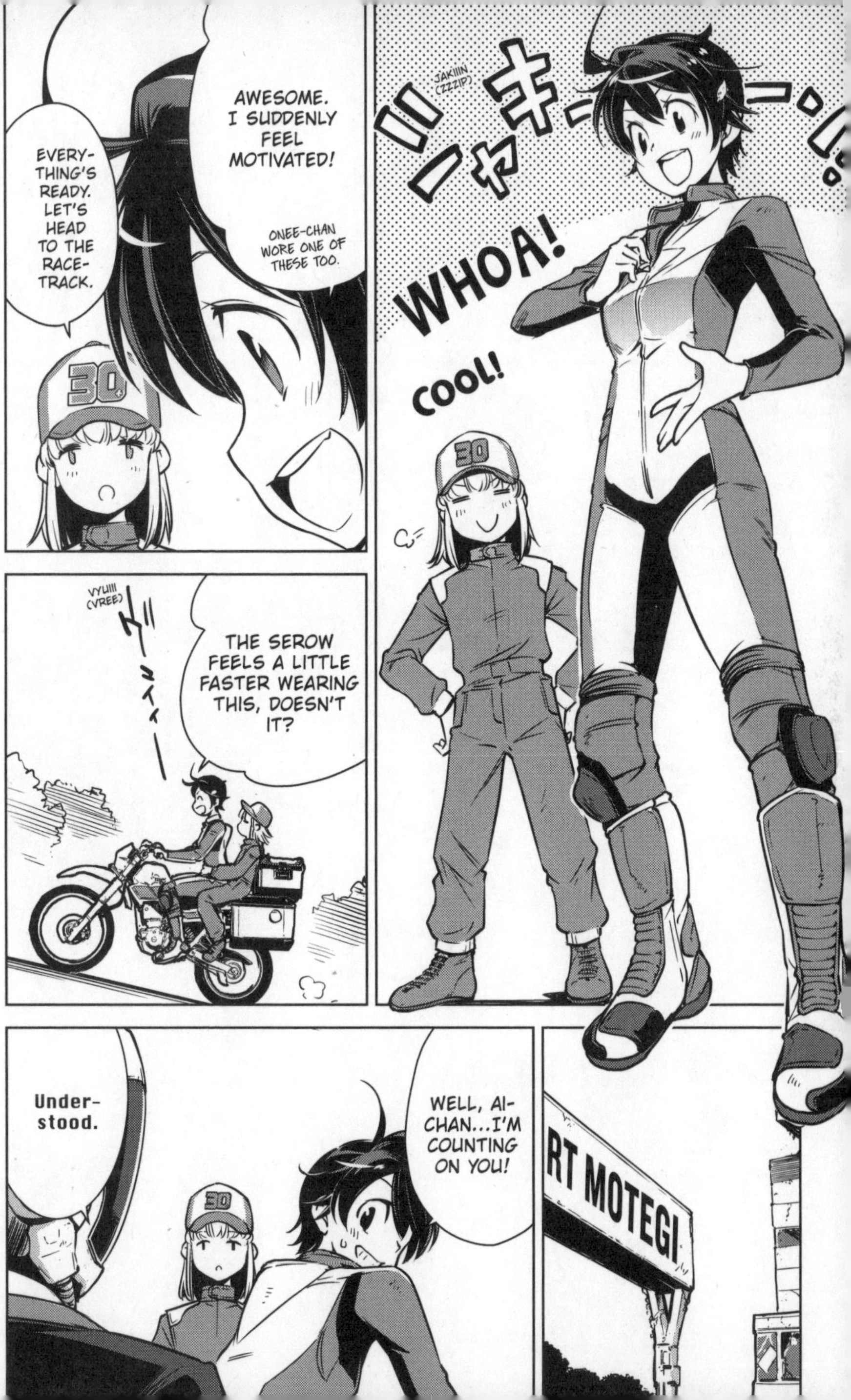
JAKIIIN (ZZZIP)
WHOA!
COOL!
AWESOME. I SUDDENLY FEEL MOTIVATED!
ONEE-CHAN WORE ONE OF THESE TOO.
EVERY-THING'S READY. LET'S HEAD TO THE RACE-TRACK.
VYUIII (VREE)
THE SEROW FEELS A LITTLE FASTER WEARING THIS, DOESN'T IT?
RT MOTEGI
WELL, AI-CHAN...I'M COUNTING ON YOU!
Under-stood.

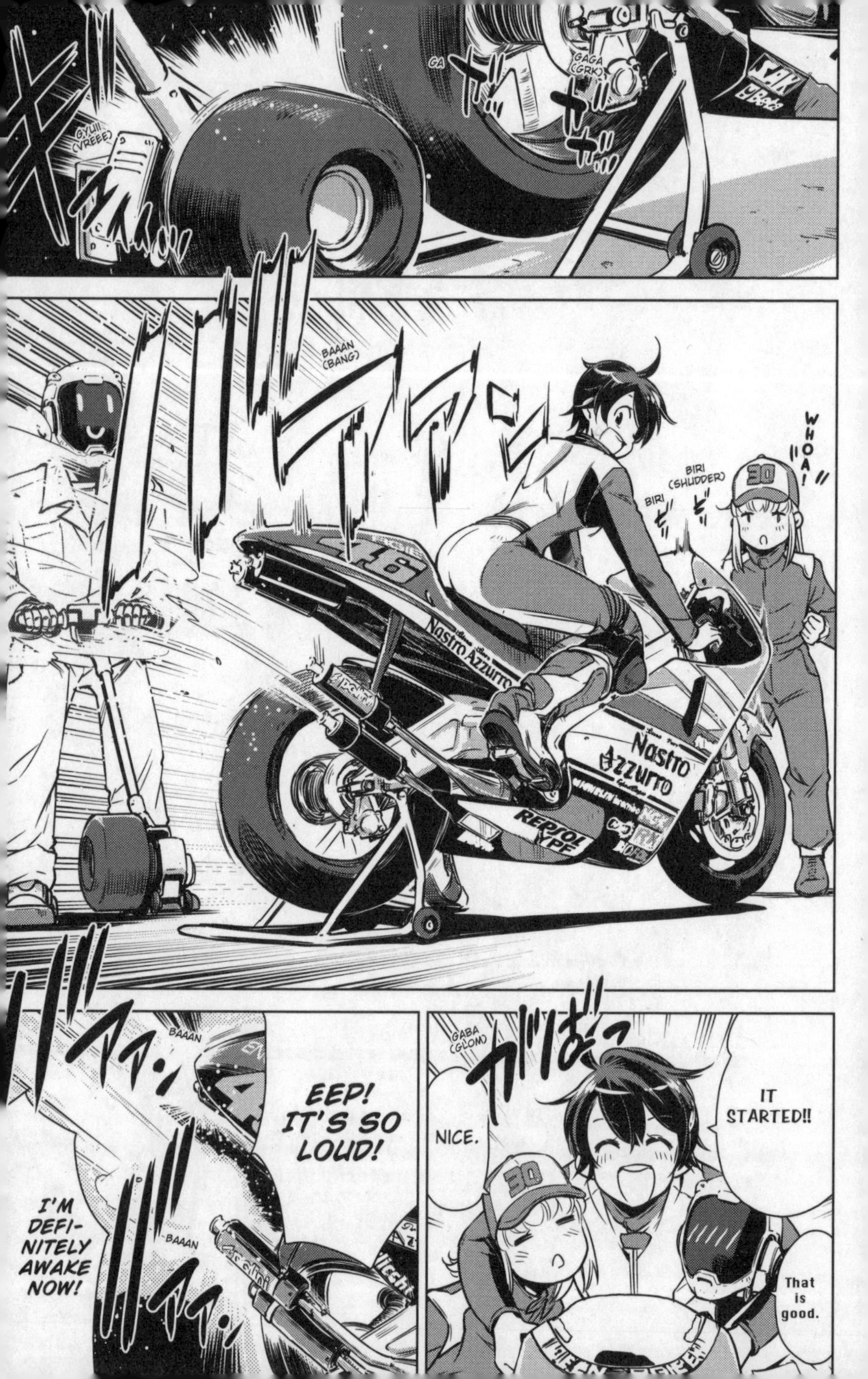
GAGA (GRK)
GA
GYUII (VREEE)
WHOA!!
BIRI (SHUDDER)
BIRI
BAAAN (BANG)
GABA (GLOM)
IT STARTED!!
NICE.
That is good.
BAAAN
EEP! IT'S SO LOUD!
BAAAN
I'M DEFI-NITELY AWAKE NOW!

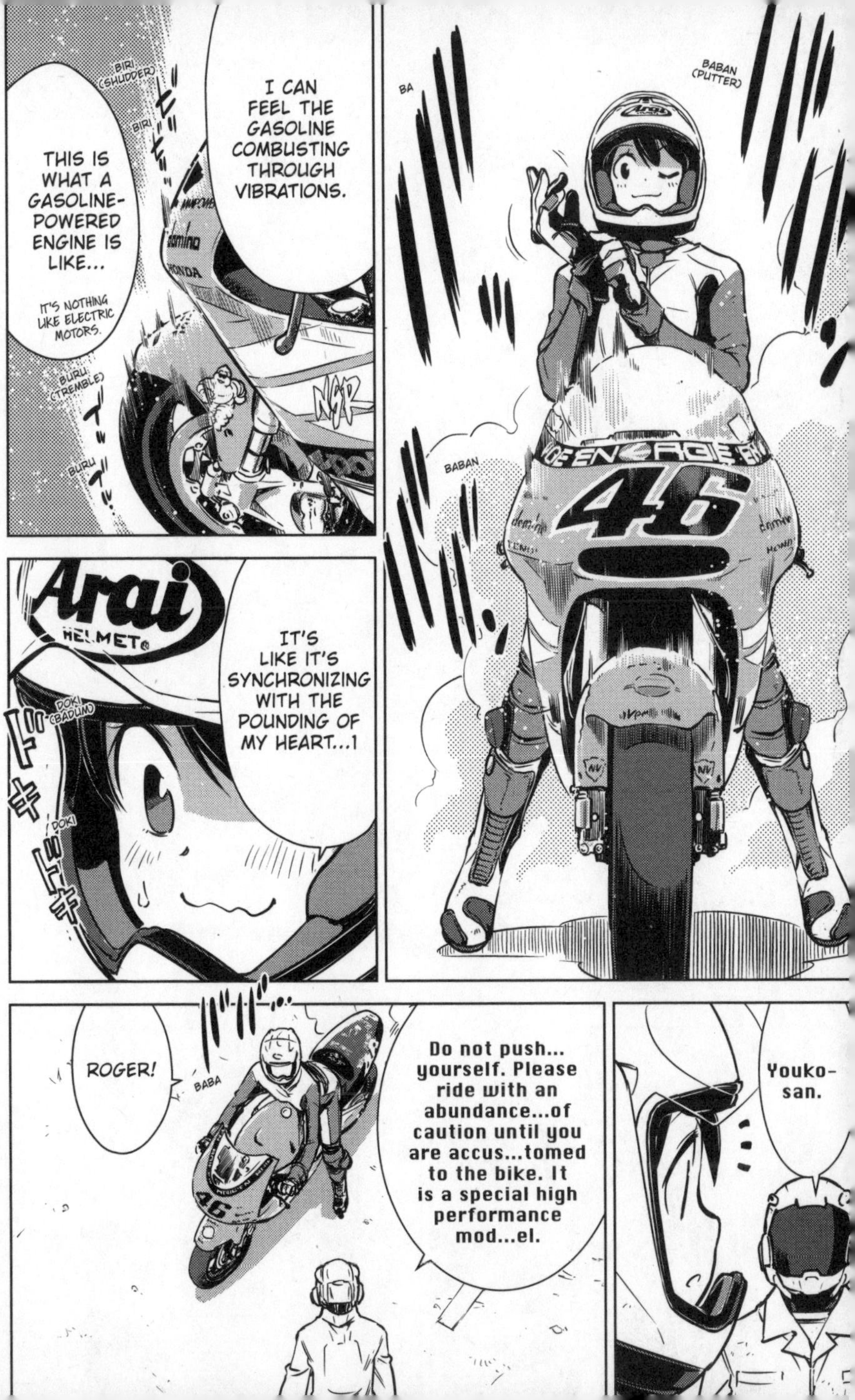

BABAN (PUTTER)
BA
BABAN
I CAN FEEL THE GASOLINE COMBUSTING THROUGH VIBRATIONS.
BIRI (SHUDDER)
BIRI
THIS IS WHAT A GASOLINE-POWERED ENGINE IS LIKE...
IT'S NOTHING LIKE ELECTRIC MOTORS.
BURU (TREMBLE)
BURU
IT'S LIKE IT'S SYNCHRONIZING WITH THE POUNDING OF MY HEART...!
Arai HELMET
DOKI (BADUM)
DOKI
Youko-san.
Do not push... yourself. Please ride with an abundance...of caution until you are accus...tomed to the bike. It is a special high performance mod...el.
ROGER!
BABA

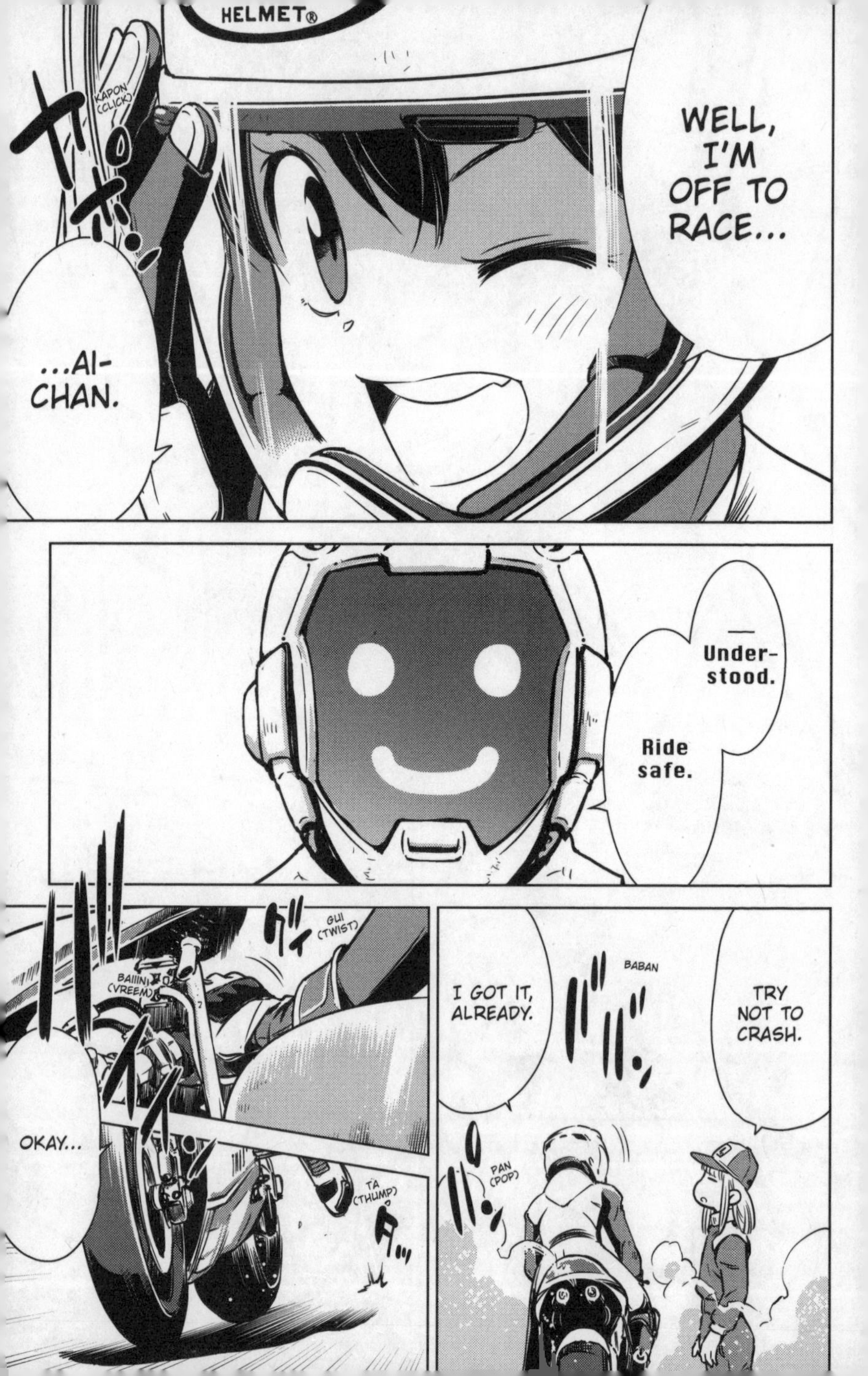
HELMET®
WELL, I'M OFF TO RACE...
KAPON (CLICK)
...AI-CHAN.
—Understood.
Ride safe.
TRY NOT TO CRASH.
BABAN
I GOT IT, ALREADY.
PAN (POP)
GUI (TWIST)
BAIIIN (VREEM)
OKAY...
TA (THUMP)

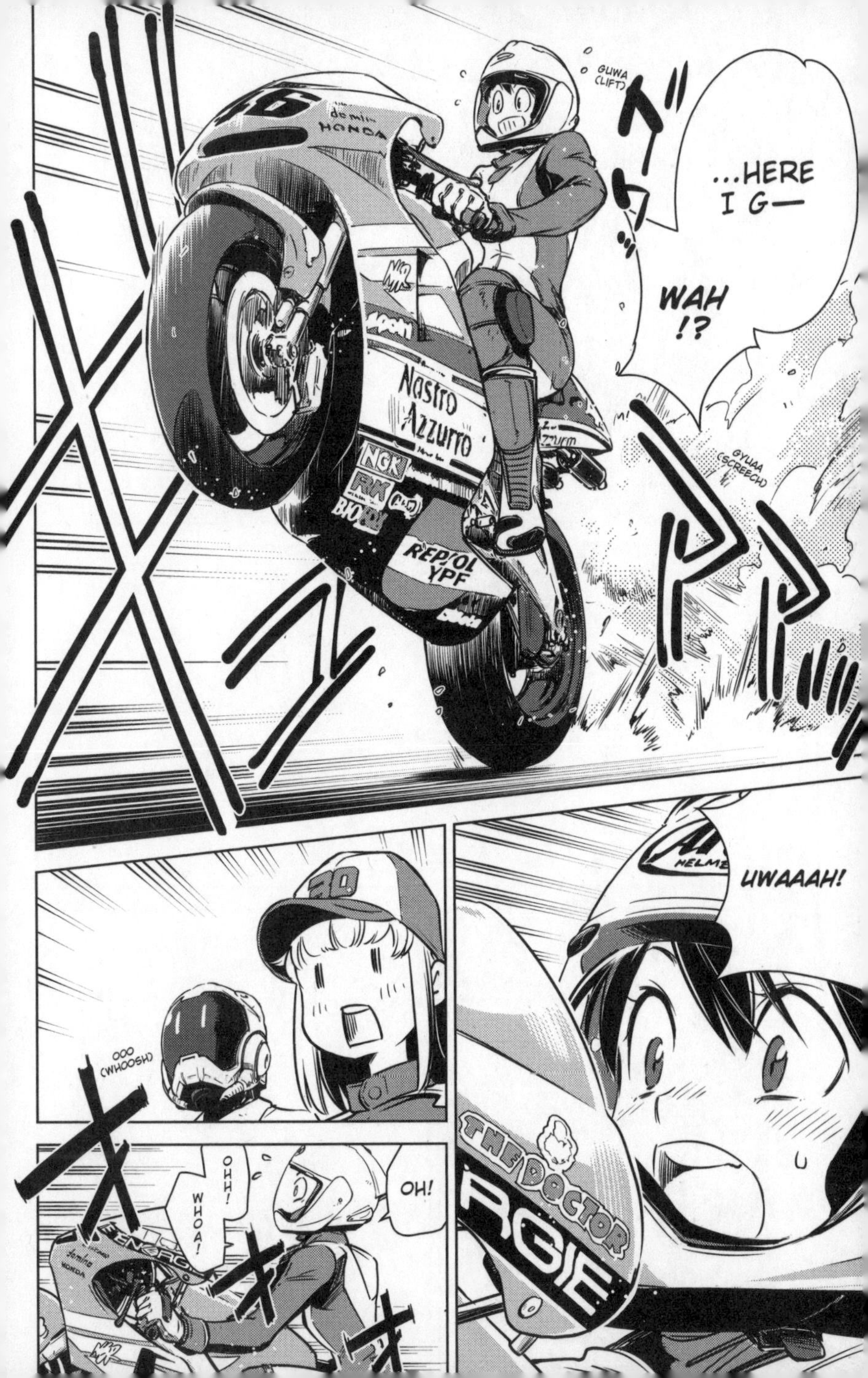
...HERE I G—
WAH !?
GUWA (LIFT)
GYUAA (SCREECH)
UWAAAH!
OOO (WHOOSH)
OH!
OHH!
WHOA!

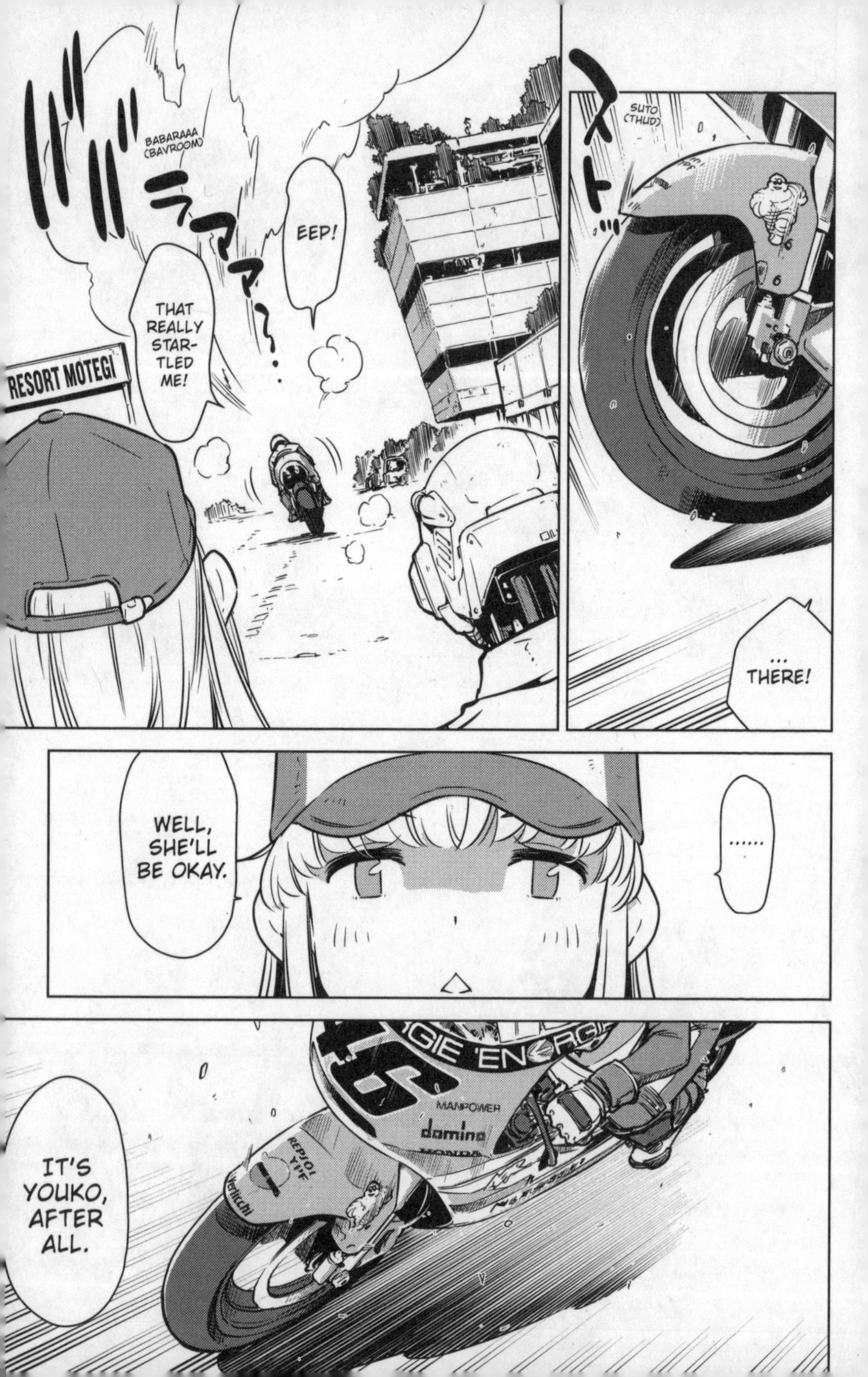
SUTO (THUD)
... THERE!
EEP!
BABARAAA (BAVROOM)
THAT REALLY STAR-TLED ME!
RESORT MOTEGI
......
WELL, SHE'LL BE OKAY.
MANPOWER
domino
IT'S YOUKO, AFTER ALL.

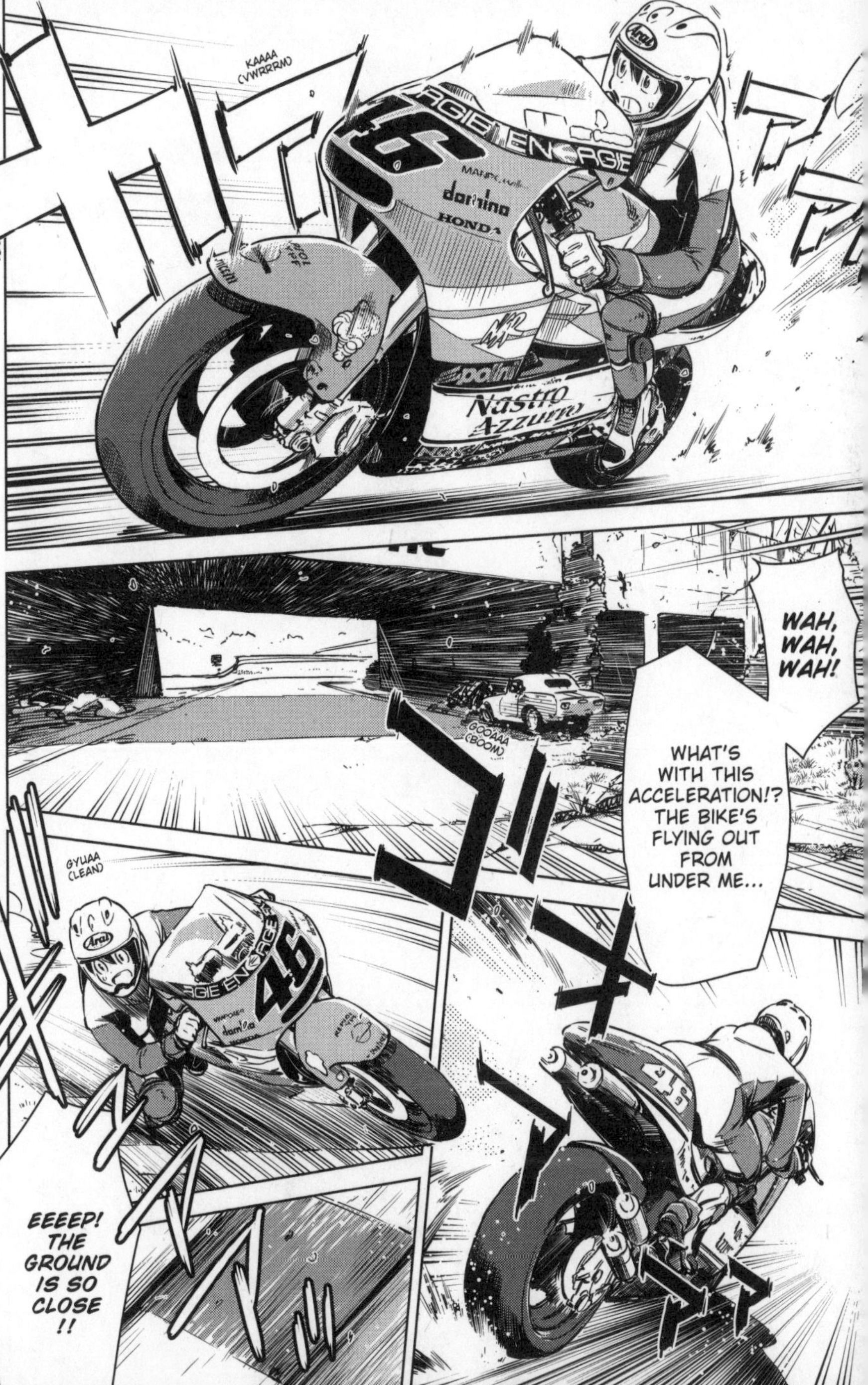
KAAAA (VWRRRM)
WAH, WAH, WAH!
GOOAAA (BOOM)
WHAT'S WITH THIS ACCELERATION!? THE BIKE'S FLYING OUT FROM UNDER ME...
GYUAA (LEAN)
EEEEP! THE GROUND IS SO CLOSE !!

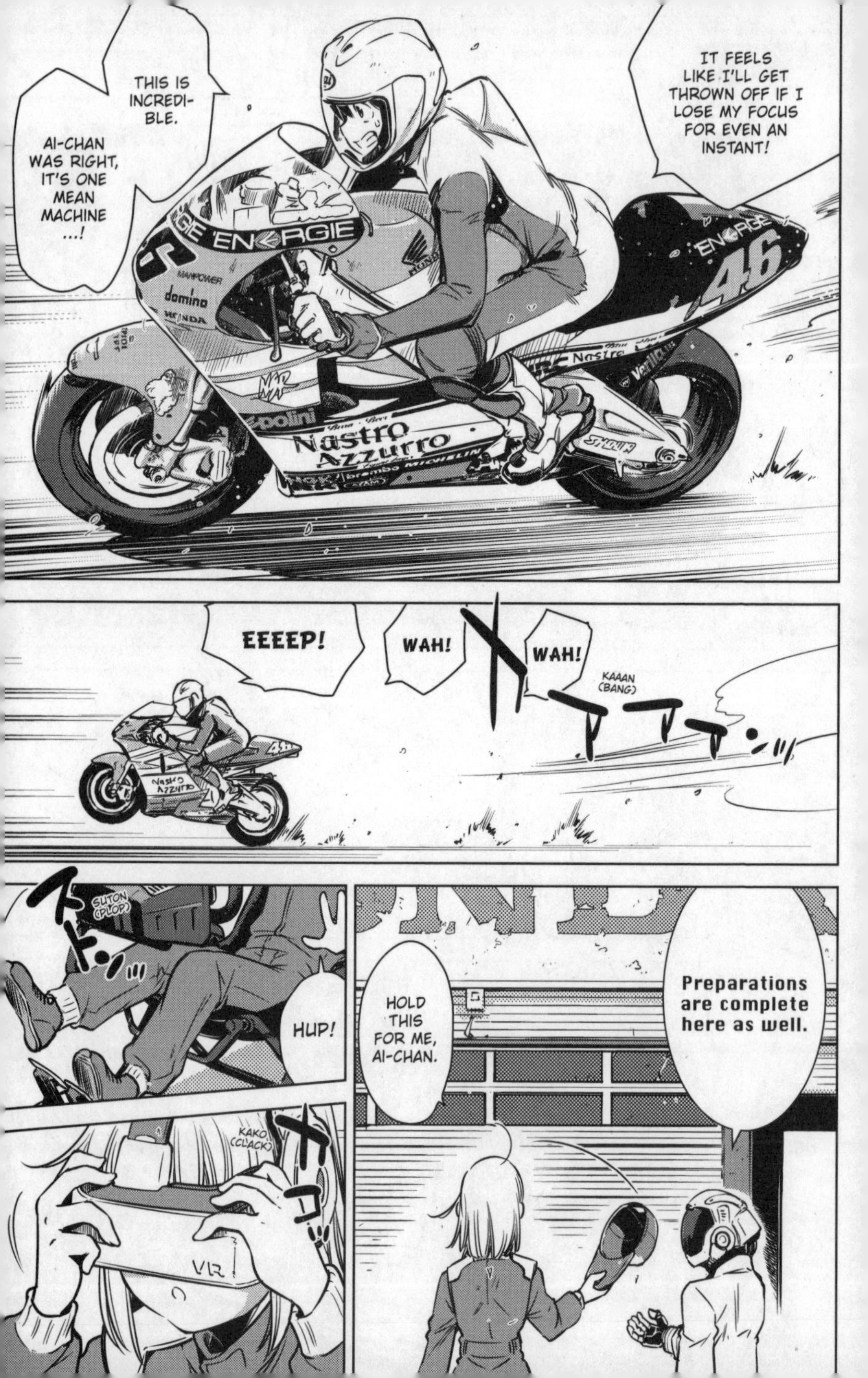
IT FEELS LIKE I'LL GET THROWN OFF IF I LOSE MY FOCUS FOR EVEN AN INSTANT!
THIS IS INCREDI-BLE.
AI-CHAN WAS RIGHT, IT'S ONE MEAN MACHINE ...!
KAAAN (BANG)
WAH!
WAH!
EEEEP!
Preparations are complete here as well.
HOLD THIS FOR ME, AI-CHAN.
SUTON (PLOP)
HUP!
KAKO (CLACK)
VR

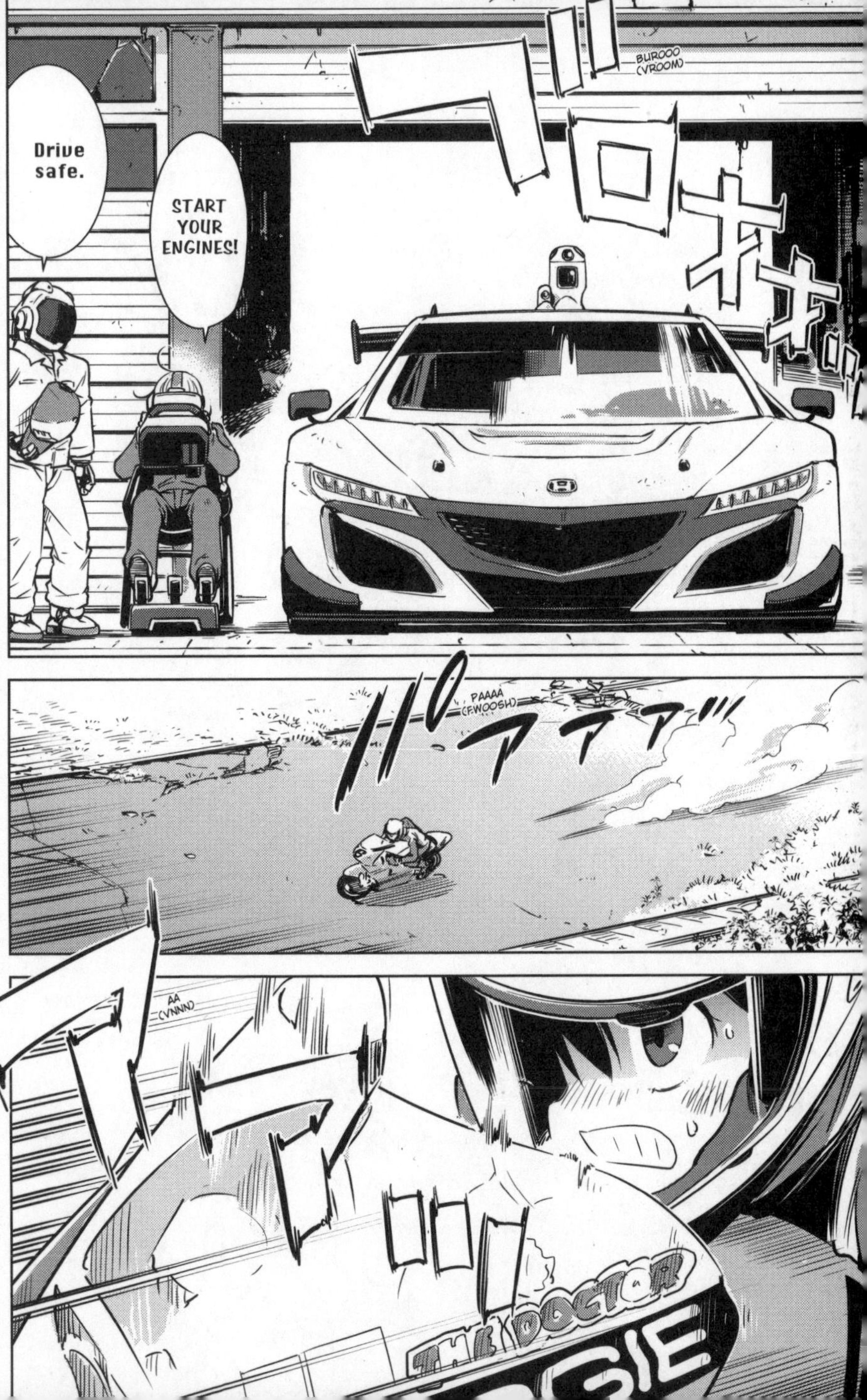
BUROOO (VROOM)
START YOUR ENGINES!
Drive safe.
PAAAA (F.WOOSH)
AA (VNNN)
THE DOCTOR

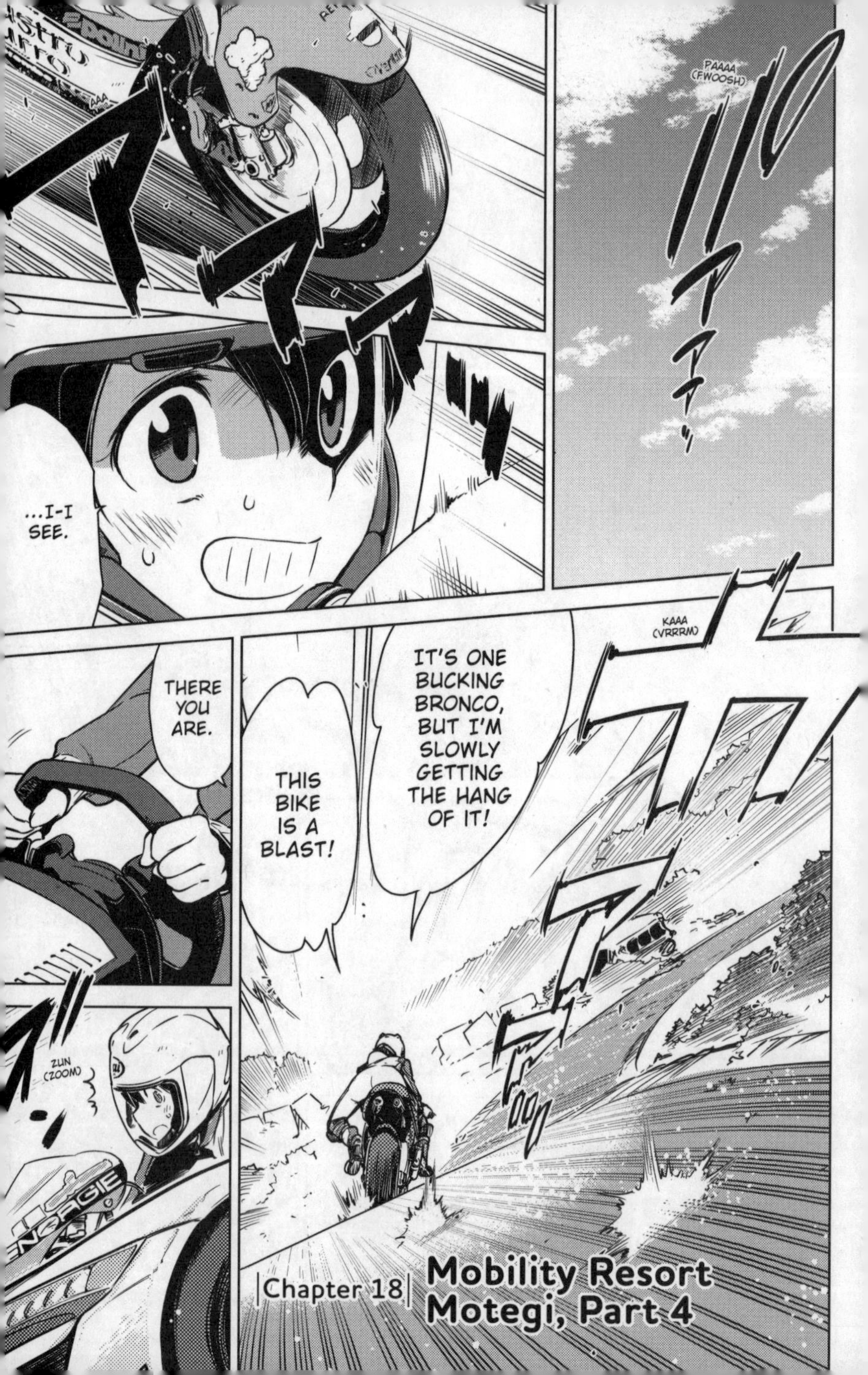
PAAAA (FWOOSH)
...I-I SEE.
KAAA (VRRRM)
IT'S ONE BUCKING BRONCO, BUT I'M SLOWLY GETTING THE HANG OF IT!
THIS BIKE IS A BLAST!
THERE YOU ARE.
ZUN (ZOOM)

Chapter 18 | Mobility Resort Motegi, Part 4

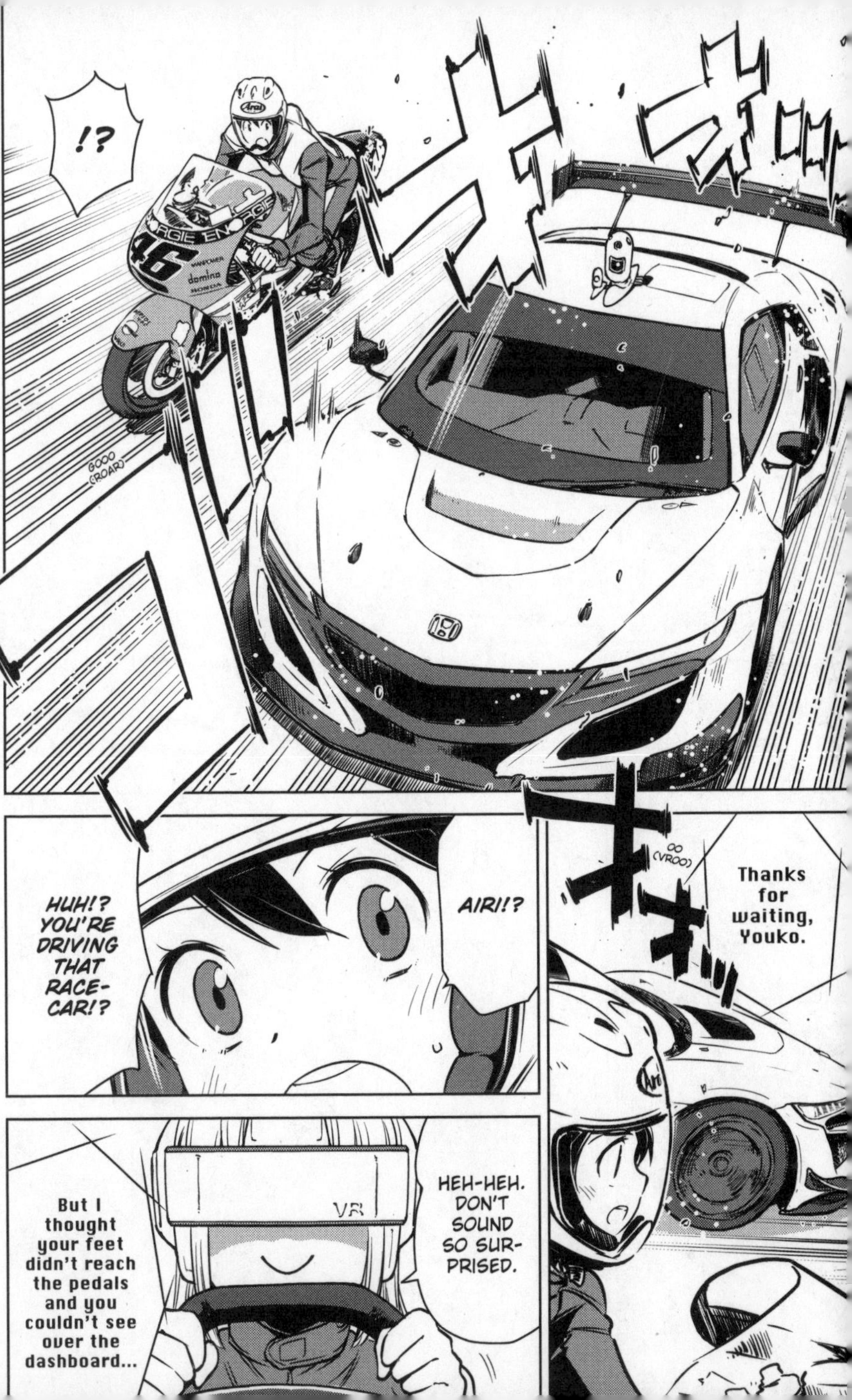
!?
GOOO (ROAR)
∞ (VROO)
Thanks for waiting, Youko.
AIRI!?
HUH!? YOU'RE DRIVING THAT RACE-CAR!?
HEH-HEH. DON'T SOUND SO SURPRISED.
But I thought your feet didn't reach the pedals and you couldn't see over the dashboard...

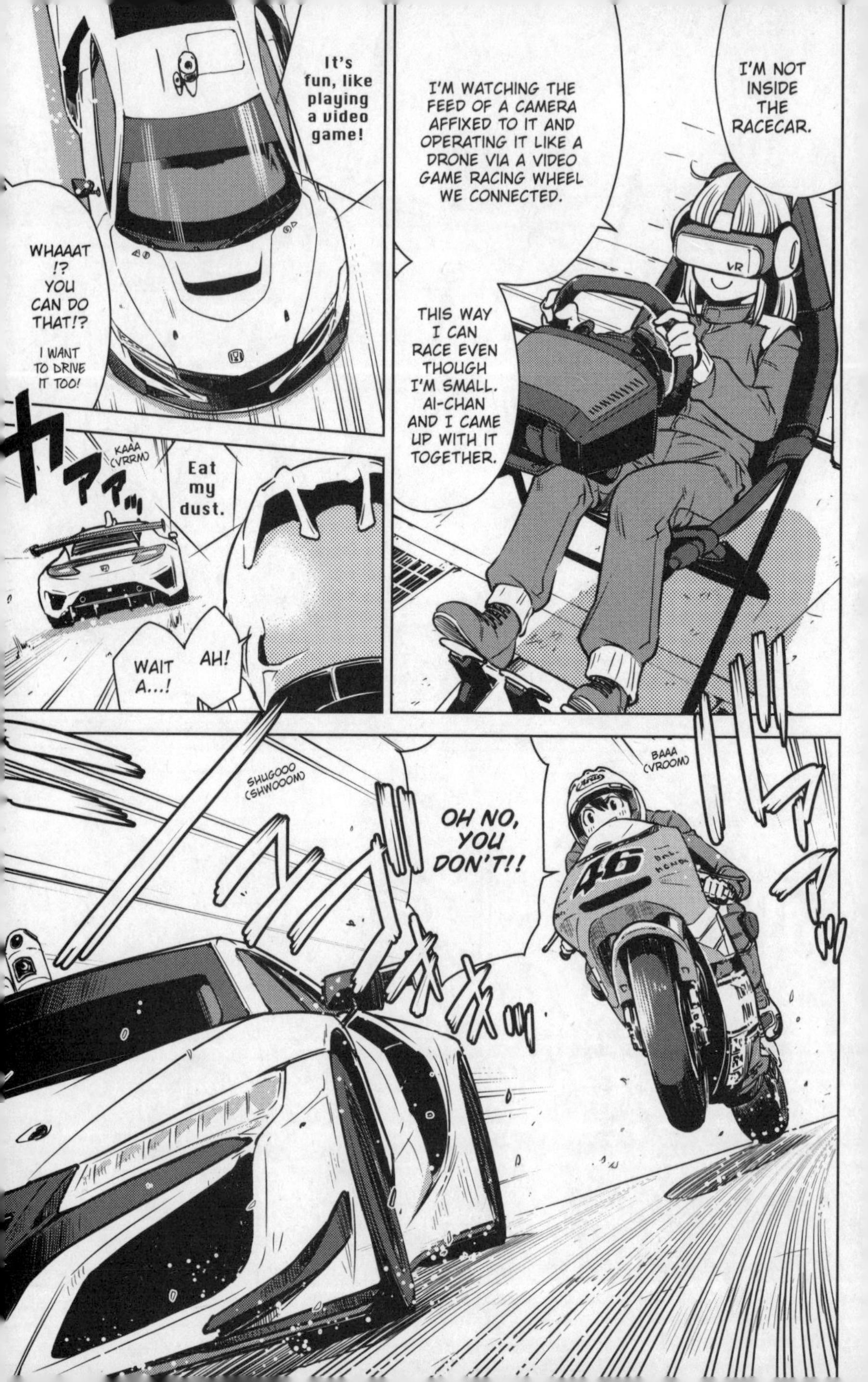
I'M NOT INSIDE THE RACECAR.
I'M WATCHING THE FEED OF A CAMERA AFFIXED TO IT AND OPERATING IT LIKE A DRONE VIA A VIDEO GAME RACING WHEEL WE CONNECTED.
THIS WAY I CAN RACE EVEN THOUGH I'M SMALL. AI-CHAN AND I CAME UP WITH IT TOGETHER.
It's fun, like playing a video game!
WHAAAT!? YOU CAN DO THAT!?
I WANT TO DRIVE IT TOO!
KAAA (VRRM)
Eat my dust.
AH!
WAIT A...!
BAAA (VROOM)
OH NO, YOU DON'T!!
SHUGOOO (SHWOOOM)

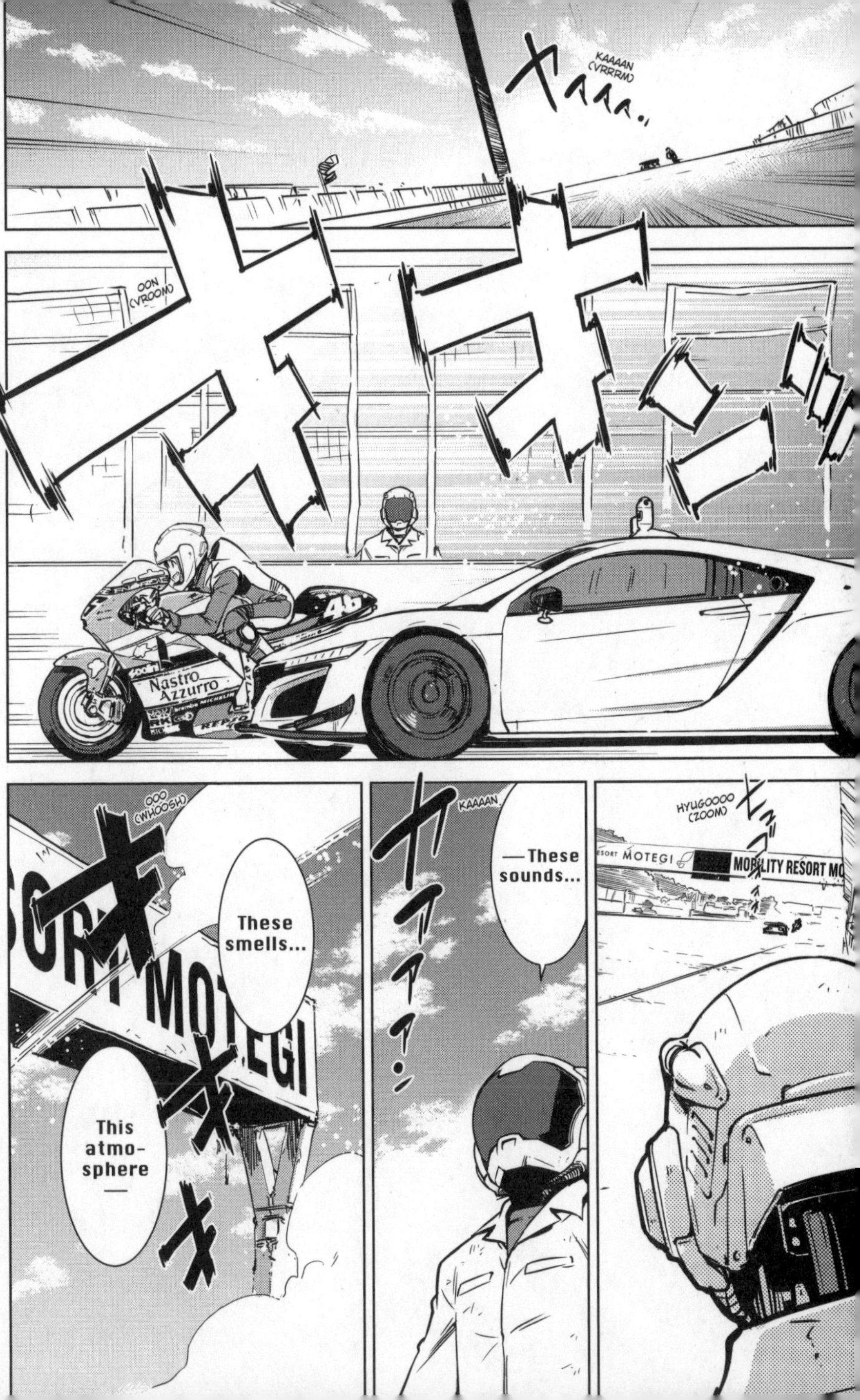
KAAAAN (VRRRM)
OON (VROOM)
Nastro Azzurro
HYUGOOOO (ZOOM)
RESORT MOTEGI
MOBILITY RESORT MO
KAAAAN
—These sounds...
OOO (WHOOSH)
These smells...
This atmo- sphere —
MOTEGI

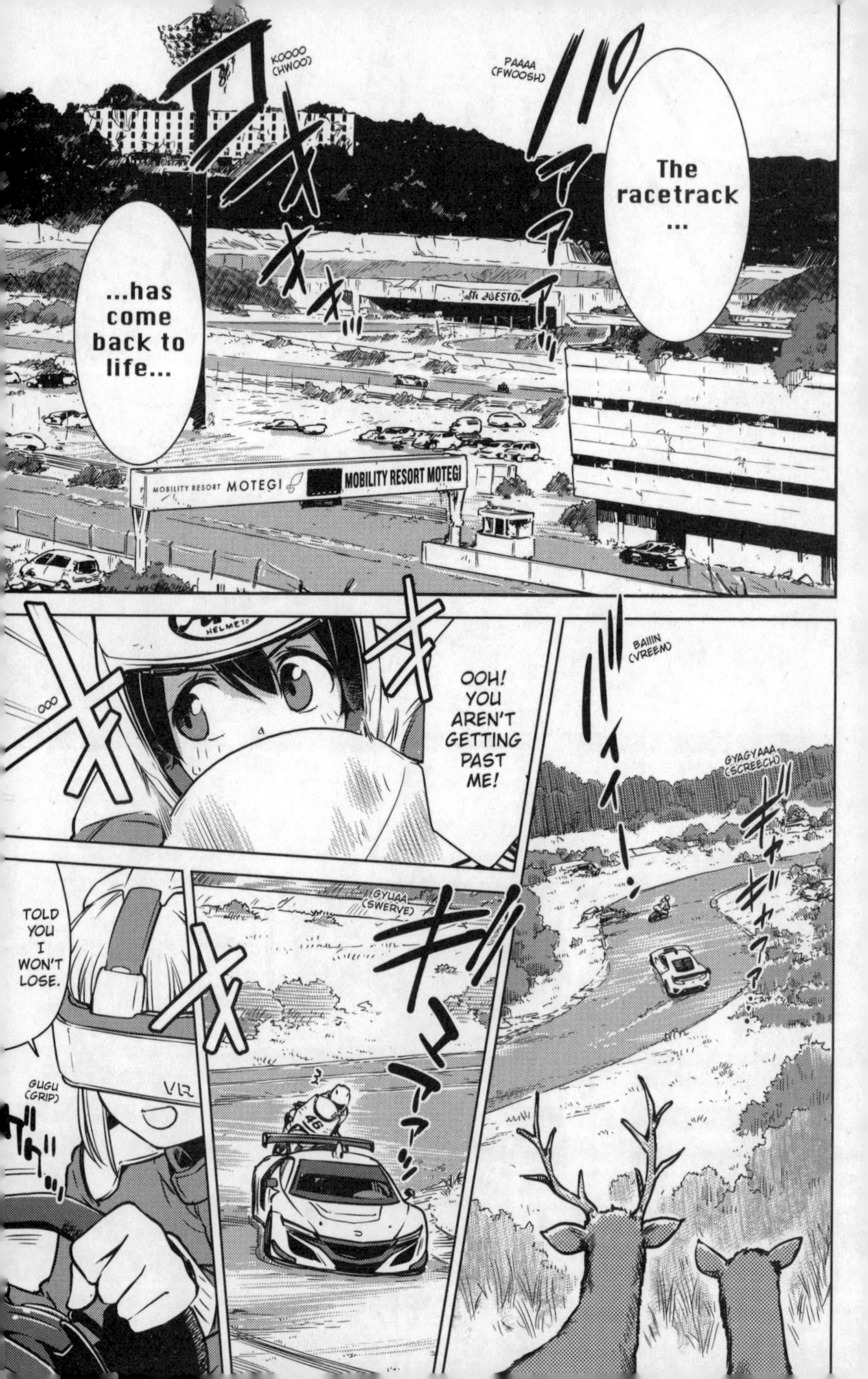
PAAAA (FWOOSH)
The racetrack ...
KOOOO (HWOO)
...has come back to life...
MOBILITY RESORT MOTEGI [redacted] MOBILITY RESORT MOTEGI
BAIIIN (VREEM)
GYAGYAAA (SCREECH)
OOO
OOH! YOU AREN'T GETTING PAST ME!
GYUAA (SWERVE)
TOLD YOU I WON'T LOSE.
GUGU (GRIP)

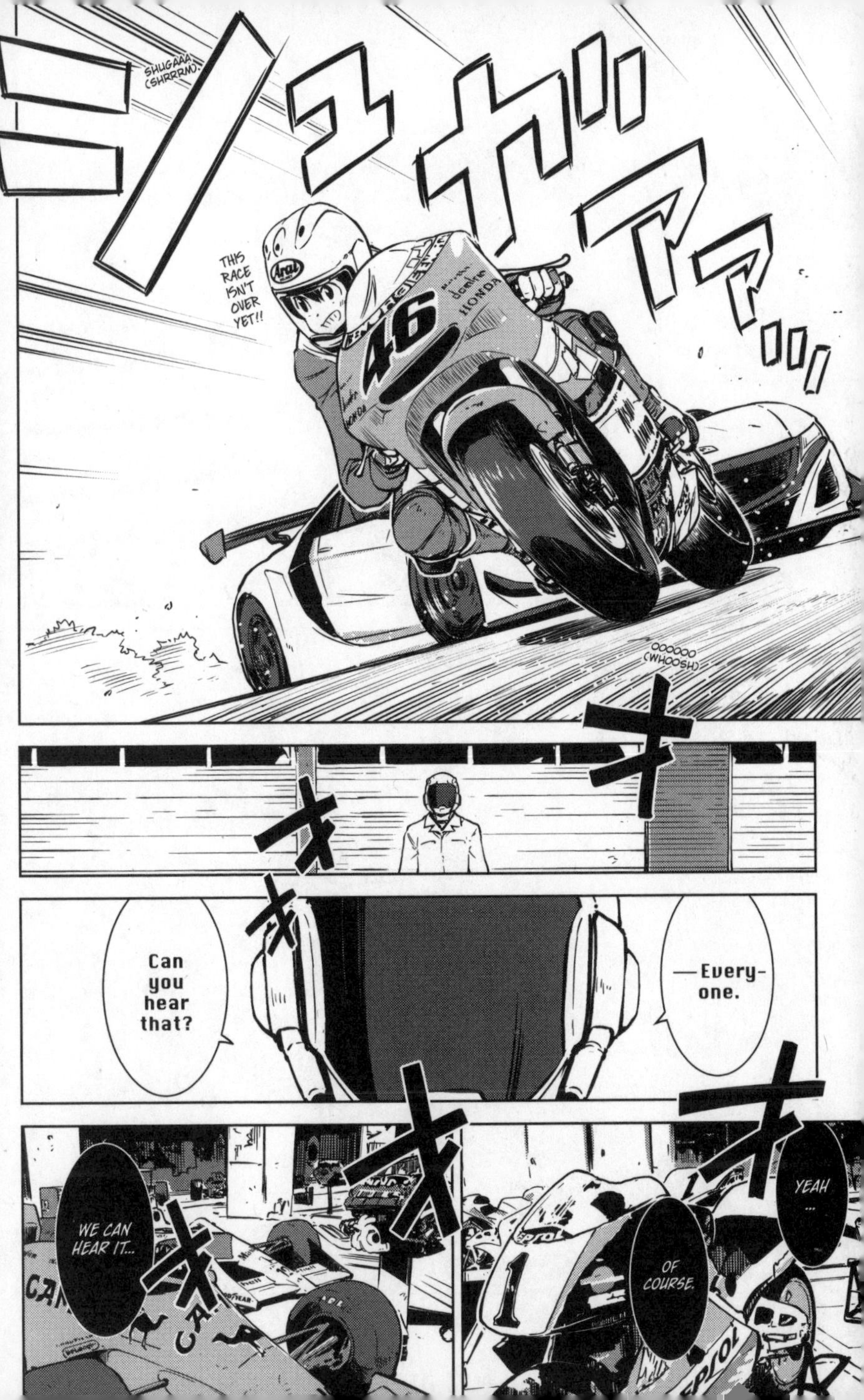
SHUGAAA (SHRRRM)
THIS RACE ISN'T OVER YET!!
OOOOOO (WHOOSH)
—Every-one.
Can you hear that?
YEAH ...
OF COURSE.
WE CAN HEAR IT...

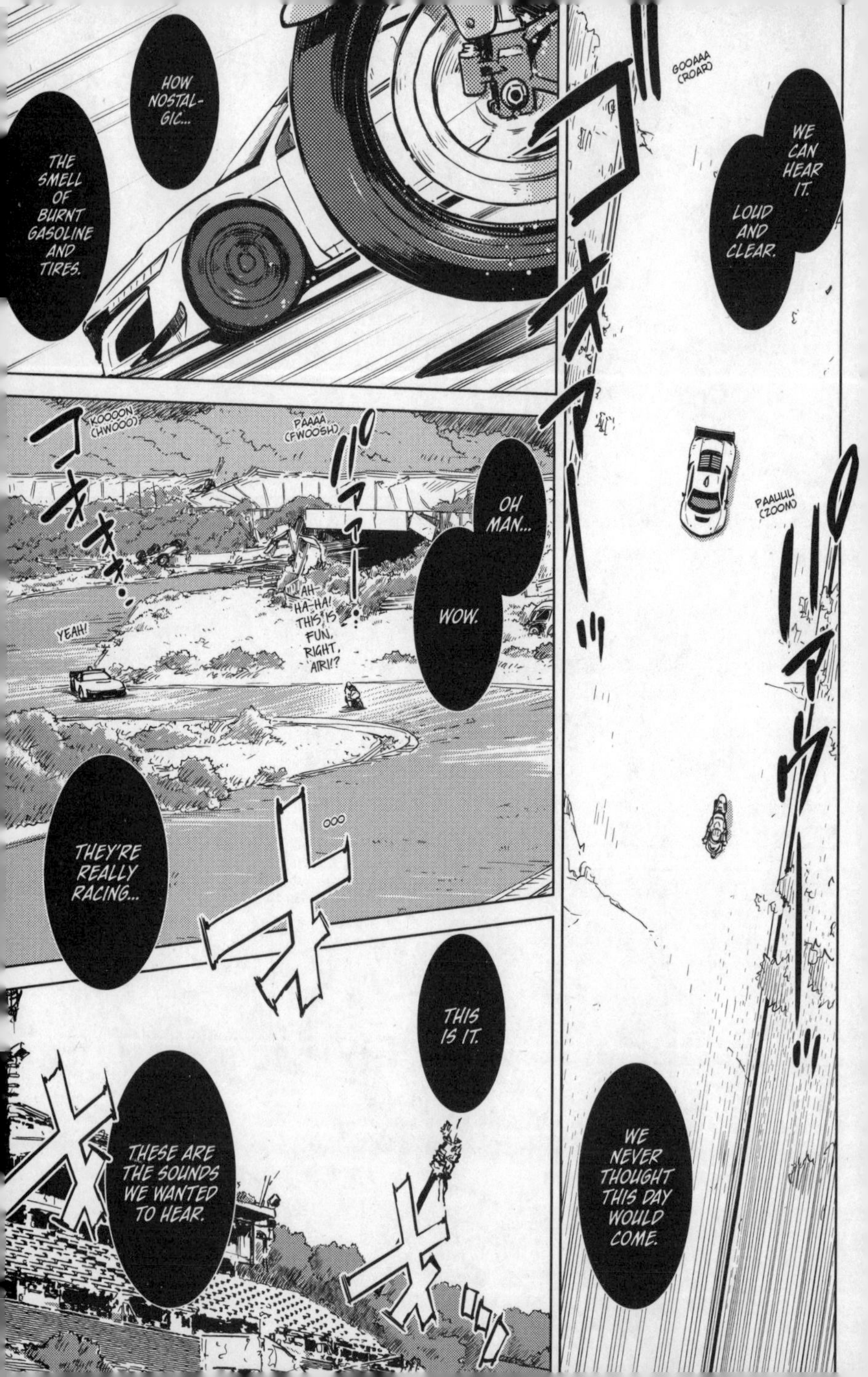
GOOOAAA (ROAR)
WE CAN HEAR IT.
LOUD AND CLEAR.
PAAUUU (ZOOM)
WE NEVER THOUGHT THIS DAY WOULD COME.
HOW NOSTAL-GIC...
THE SMELL OF BURNT GASOLINE AND TIRES.
PAAAA (FWOOSH)
KOOOON (HWOOO)
OH MAN...
WOW.
AH-HA-HA! THIS IS FUN, RIGHT, AIRI!?
YEAH!
THEY'RE REALLY RACING...
OOO
THIS IS IT.
THESE ARE THE SOUNDS WE WANTED TO HEAR.

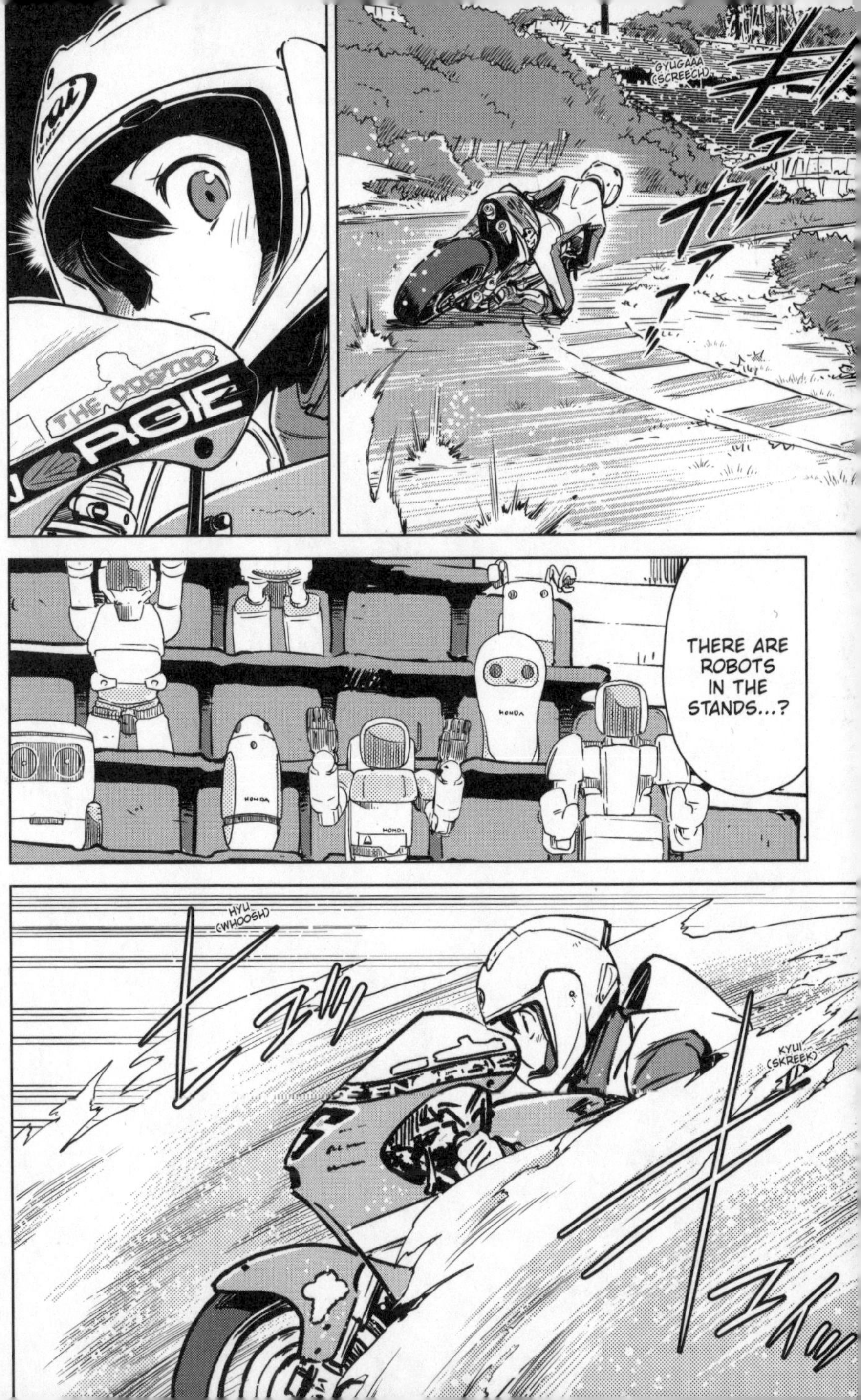
GYUGAAA (SCREECH)
THERE ARE ROBOTS IN THE STANDS...?
HYU (WHOOSH)
KYUI (SKREEK)

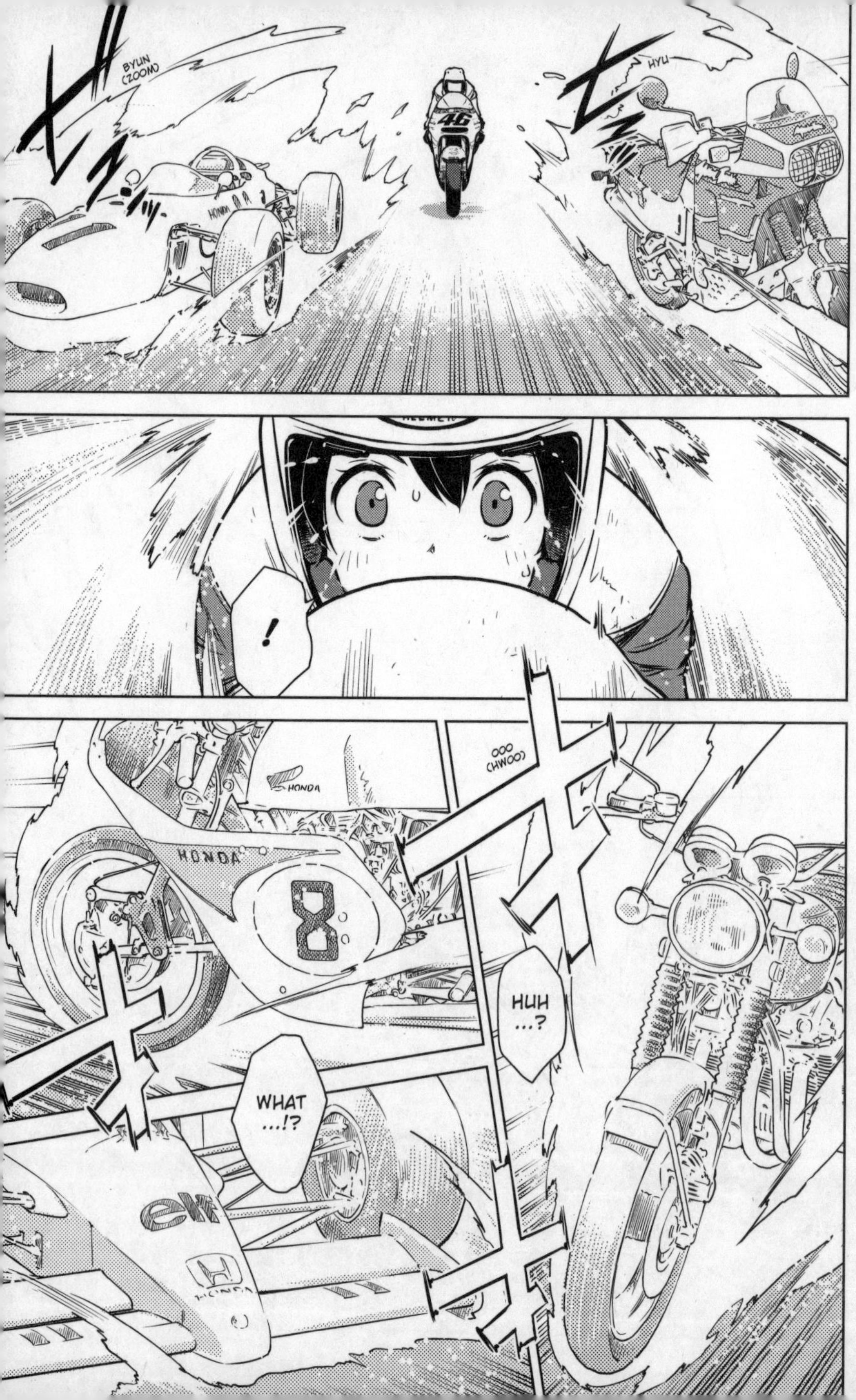
HYU
BYUN (ZOOM)
!
OOO (HWOO)
HUH ...?
WHAT ...!?

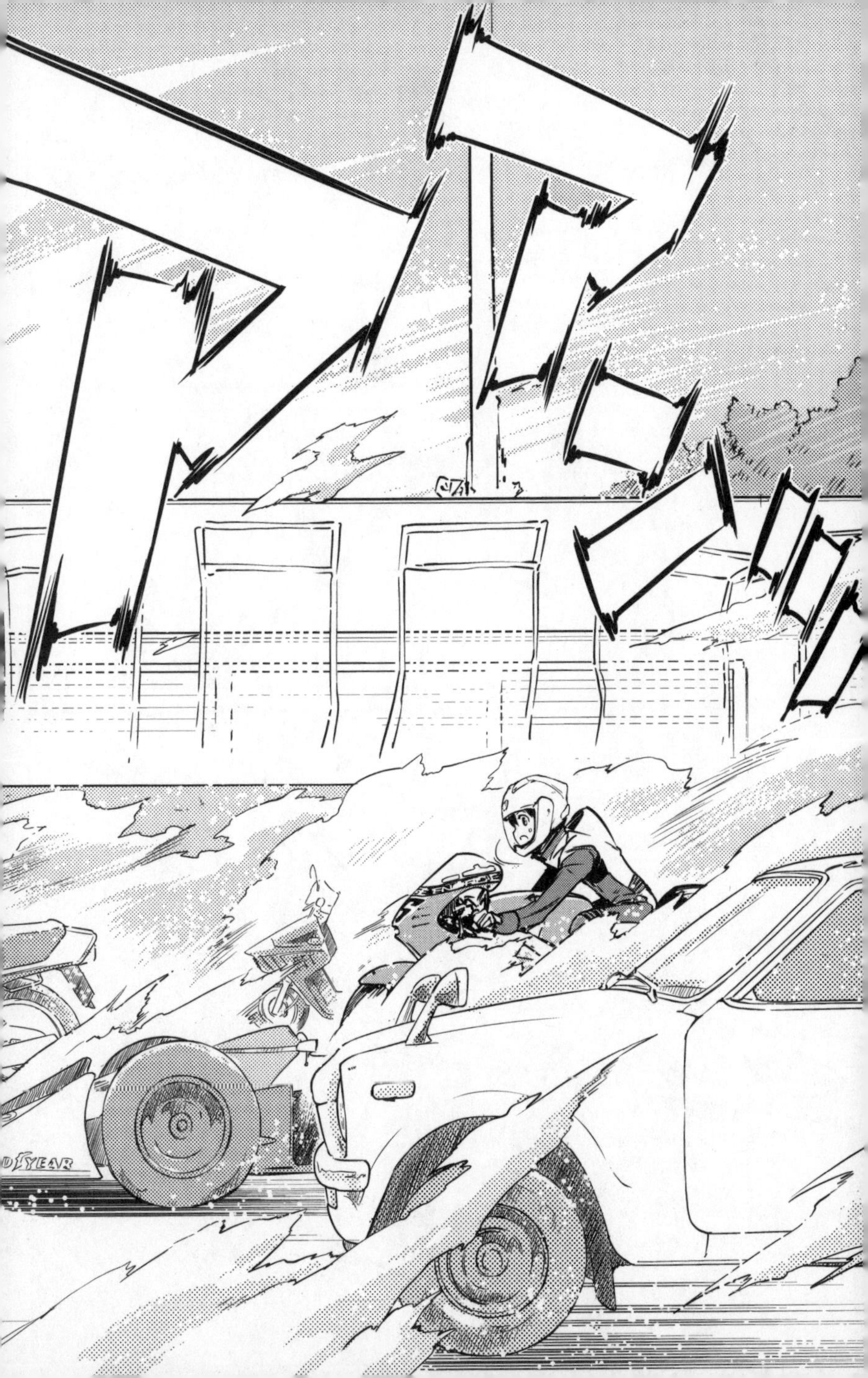

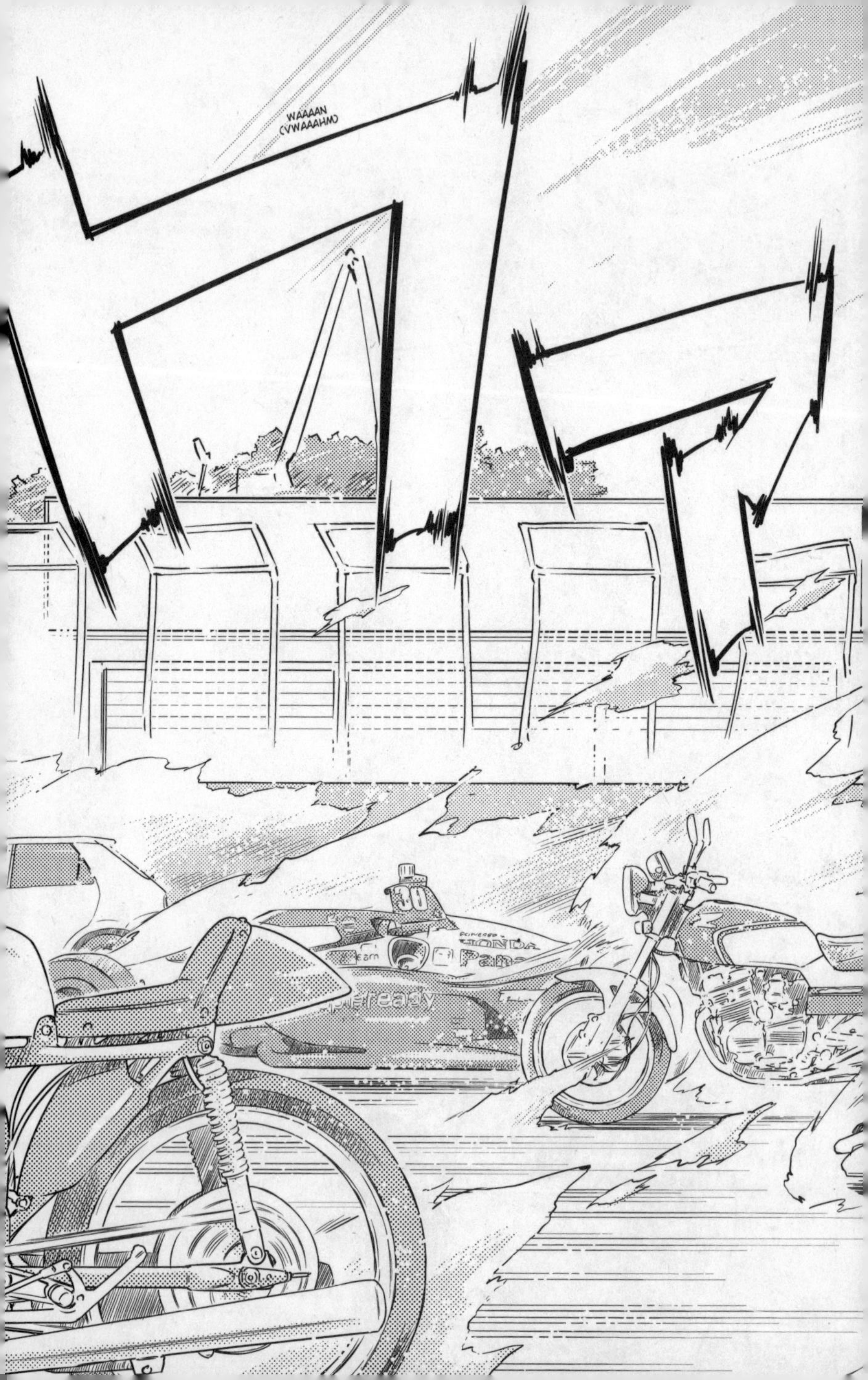
WAAAAN
(VWAAAHM)
HONDA

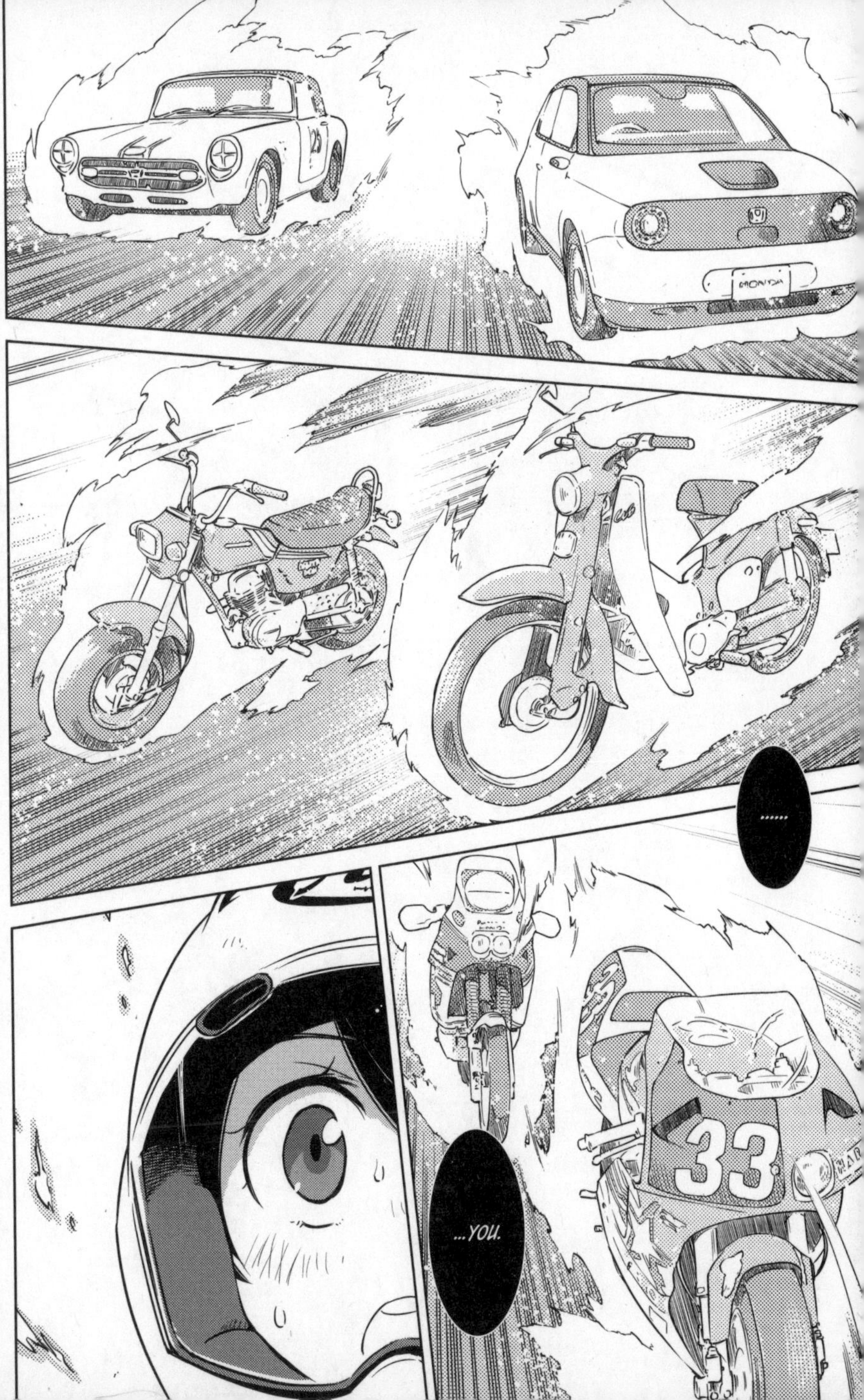
HONDA
......
...YOU.

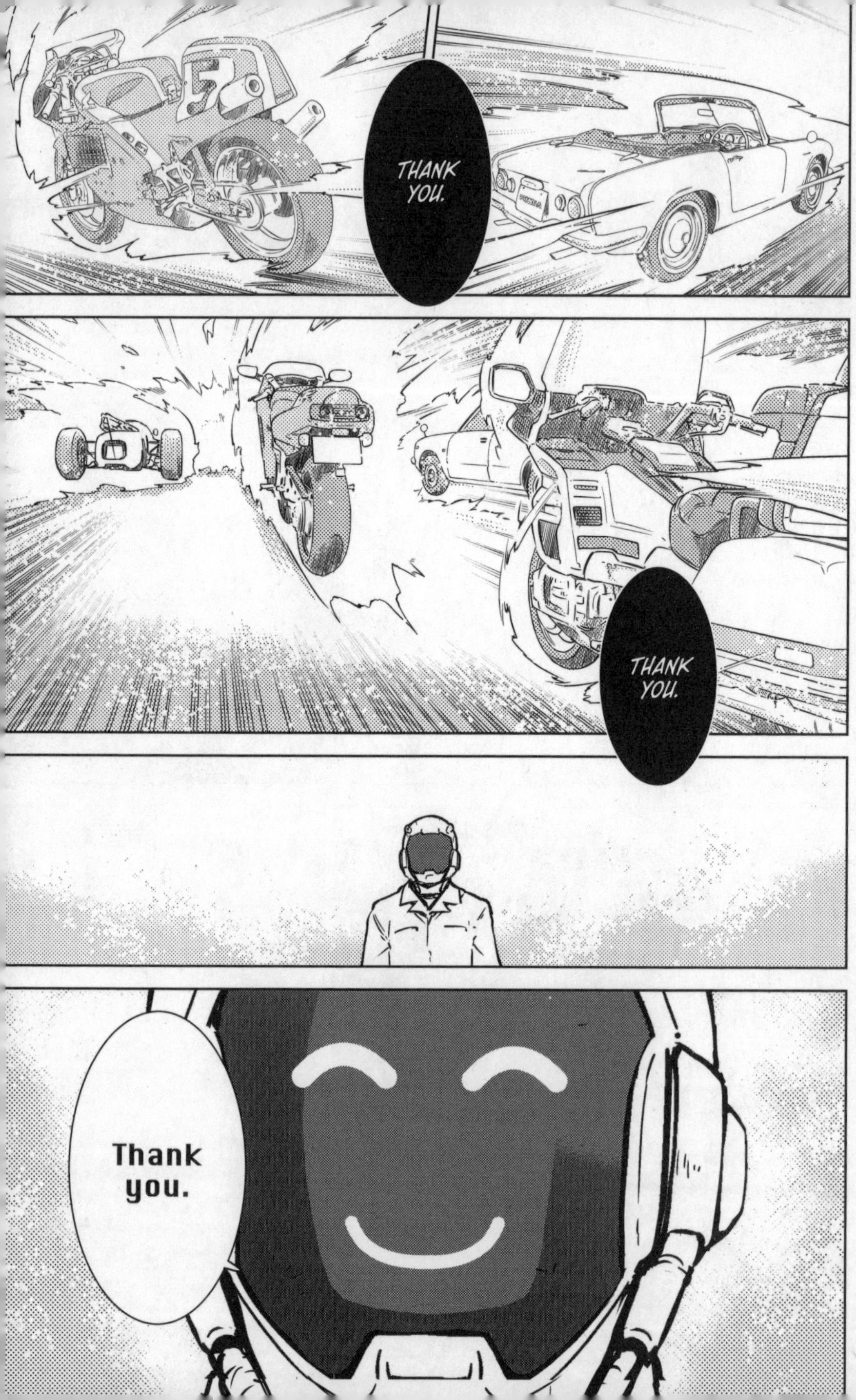
THANK YOU.
THANK YOU.
Thank you.

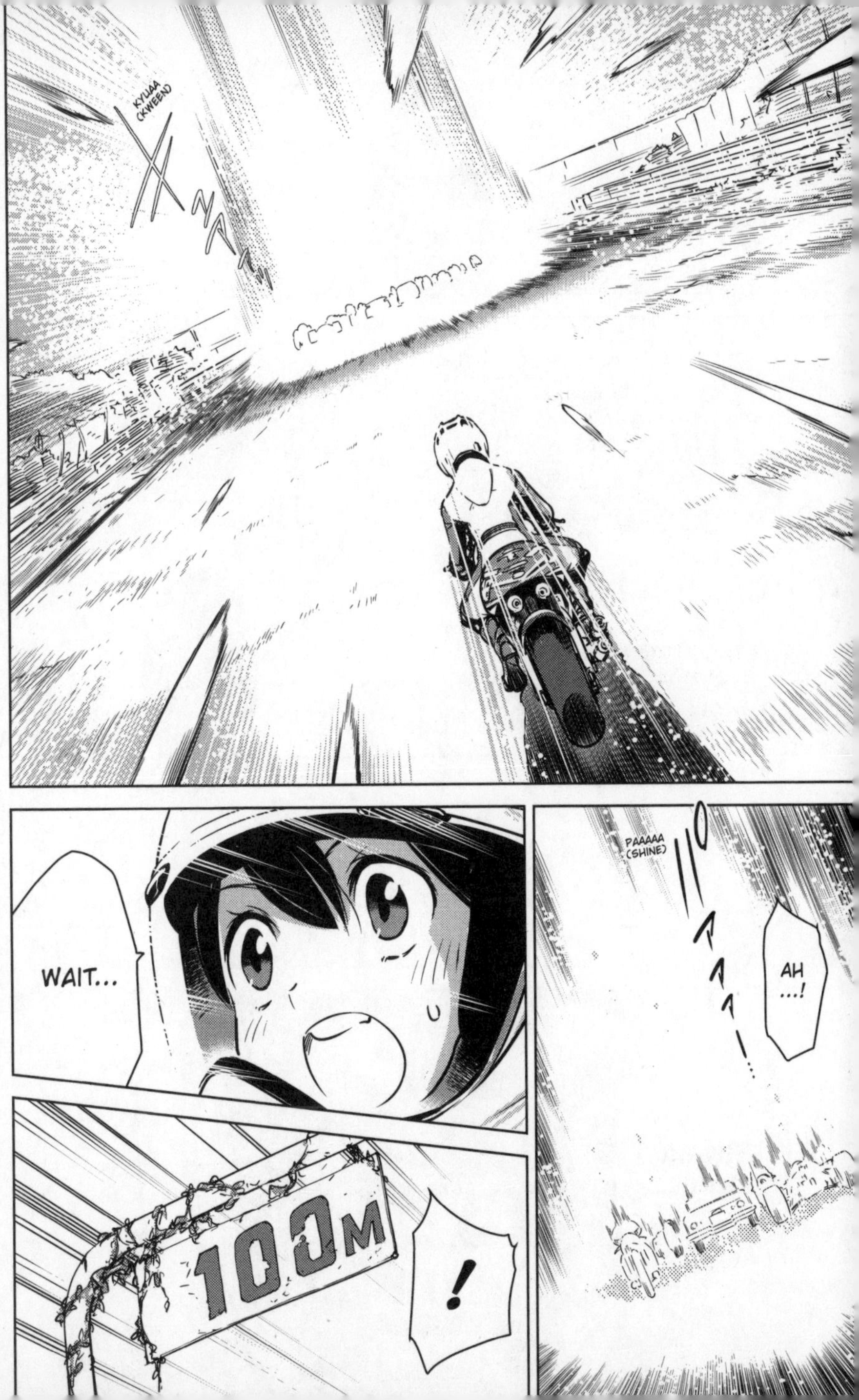
KYUAA (KWEEN)
PAAAAA (SHINE)
AH ...!
WAIT...
100M
!

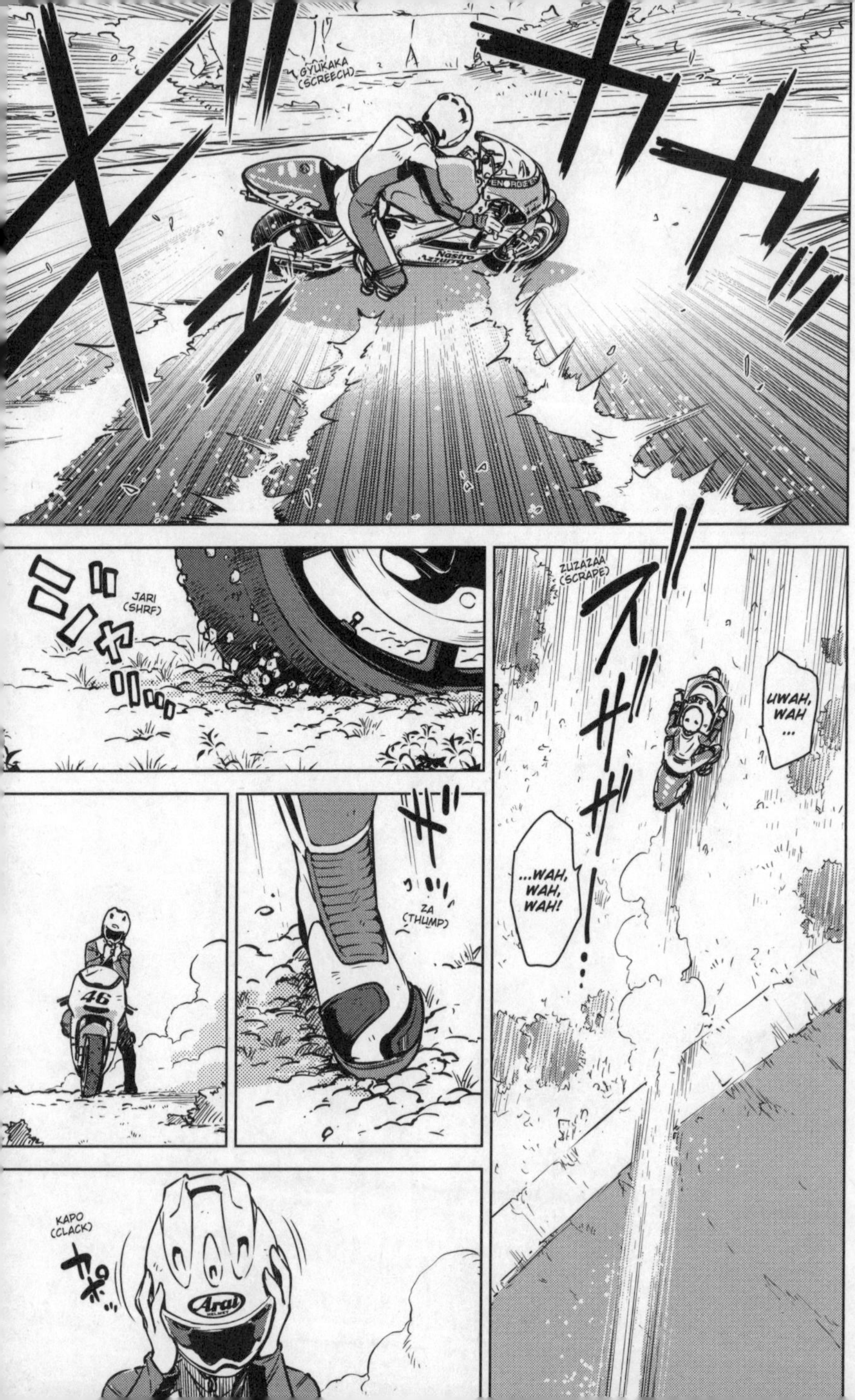
GYUKAKA (SCREECH)
ZUZAZAA (SCRAPE)
UWAH, WAH ...
...WAH, WAH, WAH!
JARI (SHRF)
ZA (THUMP)
KAPO (CLACK)

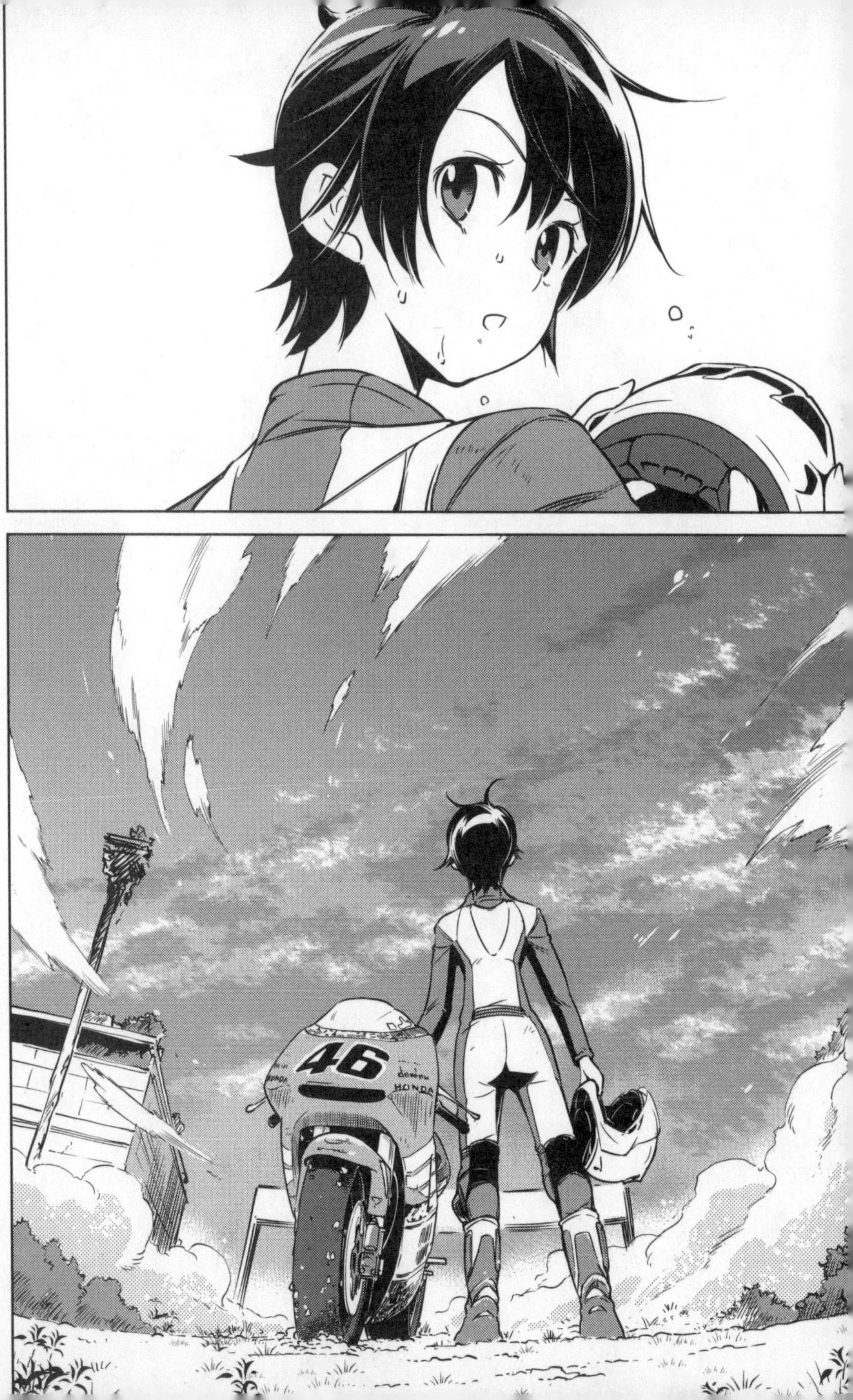
46
HONDA

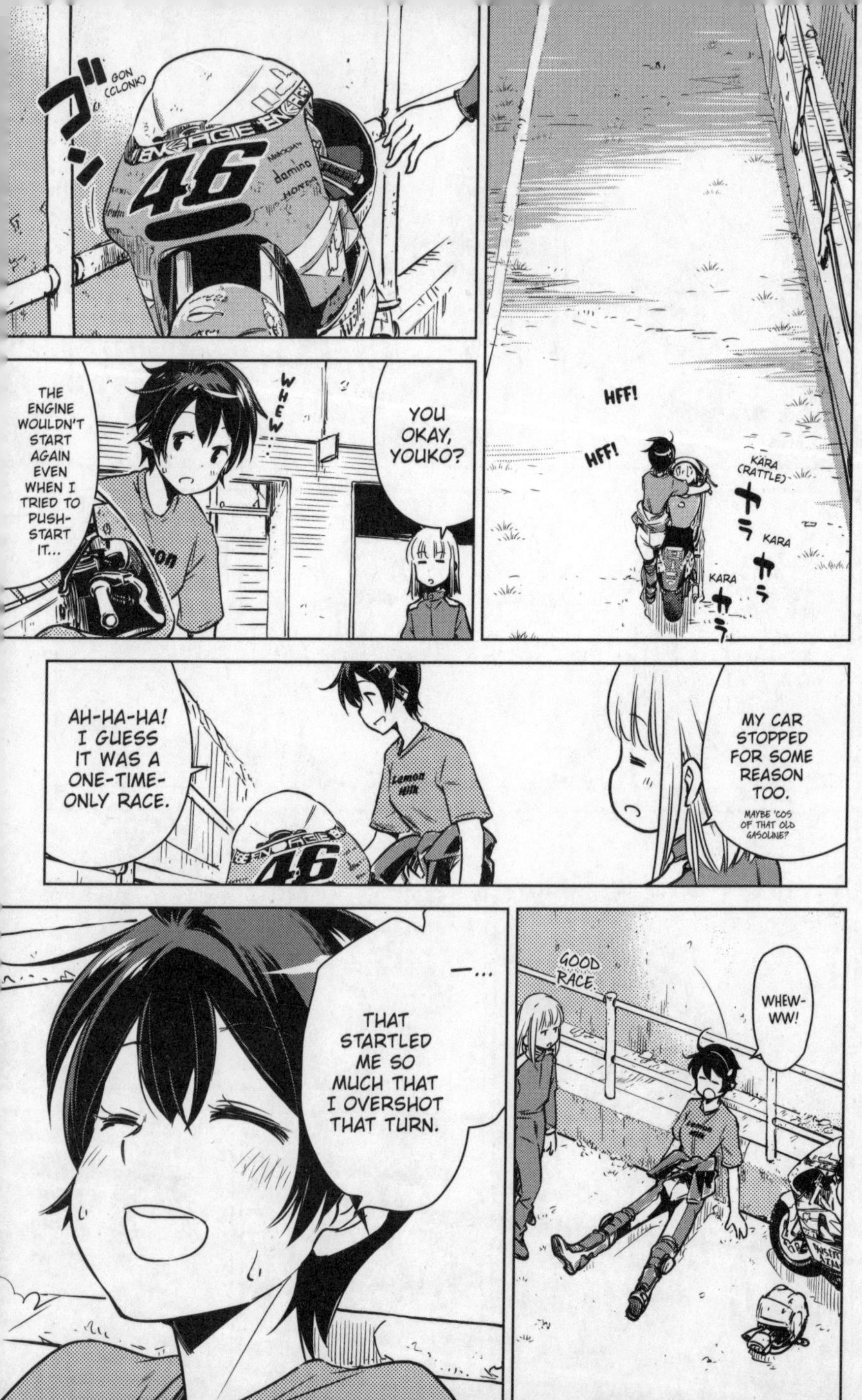
HFF!
HFF!
KARA (RATTLE)
カラ
KARA
カラ
KARA
カラ
ゴン
GON (CLONK)
YOU OKAY, YOUKO?
WHEW...
THE ENGINE WOULDN'T START AGAIN EVEN WHEN I TRIED TO PUSH-START IT...
MY CAR STOPPED FOR SOME REASON TOO.
MAYBE 'COS OF THAT OLD GASOLINE?
AH-HA-HA! I GUESS IT WAS A ONE-TIME-ONLY RACE.
WHEW-WW!
GOOD RACE.
—...
THAT STARTLED ME SO MUCH THAT I OVERSHOT THAT TURN.

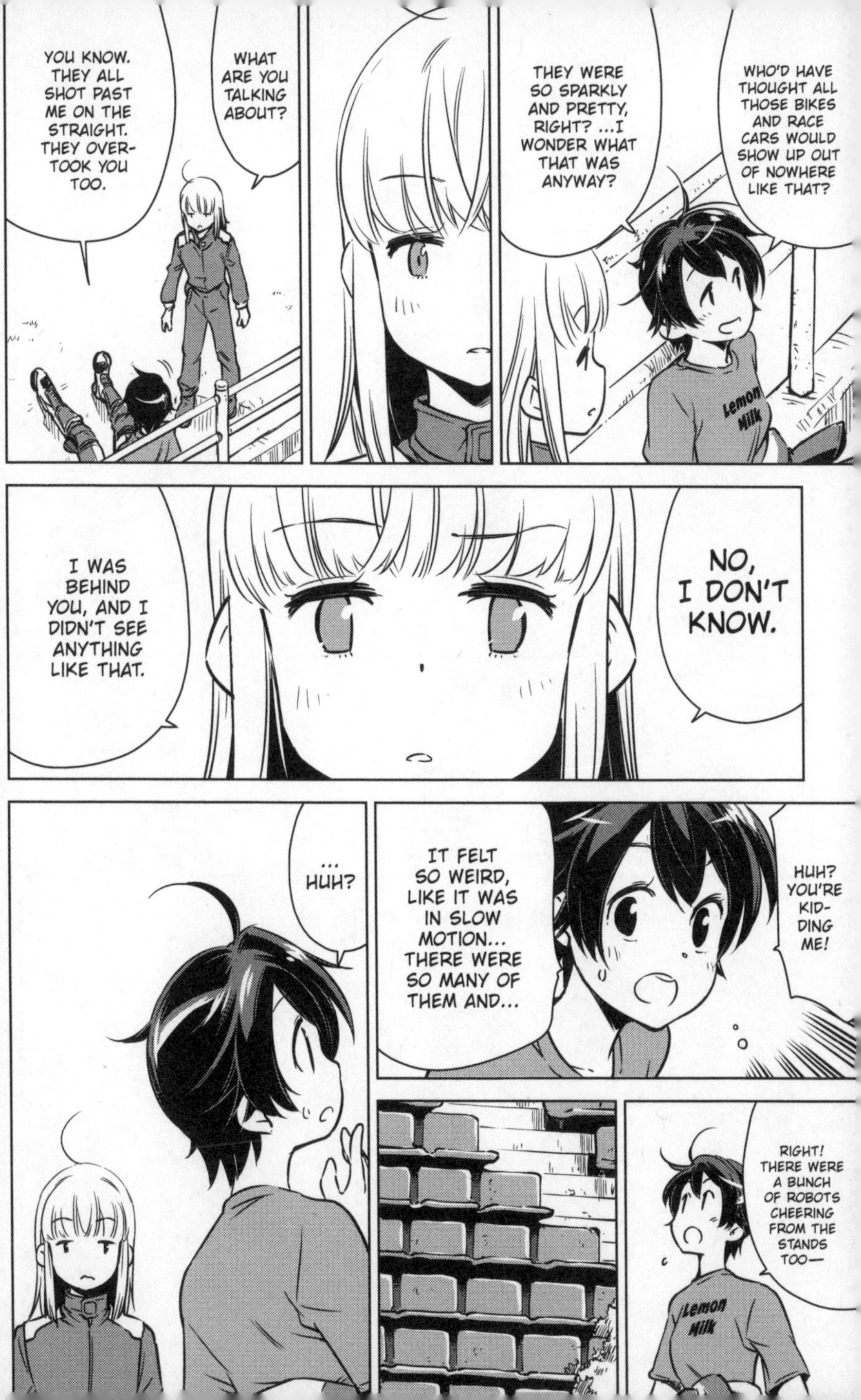
WHO'D HAVE THOUGHT ALL THOSE BIKES AND RACE CARS WOULD SHOW UP OUT OF NOWHERE LIKE THAT?
THEY WERE SO SPARKLY AND PRETTY, RIGHT? ...I WONDER WHAT THAT WAS ANYWAY?
Lemon Milk
WHAT ARE YOU TALKING ABOUT?
YOU KNOW. THEY ALL SHOT PAST ME ON THE STRAIGHT. THEY OVER-TOOK YOU TOO.
NO, I DON'T KNOW.
I WAS BEHIND YOU, AND I DIDN'T SEE ANYTHING LIKE THAT.
HUH? YOU'RE KID-DING ME!
IT FELT SO WEIRD, LIKE IT WAS IN SLOW MOTION... THERE WERE SO MANY OF THEM AND...
RIGHT! THERE WERE A BUNCH OF ROBOTS CHEERING FROM THE STANDS TOO—
Lemon Milk
... HUH?

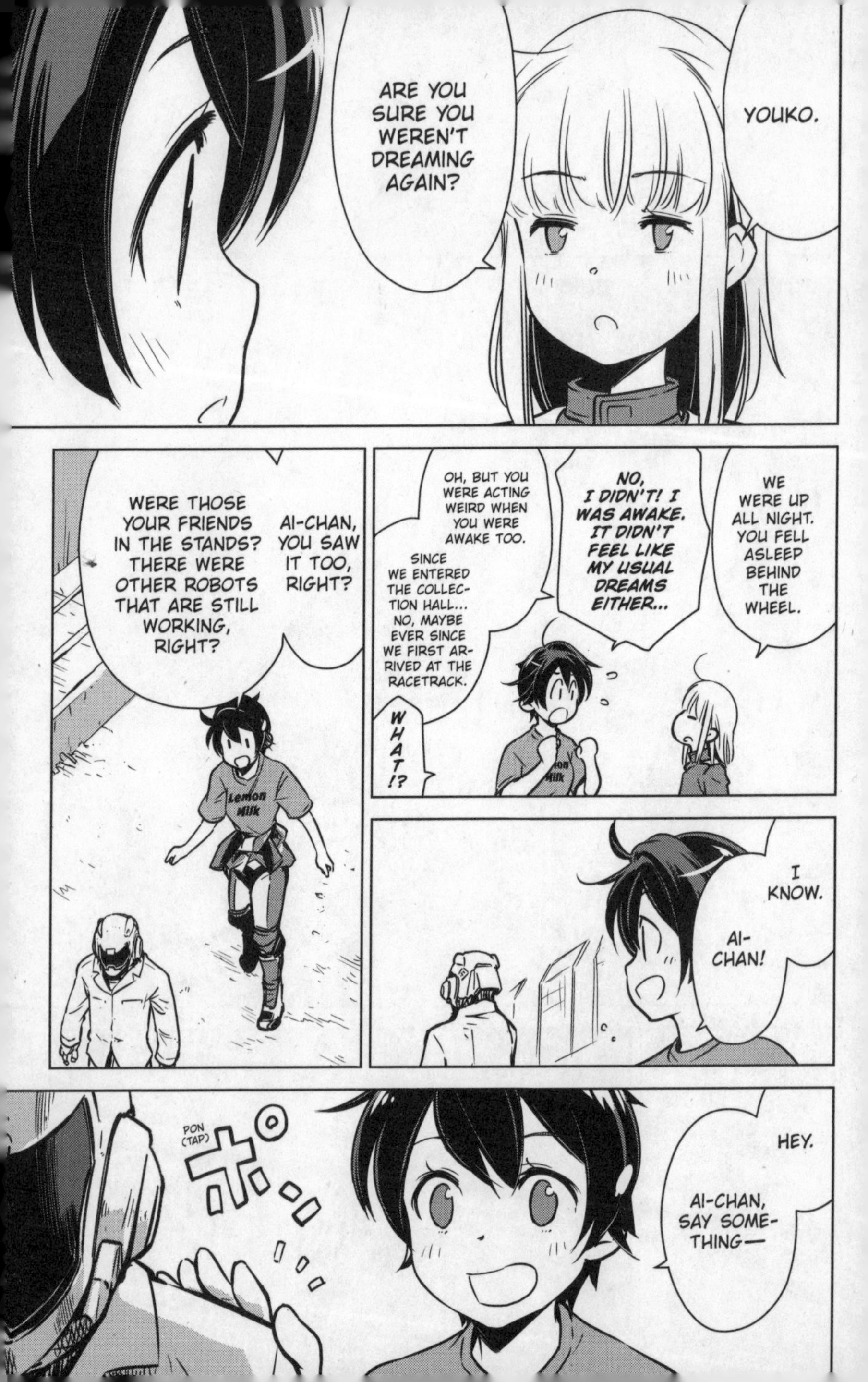
YOUKO.
ARE YOU SURE YOU WEREN'T DREAMING AGAIN?
WE WERE UP ALL NIGHT. YOU FELL ASLEEP BEHIND THE WHEEL.
NO, I DIDN'T! I WAS AWAKE. IT DIDN'T FEEL LIKE MY USUAL DREAMS EITHER...
OH, BUT YOU WERE ACTING WEIRD WHEN YOU WERE AWAKE TOO.
SINCE WE ENTERED THE COLLEC-TION HALL... NO, MAYBE EVER SINCE WE FIRST AR-RIVED AT THE RACETRACK.
WHAT!?
Lemon Milk
I KNOW.
AI-CHAN!
AI-CHAN, YOU SAW IT TOO, RIGHT?
WERE THOSE YOUR FRIENDS IN THE STANDS? THERE WERE OTHER ROBOTS THAT ARE STILL WORKING, RIGHT?
Lemon Milk
HEY.
AI-CHAN, SAY SOME-THING—
PON (TAP)

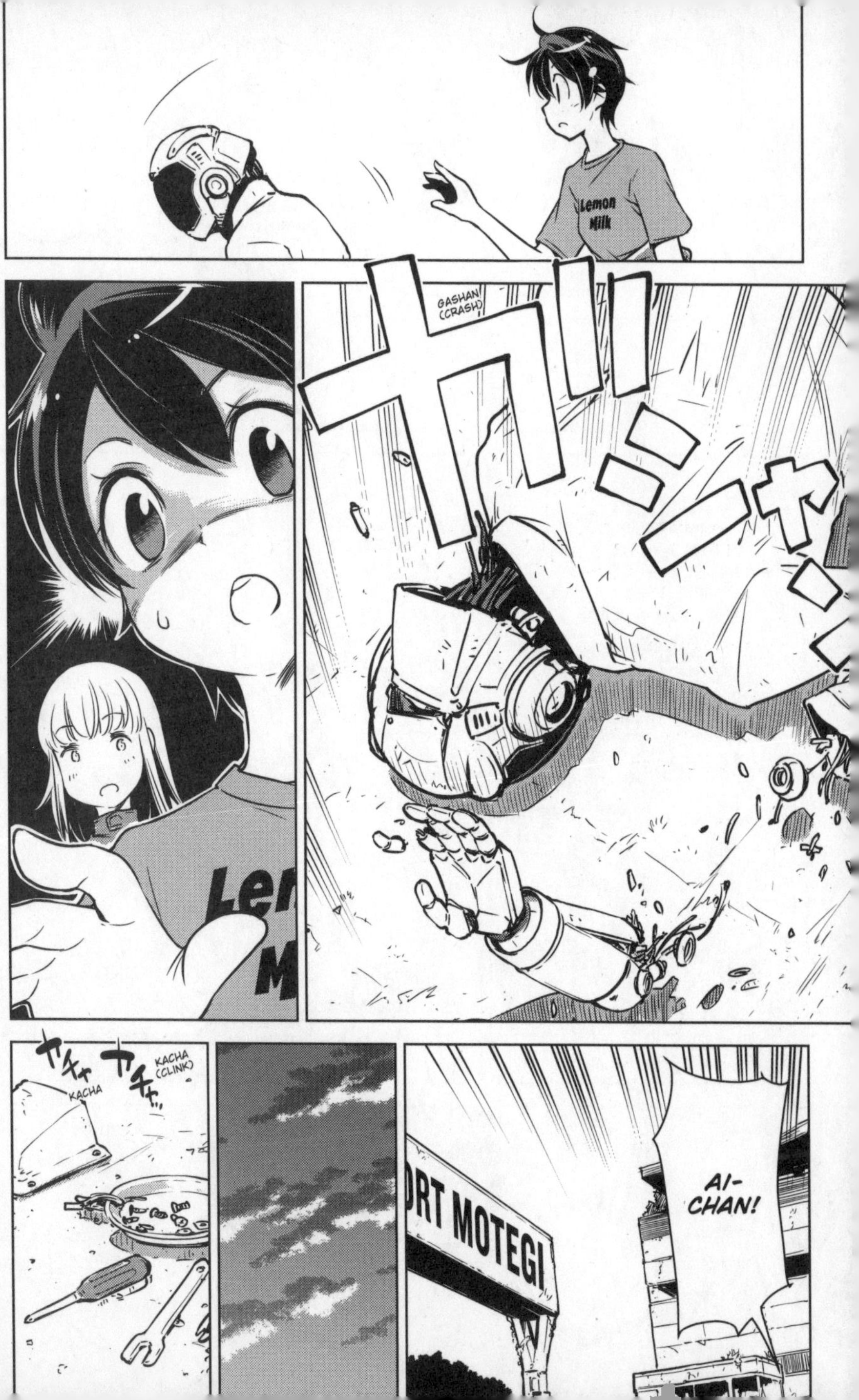
Lemon
Milk
GASHAN
(CRASH)
AI-
CHAN!
KACHA
(CLINK)
KACHA

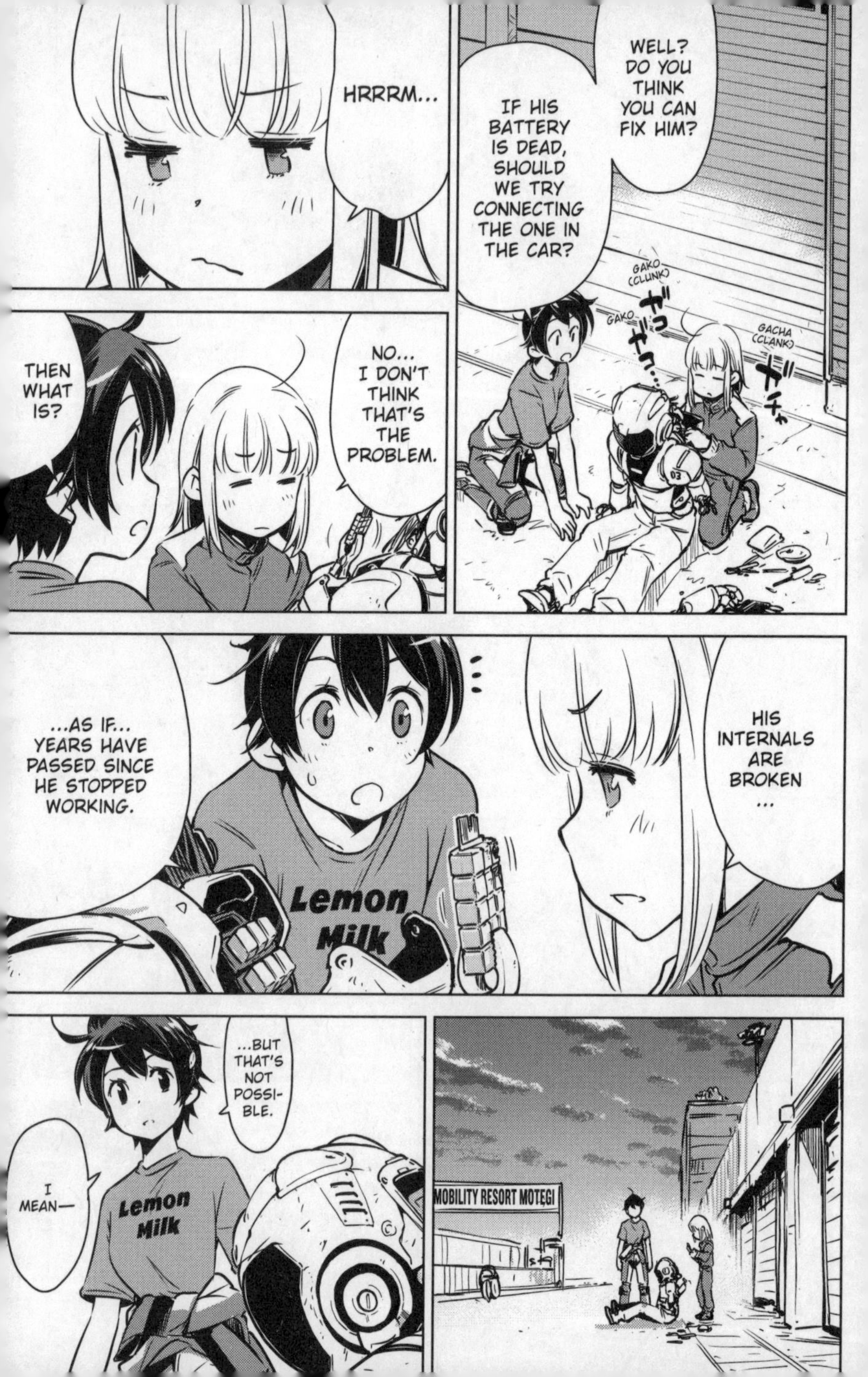
WELL? DO YOU THINK YOU CAN FIX HIM?
IF HIS BATTERY IS DEAD, SHOULD WE TRY CONNECTING THE ONE IN THE CAR?
GAKO (CLUNK)
GAKO
GACHA (CLANK)
HRRRM...
NO... I DON'T THINK THAT'S THE PROBLEM.
THEN WHAT IS?
HIS INTERNALS ARE BROKEN ...
...AS IF... YEARS HAVE PASSED SINCE HE STOPPED WORKING.
Lemon Milk
MOBILITY RESORT MOTEGI
...BUT THAT'S NOT POSSIBLE.
I MEAN—
Lemon Milk

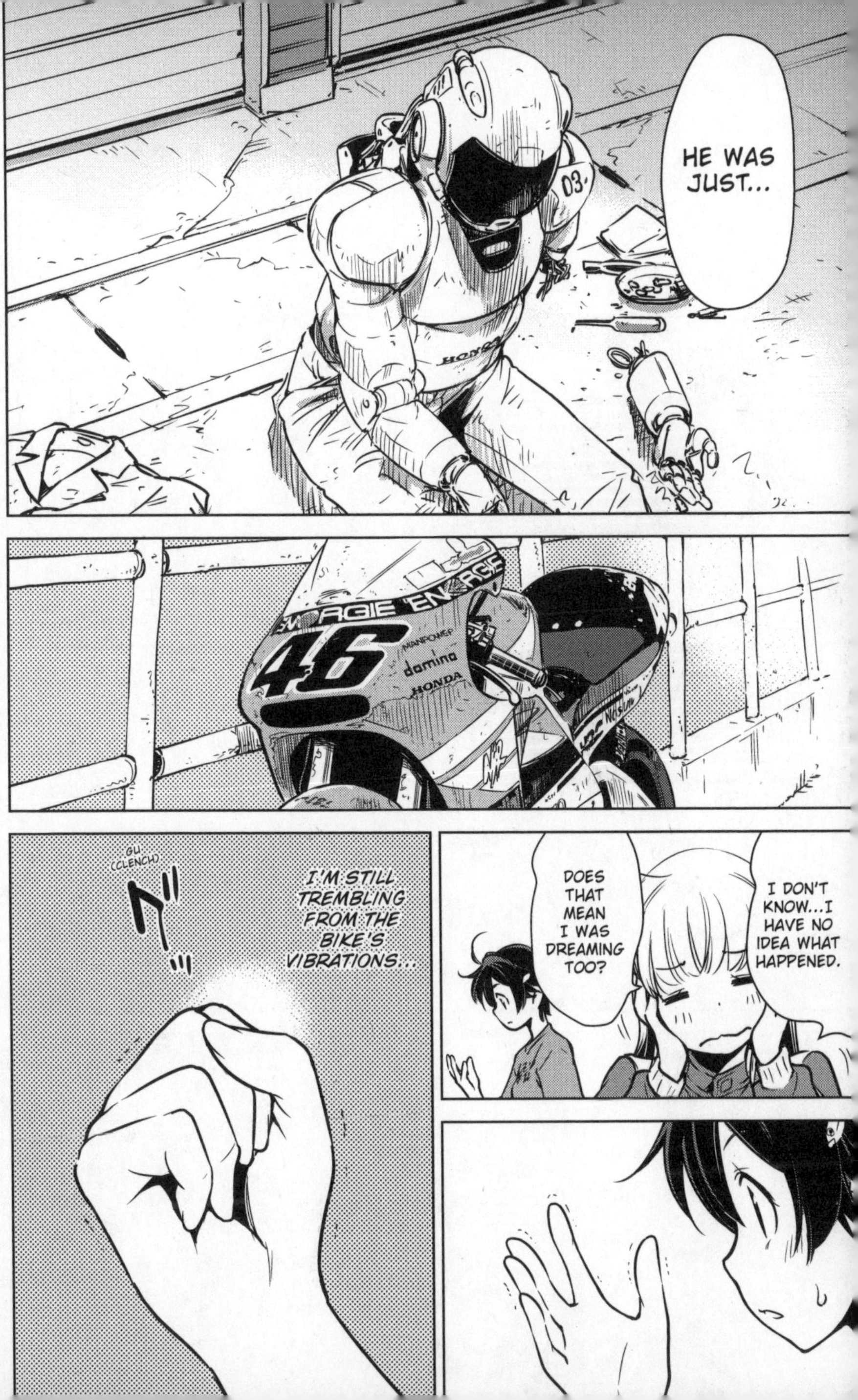
HE WAS JUST...
46
domino
HONDA
I DON'T KNOW...I HAVE NO IDEA WHAT HAPPENED.
DOES THAT MEAN I WAS DREAMING TOO?
GU (CLENCH)
I'M STILL TREMBLING FROM THE BIKE'S VIBRATIONS...

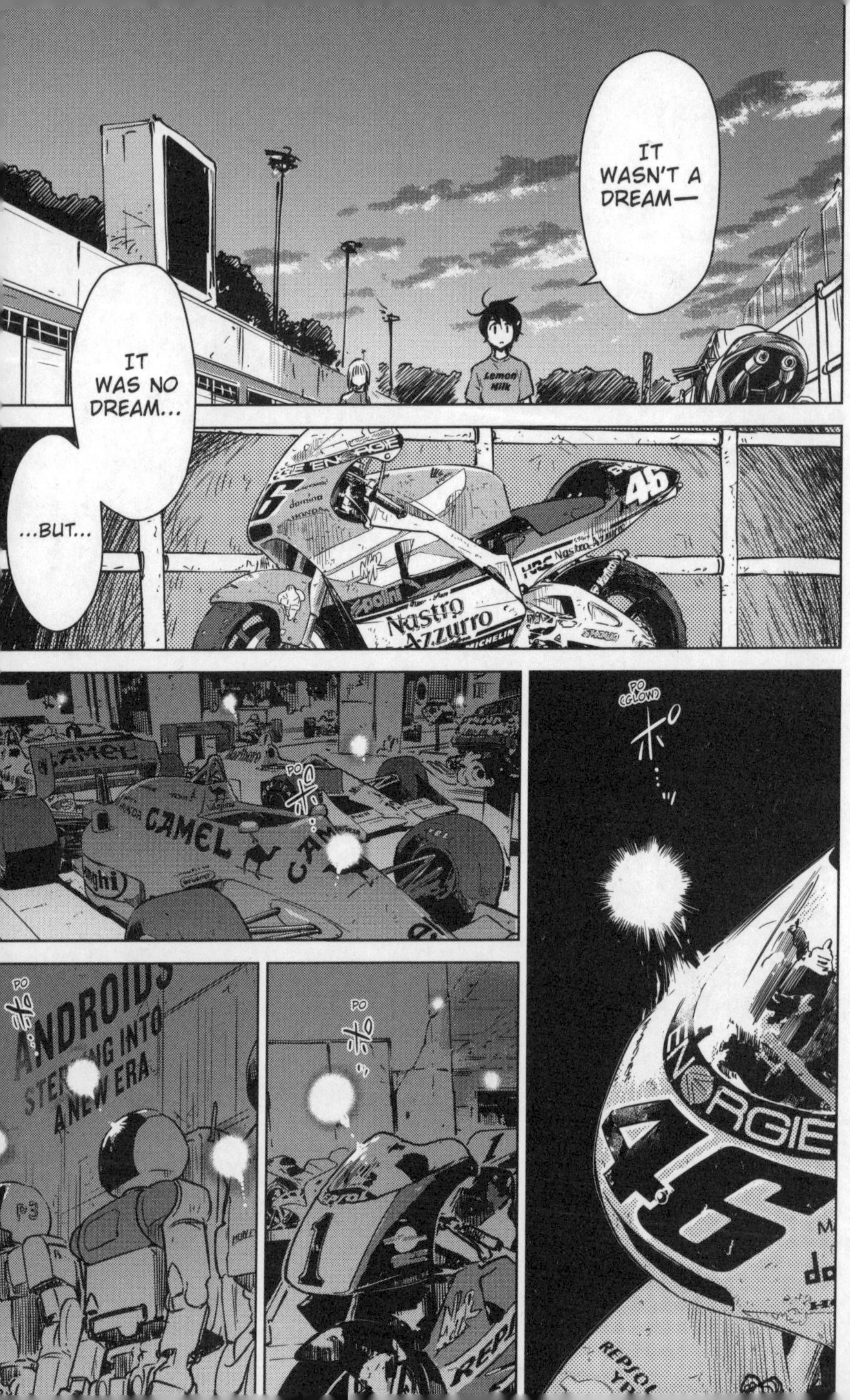
IT WASN'T A DREAM—
IT WAS NO DREAM...
...BUT...
PO (GLOW)
PO
PO
PO
ANDROIDS
A NEW ERA

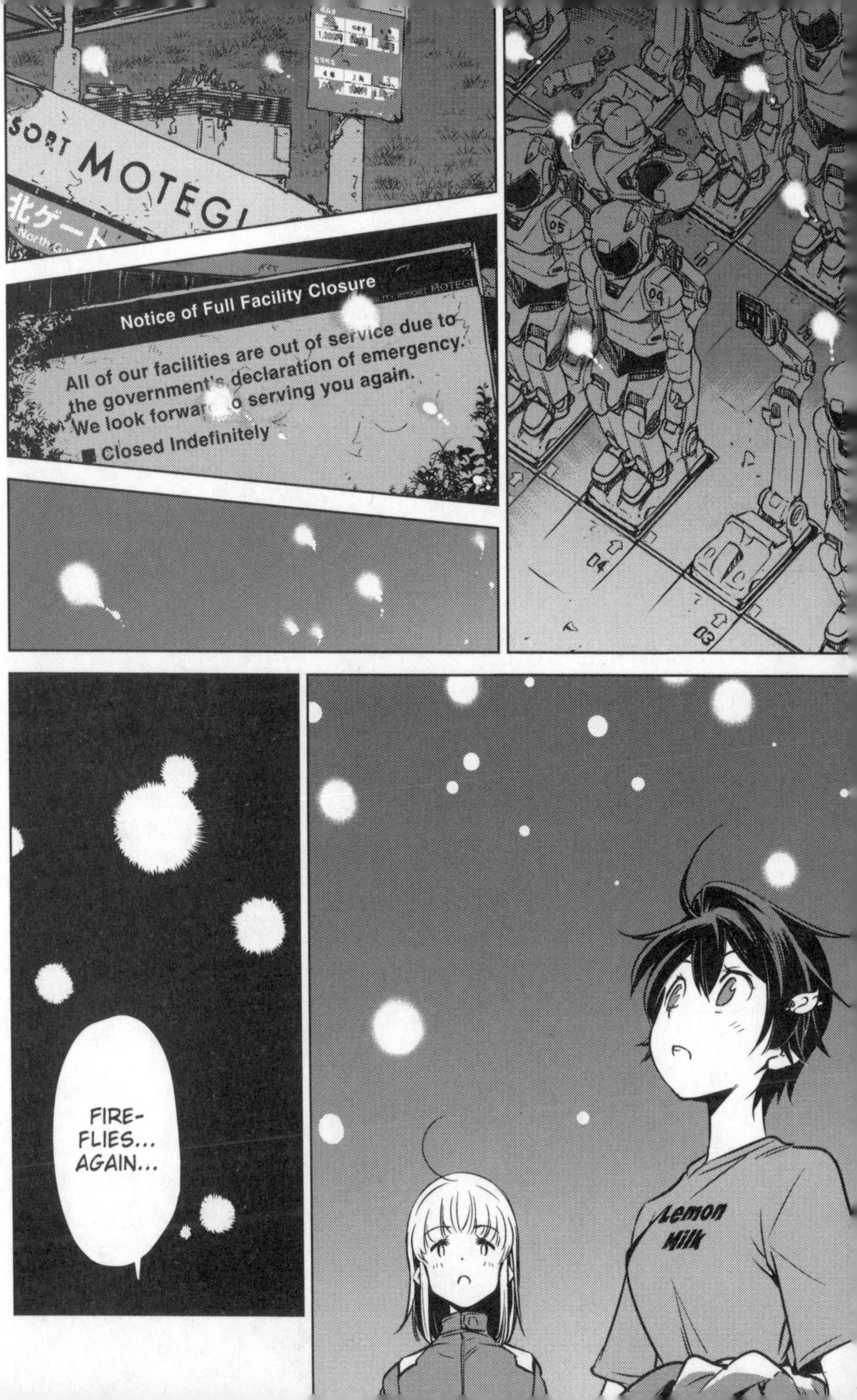
SORT MOTEGI
北ゲート
Notice of Full Facility Closure
All of our facilities are out of service due to the government's declaration of emergency.
We look forward to serving you again.
■ Closed Indefinitely
Lemon Milk
FIRE-FLIES... AGAIN...

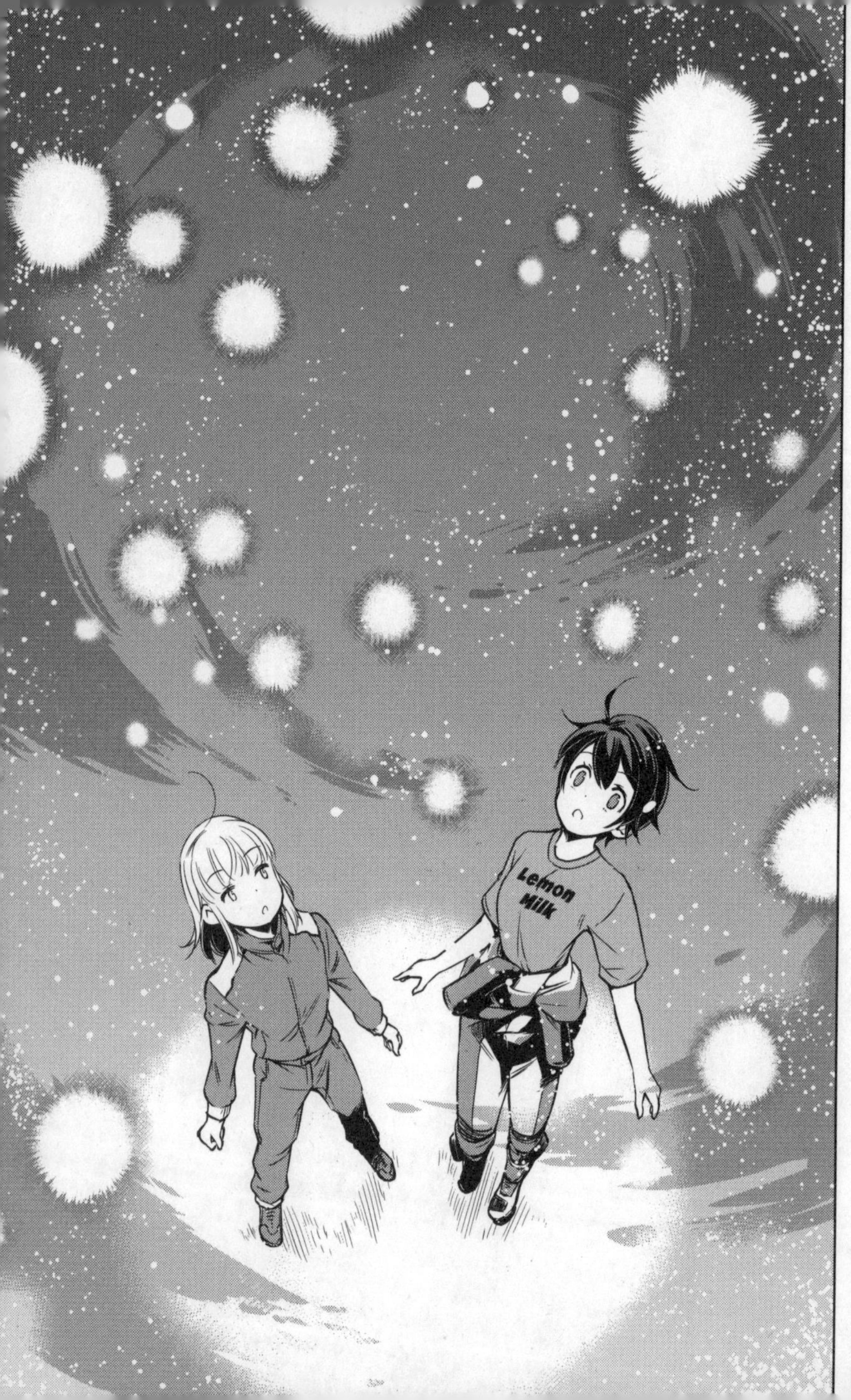
Lemon
Milk

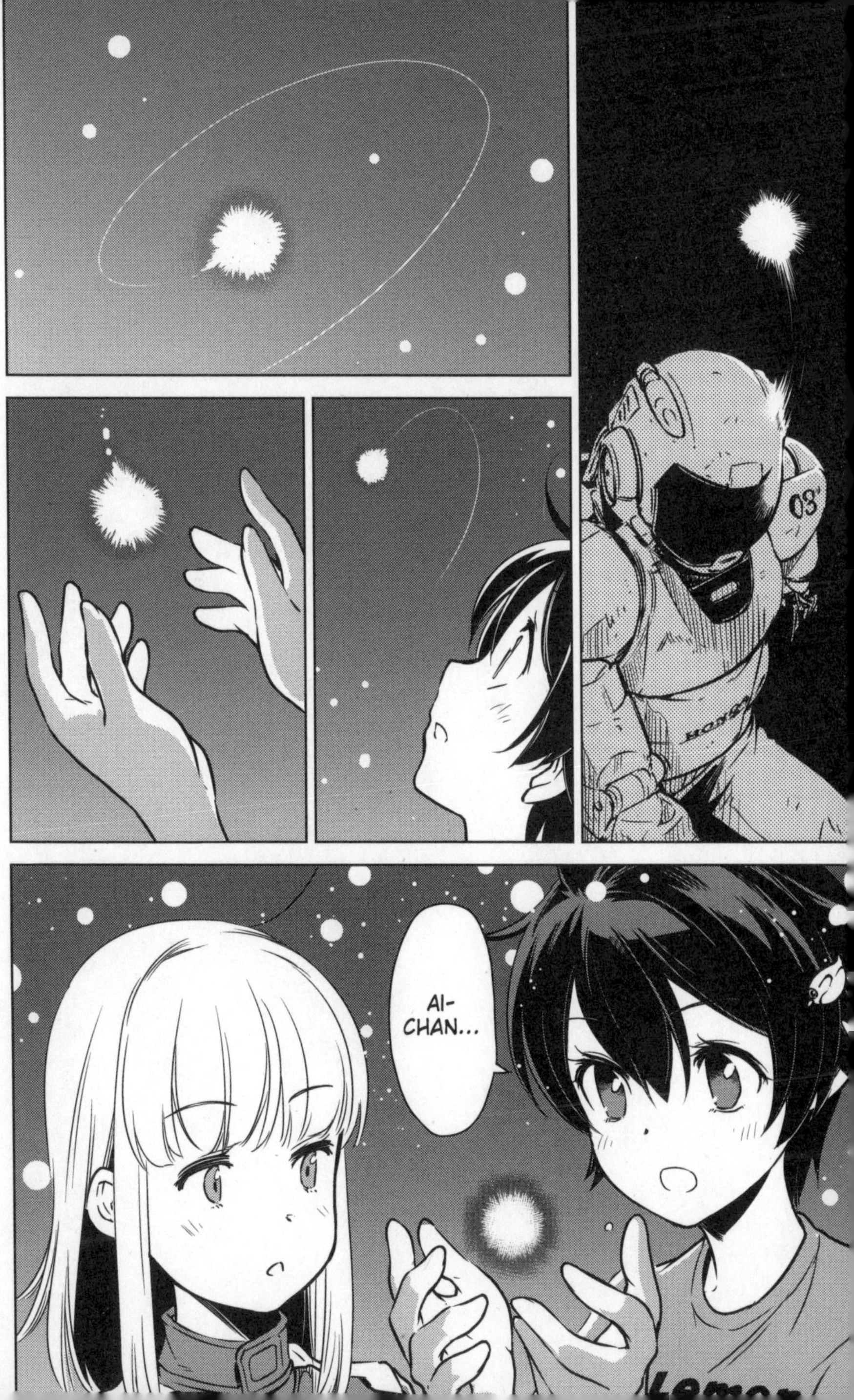
03
AI-
CHAN...

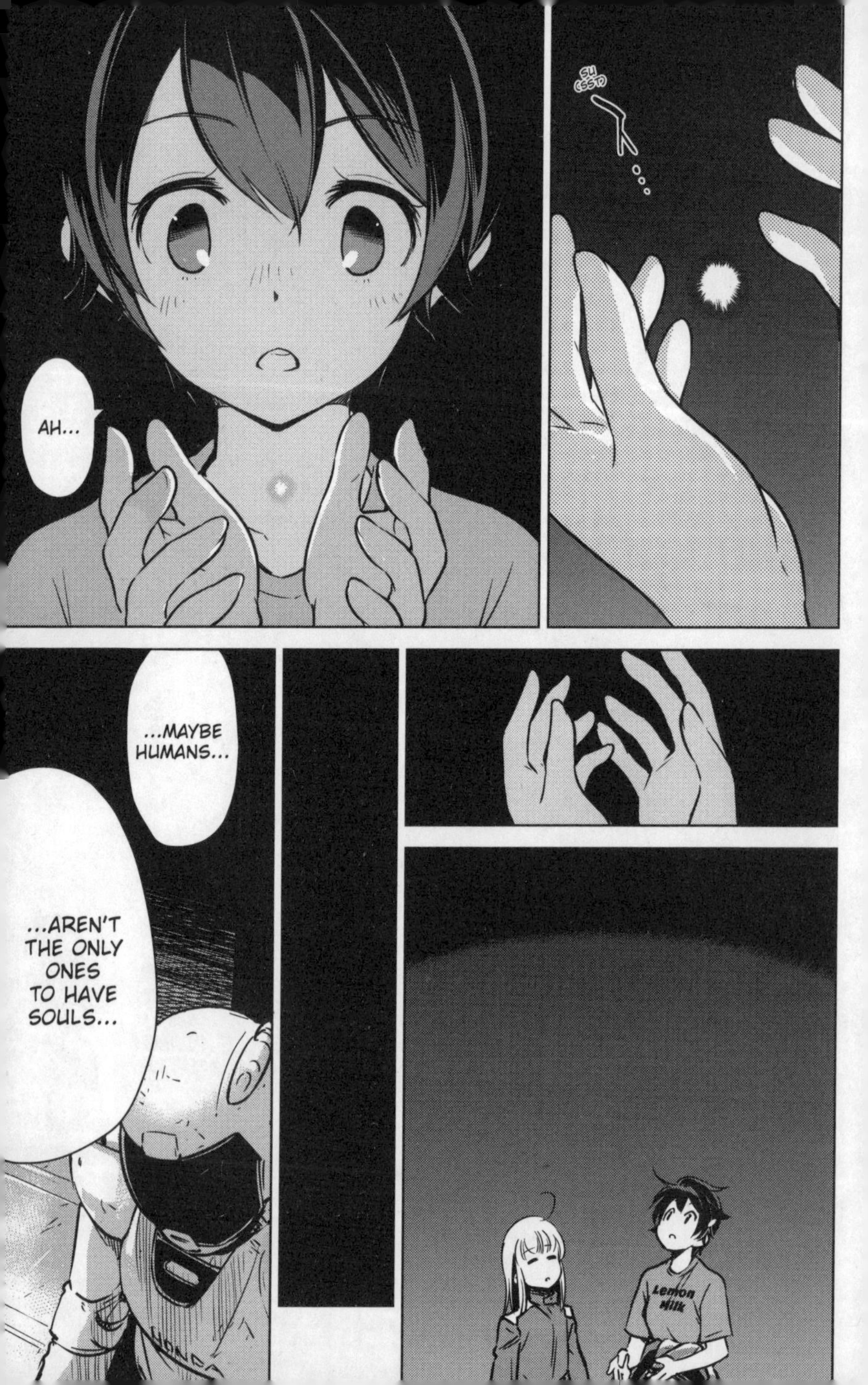
SU (SST)
AH...
Lemon Milk
...MAYBE HUMANS...
...AREN'T THE ONLY ONES TO HAVE SOULS...

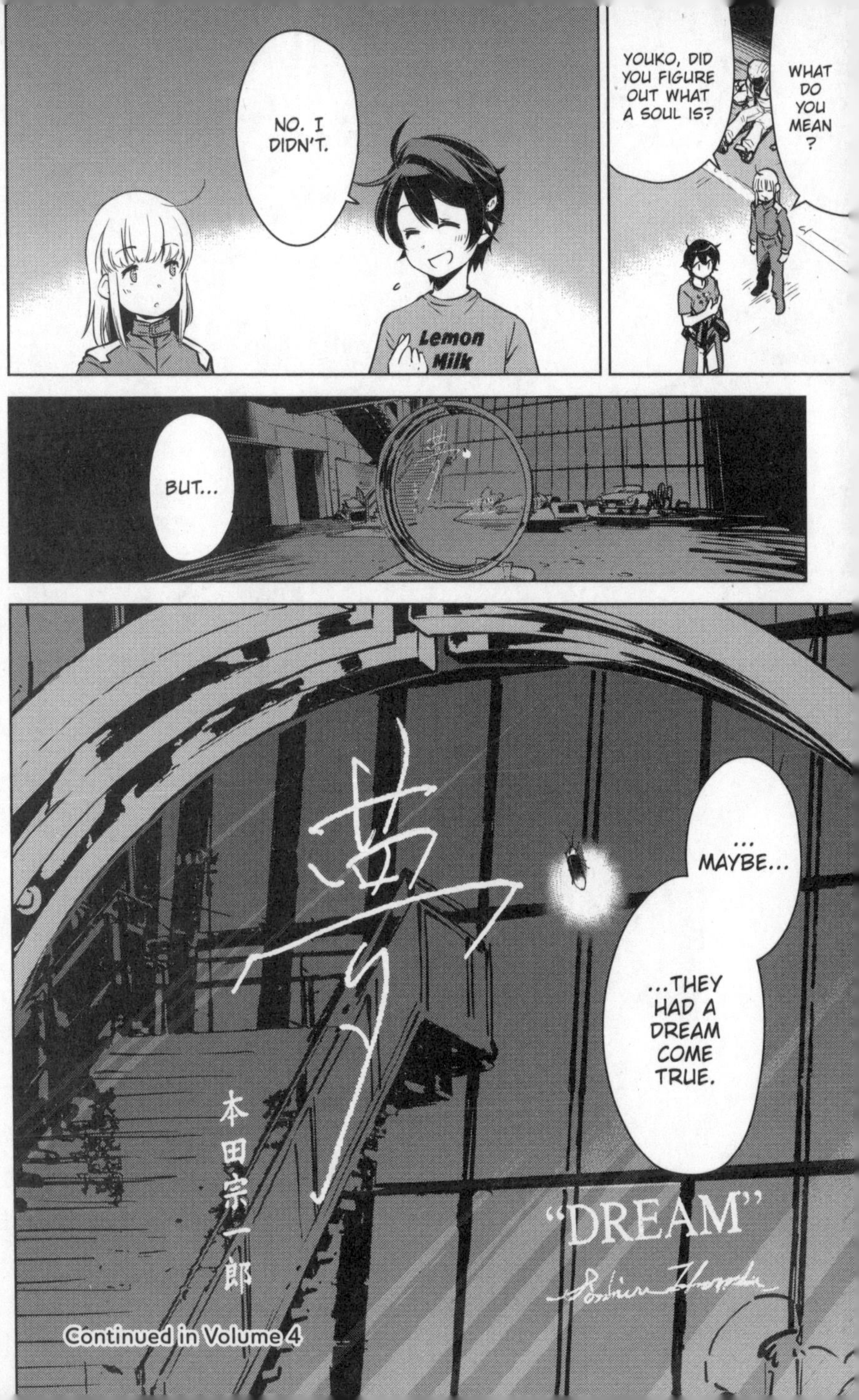
WHAT DO YOU MEAN?
YOUKO, DID YOU FIGURE OUT WHAT A SOUL IS?
NO. I DIDN'T.
Lemon Milk
BUT...
...MAYBE...
...THEY HAD A DREAM COME TRUE.
夢
本田宗一郎
"DREAM"
Continued in Volume 4

AFTERWORD

I like racetracks for no particular reason. Unlike on public roads, you can have fun riding at full throttle and work on polishing your riding skills. Now that I ride less often than when I was young, I've gotten big into racing—or rather, I ride as an easygoing breather from my manga manuscripts, and it makes me happy when my technique improves. Thinking back on it now, I can hardly believe that my experiences with motorcycle touring and racing, which were nothing more than a hobby to me, wound up being material for my manga... Life is strange.

APRIL 2022

SAKAE SAITO

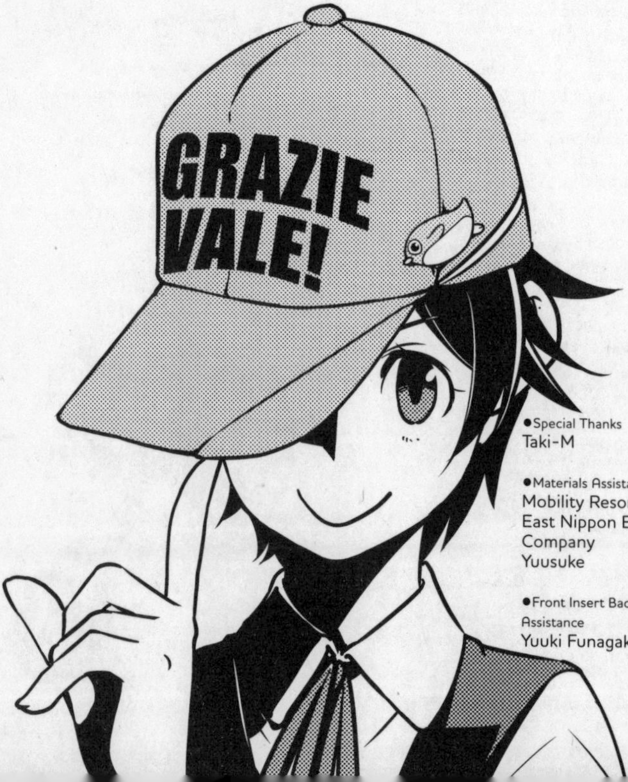
GRAZIE
VALE!

●Special Thanks
Taki-M

●Materials Assistance
Mobility Resort Motegi
East Nippon Expressway Company
Yuusuke

●Front Insert Background Art Assistance
Yuuki Funagakure

Touring After the Apocalypse

Translation: Amanda Haley
Lettering: Phil Christie

SHUMATSU TOURING Vol. 3
©Sakae Saito 2022
First published in Japan in 2022 by
KADOKAWA CORPORATION, Tokyo.
English translation rights arranged with
KADOKAWA CORPORATION, Tokyo,
through TUTTLE-MORI AGENCY, INC.,
Tokyo.

English translation © 2023
by Yen Press, LLC

Yen Press
150 West 30th Street, 19th Floor
New York, NY 10001

Visit us at yenpress.com
facebook.com/yenpress
twitter.com/yenpress
yenpress.tumblr.com
instagram.com/yenpress

First Yen Press Edition: July 2023
Edited by Yen Press Editorial: Thomas McAlister, Carl Li
Designed by Yen Press Design: Krystal Liang, Andy Swist

Library of Congress Control Number: 2022942371

ISBNs: 978-1-9753-6373-4 (paperback)
978-1-9753-6374-1 (ebook)

10 9 8 7 6 5 4 3 2 1

WOR

Printed in the United States of America